LEGAL RESEARCH AND WRITING ACROSS THE CURRICULUM: PROBLEMS AND EXERCISES

Michael D. Murray
Valparaiso University School of Law

and

Christy Hallam DeSanctis
The George Washington University Law School

FOUNDATION PRESS
2009

THOMSON REUTERS

© 2009 By THOMSON REUTERS/FOUNDATION PRESS

195 Broadway, 9th Floor
New York, NY 10007
Phone Toll Free 1–877–888–1330
Fax (212) 367–6799
foundation–press.com

Printed in the United States of America

ISBN 978–1–59941–398–3

 TEXT IS PRINTED ON 10% POST CONSUMER RECYCLED PAPER

ABOUT THE AUTHORS

Michael D. Murray is Associate Professor of Law at Valparaiso University School of Law. He has taught at the University of Illinois College of Law from 2002 to 2008, and Saint Louis University School of Law from 1998-2002. He teaches law school and undergraduate courses in Art Law, Civil Procedure, First Amendment and Censorship, International Art and Cultural Heritage, International Civil Liberties: Freedom of Expression, Introduction to Advocacy, Legal Research and Writing, Legal Writing and Analysis, and Professional Responsibility. Professor Murray is the author or coauthor of fourteen books and several law review articles on art law, civil procedure, copyright, freedom of expression, law and the health care professions, legal research and writing, and products liability. His casebook, ***Art Law: Cases and Materials*** (2004), is one of the most widely adopted casebooks in the field. Professor Murray graduated from Loyola College in Maryland and from Columbia Law School, where he was a Harlan Fiske Stone Scholar. He was a member of a national champion Jessup International Law Moot Court team at Columbia, and Notes Editor of the Columbia Journal of Transnational Law. After law school, he clerked for United States District Judge John F. Nangle of the Eastern District of Missouri and Chair of the Judicial Panel on Multidistrict Litigation. Murray also practiced commercial, intellectual property, and products liability litigation for seven years at Bryan Cave law firm in St. Louis.

Christy H. DeSanctis is Associate Professor of Legal Research and Writing and Director of the Legal Research and Writing Program at the George Washington University Law School. The Program encompasses 1L Legal Research and Writing, and Introduction to Advocacy; the Scholarly Writing and LL.M. Thesis Programs; and an in-house Writing Center. After graduating from NYU School of Law, she clerked for John W. Bissell, the former Chief Judge of the U.S. District Court for the District of New Jersey. Prior to joining the GW faculty, Professor DeSanctis practiced at the Washington, D.C., law firms of Collier Shannon Scott and Steptoe & Johnson. There, she focused on trial and appellate litigation at both the state and federal level, including in the U.S. Supreme Court, and worked on a variety of regulatory and legislative matters before federal agencies and Congress. She also published numerous articles relating to major legislative efforts with which she was directly involved, including terrorism insurance legislation and federal health and financial privacy regulations. Professor DeSanctis began teaching as an adjunct faculty member at GW in 2002; she was appointed to the fulltime faculty and assumed the Directorship of the LRW Program in 2004. In addition to teaching legal research and writing courses, she also teaches Law and Literature. She regularly speaks at conferences on legal writing and rhetoric. Professor DeSanctis also has taught several undergraduate English courses at the University of Maryland, College Park, including: Introduction to the Novel; American Literature after 1865; and Freshman Composition, a persuasive writing course based in part on theories of classical rhetoric. In addition to her J.D., Professor DeSanctis holds a Masters in English language and literature with a minor in rhetoric and composition from the University of Maryland. She is currently at work on a Ph.D. in late nineteenth and early twentieth century American Literature.

DEDICATION

To Denise, Olivia, and Dennis, who make it fun;

To my sisters, Margaret, Mary, Jeannette, Anne, and Laura, who proved to me that the benefits of a teaching career outweigh all the costs.

M.D.M.
St. Louis, MO
March 2009

To Michael B. DeSanctis, as always;

To my friends and family who have put up with me for all of these years.

C.H.D.
Washington, DC
March 2009

ACKNOWLEDGMENTS

This book is a continuation of the LRW Series at Foundation Press that we, the authors, started four years ago. We have had a great deal of assistance from editors and others at Foundation Press over the past eight years. In particular, we would like to thank Robb Westawker, who steered this current interactive book project through the production process at Foundation Press, and Heidi Boe and Bob Temple for their part in making it come to fruition. We continue to thank John Bloomquist, the Publisher of Foundation Press, for five years of helping us through each of the stages of publication, marketing, and sales of our books. And we remember fondly Steve Errick, formerly Editor of Foundation Press, for being the first to latch on to our book proposal and for never giving up on it.

Several other people also are owed our gratitude for their unwavering support of our professional endeavors and participation in the process resulting in this book. Professor Murray would like to single out his research and teaching assistants: Sasha Madlem, Robin Martinez, Tyler Pratt, and Vanessa Sheehan at Valparaiso University School of Law; Lindsay Beyer, Brian George, Aaron Goldberg, and Maurice Holman at the University of Illinois College of Law, and Renee Auderer, Jeannie Bell, Jonathan Blitz, John Challis, and Katalin Raby at Saint Louis University School of Law. We also thank the students who allowed us to use their work as writing examples: Lindsay Beyer, Jessica Bregant, Michelle Chen, Jim Davis, Jeffrey Ekeberg, Ken Halcom, James Klempir, Suleen Lee, Gerald Meyer, Greg Rubio, Vaishali Shah, Ellen Shiels, Gabriel Siegle, Joshua Watson, and Jim Williams at the University of Illinois College of Law; and Jeannie Bell, Kevin Etzkorn, Josh Knight, Kirsten Moder, Allison Price, Gaylin Rich, Jerrod Sharp, Katherine Weathers, and Cherie Wyatt at Saint Louis University School of Law. Special thanks also are due to Professor Murray's assistants over the last eight years, Kristin Takish at Valparaiso University, and Mary Parsons and Deanna Shumard at the University of Illinois, whose support above and beyond the call of duty is remarkable and much appreciated.

Professor DeSanctis would like to recognize Jessica L. Clark and Kristen E. Murray, for their outstanding assistance running the GW LRW Program in past years, friendship, unabashed humor, and superb insight on how to teach students to write well; Professor Lorri Unumb, my predecessor at GW, for teaching me not only how to teach legal writing but also how to run a great program; and all of the GW Law Dean's Fellows and Writing Fellows from 2004 to 2008 for their energy and unceasing desire to make teaching legal research and citation interesting, rewarding and fun (and the 2004-05 Writing Fellows in particular for their assistance with the Appendix in this text on grammar rules).

The authors thank their legal research and writing colleagues who reviewed and commented on the text: Kenneth Chestek (University of Indiana-Indianapolis School of Law); Jessica Clark (George Washington University); Jane Ginsburg (Columbia Law School); Terri LeClercq (University of Texas School of Law); Pamela Lysaght (University of Detroit Mercy School of Law); Joanna Mossop (Columbia Law School); Kristen Murray (Temple University, Beasley School of Law); Suzanne Rowe (University of Oregon School of Law); Ann Davis Shields (Washington University School of Law); Judith Smith (Columbia Law School); Mark Wojcik (John Marshall Law School); and Cliff Zimmerman (Northwestern University School of Law). This book is the better for their kind and generous review and input.

Professor DeSanctis also thanks the following people: Linda A. Shashoua for her unwavering support in this endeavor and all of my others, as well as her guidance, friendship, and expertise in putting thoughts into both writing (and music!); Michael S. Levine, for his seemily undying friendship (despite my attempts to ignore him) and for sharing with me his thoughts and insights from almost ten years of teaching legal writing; George D. Gopen, for teaching me everything I know about reader and listener expectations; the Hon. John W. Bissell, for the opportunity to work with a true wordsmith; Scott A. Sinder, for teaching me how to write anything in one hour (and a Supreme Court brief in a weekend! (extenuating circumstances)); Pam Chamberlain for her institutional know-how and priceless advice on how the GW program operates; and to all of the past, present and future GW LRW adjunct professors (including, in no particular order: Lisa Goldblatt, Tom Simeone, Ken Kryvoruka, Andrew Steinberg, Josh Braunstein, John Arnett, Andrea Agathoklis, Tim McIlmail, Donna McCaffrey, Scott Castle, Bill Goodrich, Susan Lynch, Erik Barnett, and many others, from whom I have learned and continue to learn an enormous amount about a practice-oriented approach to teaching legal writing). And, oh yes, Michael DeSanctis – you simply cannot be a better writer than he is, hands down (*how* do you so masterfully edit things that you know nothing about?).

PREFACE

I. INTERACTIVE TEXTS FOR LEGAL METHOD

This book is a part of Murray and DeSanctis's <u>Legal Research and Writing Series</u> of books at Foundation Press, the latest titles of which are interactive texts providing a print format of the book and an electronic format that is designed for the current generation of law students whose familiarity and comfort with on-line and computer-based learning creates a demand for teaching resources that take advantage of that familiarity and comfort level. The interactive computer-based versions of the texts add hyperlinks to on-line databases and internet-based resources and supplement the text with pop-up definitions, graphical and textual explanations and depictions, and presentations to introduce and summarize the material. The interactive versions of the text will be fully searchable and highly portable, and each page can be annotated or highlighted. The table of contents and each of the chapters will contain internal and external navigation links making them more valuable for use in class and out. The interactive texts also employ a layout that departs from the traditional, all-text casebook format through use of callout text boxes, diagrams, and color/border segregated feature sections for hypotheticals, references to scholarly debates, or other useful information for law students.

II. WRITING ACROSS THE LAW SCHOOL CURRICULUM

If this is your first encounter with the phrases "Writing Across the Curriculum" or "Writing in the Discipline," the basic educational theory behind these phrases is that students learn new material better if they both study it and apply it in tasks that represent the practice of the discipline. This is especially true in a discipline, like the law, that contains its own norms of practice and methodology. In law school, students can master the concepts of legal method and the separate areas of study in the law better if they take on problems—research problems, writing problems, and other practice-oriented problems—in the course of their study of these areas of the law, and do not confine themselves solely to research and writing practice in a legal research, legal writing, or legal method course. In other words, a student can master contracts law more completely by researching and writing about contracts problems or drafting actual contracts rather than simply reading contracts cases and being tested on contracts exam questions.

The problems in this text are provided at several levels of complexity. In <u>Part I</u> - **Research and Writing Problems Across the First Year Curriculum**, and in <u>Part V</u> - **Research and Writing Problems in Upper Division Subjects**, there are:

<u>RESEARCH AND WRITING PROBLEMS</u> that may be assigned for in-class work or a longer assignment period. These problems are concise, relatively straightforward problems that present a single issue that is typical of the kind of issues researched on a week-to-week basis in the subject area.

<u>DRAFTING PROBLEMS</u> that may be assigned for in-class work or a longer assignment period. These problems require the preparation of the kinds of documents and work product that attorneys prepare when working with client problems in the subject area. For example, they may require the drafting of a contract, a lease, a settlement agreement, jury instructions, or other client-based practice documents.

<u>WRITING IN THE LAW DISCIPLINE PROBLEMS</u> that are designed to accurately reflect the kind of client projects that actual attorneys would be assigned to handle in the practice of law. As such, they usually will require several days or more than a week's time to prepare. The problems here present multiple issues that will require significant research and analysis. The problems often require the preparation of more than one type of work product, as would be typical in a client project in the actual practice of law.

When you are working through these problems, look for <u>Key Terms</u> that we have suggested that you may use or adapt in your searches in the index or table of contents in your print sources or as search terms in your online searches. In addition, in the problems in parts I and V we have provided a <u>Launch Point</u> to start your research. It will be a case, a statute, a secondary source (an encyclopedia, treatise, law review article, or form book), an online database, or a set of search results on Westlaw or another online resource. These Launch Points will give you a place to start the searching but they are not intended to be the only source to use to complete the assignment.

Parts II, III, and IV of this text provide problems and exercises for use in a typical Legal Research and Writing, Lawyering Skills, or Legal Method class. As such, they are designed to correspond directly to the chapters and topics covered in the interactive texts in Murray and De-Sanctis's Legal Research and Writing Series. **Part II - Research and Writing Problems and Exercises in Legal Writing and Analysis** corresponds to Murray and DeSanctis, *Legal Writing and Analysis;* **Part III - Research and Writing Problems and Exercises in Legal Research Methods** corresponds to Murray and DeSanctis, *Legal Research Methods,* and **Part IV - Research and Writing Problems and Exercises in Advanced Legal Writing and Oral Advocacy: Trials, Appeals, and Moot Court** corresponds to Murray and DeSanctis, *Advanced Legal Writing and Oral Advocacy: Trials, Appeals, and Moot Court.* Parts II, III, and IV of this text provide:

> <u>QUESTIONS FOR DISCUSSION AND REVIEW</u> that can be discussed in class. These are short questions that do not require additional research and that are intended to provide a review of the topics in the chapter.

> <u>WRITING PROBLEMS</u> that may be assigned for in-class work or a longer assignment period. These problems are concise, relatively straightforward problems that present one or two issues that are designed to help you practice and master a lawyering skill involving legal writing and analysis. Most do not require additional research to complete the work.

> <u>RESEARCH EXERCISES</u> that are short, "treasure hunt" exercises that usually require you only to find one or a limited number of legal sources in order to answer a short and

simple question that is based on the same sources you are asked to locate. Most of these exercises can be performed equally well with print or online research sources.

CITATION EXERCISES that are short exercises to test your mastery of the essential lawyering skill of proper citation of authorities.

Together, the parts of this text will provide you with a comprehensive writing across the law curriculum and writing in the law discipline experience that will enable you to develop the skills necessary to practice law. This book will give you the opportunity to immerse yourself in projects to create the type of writing that is produced in law practice. The problems and exercises here are an entry into the legal discourse community. They will be focused on measuring your ability to produce accurate documents that serve the purposes of the problems presented within the context of a specific area of law. Whether researched and written by yourself or in small groups, the problems will simulate the practice of law and introduce you to the legal discourse of a new discipline. They will afford you a realistic chance to master concepts and skills necessary for law practice.

Good luck in your law study and in your career as an attorney!

TABLE OF CONTENTS

PART I: **RESEARCH AND WRITING PROBLEMS ACROSS THE FIRST YEAR CURRICULUM**

    I.   CONTRACTS
    II.   TORTS
    III.   CIVIL PROCEDURE
    IV.   PROPERTY
    V.   CRIMINAL LAW
    VI.   CONSTITUTIONAL LAW

PART II: **RESEARCH AND WRITING PROBLEMS AND EXERCISES IN LEGAL WRITING AND ANALYSIS**

    I.   INTRODUCTION TO LEGAL METHOD (Legal Writing and Analysis, Chapter 1)
    II.   RULES OF LAW AND LEGAL REASONING (Legal Writing and Analysis, Chapter 2)
    III.   THE LIFE OF A CASE, STATE AND FEDERAL COURT SYSTEMS, AND JURISDICTION (Legal Writing and Analysis, Chapter 3)
    IV.   DETERMINING THE RULE FROM A SINGLE CASE OR OTHER AUTHORITY (Legal Writing and Analysis, Chapter 4)
    V.   DETERMINING THE APPLICABLE RULE: ANALYSIS OF MULTIPLE AUTHORITIES (Legal Writing and Analysis, Chapter 5)
    VI.   ORGANIZATION OF LEGAL WRITING (Legal Writing and Analysis, Chapter 6)
    VII. THE OFFICE MEMORANDUM AND THE CLIENT LETTER (Legal Writing and Analysis, Chapter 7)
    VIII. EDITING AND FINE TUNING YOUR WRITING (Legal Writing and Analysis, Chapter 8)

IX.   LEGAL CITATION (Legal Writing and Analysis, Chapter 9)

X.   PREPARING A CASE BRIEF OR CASE ANALYSIS FOR CLASS (Legal Writing and Analysis, Appendix A)

PART III: **RESEARCH AND WRITING PROBLEMS AND EXERCISES IN LEGAL RESEARCH METHODS**

I.   INTRODUCTION TO LEGAL RESEARCH (Legal Research Methods, Chapter 1)

II.   RESEARCHING STATUTES AND CONSTITUTIONS (Legal Research Methods, Chapter 2)

III.   RESEARCHING CASE LAW (Legal Research Methods, Chapter 3)

IV.   RESEARCHING FEDERAL REGULATORY AND ADMINISTRATIVE LAW (Legal Research Methods, Chapter 4)

V.   RESEARCHING SECONDARY SOURCES OF THE LAW: ENCYCLOPEDIAS, TREATISES, LAW REVIEWS, AND PERIODICALS (Legal Research Methods, Chapter 5)

VI.   RESEARCHING LEGISLATIVE HISTORY (Legal Research Methods, Chapter 6)

VII.   RESEARCHING COURT RULES, LOCAL RULES, AND SUBJECT-SPECIFIC RESOURCES (Legal Research Methods, Chapter 7)

PART IV: **RESEARCH AND WRITING PROBLEMS AND EXERCISES IN ADVANCED LEGAL WRITING AND ORAL ADVOCACY: TRIALS, APPEALS, AND MOOT COURT**

I.   ADVERSARIAL LEGAL WRITING (Advanced Legal Writing and Oral Advocacy: Trials, Appeals, and Moot Court, Chapter 1)

II.   PRETRIAL MOTIONS (Advanced Legal Writing and Oral Advocacy: Trials, Appeals, and Moot Court, Chapter 2)

III.   <u>MOTIONS TO DISMISS (Advanced Legal</u>
         <u>Writing and Oral Advocacy: Trials, Appeals, and</u>
         <u>Moot Court, Chapter 3)</u>
IV.   <u>MOTIONS FOR SUMMARY JUDGMENT</u>
         <u>(Advanced Legal Writing and Oral Advocacy:</u>
         <u>Trials, Appeals, and Moot Court, Chapter 4)</u>
V.   <u>APPELLATE ADVOCACY: APPEALS, WRITS,</u>
         <u>AND STANDARDS OF REVIEW (Advanced</u>
         <u>Legal Writing and Oral Advocacy: Trials, Ap-</u>
         <u>peals, and Moot Court, Chapter 5)</u>
VI.   <u>APPELLATE BRIEFS (Advanced Legal Writing</u>
         <u>and Oral Advocacy: Trials, Appeals, and Moot</u>
         <u>Court, Chapter 6)</u>

PART V: **<u>RESEARCH AND WRITING PROBLEMS IN</u>**
                <u>UPPER DIVISION SUBJECTS</u>

I.   <u>REMEDIES</u>
II.   <u>COPYRIGHT</u>
III.   <u>RIGHT OF PUBLICITY</u>
IV.   <u>ADVANCED CONSTITUTIONAL LAW,</u>
         <u>FIRST AMENDMENT, AND FREEDOM OF</u>
         <u>EXPRESSION</u>

Part I

Research and Writing Problems Across the First Year Curriculum

I.   CONTRACTS

RESEARCH AND WRITING PROBLEMS

1. In order to increase sales, Bubba's Bubble Gum Company decided to develop a game where customers receive "Bubba Points" for each package of gum they purchase. After the customer purchases the package and opens the gum wrappers inside the package, the customer will see a number written on each wrapper equaling the number of points that wrapper is worth. The points on each wrapper range from 5 to 100. As the customers collect the points, they can mail them in with a game form declaring their prize choice. Typical game prizes range from free packages of gum and mp3 player cases to stereos and televisions. In order to promote this game, Bubba's took out an advertisement which explained the rules of the game and showed some of the prizes with the point total underneath. Bubba's advertised several of the "normal" prizes, but then as a joke (or so Bubba claims) it also displayed a brand new Lamborghini Murcielago automobile for only 10,000,000 "Bubba Points." Assuming the Lamborghini was a real prize, Bobby Stevie started collecting all his points and his family and friends' points. He organized an event at school and ran a website to collect more. After several months, he collected the 10 million points and sent them into Bubba's Bubble Gum Company requesting the Lamborghini.

    When Stevie's request was rejected by Bubba's on the grounds that he misunderstood the joke, he turned to your law firm to find out if he should sue Bubba's. You decide that Stevie's best theory is a breach of contract. Assume that the case could be brought in a federal court under diversity jurisdiction (for example, in the U.S. District Court for the Southern District of New York). Draft a 1-2 page client letter to Mr. Stevie detailing the likelihood of success and, in your opinion, whether he should pursue this lawsuit.

Key Terms: advertisement, offer, acceptance, contest, joke

Launch Point: *Leonard v. Pepsico, Inc.*, 88 F. Supp. 116 (S.D.N.Y. 1999), *aff'd* 210 F.3d 88 (2d Cir. 2000).

2. As Loy Dorn's attorney, you recently filed suit against Loy's partner, Pat Tictaker, for breach of an oral contract. In response to the complaint, Tictaker's attorney filed a motion to dismiss. The motion to dismiss claims that the breach of contract suit is invalid under the statute of frauds because the agreement could not be performed within one year. The facts are as follows:

In January 2005, Dorn and Tictaker entered into a oral agreement, which included the following arrangements:

Dorn agreed to continue to attend the University of California at San Diego and continue his degree in organic pharmacology. At the time of the agreement, Dorn had only completed one semester of the five year program. In addition to school, Dorn agreed to live with Tictaker, and be Tictaker's chauffeur, business secretary, and counselor on certain investments. The agreement also stipulated that Dorn would not continue his education past his pharmacology degree.

Tictaker agreed to financially support Dorn for life, including paying all the rent for the couple's San Diego apartment. Furthermore, Tictaker would open joint checking and savings accounts in Dorn's and Tictaker's names and maintain a positive balance in both of the accounts. Tictaker would also allow Dorn to charge on the couple's credit accounts, as well as give Dorn an equity half interest in all the investments Dorn counseled Tictaker on.

In November 2008, Dorn came home to find that Tictaker changed the locks on the apartment and would not let Dorn enter. Furthermore, Tictaker had emptied out the bank accounts, closed out the credit accounts, and cashed out the investments, and refused to pay Dorn any money owed to him. Dorn was still in school and had continued to follow the oral agreement prior to Tictaker's actions. The complaint for breach of oral contract was filed in January 2009.

Research and analyze Dorn's rights under this oral contract and draft 1-2 pages for the argument section of the opposition to Tictaker's motion to dismiss asserting the statute of frauds defense.

Key Terms: cohabitation agreement, "Marvin" agreement, promise to support for life, oral contract, statute of frauds

Launch Point: *Whorton v. Dillingham,* 248 Cal. Rptr. 405 (Ct. App. 4th Dist. 1988); *Byrne v. Laura,* 60 Cal. Rptr. 2d 908 (Ct. App. 1st Dist. 1997).

3. Bill Wilson is an extremely thrifty coupon-saver. While reading through the Honolulu Sunday Tribune, he came across a coupon for Aloha Washing Machine Company that offered $100.00 cash for any used washing machines with the purchase of a new Whirlpool machine from their store. Wilson collects washing machines. He already had a Whirlpool dryer and he wanted to make a matching set, so Wilson took in an old L.G. washing machine to Aloha to trade in for a new Whirlpool. When Wilson attempted to trade in the old L.G. machine, Joey, the sales manager of the store, refused to honor the coupon because the L.G. machine was worth nothing and could not be resold. Bill Wilson is wondering whether or not he can bring suit against Aloha Washing Machine Company. Research his claims against the Company and draft a 1-2 page memo on whether and on what theory or theories the Company may be liable to Wilson.

Key Terms: advertisement, offer, coupon, acceptance, tender of performance, false or misleading advertising

Launch Point: Restatement (Second) of Contracts § 26 (1981).

DRAFTING PROBLEMS

1. Med Tech, Incorporated maintains and repairs medical equipment for hospitals. In particular, Med Tech specializes in the maintenance and repair of MRI, CT Scan, and X-ray machines, as well as other technological equipment. The President of Med Tech, Michael Jones, has contacted St. Mary's Hospital in South Town, Kentucky, to repair and maintain their medical equipment. St. Mary's told Med Tech that they were interested and would review any contract Med Tech drafted. Mr. Jones has contacted your law firm in South Town because you specialize in Corporate Law and is requesting you draft a contract between Med Tech and St. Mary's. Due to a terrible downturn in the economy, Mr. Jones would like a long-term agreement of at least 8 years at a price of one million dollars per year. The customary rate in this region is $1.25 million per year, but the terms for those contracts are generally only 2-3 years. Draft a contract detailing the agreement between these two parties, taking into consideration any additional terms of the agreement you see fit.

    Key Terms: form, contract, health, healthcare facilities, maintenance contract or agreement

    Launch Point: American Jurisprudence Legal Forms 2d (AMJUR-LF); Westlaw's FORMFINDER database.

2. Philip Michaels is a swimming phenomenon who recently hit a patch of bad luck. After photographs emerged of Michaels participating in an illegal activity, he was dropped by many of his sponsors and found himself without a lot of money to pay for his current lifestyle or his training. In an effort to make some money, Michaels decided to sell some of his fourteen Olympic gold medals. Michaels figured that by selling only a few of his medals he could make enough money to maintain his lifestyle and training until the scandal blew over and he could get his sponsors back. Michaels also hoped that he would make enough money to buy back the medals he was forced to sell. Michaels found a swimming fanatic, Australian Rick Parsley, who also was a competitive swimmer in his day before having trouble with the law. Parsley is willing to buy three of Michaels' gold medals for $75,000 and has

agreed to let Michaels buy the medals back within the next five years for $125,000. Although Michaels is grateful to Parsley, Michaels wants a contract stipulating the term that matters the most to him: that Michaels has the option of buying the medals back for the agreed price within five years of the date of initial sale to Parsley. Please draft a purchase and sale contract with this option term that will bind Parsley to the agreement.

Key Terms: contract, commercial transactions, option to repurchase, buy-back

Launch Point: 12 West's Legal Forms 3d, Commercial Transactions § 16.2, Form 18.5

WRITING IN THE LAW DISCIPLINE PROBLEMS

1. In the quiet little village of Smithtown, New York stands a picturesque Victorian Style house built in the 1800s. It sits on a 5 acre lot and is approximately 200 feet from a lake. Known by the locals as "Poltergeist Mansion," the locals and the current homeowner, Thomas Jones, believe the house is haunted by at least five different spirits, all of whom can become violent. The spirits are so well-known in the region that the house has received recognition in numerous national magazines and television shows both for its beauty and its ghosts. As recently as July 2008, the house was featured on the SciFi Channel program, "Ghosthunters VI – Someone Must Get Hurt This Season." Mr. Jones, fed up with the terrifying events that occur almost every night on the premises, has decided to sell the house. Although the house is valued at $5 million, he is only asking for $3 million.

   Donny Jepp, an extremely wealthy actor who is intrigued by eccentric and atypical roles, inquired into the home. He, of course, did not live in Smithtown and was unfamiliar with the area, but he had heard of "Poltergeist Mansion" and all its "visitors." Having heard the house was for sale, Mr. Jepp became interested in purchasing the house because he had a lead role in an upcoming film involving a haunted house and he thought living in the house would help him get into character. He visited Poltergeist Mansion with Mr. Jones on one sunny Saturday morning and fell in love with it. While showing Mr. Jepp the house, Mr. Jones did not disclose to Mr. Jepp any details about the presence of spirits because Mr. Jones wasn't sure that Mr. Jepp would purchase the house if he knew everything there was to know about the ghosts and their violent ways. Mr. Jones also thought that since the house had been featured in many magazines and television shows that the word was out and Mr. Jepp could find out everything about the house if he took the time. The two men completed the contract for sale and Mr. Jepp wrote Mr. Jones a check for half the asking price as a down payment. The remaining value was to be paid in two months after Jepp's new film came out. Mr. Jones, with a huge smile on his face, wished Jepp the best of luck and left quickly before sunset. Two days later Jepp moved in.

The first night Jepp spent there, he was awakened when he heard footsteps on the third floor. Excited and intrigued by this occurrence, Jepp decided to go up to the third floor to see what he could find. When he got up there, nobody was there and the footsteps had stopped. Disappointed, Jepp went back to bed and did not hear anything again for three nights. On his fourth night in the house, Jepp was reading one of his scripts by the fireplace when the fire suddenly went out. Slightly startled by the sudden event, but enjoying the suspense it created, Jepp decided to go to the kitchen and get some more matches to light the fire. When he entered the kitchen, a steak knife flew out of the sink and stuck into the cupboard next to his head. Jepp turned around, but nobody was there. His heart was pumping as he got the matches and returned to the fireplace, only to find the fireplace poker was floating around in the air, and something (a ghost?) tried to stab him with it. Jepp grabbed the poker and the ghost disappeared. Thinking he had had enough for the night, Jepp decided to go to bed. He fell asleep, but was awakened when he felt a burning, scratching feeling on his back and chest. The pain was excruciating, almost to the point that he felt paralyzed by it. When it ended, he looked in the bathroom mirror to find that he was bleeding and that there were three long scratch marks on his body. Finally fed up with the haunting of the night, Jepp grabbed some clothes and checked into a hotel. The next evening, when he returned to the house, Jepp saw shadows in the windows and he decided that he had had enough of an experience with the haunted house and went back to the hotel. The next day, he came to your law firm wanting to rescind the contract and get his down payment back.

The managing partner of your firm thinks that Jepp's best theory to support rescinding the contract is fraud. After conducting your own research, you are to: (1) draft the argument section of a memorandum in support of a pretrial motion for summary judgment asserting the grounds for rescission of the contract based on a fraud theory; and (2) draft a client letter to Jepp explaining your research and your conclusions about his ability to rescind the contract on a fraud theory.

Key Terms: contract, real estate purchase, fraud, non-disclosure of material facts, rescission, grounds to rescind contract

Launch Point: <u>*Stambovsky v. Ackley*, 572 N.Y.S.2d 672 (App. Div. 1st Dep't 1991)</u>

2. Lilly LaTulip is a very successful florist who has owned her own floral business for the past ten years. While Lilly is doing well, she recently agreed to make all the flower arrangements for the very eccentric musician Jacko Michael. The wedding is in two weeks, and Lilly finally found the perfect colored sequined gloves for the centerpieces from Chintzy & Cheap. Although Lilly did not see the gloves in person, she saw a picture of them on Chintzy & Cheap's website. Lilly called Chintzy & Cheap to order the gloves, and in the course of their conversation about sizes and styles, the salesman mentioned that Chintzy & Cheap really knew its gloves because it had been in the same business for more than twenty years. The salesman promised to send Lilly the gloves via UPS the next day along with a signed copy of the contract for the gloves, which also established an account with Chintzy & Cheap for future business. Lilly received the gloves and the signed contract in a few days, but she was not happy with the number of sequins on the gloves. Lilly had no other complaints about the gloves or Chintzy & Cheap. With only twelve days until the wedding, Lilly was worried that she would not be able to find any gloves that would make Mr. Michael happy. She began scouring local businesses and the Internet to find the most sequined gloves she could find. With only one day until the wedding, Lilly

finally found the perfect gloves, but she never bothered to inform Chintzy & Cheap that the gloves it sent were not quite right until she received a final notice for payment after several months. Since the gloves were not exactly what she wanted, Lilly believes she should not have to pay for the gloves and should be able to return them. Analyze her claims and defenses and draft the following documents: (1) a letter asserting Lilly's rejection of the gloves addressed to Chintzy & Cheap; (2) a memorandum of law analyzing the legal position of Lilly with respect to the claims of Chintzy & Cheap; and (3) a settlement proposal stating Lilly's legal position and terms of compromise with respect to the claims of Chintzy & Cheap.

Key Terms: Uniform Commercial Code, offer or acceptance between merchants, signature requirement, statute of frauds, notice of rejection of non-conforming goods

Launch Point: Uniform Laws Annotated, UCC; American Jurisprudence Legal Forms 2d (AMJUR-LF); Westlaw's FORM-FINDER database

3. Based on the following information, prepare a memorandum analyzing whether the contract between Davis and Jiang can be enforced by specific performance:

Patricia Piao-Liang Davis is a 20 year old super-model who goes by the professional name "Piao-Liang." She was born in Nanjing, PRC in 1989, but was orphaned at four months of age, and was adopted at six months of age by Clifford and June Davis, U.S. citizens, and raised in Provo, Utah. Piao-Liang is a naturalized citizen of the United States, and is domiciled and resident in Provo, Utah. Piao-Liang has joined a group of other super-models who offer their unfertilized ova for auction on an internet site known as Dezyner-Genes.com. Although she has participated in the web site since January 2007, she has never accepted any bids to purchase her eggs.

While on a photo-shoot for Drop Dead Gorgeous magazine that took her to various locations in China (the Great Wall and Tiananmen Square in Beijing, the Bund in Shanghai, and others),

Piao-Liang was approached at West Lake in Hangzhou by a businessman, Mr. Jerry Jiang (whose Chinese name is Jiang Chuang-ping). Jiang explained that his wife was infertile, and he was interested in purchasing an ovum from Piao-Liang, and offered her $1 million for it. She was flattered and orally agreed to the transaction. The two drank baijiu and toasted each other several times to celebrate the deal. When she returned to the United States, Piao-Liang's lawyers, Hart, Charles, & LaRouche, reviewed Jiang's written proposal for the agreement concerning the sale of the ovum, and they accepted the terms, but added a forum selection and choice of law clause in the agreement, specifying that any action arising under the contract would be brought in a state or federal court in California and that the law of California would govern the contract. The contract was signed by Piao-Liang in New York, NY, on November 2, 2008, and by Jiang in Taibei, Republic of China (Taiwan), on November 4, 2008. The egg or eggs were to be delivered by June 1, 2009, and the payment of $1 million was to be made immediately upon successful fertilization and implantation.

Piao-Liang discovered in late November that Mr. Jiang is the nephew of the late General and President of the ROC, Jiang Ji-shi, better known to the world as Chiang Kai-shek. This horrified her because her Chinese family had been oppressed by the Nationalists prior to the Communist victory in China. She decided to refuse to go through with the sale, and Mr. Jiang sued her in the United States District Court for the Northern District of California.

Purchase and Sale Contract

WHEREFORE, Mr. Jerry Jiang Chuang-Ping (Buyer) and Ms. Patricia Piao-Liang Davis (Seller) wish to enter into an agreement for the transfer of at least one egg from Seller's ovaries to Buyer for the purpose of fertilization of the egg and implantation in Buyer's wife; and

WHEREFORE, the parties, Buyer and Seller, in consideration of the mutual promises stated herein and for other good and valuable consideration; and

WHEREFORE, the parties, Buyer and Seller, wish to complete this transaction at the earliest practicable time, and in no event later than June 1, 2009;

Then the parties covenant and agree to the following:

1. At the earliest practicable opportunity, and in no event later than June 1, 2009, in New York City, NY or Salt Lake City, UT, or at any other mutually agreeable location, Seller shall deliver to Buyer's OB-GYN physician one or more healthy and viable ova (i.e., eggs) from her ovaries.

2. Upon receipt and successful fertilization of the egg(s), the egg(s) are to be implanted in Buyer's wife's uterus,

3. After successful implantation of the fertilized egg(s) in Buyer's wife's uterus, without miscarriage, for twenty-one days, Buyer shall pay Seller by wire transfer to Osmond National Bank, Account No. 100223456 owned by Seller, the sum of one million United States dollars.

4. In the event that conditions 2 and 3 cannot be successfully completed with the initial supply of the egg(s) from Seller, Seller shall, within six weeks of notification by facsimile or U.S. mail by Buyer of the failure of conditions 2 or 3, supply one or more additional healthy and viable eggs to Buyer's OB-GYN physician in New York City, NY or Salt Lake City, UT, and shall continue to supply eggs in the manner described in this paragraph every six weeks until successful completion of conditions 2 and 3 of this contract.

5. Should any dispute between the parties arise under this agreement, the parties, Buyer and Seller, agree that all disputes shall be resolved in litigation that shall be filed in a state or federal court in the State of California and all conditions and terms and obligations of this contract shall be governed by and interpreted under California law.

Signed by Buyer: Signed by Seller:

_____   _____

Jerry Jiang Chuang-ping   Patricia Piao-Liang Davis
Date: November 4, 2008   Date: November 2, 2008

_____

Piao-Liang® is Beauty
234 Joseph Smith Drive
Provo, UT 84602 USA
(801) 555-piao

December 18, 2008

By Facsimile and Mail:

Mr. Jerry Jiang Chuang-ping
Two Embarcadero Center, Suite 3801
San Francisco, CA 94111-3909
Phone: 415-555-7779
Fax: 888-555-7789

To Mr. Jiang:

I am canceling the deal. I never knew you were connected with the Nationalists. This changes everything. I no longer want to undergo the procedure for you or anyone else.

Sincerely,
Piao-Liang Davis

_____

UNITED STATES DISTRICT COURT
NORTHERN DISTRICT OF CALIFORNIA

JIANG CHUANG-PING,	)	
	)	
Plaintiff,	)	No. 2:06-CV-2345-K
v.	)	(Judge Kimball)
	)	
PATRICIA PIAO-LIANG DAVIS,	)	JURY TRIAL DE-
A/K/A "PIAO-LIANG",	)	MANDED
	)	
Defendant.	)	

COMPLAINT

NOW COMES Plaintiff Jiang Chuang-ping ("Plaintiff"), and for his complaint against Defendant Patricia Piao-Liang Davis, also known as the supermodel "Piao-Liang" ("Defendant"), states as follows:

PARTIES

1. Plaintiff is a citizen and resident of the City of San Francisco, State of California, and the United States of America. He is domiciled in the State of California in this Northern District of California.

2. Defendant Piao-Liang is a citizen and resident of the State of Utah, United States of America, and is domiciled in Provo, Utah.

JURISDICTION AND VENUE

3. This Court has subject matter jurisdiction over this action under 28 U.S.C. § 1332(a)(1) in that Plaintiff and Defendant have diverse citizenship, and the matter involves over $75,000 in controversy.

4. Personal jurisdiction exists over Defendant because Defendant was served with process in this State and District.

5. Defendant and Plaintiff entered into the Contract attached hereto as Exhibit 1 ("Contract") on November 2 and November 4, 2008, respectively.

6. The contract provides for suit to be brought in a federal court in California and the Contract is to be governed by California law. Contract, section 5.

7. Venue is proper in this district pursuant to the forum selection clause in section 5 of the Contract and pursuant to 28 U.S.C. § 1391 in that Defendant was served with process within this District and Division, and the subject matter of the Contract is present in this District.

COUNT I - BREACH OF CONTRACT

8. On November 2, 2008, Defendant entered into the Contract, promising to deliver to Plaintiff's OB-GYN physician one or more healthy and viable ova from her ovaries at the first available opportunity and no later than June 1, 2009. Upon receipt and successful fertilization and implantation of the egg(s) in Plaintiff's wife's uterus, Plaintiff was to pay Plaintiff by wire transfer the sum of one million United States dollars.

9. On December 18, 2008, Defendant phoned Plaintiff and repudiated the contract by stating that she would not perform her obligations. She then, on that same day, sent by facsimile transmission and U.S. Mail the letter attached hereto as Exhibit 2, again repudiating the Contract and refusing to perform her obligations under the Contract.

10. Plaintiff was and remains ready to perform his obligations under the Contract, and there are no other conditions precedent to the agreement that would prevent its performance.

11. Defendant breached its agreement with Plaintiff by anticipatory repudiation.

12. Plaintiff has no available alternative remedy at law that could replace or compensate Plaintiff for the unique value of the subject matter of the Contract, and seeks specific performance of the Contract, and such further and other relief as the Court deems proper in the circumstances.

COUNT II - SPECIFIC PERFORMANCE

13. Plaintiff realleges the allegations of paragraphs 1-12 of this complaint as though set forth fully in this paragraph.

14. Plaintiff comes to this court seeking equity, with clean hands, and with the equities in his favor. Plaintiff has no available alternative remedy at law. The public policy of this jurisdiction favors the upholding and enforcement of contracts for the provision of a unique subject matter.

15. Defendant has repudiated and breached her obligations under the Contract. The equities and public policy are against Defendant.

16. Plaintiff seeks specific performance of the Contract.

WHEREFORE, Plaintiff requests the Court to order Defendant to deliver to Plaintiff's OB-GYN physician one or more healthy and viable ova from her ovaries at the first available opportunity and no later than June 1, 2009, and to award Plaintiff such further and other relief as the Court deems proper in the circumstances.

JURY TRIAL DEMANDED.

FINLEY & MOORE, LLP

By:_____

       Miriam O. McGuinnis, Ut Bar No. 02112
       114 Market Street, Suite 2800
       Salt Lake City, Utah 84101
       Phone: 801-555-SU4U

       Attorneys for Plaintiff Jiang Chuang-ping

_____

Key Terms: contract, enforceability, subject matter, enforcement against public policy

Launch Point: <u>17A Am. Jur. 2d Contracts § 237</u>.

II.   TORTS

RESEARCH AND WRITING PROBLEMS

1. To promote its upcoming annual rodeo show, Mayor Spur decided all the Rodeo Town, Texas citizens should dress in western attire for the entire week. The Mayor made his pitch on every country music station received by Rodeo Town and in the local Lone Star Chronicle newspaper. In his announcements, the Mayor warned that if individuals are caught not wearing the western outfits during rodeo week, they will be lassoed by cowboys patrolling the streets and taken to the town square where they will be dressed like a rodeo clown and made to sell tickets to the rodeo. They must do this until they sell two tickets. If the captured person want to, they can forego the humiliation and purchase the tickets themselves.

    During rodeo week, your client, Panicky Patty, visited Rodeo Town, but was not wearing any cowboy attire. As she walked through the streets, Lassoing Larry, the town sheriff, charged towards her on foot circling the lasso over his head and yelling,

"Let's get her!" Panicky panicked and started running away from the sheriff. Panicky tried to run into a nearby store, but as she did so, she slipped and fell against the glass door of the store, breaking the glass and severely cutting her hand and wrist in several places. Mayor Spur, fearing liability, has come to your law office, Bronco & Bull LLP, since your office has litigated hundreds of tort cases. The senior partners have called on you, the youngest attorney in the firm, to draft a 1-2 page memo discussing the likelihood of liability by the sheriff or mayor or the city itself. If there are potential defenses, list them but do not discuss them in detail because another associate will focus on them. Do not analyze negligence theories. Instead, your memo should focus on: (1) potential liability of the city for intentional torts; and (2) whether the mayor or the sheriff can be sued for an intentional tort.

Key Terms: assault, battery, agent, implied or apparent agency, master-servant, respondeat superior liability

Launch Point: *Moore v. El Paso Chamber of Commerce*, 220 S.W.2d 327 (Tex. Civ. App. 1949)

2. A professional firefighter for a local community in Michigan was injured fighting a house fire that was started when the homeowner fell asleep with a cigarette in her hand. When the firefighters arrived at the house, all of the occupants had already escaped the blaze. While trying to put out the blaze in the house, the firefighter fell from the second story and broke both of his legs. After an investigation, the fire department determined that the firefighter fell because the homeowners failed to replace the railing along the stairs and the landing after having some remodeling done in the house several years ago. Draft 1-2 pages analyzing whether the firefighter has a cause of action against the homeowners.

Key Terms: homeowner, premises liability, unsafe condition, guest or invitee, emergency, public officer or employee, assumption of risk

Launch Point: 62 Am. Jur. 2d, Premises Liability §§ 67, 431;
Jay Berger, *Has the Michigan Firefighter's Rule Gone Up in Smoke?
An Analysis of the Wilful and Wanton Exception*, 44 Wayne L. Rev.
1555 (1998)

3. A masked man stormed into a local bank with his gun drawn de-
    manding money from the tellers. When the tellers hesitated, the
    robber grabbed a young teller by her hair and pointed the gun at
    her head. The man threatened to shoot the teller if the others tell-
    ers did not put all the money into the duffel bag he threw at them.
    While the other tellers frantically placed the money into the bag,
    the man kept the gun pointed at the young teller's head jabbing
    it into her temple whenever he shouted at the tellers to hurry
    up. After several minutes, the tellers filled the bag with money,
    and the robber quickly left the bank before the police arrived.
    The young teller collapsed immediately and had to be taken to
    the hospital. Later, the employees learned that the same man at-
    tempted to rob another bank earlier the same day and shot three
    tellers who did not give him enough money. The police were not
    able to find the robber for several months. Since the robbery, the
    young teller, who only worked part time while attending college,
    refused to leave her home. The teller's parents noticed that their
    daughter began to lose weight, could not sleep, seemed skittish
    around other people, particularly men, quit her job, and dropped
    out of school. After six months, the police arrested the robber
    and charged him with several armed robberies. The young teller
    is thinking about filing a civil lawsuit against the robber. Analyze
    in 1-2 pages: (1) what tort claims the young teller might assert
    against the robber assuming he is not judgment proof; and (2) for
    each claim, state the elements that must be proved by the young
    teller.

    Key Terms: battery, assault, intentional infliction of emotional
    distress, outrageous conduct, restitution for victim of crime

    Launch Point: Restatement 2d of Torts § 46; 92 A.L.R. 5th 35.

4. Recently, a friend of yours from law school named Jim Conway
    came to see you regarding a situation that occurred at his law
    firm in Chandler, Arizona. Jim told you that a colleague of his,

John Knotts, borrowed Jim's legal writing book from the top shelf of Jim's office in the law firm where John and he worked. John was drafting his first appellate brief since passing the bar, his first in over ten years, and he wanted to make sure he brushed up on his techniques. John never borrowed the book before and never asked Jim's permission to borrow the book this time. Unfortunately, John stayed up all night reading the book while drinking Koffeebuc's Kappucinos, and in the early morning hours, John fell asleep and accidentally knocked a cup of coffee all over the opened book lying on his desk. The coffee soaked in and stained many of the pages badly and caused them to become stuck together in clumps, making several chapters of the book virtually unreadable. When John saw Jim that morning, he apologized and offered to replace the book at its fair market value of approximately $80, which John determined after looking at the price of this edition of the book on several online book dealers. After listening to John, Jim was devastated because to him the book was an invaluable collector's item worth much more than $80. The book was a first edition that was misprinted because the title on the spine ran from the bottom of the book to the top, instead of top to bottom. Furthermore, Jim's law school Legal Writing professor, the author of the book, had autographed Jim's copy. Then the professor went on to become a Supreme Court justice. To Jim, the book is invaluable. Jim wants to know what, if any, types of claims he may have against John and what damages he might recover. Please respond to Jim in the form of a client letter stating and explaining his options under Arizona law.

Key Terms: conversion or destruction of property, damages, value to owner

Launch Point: Restatement (Second) of Torts § 927 (1979).

DRAFTING PROBLEMS

1. Sammy Brown was a professional baseball player and future hall-of-famer, who had a habit of smoking 2 packs of cigarettes while in the dugout. He still had three years on his contract when, on one scorching August day, he passed out while hustling out a double. He was rushed to the hospital where the doctor, Dr.

Smith, diagnosed him with heat exhaustion. The doctor, however, did not order a CT scan, which some doctor's consider the proper standard of care whenever an individual goes unconscious and is admitted to the emergency room. Later that evening, while in his hospital bed, Sammy suffered a stroke and died. It turns out that Sammy had a brain aneurysm, which could have been detected had the doctor ordered a CT scan when he entered the emergency room.

Mrs. Brown, distraught and knowing the value of her husband's career, is suing the doctor for medical malpractice and the wrongful death of Sammy because he breached the proper standard of care. Mrs. Brown is seeking over ten million dollars in damages. You are Dr. Smith's attorney and you know that if you go to trial, you will likely lose and the damages will be huge, quite possibly over ten million dollars. As a result, you want to minimize the damages by offering Mrs. Brown a settlement. After two months of negotiations, Mrs. Brown agrees to settle for seven million dollars. Draft a structured settlement agreement between Ms. Brown and the doctor. You may draw from standard forms but please cite each source that you draw from.

Key Words: Structured settlement, settlement agreement, release

Launch Point: American Jurisprudence Trials, 4 AMJUR TRIALS 289; West's Legal Forms (West-LF) - General Settlement Agreements

2. The police department of Tarrytown, Rhode Island, has had difficulty coping with a local rock band called "Crunch" whose outdoor concerts have on several occasions devolved into riots in which real and personal property has been damaged or destroyed, and several attendees or bystanders at or near the concert site have been injured. The police officers have often become disoriented and separated from their units and their commanding officers in the rioting crowds which has prevented the units from controlling the situation. In order to maintain cohesiveness in the ranks and improve the tactical positioning of officers involved in riot control, the police department wishes to impose new regulations on

the police: sergeants and lieutenants who are on the scene must wear bright white patrol shirts instead of the blue shirts worn by the other police officers, and they are not to cover up the shirts with the usual flak jackets and riot gear worn by the other officers. The plan is to allow all of the unit police officers to be able to quickly identify the commander at the scene and be better able to maintain a tactical position around that person. Several town council members have expressed concerns that these new regulations might expose the town to civil law suits from the sergeants and lieutenants who might be injured at the scene in part because they will "stand out" from the other officers, presenting a more attractive target for the rioters, and they will not be wearing the protective gear worn by the other officers at the scene.

As a young member of the town counselor's staff, you have been asked to research and draft a short report to the town council (1-3 pages) on whether the town might be exposed to liability for civil claims by the sergeants and lieutenants who will be subject to the new regulations. In this report, you should lay out the claims that might be asserted and the requirements (elements) of these claims and report on those claims that are precluded by state law.

Key Terms: injury on duty, benefits, remedy, police officers, municipal corporations, agents, employees

Launch Point: *Kaya v. Partington*, 681 A.2d 256 (R.I. 1996)

WRITING IN THE LAW DISCIPLINE PROBLEMS

1. In 2008, Donny Brown was a duly-authorized and licensed driver of a taxi cab for the Speedy Cab Company in New York City. As he drove the streets looking for and transporting his fares, Mr. Brown carried two, five gallon containers full of gasoline in the trunk of his cab. Mr. Brown had the containers full of gasoline because in addition to his salary, he also received tips and a small percentage of the fares he collected every week. He figured that if he could reduce the number of hours spent driving to the gas station he would be able to maximize his weekly income. After all, it often took him at least an hour to get to a gas station in Manhattan (they are few and far between in the crowded city, and

there almost always is traffic) and to tank up at the station and get back to the busier streets where fares most likely would be found. Brown did not tell anyone at Speedy Cab Company that he was carrying extra gas around in the trunk of his cab, and in fact no one at the company knew he was doing this, although a careful inspection of Brown's weekly logs might have revealed that Brown was unusually efficient and productive for longer periods of time compared to other hack drivers who tanked up more frequently.

Unfortunately, one day in 2008, a second cab crashed into the rear of Mr. Brown's cab and the two containers full of gasoline ignited and exploded in a massive fireball. Mrs. Betty Jones, a bystander who was collecting money for charity on the sidewalk near the crash site, suffered third degree burns over 90% of her body. She is now suing the Speedy Cab Company claiming it was negligent because it allowed Mr. Brown to carry the gasoline containers in the trunk of the car, thereby endangering its passengers and anyone else in the vicinity.

You represent the Speedy Cab Company and refuse to pay any damages because you believe your client is not liable. Your assignment is to draft: (1) a stipulation of the facts, and (2) the argument section of a memorandum in support of a motion for summary judgment in favor of the Speedy Cab Company on Mrs. Jones's negligence claim.

Key Terms: negligence, causation, proximate cause, duty of care, chain of causation, liability

Launch Point: *Palsgraf v. Long Island Railroad Co.*, 162 N.E. 99 (N.Y. 1928)

2. Your client, General Hospital, has engaged your firm to investigate its chances of success in defending a negligence action brought by Nick York. The facts are as follows:

Nick York, now widowed, was married to Fran York for 15 years. On June 2, 2008, Fran was diagnosed with bipolar disorder (f/k/a manic depressive disorder). She began seeing Dr. Marcia Rubino, a psychiatrist, once a week to help alleviate the symptoms of her illness. On June 26, 2008, Fran lapsed into one of her deep depressive "spells" and voluntarily admitted herself into the psychiatric ward of General Hospital.

Upon entering the ward, Fran was stripped searched, a common practice at the hospital when admitting a psychiatric patient. Fran's lower arms and wrists were scarred, appearing to be cut in three places. The cuts did not appear to be severe enough to be life-threatening, but still were reported in Fran's file. The hospital then set up an initial appointment with the hospital's resident psychiatrist, Dr. Patricia Martin, as is done with all incoming psychiatric patients. Dr. Martin confirmed the diagnosis of bipolar disorder and assigned Fran to a room in a closed ward where she would be supervised 24 hours a day.

After several days in the hospital, on July 1, 2008, Dr. Martin gave orders for Fran to be reassigned to a room in an open ward. Dr. Martin thought that Fran was improving, and that the change would benefit her recovery. An open ward allows one nurse at a time to monitor the room, which has two patients. The nurse visits the room and checks on the patients at least three times during any 24 hour period, but the patients are not constantly under surveillance as they are in the closed ward. The doors of the patients' rooms are not locked and the patients are free to walk around the ward. The open ward is designated for patients not displaying any suicidal tendencies. This is because it has been shown that more freedom helps patients with mental disorders to improve faster.

During her stay in the open ward, on two occasions Fran was found laying at the bottom of a single flight of stairs leading from one floor of the hospital to another floor. Fran was unhurt in each of these incidents. No one witnessed the incidents, but the nurses or orderlies who found Fran at the bottom of the stairs reported that it appeared the incidents were accidental. Fran herself described them as incidents where she "slipped or lost her grip on the railing." The incidents were noted in Fran's chart as accidental falls. There were no other incidents while Fran was assigned to the open ward.

On July 5, 2008, the nurses of General Hospital started a 72 hour work stoppage in order to send management a message and as part of their efforts to organize a collective bargaining unit in the United Medical Workers Union. General Hospital hired replacement nurses, most of whom were retired nurses and physicians' assistants, while others were nurses reassigned to General Hospital from other hospitals in the SHG Hospital Network. Even so, General Hospital was forced to maintain a "minimum staffing condition code yellow" status for the time period of 6:00 a.m. on July 5 through 6:00 a.m. on July 8, 2008. This is sometimes referred to by hospital staff as putting out a "skeleton crew."

On July 6, 2008, the night nurse, a retiree of General Hospital called back into service, checked on Fran at approximately 11:30 p.m. and even helped her get ready for bed. As per standard hospital procedure in the open wards, no other checks were made on Fran until July 7, 2008, at 7:08 a.m., when the morning shift nurse found Fran dead in her bathroom. Cause of death was massive bleeding from cuts across her wrists. Fran had shattered the bathroom mirror and used a shard of glass to cut her wrists. The medical examiner's report placed the time of death between 1:00 a.m. and 4:00 a.m.

Nick York is now planning on suing General Hospital for negligence. In a letter written to the hospital ombudsman, Mr. Ronald Pearson, Nick claimed that if the hospital had been more diligent in diagnosing Fran, it would have realized she had suicidal tendencies and would have placed her in the closed ward where there was greater supervision. With greater supervision, Fran might still be alive.

Research and draft a memorandum on whether or not General Hospital is likely to be successful in defending the threatened negligence and wrongful death action.

Key Terms: negligence, professional negligence, malpractice, suicide, mental health, depression

Launch Point: *Bunting v. Huckstep*, 853 S.W.2d 448 (Mo. Ct. App. E. Dist. 1993)

3. Your firm needs to analyze the claim of a new client, Victor Emmanuel Chandelbise. Please determine whether Victor can bring a strict products liability action against Homenides de Histangua Hospital and the surgeon and inventor, Dr. Finache. Attached is an article from the newspaper that gives some details about the event:

St. Louis Post-Dispatch
St. Louis woman dies from her heart valve failure

Date: September 15, 2008
By: Romain Tournel

At 3:30 a.m. on September 14, a St. Louis woman, Yvonne Chandelbise, died from cardiac arrest en route to Barnes Hospital. The cause of the 43 year old woman's death was apparently related to her Keltic VII heart valve. Chandelbise was one of the first recipients of the Keltic VII heart valve, invented by famed local surgeon Dr. Walter Finache and a team of scientists working at the Homenides de Histangua Hospital in Webster Groves, Missouri.

Chandelbise received the heart valve in March 2008 after several years of severe cardiovascular problems. Her husband, Victor Emmanual Chandelbise, reported that the valve worked fine for several months, but then his wife started hearing audible clicking as the valve opened and shut. Soon after, on September 12, Yvonne saw a news story on Spinline news program that reported that several Keltic VII heart valves had failed, causing fragments of the lining of the valves to break off and to spin into the bloodstream causing fatalities. The story mentioned that the failure of the valves often was preceded by audible sounds from the valves.

Yvonne was greatly disturbed by the news, and suffered several panic attacks on September 12 and 13 following the airing of the news story. Early in the morning of September 13, Yvonne awoke in the middle of the night and her husband reported that she "was in a full blown panic attack," and she made statements to the effect that the clicking sounds from her heart valve were getting louder. She then went into cardiac arrest, and died en route to the hospital.

This was the first such report of a potential failure-related death attributable to the Keltic VII heart valve in the state of Missouri. Neither Dr. Finache nor Homenides de Histangua Hospital chose to comment on this matter. Yvonne Chandelbise is survived by her husband and a son, Camille Chandelbise.

These are the facts as told by Victor Chandelbise:

- Yvonne had a bad heart condition ("end stage degradation of heart muscle tissue"). Her Keltic VII valve was implanted on March 17, 2008. She was happy with its performance on April 12 when she signed a patient survey giving Dr. Finache high marks. Victor reported that the valve was helping her quality of life all the way to September 13, 2008, when she saw the Spinline TV program.

- Yvonne heard her valve clicking in the week following the implantation surgery. Dr. Finache had predicted that she might hear the noise of a mechanical valve opening and shutting, and he listened to the valve at her four week check up and ran other tests and reported that the valve sounded and was operating normally. When Yvonne noticed that the clicking sounds were getting louder over the course of the summer, Yvonne twice called Dr. Finache, once in July and once in August, to discuss the clicking sounds, and she was assured on each occasion by Dr. Finache that the clicking by itself was no cause for concern as long as she had no other symptoms of heart problems (shortness of breath, chest pains, or overall weakness).

- Her heart failure was preceded by her viewing the Spinline TV news story that the Kelvic VII heart valve had failed on six prior occasions, breaking into pieces that swirled in the blood causing death. Enhanced clicking noise preceded these other six incidents. The first of these incidents was in June 2008 and the last was in mid-August 2008.

- Yvonne's heart valve apparently did not malfunction or fail in the way that the other six valves did. It did not break apart. It did have extraordinarily loud clicking noises, especially in the time period immediately preceding Yvonne's death. This clicking (combined with the information from the TV story about what the clicking might mean) created the panic that preceded her heart failure.

- A family lawyer friend had Victor go and obtain an engineering diagnostic report. This report confirmed many of the findings of the autopsy report of Barnes Jewish Hospital regarding the performance of Yvonne's Keltic VII valve. Both reports confirmed that Yvonne's heart valve did not malfunction or fail, it did not break apart, but it did have extraordinarily loud clicking noises. The autopsy concluded that the Keltic VII heart valve played no role in her fatal heart attack which occurred in the opposite side of her heart from where the valve was implanted.

- You should assume that these heart valve devices are not regulated by the FDA and not covered by the Medical Device Amendments (MDA) to the FDA regulations. Thus, Missouri law applies, not federal law. All the events occurred and all persons involved in these events lived and acted in St. Louis County, Missouri.

- For the time being, you should ignore the difficulties we might face in proving any action against potential defendants. Issues of how we might prove the case or what proof would be necessary, and any other evidentiary issues should be put aside for now.

The two questions that you should answer in your memorandum are: (1) Can Victor Chandelbise state a viable products liability cause of action against the Homenides de Histangua Hospital – a health care provider – for strict liability for failure to warn? and (2) Can Victor Chandelbise state a viable products liability cause of action against Dr. Finache, the surgeon who implanted the valve and the designer and manufacturer of the heart valve, for strict liability for failure to warn? In particular, you should focus on the defect requirement (definition of defect and whether the valve can meet that requirement) and the causation requirement, and do not focus on other requirements for a strict liability failure to warn cause of action.

Key Terms: strict liability, products, failure to warn, heart valve, defect, malfunction, causation

Launch Point: *Spuhl v. Shiley, Inc.*, 795 S.W.2d 573 (Mo. Ct. App. E. Dist. 1990)

III.   CIVIL PROCEDURE

RESEARCH AND WRITING PROBLEMS

1. Ralph has had a long-standing beef with his old buddy Norton for stealing food out of his icebox over the course of many years. Ralph would like to sue him in North Carolina, where Ralph now lives in retirement, but Norton still lives in New York City. One day, while having a beer at a bar across the street from the main terminal of the local airport, Ralph saw Norton walk out of the airport and cross the street and walk into the bar. The two former neighbors embraced and Norton told the tale of his plane losing a section of the rudder forcing them to make an emergency landing at the airport. Ralph wasted no time in serving Norton with the North Carolina court's summons and complaint that he had with him, suing him for his past mooching. Norton said, "Thanks a lot, Ralphie boy!" and stormed out, and flew home on the next plane out. Based on these facts, draft 1-2 pages: (1) analyzing whether the North Carolina court can exercise jurisdiction over Norton; (2) analyzing whether Norton can sue Ralph back in the same action in North Carolina for swindling him out of money in a futile scheme to renovate a hotel in New Jersey; and (3) determining the alternative fora where Norton might sue Ralph for his claims arising from the hotel scheme.

    Key Terms: personal jurisdiction, service while present in the forum, "gotcha" service, supplemental jurisdiction, same case or controversy

    Launch Point: <u>4 Wright & Miller, Federal Practice and Procedure 3d §§ 1064</u>, <u>1065</u>, <u>13D Wright & Miller, Federal Practice and Procedure 3d § 3567</u>

2. Jane moved from Manchester, England, to the State of Ohio, U.S.A., and opened a coke processing plant near the Ohio River in Cincinnati. She put it into operation and almost immediately released a huge cloud of noxious fumes that drifted over the river and caused injuries to people strolling in Walker Park in Dayton, Kentucky. Jane was so distraught, she closed down the plant that same day, and never reopened it. She immediately retired to

Arizona and from then on has never left Arizona. Based on these facts, draft 1-2 pages: (1) analyzing whether the injured parties in Kentucky can sue Jane in a Kentucky court; (2) analyzing whether the injured parties in Kentucky can sue Jane in an Ohio court; and (3) determining the alternative fora where the injured parties in Kentucky might sue Jane.

Key Terms: personal jurisdiction, long-arm statute, tort, personal injury with effects in state

Launch Point: <u>4 Wright & Miller, Federal Practice and Procedure 3d § 1068</u>; <u>4A Wright & Miller, Federal Practice and Procedure 3d § 1069</u>

3. Sue is an artist living and working in Bangor, Maine, who sued her landlord, who also is a citizen and resident of Bangor, Maine, in the Maine District Court, District III, Bangor, for taking pictures of her artwork and selling the photographs in violation of her copyright. Before she knows it, her case winds up in the United States District Court for the District of Maine, Bangor Office. Draft 1-2 pages: (1) analyzing whether removal was appropriate; and (2) analyzing whether, now that the case is in federal court, Sue can add a state law property damage claim to her complaint seeking the value of a painting that the landlord crushed when he slammed open the door to her apartment?

    Key Terms: copyright jurisdiction, copyright preemption, federal question, supplemental jurisdiction, same case or controversy

    Launch Point: <u>13D Wright & Miller, Federal Practice and Procedure 3d §§ 3567, 3582</u>

4. Clara is a citizen and resident of South Dakota. Clara's home-made roach killer recipe was so effective that all of her neighbors wanted to use it. She slapped some handwritten labels on some mason jars and filled them with the roach killer and sold them to her friends and neighbors. One neighbor, who also is a citizen and resident of South Dakota, accidentally took a swig of the roach killer thinking it was the jar of corn whisky he had stashed under the sink, and suffered a serious injury. A friend told Clara

she had better retain a lawyer that knows her way around federal law. Draft 1-2 pages analyzing whether the neighbor's claim can be brought in federal court and on what basis or bases would jurisdiction in federal court be appropriate.

Key Terms: subject matter jurisdiction, federal court, insecticide, labeling, federal preemption

Launch Point: *Bates v. Dow Agrosciences LLC*, 544 U.S. 431 (2005)

5. Bobo is a citizen and resident of Cape Code, Massachusetts. He had his seaside newsstand destroyed by a crowd of tourists that swarmed the stand when it was rumored that Bobo had retrieved John F. Kennedy Jr.'s watch from the ocean and had it on display at the stand. Through diligent effort, Bobo determined that the tourists were citizens and residents of New York City, Boston, Philadelphia, Washington D.C., and Baltimore. Draft 1-2 pages analyzing: (1) whether it is possible to sue all of the tourists for negligence in one court (and be sure to identify which court that would be); and (2) whether it is possible to sue all of the tourists for negligence in a federal court.

Key Terms: jurisdiction, minimum contacts, injury or damages caused in forum, diversity

Launch Point: *Harlow v. Children's Hosp.*, 432 F.3d 50 (1st Cir. 2005); *Connectu LLC v. Zuckerberg*, 522 F.3d 82 (1st Cir. 2008)

DRAFTING PROBLEMS

1. Review the facts of Civil Procedure—Writing in the Law Discipline Problem 1 below (Grumbacher v. Elwood "Lion" Forest). Draft interrogatories, requests for production of documents and things, and requests for admissions on the merits of the case (*i.e.*, not relating to venue) for the discovery phase of this litigation on behalf of whichever side you are assigned or choose to represent.

Key Terms: right of publicity; public figure or celebrity; sports; matter of public interest; use of name, image or likeness without consent; First Amendment right of free expression; artistic expression; merchandise

Launch Point: 3A West's Fed. Forms 5th, District Courts-Civil § 3492

2. Review the facts of Civil Procedure—Writing in the Law Discipline Problem 2 below (Jiang v. Piao-Liang). Draft interrogatories, requests for production of documents and things, and requests for admissions on the merits of the case (*i.e.*, not relating to venue) for the discovery phase of this litigation on behalf of whichever side you are assigned or choose to represent.

Key Terms: contract, body part, body tissue, egg, ova, specific performance

Launch Point: 3A West's Fed. Forms 5th, District Courts-Civil § 3492

WRITING IN THE LAW DISCIPLINE PROBLEMS

1. Research and draft a memorandum in support of motion to transfer venue or a memorandum in opposition to motion to transfer venue depending on whichever side you are assigned or choose to represent.

MEMORANDUM

TO: Junior Associate

FROM: Senior Partner

DATE: January 18, 2009

RE: <u>Grumbacher v. Elwood "Lion" Forest</u>

SUBJECT: Motion to Transfer Venue

Defendant Elwood "Lion" Forest is the most famous Native American golfer on the PGA tour. Since his bursting onto the professional golfing scene in 1999, after winning four consecutive PGA Amateur titles, he has continued to excel, winning ten of the "major" tournaments in the last seven years, and winning the same major (the British Open) in three consecutive years, 2005, 2006, and 2007. He has received an enormous amount of attention from the United States and world press. In the last three years, he has been on the cover of over 180 newspapers and more than 250 sports and news magazines. He has received close to $90 million in product endorsement contracts in 2008, including a deal with TropoOrangie Products for $45 million that put his face on the label of orange juice cartons the world over.

Plaintiff Newton Grumbacher is an artist living in Chicago, Illinois. His medium is oil paint, and he paints outdoors as much as possible. Once, he attended a PGA event at Kemper Lakes Course in Deerfield, Illinois, and saw Lion Forest in action. He sketched the golfer making several shots, and went back to his studio and completed a painting of the golfer in the midst of one of his signature shots. Friends of the artist thought the painting was fantastic, and they encouraged Grumbacher to make some prints of the painting. Grumbacher created a limited series of 200 prints which he began to sell for $600/each. He also created a line of coffee mugs ($8) and golf towels ($10). All the prints, mugs and towels have the same image on them, the painting of Lion Forest with Grumbacher's name emblazoned across the bottom of the picture.

Lion Forest saw one of the golf towels at an event, and became furious. He immediately had his lawyers draft up a threatening cease and desist letter to Grumbacher. (Complaint, exhibit 1). The letter demanded that Grumbacher cease the distribution or sale of any prints, mugs, towels, or any other article that features the likeness of Lion Forest produced without the consent of Mr. Forest, and retrieve and destroy all existing examples of such items, within 10 days, or Mr. Forest would sue Mr. Grumbacher under Illinois and Federal law for violation of Mr. Forest's right of publicity.

Grumbacher, being no stranger to controversy, got the jump on Mr. Forest and sued him in the Northern District of Illinois for declaratory judgment under Federal False Designation of Origin Act, 15 U.S.C. § 1125 and the Illinois Right of Publicity Act, 765 Ill. Comp. Stat. 1075/30 et seq.

Our first task is draft a court brief (Memorandum in Support/Opposition) regarding the Motion to Transfer Venue filed by Defendant Forest. See attached court file. Use the declarations in the court file when you are drafting your memorandum.

UNITED STATES DISTRICT COURT
NORTHERN DISTRICT OF ILLINOIS
EASTERN DIVISION

NEWTON W. GRUMBACHER,	)	
	)	
Plaintiff,	)	No. 02-C-9345
v.	)	(Judge Ruben Castillo)
	)	
ELWOOD FOREST, A/K/A "LION"	)	
FOREST,	)	JURY TRIAL
	)	DEMANDED
	)	
Defendant.	)	

COMPLAINT

NOW COMES Plaintiff Newton W. Grumbacher ("Plaintiff"), and for his complaint against Defendant Elwood Forest, also known as the professional golfer "Lion" Forest ("Defendant"), states as follows:

PARTIES

1. Plaintiff is a citizen and resident of the City of Chicago, Cook County, State of Illinois. He is domiciled in the State of Illinois.

2. Defendant Lion Forest is a citizen and resident of the State of Florida, and is domiciled in West Palm Beach, Florida.

JURISDICTION AND VENUE

3. This Court has subject matter jurisdiction over this action under 28 U.S.C. § 1332(a)(1) in that Plaintiff and Defendant have diverse citizenship, and the matter involves over $75,000 in controversy.

4. This Court further has subject matter jurisdiction over this action under 28 U.S.C. § 1331, in that the action arises under federal law, the Federal False Designation of Origin Act, 15 U.S.C. § 1125. This court has supplemental jurisdiction over the portion of the claim that involves the Illinois Right of Publicity Act, 765 Ill. Comp. Stat. 1075/30 et seq.

5. Venue is proper in this district pursuant to 28 U.S.C. § 1391(a)(2) because a substantial part of the events or omissions giving rise to the claims occurred in this district.

COUNT I - DECLARATORY JUDGMENT

6. On June 2, 2008, Plaintiff saw Defendant in person participating in a golf tournament at Kemper Lakes Country Club in Deerfield, Illinois.

7. On that date, Plaintiff made five sketches of Defendant playing golf. Later, he used these sketches to produce an oil on canvas painting which depicts Defendant playing golf.

8. The painting is an artistic creation and a work of art, embodying ideas and images, and reflecting Plaintiff's artistic interpretation and skill. Thus, Plaintiff's painting is protected under state and federal law, including the Federal False Designation of Origin Act, 15 U.S.C. § 1125, and the Illinois Right of Publicity Act, 765 Ill. Comp. Stat. 1075/30 et seq., from claims of infringement or violation of Defendant's rights of publicity.

9. Defendant is a famous public figure. He is one of the most famous golfers currently active on the PGA circuit. His name and image are well know all across the world. Defendant excels at his sport, winning ten of the major tournaments in seven years, and winning the same major (the British Open) in three consecutive years, 2005, 2006, and 2007. He has received an enormous amount of attention from the United States and world press. In the last three years, he has been on the cover of over 180 newspapers and more than 250 sports and news magazines. He has received close to $90 million in product endorsement contracts in 2008, including a deal with TropoOrangie Products for $45 million that put his face on the label of orange juice cartons the world over. Defendant is a subject worthy of news attention and depiction. Thus, Plaintiff's painting is protected under state and federal law, including the Federal False Designation of Origin Act, 15 U.S.C. § 1125, and the Illinois Right of

Publicity Act, 765 Ill. Comp. Stat. 1075/30 et seq., from claims of infringement or violation of Defendant's rights of publicity.

10. Plaintiff has made derivative works of his painting, including a limited edition of 200 high quality, serigraph transfer, individually numbered and signed prints of the painting worth at least $600 each. Plaintiff has also produced coffee mugs and golf towels bearing the same image of the painting. The image of the painting is modified so as to add the artist's last name on each of the prints, mugs and towels.

11. In that the original painting is protected under state and federal law, including the Federal False Designation of Origin Act, 15 U.S.C. § 1125, and the Illinois Right of Publicity Act, 765 Ill. Comp. Stat. 1075/30 et seq., from claims of infringement or violation of Defendant's rights of publicity, each derivative work produced by the same artist is also protected from claims of infringement or violation of Defendant's rights of publicity.

12. On December 1, 2008, Defendant sent by facsimile transmission and U.S. Mail the letter attached hereto as Exhibit 1, threatening Plaintiff and demanding that Plaintiff cease and desist production, distribution and sale of all prints, mugs, towels, and any other "derivative works" of the painting without the consent of Defendant. The letter also calls for Plaintiff to destroy the original painting of Defendant and all prints, mugs, towels, and other "derivative works" of the painting now and in the future possession of Plaintiff. The letter threatened a lawsuit within ten days of the letter if its terms were not followed.

13. An actual case and controversy exists between Plaintiff and Defendant based on the letter and the threats of legal action concerning Plaintiff's art contained therein.

WHEREFORE, Plaintiff requests the Court to order a declaratory judgment in favor of Plaintiff and against Defendant, ordering and decreeing that Plaintiff has the right to produce, sell, and distribute the painting of Defendant and prints, mugs, and towels bearing the image depicted in the original painting, and to award Plaintiff such further and other relief as the Court deems proper in the circumstances.

JURY TRIAL DEMANDED.

SMITH, MAPLE, & RUSH, P.C.

By:_____

Andres Smith
Ill. Bar No. 6157980
111 South Michigan Avenue
Chicago, Illinois, 60603-6110
Fax: 800-555-SU4U

Attorneys for Plaintiff
Newton W. Grumbacher

Filed: December 8, 2008

E. Lion Forest
18 Golfview Road
West Palm Beach, Florida 33406

December 1, 2008

By Facsimile and Mail:
Mr. Newton W. Grumbacher
234 Warsaw Street
Chicago IL 60609

Dear Sir:

I have engaged the law firm of Rogers, Alben, & Dana to investigate your unauthorized production, sale, and distribution of items bearing my image and likeness without my authorization. This is a violation of my rights under Illinois and federal law. I never authorized you or anyone else associated with you to produce, distribute or sell any item or derivative work that bears my image and likeness. You have produced no less than one oil painting, 200 (more or less) serigraph reprints of the oil painting, and numerous other derivative works, including but not limited to coffee mugs and towels. Please accept this as my demand that you cease production, distribution and sale or all items described above. Please take all necessary means to collect back any items whose sale is not yet final. And, within ten (10) days of the date of this letter, please provide proof to me at the above address of the destruction of all items described in this letter, including one oil painting, 200 (more or less) serigraph reprints of the oil painting, and numerous other derivative works, including but not limited to coffee mugs and towels, all of which bear my image and likeness.

If you fail to comply with the demands of this letter, within eleven (11) days of the date of this letter, I will initiate suit against you for injunctive relief, statutory and civil damages, in a court of law.

Sincerely,

E. Lion Forest

UNITED STATES DISTRICT COURT
NORTHERN DISTRICT OF ILLINOIS
EASTERN DIVISION

NEWTON W. GRUMBACHER,	)	
	)	
Plaintiff,	)	No. 00-C-9345
v.	)	Judge Ruben Castillo
	)	
ELWOOD FOREST, A/K/A "LION"	)	
FOREST,	)	
	)	
Defendant.	)	

MOTION TO TRANSFER VENUE

NOW COMES defendant Elwood "Lion" Forest (Defendant), and moves this Court pursuant to 28 U.S.C. § 1404, to transfer this action to the United States District Court for the Southern District of Florida, West Palm Beach Division. In support of this motion, Defendant states:

Defendant recognizes that venue is appropriate in this district because a portion of the events of this case did occur in this district. Nevertheless, as described in the attached Declarations of Elwood Forest and Scott Skiptracer, this action should be transferred for the convenience of the parties and witnesses and in the interest of justice. Venue is appropriate in the United States District Court for the Southern District of Florida, West Palm Beach Division because defendant resides there.

WHEREFORE, Defendant Elwood Forest prays the Court will transfer this action to the United States District Court for the Southern District of Florida, West Palm Beach Division and award Defendant costs and expenses and such further and other relief as the Court deems appropriate in this matter.

ROGERS, ALBEN, & DANA

By:_____

Randal Alben
Ill. Bar No. 5322445
1010 Wacker, Suite 200
Chicago, IL 60602
Phone: (312) 555-9900
Fax: (312) 555-9901

Attorneys for Defendant E. Lion Forest

UNITED STATES DISTRICT COURT
NORTHERN DISTRICT OF ILLINOIS
EASTERN DIVISION

NEWTON W. GRUMBACHER,	)	
	)	
Plaintiff,	)	No. 00-C-9345
v.	)	Judge Ruben Castillo
	)	
ELWOOD FOREST, A/K/A "LION"	)	
FOREST,	)	
	)	
Defendant.	)	

DECLARATION OF ELWOOD FOREST

I, Elwood "Lion" Forest, of lawful age, do swear under penalty of perjury of the laws of the United States and the State of Illinois that I have first hand information concerning the following and the following information is true and correct:

1. I am 29 years old. I am a citizen and resident of Florida. I reside at 18 Golfview Road, West Palm Beach, Florida 33406.

2. My career and my own personal business and promotional activities are based in West Palm Beach, Florida. All of the witnesses to my personal affairs, promotions and publicity—including my agent, Guy Smith, my personal manager, Bea Jones, and my accountant and financial planner, Bill Murphy—are residents of the West Palm Beach area. None of these witnesses are amenable to process in the United States District Court for the Northern District of Illinois. All of the documents, exhibits, and other evidence of my fame, advertising, and promotional activities are located at 18 Golfview Road, West Palm Beach, Florida.

3. As a professional golfer, I travel a great deal, and on occasion I have traveled to the Northern District of Illinois for tournaments. I have

only been in the Northern District of Illinois four times in the last seven years, having attended the last three Kemper Lakes Skins tournaments at Kemper Lakes Country Club in Deerfield, Illinois, and once attended the TropoOrangie Pro Am tournament at Tamarack Golf Club in Northern Illinois. Other than these short, six day appearances, I have had no connection whatsoever to the Northern District of Illinois.

4. I have no advertising or promotional agreement with any corporation that is incorporated in or has its principle place of business in the State of Illinois.

FURTHER DECLARANT SAYETH NAUGHT.

Sworn to under penalty of perjury on this 29th day of December 2008.

_____

Elwood "Lion" Forest

_____

UNITED STATES DISTRICT COURT
NORTHERN DISTRICT OF ILLINOIS
EASTERN DIVISION

NEWTON W. GRUMBACHER,	)	
	)	
Plaintiff,	)	No. 00-C-9345
v.	)	Judge Ruben Castillo
	)	
ELWOOD FOREST, A/K/A "LION"	)	
FOREST,	)	
	)	
Defendant.	)	

DECLARATION OF SCOTT SKIPTRACER

I, Scott Skiptracer, of lawful age, do swear under penalty of perjury of the laws of the United States and the State of Illinois that I have first hand information concerning the following and the following information is true and correct:

1. I am 38 years old. I am a citizen and resident of Chicago, Illinois.

2. I am a duly licensed and authorized private investigator and process server in the State of Illinois. I am licensed and authorized to do business in Cook County, City of Chicago, and Lake County, Illinois.

3. I was engaged by Defendant Forest to gather information regarding the above captioned matter.

4. Plaintiff Grumbacher is a citizen and resident of Chicago, Illinois whose maintains a household at 234 Warsaw Street, Chicago IL 60609. He maintains a studio and work space at 427 Addison, Chicago IL 60609. It is believed that the articles—serigraph prints, golf towels, and mugs bearing the unauthorized image of defendant and described in the complaint—were created at this studio and workspace. I observed a quantity of the described towels and mugs in the studio and workspace on December 28, 2008.

5. Plaintiff also maintains a semi-permanent residence in Greenacres, Florida in the vicinity of West Palm Beach, Florida. He has a small apartment above the garage of the home in Greenacres belonging to his aunt, Viridian Green. Neighbors reported to me that Plaintiff makes annual visits to this apartment, sometimes staying for up to two months in the winter.

6. Plaintiff has an ongoing relationship with the Coral View Gallery in Palm Springs, Florida, which is the close vicinity of West Palm Beach, Florida, and he has an ongoing relationship with the Marino Gallery in Miami, Florida, located in the jurisdiction of the United States District Court for the Southern District of Florida.

7. According to the 2006 General Service Administration Statistics on Federal Courts (Feb. 2007), the average time from filing to trial for a civil action in the United States District Court for the Southern District of Florida, West Palm Beach Division is 12 months whereas the average time from filing to trial for a civil action in the United States District Court for the Northern District of Illinois, Eastern Division is eighteen months to twenty four months.

FURTHER DECLARANT SAYETH NAUGHT.

Sworn to under penalty of perjury on this 12th day of January 2009.

_____

Scott Skiptracer

_____

UNITED STATES DISTRICT COURT
NORTHERN DISTRICT OF ILLINOIS
EASTERN DIVISION

NEWTON W. GRUMBACHER,	)	
	)	
Plaintiff,	)	No. 00-C-9345
v.	)	Judge Ruben Castillo
	)	
ELWOOD FOREST, A/K/A "LION"	)	
FOREST,	)	
	)	
Defendant.	)	

DECLARATION OF NEWTON GRUMBACHER

I, Newton Grumbacher, of lawful age, do swear under penalty of perjury of the laws of the United States and the State of Illinois that I have first hand information concerning the following and the following information is true and correct:

1. I am 40 years old. I am a citizen and resident of Chicago, Illinois. My permanent residence is located at 234 Warsaw Street, Chicago IL 60609. I have a studio and work space at 427 Addison, Chicago IL 60609. All of the works of art described in the complaint—the original painting of defendant and the original works of art in the form of serigraphs, art towels, and ceramic art pieces—were created and are located at my home address or my studio in Chicago, Illinois. None of the articles described in the complaint were created in the State of Florida or are located in the State of Florida.

2. From time to time I vacation in Greenacres, Florida, never more than twice a year, and usually for only two weeks at a time. None of the art involved in this matter was conceived or created in Florida. I maintain an ongoing relationship with the Coral View Gallery in Palm Springs, Florida, and the Marino Gallery in Miami, Florida, but none of the art works involved in this action and described in the complaint have ever been displayed or otherwise shown or ever even located in the State of Florida.

3. All of my witnesses, including my secretary, Carol Lander, and my studio assistant, Al Moore, have their permanent residence in Chicago and are not amenable to process in the United States District Court for the Southern District of Florida.

FURTHER DECLARANT SAYETH NAUGHT.

Sworn to under penalty of perjury on this 14th day of January 2009.

_____

Newton Grumbacher

_____

Key Terms: venue, transfer to more convenient forum

Launch Point: 28 U.S.C. §§ 1404, 1406

_____

2. Based on the following information, prepare a memorandum in support of the motion to dismiss or a memorandum in opposition to this motion depending on whichever side you are assigned or choose to represent.

_____

Patricia Piao-Liang Davis is a 20 year old super-model who goes by the professional name "Piao-Liang." She was born in Nanjing, PRC in 1989, but was orphaned at four months of age, and was adopted at six months of age by Clifford and June Davis, U.S. citizens, and raised in Provo, Utah. Piao-Liang is a naturalized citizen of the United States, and is domiciled and resident in Provo, Utah. Piao-Liang has joined a group of other super-models who offer their unfertilized ova for auction on an internet site known as Dezyner-Genes.com. Although she has participated in the web site since January 2007, she has never accepted any bids to purchase her eggs.

While on a photo-shoot for Drop Dead Gorgeous magazine that took her to various locations in China (the Great Wall and Tiananmen Square in Beijing, the Bund in Shanghai, and others), Piao-Liang was approached at West Lake in Hangzhou by a businessman, Mr. Jiang "Jerry" Chuang-ping. Mr. Jiang explained that his wife was infertile, and he was interested in purchasing an ovum from Piao-Liang, and offered her $1 million for it. She was flattered and orally agreed to the transaction. The two drank baijiu and toasted each other several times to celebrate the deal. When she returned to the United States, Piao-Liang's lawyers, Hart, Charles, & LaRouche, reviewed Mr. Jiang's written proposal for the agreement concerning the sale of the ovum, and they accepted the terms, but added a forum selection and choice of law clause in the agreement, specifying that any action arising under the contract would be brought in a state or federal court in California and that the law of California would govern the contract. The contract was signed by Piao-Liang in New York, NY, on November 2, 2008, and by Mr. Jiang in Taibei, Republic of China (Taiwan), on November 4, 2008. The egg or eggs were to be delivered by June 1, 2009, and the payment of $1 million was to be made immediately upon successful fertilization and implantation.

Jerry Jiang, age 56, is a naturalized American citizen who owns a controlling interest in and supervises four factories producing computer memory chips in Taibei. He was born in Taibei in 1953. He immigrated to the United States in 1979, and was naturalized as a U.S. citizen in 1984. Although he first settled in San Francisco, he now lives and works seven months of the year in Taiwan, and owns a condominium in Taibei. The rest of the year he travels or stays at one of his two homes in San Francisco, California and Aspen, Colorado. His wife, Sun Li, travels with him and stays wherever he is staying throughout the year. (The couple have no children and cannot have any because Sun Li is infertile.) Jiang and Sun have followed this routine every year for the last twelve years, but Jiang has made it known that he intends to retire to Taiwan when he turns 65. He has a California driver's license and a U.S. Passport, but he is still recognized by the government of the Republic of China as having dual-citizenship, and also has a Republic of China passport. He votes, registers his car, and pays taxes in California, but he also pays taxes in Taiwan.

Piao-Liang discovered in late November that Mr. Jiang is the nephew of the late General and President of the ROC, Jiang Ji-shi, better known to the world as Chiang Kai-shek. This horrified her because her Chinese family had been oppressed by the Nationalists prior to the Communist victory in China. She decided to refuse to go through with the sale, and Mr. Jiang sued her in the United States District Court for the Northern District of California.

Piao-Liang has filed a motion to dismiss for lack of subject matter jurisdiction.

UNITED STATES DISTRICT COURT
NORTHERN DISTRICT OF CALIFORNIA

JIANG CHUANG-PING,	)	
	)	
Plaintiff,	)	No. 2:06-CV-2345-K
v.	)	(Judge Kimball)
	)	
PATRICIA PIAO-LIANG DAVIS,	)	
A/K/A "PIAO-LIANG",	)	JURY TRIAL
	)	DEMANDED
	)	
	)	
Defendant.	)	

<u>COMPLAINT</u>

NOW COMES Plaintiff Jiang Chuang-ping ("Plaintiff"), and for his complaint against Defendant Patricia Piao-Liang Davis, also known as the supermodel "Piao-Liang" ("Defendant"), states as follows:

<u>PARTIES</u>

1. Plaintiff is a citizen and resident of the City of San Francisco, State of California, and the United States of America. He is domiciled in the State of California in this Northern District of California.

2. Defendant Piao-Liang is a citizen and resident of the State of Utah, United States of America, and is domiciled in Provo, Utah.

JURISDICTION AND VENUE

3. This Court has subject matter jurisdiction over this action under 28 U.S.C. § 1332(a)(1) in that Plaintiff and Defendant have diverse citizenship, and the matter involves over $75,000 in controversy.

4. Personal jurisdiction exists over Defendant because Defendant was served with process in this State and District.

5. Defendant and Plaintiff entered into the Contract attached hereto as Exhibit 1 ("Contract") on November 2 and November 4, 2008, respectively.

6. The contract provides for suit to be brought in a federal court in California and the Contract is to be governed by California law. Contract, section 5.

7. Venue is proper in this district pursuant to the forum selection clause in section 5 of the Contract and pursuant to 28 U.S.C. § 1391 in that Defendant was served with process within this District and Division, and the subject matter of the Contract is present in this District.

COUNT I - BREACH OF CONTRACT

8. On November 2, 2008, Defendant entered into the Contract, promising to deliver to Plaintiff's OB-GYN physician one or more healthy and viable ova from her ovaries at the first available opportunity and no later than June 1, 2009. Upon receipt and successful fertilization and implantation of the egg(s) in Plaintiff's wife's uterus, Plaintiff was to pay Plaintiff by wire transfer the sum of one million United States dollars.

9. On December 18, 2008, Defendant phoned Plaintiff and repudiated the contract by stating that she would not perform her obligations. She then, on that same day, sent by facsimile transmission and U.S. Mail the letter attached hereto as Exhibit 2, again repudiating the Contract and refusing to perform her obligations under the Contract.

10. Plaintiff was and remains ready to perform his obligations under the Contract, and there are no other conditions precedent to the agreement that would prevent its performance.

11. Defendant breached its agreement with Plaintiff by anticipatory repudiation.

12. Plaintiff has no available alternative remedy at law that could replace or compensate Plaintiff for the unique value of the subject matter of the Contract, and seeks specific performance of the Contract, and such further and other relief as the Court deems proper in the circumstances.

COUNT II - SPECIFIC PERFORMANCE

13. Plaintiff realleges the allegations of paragraphs 1-12 of this complaint as though set forth fully in this paragraph.

14. Plaintiff comes to this court seeking equity, with clean hands, and with the equities in his favor. Plaintiff has no available alternative remedy at law. The public policy of this jurisdiction favors the upholding and enforcement of contracts for the provision of a unique subject matter.

15. Defendant has repudiated and breached her obligations under the Contract. The equities and public policy are against Defendant.

16. Plaintiff seeks specific performance of the Contract.

WHEREFORE, Plaintiff requests the Court to order Defendant to deliver to Plaintiff's OB-GYN physician one or more healthy and viable ova from her ovaries at the first available opportunity and no later than June 1, 2009, and to award Plaintiff such further and other relief as the Court deems proper in the circumstances.

JURY TRIAL DEMANDED.

FINLEY & MOORE, LLP

By:_____

Miriam O. McGuinnis
Ut Bar No. 02112
114 Market Street, Suite 2800
Salt Lake City, Utah 84101
Phone: 801-555-SU4U
Fax: (312) 555-9901

Attorneys for Plaintiff Jiang Chuang-ping

Purchase and Sale Contract

WHEREFORE, Mr. Jerry Jiang Chuang-Ping (Buyer) and Ms. Patricia Piao-Liang Davis (Seller) wish to enter into an agreement for the transfer of at least one egg from Seller's ovaries to Buyer for the purpose of fertilization of the egg and implantation in Buyer's wife; and

WHEREFORE, the parties, Buyer and Seller, in consideration of the mutual promises stated herein and for other good and valuable consideration; and

WHEREFORE, the parties, Buyer and Seller, wish to complete this transaction at the earliest practicable time, and in no event later than June 1, 2009;

Then the parties covenant and agree to the following:

1. At the earliest practicable opportunity, and in no event later than June 1, 2009, in New York City, NY or Salt Lake City, UT, or at any other mutually agreeable location, Seller shall deliver to Buyer's OB-GYN physician one or more healthy and viable ova (i.e., eggs) from her ovaries.

2. Upon receipt and successful fertilization of the egg(s), the egg(s) are to be implanted in Buyer's wife's uterus,

3. After successful implantation of the fertilized egg(s) in Buyer's wife's uterus, without miscarriage, for twenty-one days, Buyer shall pay Seller by wire transfer to Osmond National Bank, Account No. 100223456 owned by Seller, the sum of one million United States dollars.

4. In the event that conditions 2 and 3 cannot be successfully completed with the initial supply of the egg(s) from Seller, Seller shall, within six weeks of notification by facsimile or U.S. mail by Buyer of the failure of conditions 2 or 3, supply one or more additional healthy and viable eggs to Buyer's OB-GYN physician in New York City, NY or Salt Lake City, UT, and shall continue to supply eggs in the manner described in this paragraph every six weeks until successful completion of conditions 2 and 3 of this contract.

5. Should any dispute between the parties arise under this agreement, the parties, Buyer and Seller, agree that all disputes shall be resolved in litigation that shall be filed in a state or federal court in the State of California and all conditions and terms and obligations of this contract shall be governed by and interpreted under California law.

Signed by Buyer: Signed by Seller:

_____   _____
Jerry Jiang Chuang-ping   Patricia Piao-Liang Davis
Date: November 4, 2008   Date: November 2, 2008

Piao-Liang® is Beauty
234 Joseph Smith Drive
Provo, UT 84602 USA
(801) 555-piao

December 18, 2008

By Facsimile and Mail:

Mr. Jerry Jiang Chuang-ping
Two Embarcadero Center, Suite 3801
San Francisco, CA 94111-3909
Phone: 415-555-7779
Fax: 888-555-7789

To Mr. Jiang:

I am canceling the deal. I never knew you were connected with the Nationalists. This changes everything. I no longer want to undergo the procedure for you or anyone else.

Sincerely,
Piao-Liang Davis

UNITED STATES DISTRICT COURT
NORTHERN DISTRICT OF CALIFORNIA

JIANG CHUANG-PING,	)	
	)	
Plaintiff,	)	No. 2:06-CV-2345-K
v.	)	
	)	
PATRICIA PIAO-LIANG DAVIS,	)	
	)	
Defendant.	)	

MOTION TO DISMISS

NOW COMES defendant Patricia Piao-Liang Davis ("Piao-Liang"), and moves this Court pursuant to Fed. R. Civ. P. 12(b)(1), to dismiss this action for lack of subject matter jurisdiction.

Plaintiff seeks this Court to take jurisdiction over the subject matter of this action under 28 U.S.C. § 1332(a)(1), alleging diversity of citizenship of the parties and a proper jurisdictional amount. Diversity cannot be met by Plaintiff because Plaintiff is not a citizen or resident of any State of the United States, and does not possess diverse citizenship within the meaning of 28 U.S.C. § 1332(a)(1). In that Plaintiff is not a citizen and resident of any state of the United States for diversity purposes, this fact defeats the assertion of diversity jurisdiction over the subject matter of this action, and the action must be dismissed.

WHEREFORE, Defendant Piao-Liang prays the Court dismiss this action and award Defendant costs and expenses and such further and other relief as the Court deems appropriate in this matter.

Respectfully Submitted,

HART, CHARLES, & LAROUCHE P.C.

By:_____

Attorneys admitted *pro hac vice* by Order of Court dated 1/6/2009	Sandra LaRouche Mo. Bar No. 41044 1010 Walnut Street, Suite 200 St. Louis, Missouri 63101 Phone: (314) 555-9900 Fax: (314) 555-9901
	Attorneys for Defendant Patricia Piao-Liang Davis

UNITED STATES DISTRICT COURT
NORTHERN DISTRICT OF CALIFORNIA

JIANG CHUANG-PING,   )
)
            Plaintiff,   )   No. 2:06-CV-2345-K
v.   )
)
PATRICIA PIAO-LIANG DAVIS,)
)
           Defendant.   )

<u>DECLARATION OF JERRY JIANG CHUANG-PING</u>

I, Jiang "Jerry" Chuang-ping, of lawful age, do swear under penalty of perjury of the laws of the United States and the State of California that I have first hand information concerning the following and the following information is true and correct:

1. I am 56 years old. I am a naturalized United States citizen, and I reside in San Francisco, CA.

2. I am the president and CEO of Jiang Memory Solutions, Ltd., a corporation that has production and distribution facilities in San Jose, CA, Salt Lake City, UT, Redmond, WA, Festus, MO, and Taibei, Republic of China. I supervise four factories producing computer memory chips in Taibei, and the distribution facilities in the United States. Because of these responsibilities, I travel a great deal and am outside the United States on business and for recreation for months at a time. It is common for my business to require me to spend seven or more months outside the United States each year.

3. I have considered California to be my and my wife's home since we immigrated there in 1979. I have no desire to settle in any other state of the United States. My wife and I plan to stay in California for the

indefinite future. I have a United States passport and a California driver's license. I have owned a house at 231 Cobb Hill Drive in San Francisco for eleven years, and have leased office space at Two Embarcadero Center, Suite 3801, San Francisco, CA 94111-3909, for seven years. I am registered to vote in California. I have paid taxes to the City and County of San Francisco, the State of California, and the United States from 1979 to the present. I own three vehicles registered in California.

4. I have four bank accounts at BankofAmerica in San Francisco and two bank accounts at BankofAmerica, New York. I also have one account at IBJ Schroeder in Tokyo, Japan, and four accounts at Guomin Bank, Taibei, Republic of China. My checking and commercial line of credit account at BankofAmerica, New York is the largest account I own measured by amount of deposit.

FURTHER DECLARANT SAYETH NAUGHT.

Sworn to under penalty of perjury on this 29th day of December 2008.

Jerry Jiang Chuang-ping

UNITED STATES DISTRICT COURT
NORTHERN DISTRICT OF CALIFORNIA

JIANG CHUANG-PING,	)	
	)	
Plaintiff,	)	No. 2:06-CV-2345-K
	)	
v.	)	
	)	
PATRICIA PIAO-LIANG DAVIS,	)	
	)	
Defendant.	)	

DECLARATION OF CHAIM ESCOBAR

I, Chaim Escobar, of lawful age, do swear under penalty of perjury of the laws of the United States and the State of California that I have first hand information concerning the following and the following information is true and correct:

1. I am 36 years old. I am the owner and operator of Chaim's Search and Serve, a private investigatory service in San Francisco, CA.

2. I have personally investigated and obtained the following information about Mr. Jiang Chuang-ping, a/k/a Jerry Jiang, the plaintiff in the above captioned matter.

3. Jerry Jiang was born in Taibei, Taiwan in 1953. He immigrated to the United States in 1979, and was naturalized as a U.S. citizen in 1984.

4. Jiang owns a controlling interest in and supervises four factories producing computer memory chips in Taibei. These factories are his primary source of employment and income.

5. Although he first settled in San Francisco, he now lives and works seven months of the year in Taiwan, and owns a condominium in Taibei. The rest of the year he travels or stays at one of the two homes he owns in San Francisco, California and Aspen, Colorado. His wife, Sun Li, travels with him and stays wherever he is staying throughout the year.

6. Jiang and Sun have followed this routine of living seven or more months in Taiwan every year for the last twelve years.

7. Through interviews with his neighbors, Cliff Zhang and Will Xu, and employees Rajin Sihgn, Carol Patel, and Charlie Wu at his San

Jose plant, I have learned that Jiang regularly states that he intends to retire to Taiwan when he turns 65.

8. Jiang has a California driver's license and a U.S. Passport, but he is recognized by the government of the Republic of China as having dual-citizenship, and also has a Republic of China passport. He uses the Republic of China passport on trips throughout Asia, but never when he flies back and forth to the United States.

9. Jiang has four bank accounts in Taibei, Taiwan at the Guomin Bank (National Bank of Taiwan). He has other accounts across the globe in Tokyo, New York, and San Francisco, but his two most active accounts in terms of number of deposits, wire transfers, checks drawn, and other transactions are both at Guomin Bank in Taiwan. He has paid corporate income taxes and personal income taxes and property taxes to Taiwan every year since 1970 (the earliest year such records are available).

FURTHER DECLARANT SAYETH NAUGHT.

Sworn to under penalty of perjury on this 9ᵗʰ day of January, 2009.

_____

Mr. Chaim Escobar

_____

Key Terms: diversity jurisdiction, dual citizenship, not a citizen of any state

Launch Point: 28 U.S.C. § 1332(a)(1); *Coury v. Prot*, 40 F.3d 385 (5th Cir. 1994)

IV.   PROPERTY

RESEARCH AND WRITING PROBLEMS

1. Donny Default has a tendency to be late paying his sewer utility bill despite constant reminders from his landlord, Lizzy Lu.
Unknown to Lizzy, Donny did not pay his last sewer utility bill
before moving out of Lizzy's apartment building. In order to recover payment, the City of Valparaiso, Indiana has transferred the
balance to Lizzy's account and has threatened to place a lien upon
Lizzy's land if she does not pay.

Lizzy does not think the City has the power to do this and wants
to challenge the City's actions. Lizzy came to your law office seeking a professional opinion. Draft a 1-2 page client letter to Lizzy
detailing the likelihood of success and in your opinion, whether
she should continue challenging the City's actions.

Key Terms: tenant, landlord, utility fee (bill, payment, charge),
penalty

Launch Points: <u>IND. CODE § 36-9-23-25 (2009)</u> ; *Pinnacle Properties Development Group, LLC v. City of Jeffersonville*, 893 N.E.2d
726 (Ind. 2008)

2.   A young couple recently purchased the home of their dreams,
which is a one hundred year old Tudor with original fixtures and
wood in a quiet neighborhood in Billings, Montana. When the
couple purchased the home, they noticed a second driveway that
ran alongside their own driveway and to another home that sat
farther back on a separate plot of land. The couple loved their
new house so much that they did not mind the second driveway
being so close to their own, but after a few months of living in
their dream house, the couple noticed that the owners of the other
home came and went at unusual times of day and night. In addition to the time, the other owners had loud vehicles that woke
up the new couple each time they drove down the driveway. After
trying to reason with their loud neighbors, the young couple decided to hire an architect to do some work on their dream home,
which included placing sound proofing in the rooms that were the

closest to the other driveway. While applying for building permits, the young couple and their architect realized that the other driveway was actually located on their property. The young couple approached the other homeowners one more time to discuss their findings and learned that the neighbors bought their house more than thirty years ago with the driveway in the same place it is now. The other homeowners claimed to have no other way to enter their property from the street and also admitted that they had always assumed the driveway was part of their land. Draft 1-2 pages analyzing who has the best claim to the driveway property and why.

Key Terms: easement, adverse possession, easement by necessity, easement by prescription

Launch Point: <u>25 Am. Jur. 2d, Easements and Licenses § 50</u>; <u>3 Am. Jur. 2d, Adverse Possession § 20</u>; *Keebler v. Harding*, 807 P.2d 1354 (Mont. 1991)

3. Bobby Brown owns a home in Beauville, Illinois. Brown rents this home out to Rod Axle. In their lease agreement, Axle is responsible for maintaining the exterior of the home by cutting the grass, weeding and plowing the snow in the winter. One hot, sunny afternoon, Axle was weeding and tilling the land to make a garden along the back fence of the home. While digging a hole for new bulbs he was planting, Axle hit something hard. After digging around and clearing out around the object that was buried in the ground, he found it to be a metal box. Inside the box, Axle discovered $250,000 cash. For two days, Axle lay awake at night wondering if he should call Bobby. Bobby has a bad temper and Axle knew that if Bobby found out there was money there, Bobby would not only want the money but would go to any length to get it and keep it. Axle thought he should be able to keep at least half of it because he found it. Axle finally decided to call Bobby, who flew off the handle as Axle had expected, and Bobby refused to allow Axle to keep any of it and threatened to sue him if he didn't turn over the money to Bobby.

Axle has come to your office wondering what his options are. Please research and draft a 1-2 page memo on a finder's rights to this kind of property.

Key Terms: treasure trove, finder's rights, possession, true owner's rights, land owner's rights

Launch Point: *Hannah v. Peel*, [1945] 1 K.B. 509 (King's Bench Division 1945); *Michael v. First Chicago Corp.*, 487 N.E.2d 403 (Ill. App. Ct. 2d Dist. 1985)

DRAFTING PROBLEMS

1. Dotty Jones is the owner and landlord of Law School Condominiums in Chicago, Illinois, who plans to convert many of her condos to rental units and lease them to law students. She has never leased property before and wants to create a standard lease form. She decided to call your firm because she heard from a friend that your firm specializes in property management. Draft a standard lease form for Ms. Jones. Other than price and term, you should also take into consideration pets, sub-leases, rental insurance, parking, utilities, damage caused, security deposits, and any other topics you believe would be beneficial to Ms. Jones. You may draw from standard forms and even your own lease agreements, but please cite each source that you draw from.

   Key Terms: lease, rental property, multi-family, residential

   Launch Point: American Jurisprudence Legal Forms, General Lease Form § 253:1132

2. Your client, Terri Jones, and Bob Randolph were married for two years and had one child, James Jones. The couple is now divorced and James is three-years-old. Upon separation, Terri was given full custody of James and Bob was required to pay child support to Terri. Since the separation, Bob has neglected to pay the child support and the unpaid total has amounted to $35,000. Terri Jones, being a single mother and fallen on hard times, needs that money to support her child. She has come to your law firm and

wants you to place a lien upon Bob's property for the amount owed. The current address of your client is 652 N. Main St., Kalamazoo, Michigan 30863. Bob's current address is 234 W. Chestnut, Kalamazoo, Michigan 30863. In order to complete this assignment, you will have to conduct some preliminary research on Michigan's current law regarding liens to enforce child support in order to prepare a lien form that is satisfactory under the law. You may draw from standard forms but please cite each source that you draw from.

Key Terms: lien, non-payment, child support, divorce decree, child custody

Launch Point: *Walters v. Leech*, 279 Mich. App. 707, --- N.W.2d ----, 2008 WL 2811499 (Mich. Ct. App. 2008); West's Legal Forms, General Settlement Agreements; American Jurisprudence Legal Forms

3.   Ronald and Melanie Rump were recently house hunting in Idaho near their favorite ski resort and fell in love with a charming, contemporary farm house, which the Rumps believed would be a perfect weekend escape from their summer home in Vail, Colorado, and their mid-winter home in Sun Valley, Utah. Although the home was listed at $2.5 million, the couple submitted an offer for $3.0 million, which the sellers accepted that same day. The only problem is that the sellers, Nate and Donna Tate, have not purchased another home, and they have eight children, which makes it very difficult for them to find a new residence quickly. Although the Rumps want to start putting their touches on the house as soon as possible, they understand the Tate's housing situation. The Rumps do not want to give up the house, and they suggested a plan where the Rumps and Tates will sign a contract for the house in the next few days and allow the Tates to remain in the house on a month-to-month tenancy for several months (no more than six months) until they find a new home. Ronald Rump wants to make sure the contract contains language that if something happens to the home between the date the contract is signed and the date the Rumps take possession that the Tates will be liable for any repairs or damages. He also wants to make sure that he and his wife can take possession immediately if the

Tates do not find a new house within six months. Please write a real estate contract containing language that satisfies the Rumps' requirements. You may draw from standard forms but please cite each source that you draw from.

Key Terms: real estate sales contract, holdover tenancy

Launch Point: 15B Am. Jur. Legal Forms 2d Ch. 219, Summary—real estate contract forms and provisions; *Holscher v. James, 860 P.2d 646 (Idaho 1993)*

WRITING IN THE LAW DISCIPLINE PROBLEMS

1. Your firm has a new client, South Beach Towers, which is an apartment complex located in South Miami Beach, Florida. Your firm's first assignment is to draw up a new standard lease agreement, which the complex can begin using immediately. One of the partners in your firm has given you some details that South Beach Towers requires in its lease agreements, but any information not given is up to your discretion. Some of the information, like the name of the tenant and number of the unit, will be filled in by the South Beach Towers staff, so leave those areas blank with a description of what goes in the spot. Please incorporate the following **Key Terms** in a lease agreement for one bedroom, unfurnished, studio apartments leased by South Beach Towers:

   Key Terms: All leases are for a one year initial term and year-to-year tenancy; Address is 1800 East Ave, Miami Beach, FL 33139; rent is $1200 per month, tax is $50 of total payment; payment is due by 5th of each month; security deposit of $1200 due at time of signing; advance rent $2400 due at time of signing; no pets; late charge of $25; overnight guests okay; may make superficial alterations to apartment but not affecting load-bearing features; landlord will pay heat, water, trash disposal, air conditioning; may not assign or sublease without express, written approval of South Beach Towers

   Launch Point: 19A West's Legal Forms 3d, Real Estate Transactions § 48:4, Apartment Lease-Florida

2. Samantha Stein and Gertrude Powers have been neighbors on ad-
    joining properties in Trenton, New Jersey, since the early 1970s
    up until the present. Both women are avid growers of sunflowers,
    competing annually in the South Westchesterton County Fair for
    the largest and brightest flowers. Since 1987, their gardens have
    been separated only be a small wire fence that runs at a slightly
    crooked angle jetting into Samantha's property. Twenty-one years
    ago, Gertrude had installed a sprinkler system in her backyard to
    irrigate her sunflowers. The company responsible for installing
    the sprinkling system was required to do a survey of the land be-
    fore installation. It was brought to Gertrude's attention that her
    sunflower garden was growing three feet into Samantha's property
    line.

    Gertrude worked during her younger life for a property lawyer
    and had acquired knowledge about adverse possession. Gertrude
    had always planned to put a pool in her backyard, but her yard
    was very narrow and she needed the three extra feet for the pump
    system. Gertrude patiently waited until the statutory time period
    was over, and at the South Westchesteron County Fair, revealed
    to Samantha the news: that she hated sunflowers all along, and
    that she was building a pool which needed that three foot patch
    of soil.

    Samantha has brought a lawsuit to enjoin Gertrude from taking
    possession of the land. Gertrude has countersued to quiet title
    to the three foot wide parcel on the basis of adverse possession.
    You represent Gertrude in the litigation. Research and draft the
    following: (1) a stipulation of facts including all the material facts
    necessary for Gertrude to recover on her counterclaim; (2) a mo-
    tion for summary judgment in favor of Gertrude on her counter-
    claim.

    Key Terms: property, adverse possession

    Launch Point: *Mannillo v. Gorski*, 255 A.2d 258 (N.J. 1969)

V.   CRIMINAL LAW

RESEARCH AND WRITING PROBLEMS

1.   The Governor of Virginia, George Macaque, and his wife, Tori Barr Macaque, were riding in a convertible during the Fourth of July Parade in Alexandria, Virginia. There were state police security detail officers walking alongside the vehicle but there was no bulletproof glass or other barriers surrounding the governor and his wife. A man in the crowd, Cory Joseph Plumber, began pelting Governor and Mrs. Macaque with tomatoes and shouting a torrent of words and expletives about the governor's agricultural policies that allegedly were ruining the tomato industry. Shocked and embarrassed, the Macaques tried to crouch down low in the vehicle to avoid getting hit. The tomatoes on the leather seats, however, caused the governor to slip and fall awkwardly, breaking his arm. Governor Macaque has asked the state attorney general to inquire what charges can be brought against Plumber, and the attorney general has approached you, the youngest assistant attorney general in the office, to draft a 1-2 page memo outlining the crimes and elements of the crimes that may be charged against Plumber.

   Key Terms: criminal law, battery, assault, threaten, injury, harm, governor

   Launch Point: Va. Code Ann. § 18.2-60.1 (1982)

2.   Mary Q. Contrary and Neville Deershead worked together as heavy equipment operators for the State of Illinois. One day Mary and Neville got into a very heated argument about Neville's ego. Neville was always talking about himself, how good he was at their job, and how he was so much better than Mary at operating the large cranes at their work site. During this argument Mary told Neville, "If you don't be quiet I am going to shoot you!" This shut Neville up, and a couple of weeks passed in which Mary and Neville were getting along fine. One day however, Neville talked the foreman into assigning him the heavy crane work for the day while Mary was forced to work on the ground with the maintenance crew. This infuriated Mary, who left at lunchtime and

returned to the work site with a gun. Intending to shoot Neville, Mary yelled, "Hey Neville, how great do you think you'll be at dying?" As Neville turned around he saw that Mary had a gun and he immediately started to drop to the ground. At that same moment, Mary fired her gun in the direction of Neville, and hit Poorguy Paul in the chest because Poorguy was standing directly behind the spot where Neville was. Poorguy died from his gunshot wound. When Mary was arrested she told the police, "I never meant to shoot that Poorguy!"

You work for the newly-elected town prosecutor of Littleton, Illinois, who has had little experience with criminal law up to this point in his career. Your boss asks you to research and draft a 1-2 page memo answering the question of whether the prosecutor can charge Mary with the murder of Poorguy Paul and the attempted murder of Neville Deershead.

Key Terms: criminal law, transferred intent, murder, attempted murder, lesser included offenses, merged offenses, single act

Launch Point: *People v. Conley, 713 N.E.2d 131 (Ill. App. Ct. 1st Dist. 1999)*; *People v. Burrage, 645 N.E.2d 455 (Ill. App. Ct. 1st Dist. 1994)*; *People v. Garrett, 576 N.E.2d 331 (Ill. App. Ct. 1st Dist. 1991)*

DRAFTING PROBLEMS

1. On January 5, 2005, your client, seventy-five year-old Ms. Parker, was in her bank when two burglars entered with shotguns. The burglars demanded the customers put their hands above their head, while the bank tellers empty the drawers. Unknown to the burglars, Ms. Parker began carrying a 9mm handgun in her purse after she was robbed at gunpoint a year ago. Flashing back to her previous experience and fearing for her life, Ms. Parker pulled out her gun and shot one of the burglars in the back, completely emptying her handgun and killing the burglar. Nobody else was injured in the shooting and the second burglar fled immediately fearing for his life because the shotguns were not loaded. The burglar was subsequently apprehended and convicted. Ms. Parker

was also tried for the murder of the first burglar. You propose to the jury that Ms. Parker acted in her own self-defense and in the defense of others. The judge has asked you and the prosecutor to draft separate jury instructions both on the second degree murder charge and the two affirmative defenses you have raised. First, draft the two instructions in your role as counsel for Ms. Parker. For extra credit, draft two instructions that the prosecutor might submit. You may draw from model instructions or from case law, but please cite each source that you draw from.

Key Terms: jury instructions, second degree murder, self defense, defense of others,

Launch Point: Jury Instruction Databases

2. A client of yours came to your West Virginia office the other day and told you that his son, Justin, was in trouble. Justin was arrested for first-degree murder after his girlfriend was found dead in her apartment in Charleston, West Virginia. The police found Justin's blood, his DNA, and his fingerprints all over the girl's apartment. The murder weapon has not been found at this time. The son has a history of mental illness and has been in and out of psychiatric hospitals most of his life. Justin also takes medicine for bipolar disorder. Recently, Justin told his parents that his girlfriend admitted to seeing another man, but they were trying to work out their relationship because the girlfriend recently gave birth to Justin's child. A few days before his arrest Justin confided to his parents that he caught his girlfriend with the other man when he went to visit her and his son. Justin admitted to his parents that he was enraged to find another man with his girlfriend, but he doesn't remember much else of that day. Based on these facts, determine whether Justin has any defenses to the murder charge or might be entitled to a charge less than first-degree murder. Draft the jury instructions that outline what you have to prove for Justin's best defense or lesser charge. For extra credit, draft instructions that the prosecutor might submit on each of the topics that you drafted on Justin's behalf. You may draw from model instructions or from case law, but please cite each source that you draw from.

Key Terms: jury instructions, not guilty by reason of insanity, guilty but mentally ill, second degree murder, heat of passion

Launch Point: <u>Jury Instruction Databases</u>

WRITING IN THE LAW DISCIPLINE PROBLEMS

1. You are an assistant public defender in Vermont, and you have been assigned to represent Franklin Louis Robert ("Robert"). Robert is accused of murdering his mother with a hammer. The only evidence against Robert is that he was found the day after the murder in possession of his mother's car and her laptop computer, and Robert's DNA was detected on the murder weapon. After the police arrested Robert and he signed a statement acknowledging that he understood his rights, but before he was appointed any representation Robert signed a sworn statement admitting to the murder.

    In your discussions with Robert, you have become increasingly concerned about his mental capability. Any time you question Robert regarding his mother's death he refuses to admit that she is dead. Robert claims that his mother simply ran away and will eventually return to the area. Furthermore, Robert refuses to let you or anyone else on your staff shake his hand. Robert's cooperation also fluctuates, and on certain days, he refuses to talk to you at all and will only talk to other individuals in your office. On other days, Robert willingly talks to you, but no one else.

    When you question other family members, Robert's mental capacity always becomes an issue. Robert's father admits that Robert attended Oxford University and had a successful career as a professor of mathematics at U.C. Berkeley until he took a trip to Indonesia in 2006. After being in Indonesia for over a year, Robert returned to the states and lived once again in Oakland, California. When Robert would return to Vermont for family visits, he acted strangely and often made odd comments about a "manifesto" and a "new order of living without carbon-emitting machinery." At one point in May 2008, Robert even threatened to kill his mother if she didn't help him by typing up his notes that he kept in various journals and papers so that he could submit them for publication. Robert's mother did not press charges against her son because she thought he was just going through a rough time, and in any event, Robert abruptly left and returned to California within a day of his making the threat. Until Robert was arrested for his mother's murder, no one else in the family knew that he had returned to Vermont from California.

With all of Robert's problems, you are finding it very difficult to defend him. Besides being uncooperative, Robert's insistence on his mother being alive has left you dumbfounded. You have discussed an insanity defense with Robert, but he will not even consider it. He asserts that, "Only crazy people need an insanity defense, and I'm not crazy." He considers it a personal insult that you would suggest that he appear in front of his neighbors on the jury and in the courtroom and assert that he was crazy. He states that, "No one is going to take my book on the 'new order of carbon-free life' seriously when I get around to publishing it if I stand up in court and assert that I am a certifiable nut-case."

In Vermont, case law indicates that the court system cannot force an insanity defense on a defendant, but you have heard that other jurisdictions have begun to do just that. Earlier, you remember reading an article titled "Hendricks v. People: Forcing the Insanity Defense on an Unwilling Defendant," by Robert D. Miller, MD, PhD, which you want to reread before you do anything else.

First, research and draft a memorandum on the likelihood that you will be able to persuade the Vermont trial court to accept a plea of not guilty by reason of insanity against Robert's will. Second, prepare a pre-trial motion requesting the trial judge to require Robert to participate in a mental examination to determine if he qualifies for an insanity defense.

Key Terms: insanity defense, mental examinations, unwilling defendant, involuntary insanity defense

Launch Point: Robert D. Miller, *Hendricks v. People: Forcing the Insanity Defense on an Unwilling Defendant*, available at http://www.jaapl.org/cgi/reprint/30/2/295.pdf; *State v. Tribble*, 892 A.2d 232 (Vt. 2005)

2. The following facts are not in dispute: At 8 p.m. on October 27, 2007, Memphis police were staking out an address with the hope of apprehending two suspected felons who were believed to be coming to that address to sell stolen narcotics. The suspects arrived at the address with the stolen narcotics. Before arrests could be made, however, the suspects spotted the police and fled in their car at a high rate of speed with the police in pursuit. Eventually, the suspects abandoned their vehicle, separated and fled on foot. The police exchanged gunfire with one suspect as he fled. This suspect later entered the house of Jimmy Daniels and hid in the front closet. Daniels fled the premises and notified the police. The police immediately surrounded the house and shortly thereafter called the Western Tennessee SWAT team to the scene. The SWAT (Special Weapons And Tactics) team consists of per-sonnel specially trained to deal with barricaded suspects, hostage-taking, or similar high-risk situations. Throughout the standoff, the police and SWAT team used a bullhorn and telephone in at-tempts to communicate with the suspect. The police, receiving no response, continued efforts to establish contact with the suspect until around 11:30 p.m. At that time the SWAT team decided to fire at least 25 rounds of "tear gas" into the house in an attempt to expel the suspect. The team delivered the tear gas to every level of the house, breaking virtually every window in the process. In addition to the tear gas, the SWAT team cast three concussion grenades into the house to confuse the suspect. The team then entered the home and apprehended the suspect crawling out of a basement window.

The tear gas and flash-bang grenades caused extensive damage to the Daniels' house. For example: a pink film from the tear gas covered the walls and furniture; some walls were dented from the impact of the tear gas canisters; one tear gas canister went through one of the upstairs walls. Daniels alleges damages of $80,000. The City of Memphis and the Western Tennessee SWAT team denied Daniels' request for reimbursement. Daniels has now filed suit against the City and the SWAT team to recover his damages. You represent the City and the SWAT team in this case. Draft a motion for summary judgment in favor of the City and the SWAT team on Daniels' claims.

Key Terms: public necessity, law enforcement, destroyed property, eminent domain, taking

Launch Point: Charles E. Cohen, *Takings Analysis of Police Destruction of Innocent Owners' Property in the Course of Law Enforcement: The View From Five State Supreme Courts*, 34 McGeorge L. Rev. 1 (2002)

VI. CONSTITUTIONAL LAW

RESEARCH AND WRITING PROBLEMS

1. The Mayor of Springfield, Wisconsin, wants to implement a job training program for ex-felons. In particular, she wants to help men find legitimate work because studies show that men have a harder time finding employment after incarceration than women. She knows courts are highly skeptical of gender discrimination when the discrimination exists on the face of the law, so she does not want to limit the program on its face to men. But the Mayor thinks that if she can write a program to train ex-felons only when they were imprisoned for certain crimes that are committed more often by men, then she believes that even if the discrimination will have a disparate impact on women, the level of impact will be acceptable and her program will be justified. You are to research: (1) the two ways to prove gender discrimination; (2) the appropriate level of scrutiny for gender discrimination; and (3) draft a 1-2 page memo to the Mayor discussing the validity of this program.

Key Terms: discrimination, classification, level of scrutiny, gender, disparate impact, justification

Launch Points: *Craig v. Boren*, 429 U.S. 190 (1975)—proper level of scrutiny; *Korematsu v. United States*, 323 U.S. 214 (1944)—discussing classification on the face of the law; *Washington v. Davis*, 426 U.S. 229 (1976)—discussing facially neutral laws with a discriminatory impact.

2. The State of Georgia has a law requiring all cities with professional fire departments to fill job openings based on a written and physical exam. Candidates are ranked according to their combined score with the highest candidate being ranked first in line for any job offers. The City of Clayville, which is 98% African-American, has changed its exam to place all applicants who live within the City at the top of the list, regardless of their overall exam score. Joe Shoe, who is white and a non-resident of Clayville, took the test last year and had the highest combined score. Yet, when the City had a job opening, it offered the job to an African-American who lives in Clayville but was near the bottom of the list based on his combined test scores. Mr. Shoe thinks that the city of Clayville has discriminated against him because he is white and does not live in the city. In 1-2 pages, analyze Mr. Shoe's chances of success if he decides to file suit against the City challenging their employment decision and their hiring policy. Include in your analysis the level of scrutiny that would used by the courts to assess the hiring policy.

    Key Terms: discrimination, hiring, race or color, reverse-discrimination, public employment, racial quotas or percentages

    Launch Point: *Local No. 93, Intern. Ass'n of Firefighters, AFL-CIO C.L.C. v. City of Cleveland,* 478 U.S. 501 (1986); *Attorney General of New York v. Soto-Lopez,* 476 U.S. 898 (1986); *Guardians Ass'n v. Civil Service Com'n of City of New York,* 463 U.S. 582 (1983)

3. With the economic downturn and states trying to find ways to save money, the legislature in New Mexico is proposing a change to its unemployment benefits for legal aliens. In addition to meeting all the requirements for workers applying for unemployment benefits, the legislature wants to add language to the New Mexico statute requiring legal aliens to have lived in New Mexico for a minimum of fifteen years before being eligible to receive unemployment benefits. The legislature believes that the government interest in reserving resources for New Mexico residents is a strong interest that would be upheld if challenged because of the hard economic times facing its citizens. The Governor of New Mexico has her doubts about the legality of the statute, and as a former

lawyer herself, she would like you to draft a short memo (1-2 pages) discussing the legality of the proposed legislation.

Key Terms: aliens, benefits, government, equal protection

Launch Point: *Plyler v. Doe, 457 U.S. 202 (1982)*; *Graham v. Richardson, 403 U.S. 365 (1971)*

4. Vijay Patel is recently going through divorce proceedings with his soon to be ex-wife Latika Gupta. They have a daughter, Krishan-ti Patel, who attends the South Haven Unified Public School in Bakersfield, California. In 2007, the California State Legislature passed a law requiring all schools, public, private, or religious, to begin each day saying the Pledge of Allegiance while facing the American flag with their right hand over their hearts. In adher-ence to this rule, to begin the school session, the administration at South Haven requires the teachers to lead the students in the Pledge of Allegiance. The Pledge of Allegiance contains the words "under God." Mr. Patel, a devout Hindu who believes in many gods, views that the School District's enforcement of the Califor-nia law violates the Establishment Clause of the First Amendment of the United States Constitution. Latika Gupta is not as upset about the state's and the school district's actions, but she has in-formed Mr. Patel that she will not oppose his efforts to challenge the state law. Research and draft 1-2 pages analyzing whether Mr. Patel has standing to bring this First Amendment claim.

Key Terms: constitutional law, first amendment, establishment clause, standing

Launch Point: *Elk Grove Unified School Dist. v. Newdow, 542 U.S. 1 (2004)*

DRAFTING PROBLEMS

1. The State of Georgia requires all cities with professional fire de-partments to fill job openings based on a written and physical exam. Normally, candidates are ranked according to their com-bined score with the highest candidate being ranked first in line

for any job offers. The City of Clayville, which is 98% African-American, wants to draft a law to redress years of racial discrimination that has prevented African-American firefighters from being hired or promoted in numbers that reflect the racial make-up of the City. It is considering changing its hiring policy to place all applicants who live within the City at the top of the list, regardless of their overall exam score. Draft the text of a statute that would create a hiring system that would address the racially unbalanced composition of the fire department but still would pass muster under the United States Constitution. You may adopt, modify, or reject the proposed hiring system suggested by the City.

Key Words: discrimination, hiring, race or color, public employment, racial quotas or percentages

Launch Point: *Local No. 93, Intern. Ass'n of Firefighters, AFL-CIO C.L.C. v. City of Cleveland*, 478 U.S. 501 (1986); *Attorney General of New York v. Soto-Lopez*, 476 U.S. 898 (1986); *Guardians Ass'n v. Civil Service Com'n of City of New York*, 463 U.S. 582 (1983)

WRITING IN THE LAW DISCIPLINE PROBLEMS

1. You represent the City of Smalltown, Washington, and you just finished having a meeting with the Mayor, Chief of Police, and Fire Chief. With the recent budget problems, the City has had to make significant cutbacks, including overtime and maintenance. While the City has not had to let any employees go, many employees feel that the City is neglecting crucial areas and are concerned that the citizens are in danger if changes are not made soon. The department heads believe that the employees are being spiteful because they are no longer receiving the overtime hours many of them depended upon. Recently, the Washington Supreme Court overturned a Smalltown firefighter's dismissal on First Amendment freedom of speech grounds. The firefighter, who averaged approximately seventy-five hours of overtime per pay period before overtime was cut out, wrote a scathing letter to the local newspaper's editor accusing the City of placing its residents in danger because of insufficient manpower. The Fire Chief fired the firefighter under Revised Code of Washington, Title 41,

chapter 41.08.080(2) for conduct injurious to the public peace and welfare. The Civil Service Board upheld the firing, and the firefighter appealed in the courts. Under the *Pickering* Test, the Supreme Court found that the firefighter was within his rights to make the statements he made under the Washington Constitution, as well as the U.S. Constitution. Similar cases of discipline by the Smalltown police department have been overturned, too.

In the meeting, the department heads would like you, the assistant city counselor, to research the possibility of enacting a constitutionally permissible city ordinance that prohibits public employees from undertaking destructive criticism that is injurious to the public peace and welfare even if the employees are claiming to have the citizens' best interests at heart but really are only interested in their own well-being. The ordinance should allow the City to reprimand, demote, or fire these public employees. Both the police department and the fire department have civil service boards which review all disciplinary actions, and the department heads would like the ordinance to provide that these merit boards will not review actions undertaken pursuant to the ordinance if this kind of provision is permissible under the federal and state constitutions. Research and draft a report on whether this type of ordinance is possible under the federal and state constitutions' free expression protections for public employees and what would be the requirements or limitations of the ordinance under these constitutional protections. If the ordinance is possible, then draft an ordinance that would withstand a challenge under the federal and state constitutions' free expression clauses.

Key Terms: matter of public concern, public employee, *Pickering* Test, disciplinary grounds, First Amendment, merit system

Launch Point: U.S. Const. amend. I; Wash. Const. art. I, § 5, Revised Code of Washington, Title 41, chapters 41.08, 41.12; 15A Am. Jur. 2d Civil Service § 1; 63C Am. Jur. 2d Public Officers and Employees § 200

Part II:

RESEARCH AND WRITING PROBLEMS AND EXERCISES IN LEGAL WRITING AND ANALYSIS

I. INTRODUCTION TO LEGAL METHOD (Legal Writing and Analysis, Chapter 1)

QUESTIONS FOR DISCUSSION AND REVIEW

1. Identify your citizenship relationships. What municipality, village, or township do you live in? What county? What state? What are the legislative, executive and judicial entities called in these areas?

2. What are the three main primary sources of the law?

3. When can secondary authority define the law of a given area?

4. Do the following sources sound like primary or secondary sources of the law? Explain why:

   Aldermanic decree

   Corpus Juris Secundum legal encyclopedia

   Environmental Protection Agency regulation

   Congressional subcommittee report on pending legislation

   Farnsworth's treatise on Contracts

   McKinney's Consolidated Laws of New York Annotated

II.   RULES OF LAW AND LEGAL REASONING (Legal Writing and Analysis, Chapter 2)

QUESTIONS FOR DISCUSSION AND REVIEW

1. What is the difference between a rule of law with three required elements and one that has a balancing test?

2. Authorities always state rules of law in outline form—true or false?

3. Rule-based reasoning is the basic logical form used in legal writing, but how can the other forms of argument be used to buttress the legal conclusions you are communicating?

4. Where is narrative reasoning most often employed in legal writing?

5. When might a policy-based argument be the only argument you raise?

6. Why is analogical reasoning of special importance in England and the United States?

WRITING PROBLEMS

1. Break down the following rules into an outline of the elements or factors. In brackets that follow each rule, we have suggested the number of elements that the rule should be broken down into:

    A.   Every person who, under color of any statute, ordinance, regulation, custom, or usage, of any State or Territory or the District of Columbia, subjects, or causes to be subjected, any citizen of the United States or other person within the jurisdiction thereof to the deprivation of any rights, privileges, or immunities secured by the Constitution and laws, shall be liable to the party injured in an action at law. <u>42 U.S.C. § 1983 (1994)</u>. [2 elements]

B.   Summary judgment shall be rendered forthwith if the pleadings, depositions, answers to interrogatories, and admissions on file, together with the affidavits, if any, show that there is no genuine issue as to any material fact and that the moving party is entitled to a judgment as a matter of law. <u>Fed. R. Civ. P. 56(c)</u> [2 elements]

C.   To have standing, a party must show that he personally has suffered some actual or threatened injury as a result of the putatively illegal conduct of the defendant, and that the injury fairly can be traced to the challenged action and is likely to be redressed by a favorable decision. See <u>Valley Forge Christian College v. Americans United for Separation of Church and State, Inc., 454 U.S. 464, 472 (1982)</u>. [4 elements]

D.   Any person, having the intent to commit a felony, assault or theft therein, who, having no right, license or privilege to do so, enters an occupied structure, such occupied structure not being open to the public, or who remains therein after it is closed to the public or after the person's right, license or privilege to be there has expired, or any person having such intent who breaks an occupied structure, commits burglary. <u>Iowa Code § 713.1 (1999)</u>. [5 elements]

2. Assume the basic rule on dog-bite liability in Apex is: (1) defendant's ownership of the dog; (2) injury caused by the dog; and (3) lack of provocation of the dog by the plaintiff.

There are three cases in Apex dealing with dog bite liability:

Case 1:   A seven year old boy was on a neighbor's porch grabbing and pulling the ears of the neighbor's dog and poking the dog in the stomach. The boy was told several times by the neighbor to stop what he was doing and leave, but the boy continued until the dog bit him once on the cheek. The court held that the dog's owner was not liable for the damage caused by the dog because: (a) the boy had no right to remain on the neighbor's property; (b) the dog had a right to defend itself; and (c) even though the boy was a minor, he still provoked the attack.[1]

Case 2:   A three year old girl was playing jump rope on a neighbor's front porch near the neighbor's dog. She accidentally jumped on dog's tail. The dog yelped and scratched the girl on her leg with its front paws. The court held that the dog owner is not liable for the dog's attack because: (a) even unintentional acts can constitute provocation of a dog; and (b) the attack was proportionate to the amount of provocation.[2]

Case 3:   A door-to-door salesman, age 29, was going from house to house selling magazine subscriptions. He climbed up the front steps to dog owner's house. There was no dog in sight. As soon as he rang the bell, a dog jumped out and barked at him menacingly. He tried to move off the porch, but the dog followed his every move and was blocking him from leaving. The salesman sprayed the dog with pepper spray, which only partially hit the dog, and the dog jumped on the salesman and bit him several times before the man could run off. The court held that the dog owner was liable

---

1 Based on *Siewerth v. Charleston*, 231 N.E.2d 644 (Ill. App. Ct. 1967) The Illinois line of dog-bite cases has proved fruitful for legal analysis. See Diana V. Pratt, *Legal Writing: A Systematic Approach* (1999); Robin S. Wellford, *Legal Analysis and Writing* (1997).

2 Based on *Nelson v. Lewis*, 344 N.E.2d 268 (Ill. App. Ct. 1976).

for the salesman's injuries because: (a) the salesman was using public sidewalks and going about his lawful business in a peaceful way prior to dog's attack; (b) the spraying of the dog with pepper spray was only undertaken after the salesman was trapped by the dog; and (c) use of pepper spray or other action taken purely in self-defense did not constitute provocation.[3]

A.   Consider the following set of facts:

Client was returning to a party to retrieve his car keys. He had consumed a little alcohol at the party. It was past 1:00 a.m., and it was dark on the street where he had been at the party. The houses on the street were very similar in appearance. Client walked around to the back of a house where he thought the party was going on. It was the wrong house. In the darkness he tripped over a German shepherd sleeping behind the house. The dog got mad and bit client on the leg.

1.   Draft a short statement of facts regarding client's situation employing narrative reasoning. Try not to add new facts that change the legal analysis of the situation (e.g., the client kicked the dog, rather than tripped over the dog), but you are welcome to elaborate on and color in or characterize the facts provided above.

2.   Draft a short section employing rule-based reasoning which applies the Apex dog-bite rule to the facts of client's situation.

3.   Draft one or two paragraphs employing analogical reasoning using one or more of the cases (Cases 1, 2, 3) provided above.

---

3 Based on *Steichman v. Hurst*, 275 N.E.2d 679 (Ill. App. Ct. 1971), and *Dobrin v. Stebbins*, 259 N.E.2d 405 (Ill. App. Ct. 1970).

B.   Consider the following set of facts:

Client accidentally threw a football into a neighbor's back yard. Client knew the neighbor had a large Doberman pinscher that normally was tethered in the front yard. He peeked over the fence and did not see the dog anywhere near his football. He jumped the fence, grabbed the football, and was running back to the fence when the dog came out from behind some bushes and ran over and caught client and bit him several times on the rear end before he could get over the fence.

1.   Draft a short statement of facts regarding client's situation employing narrative reasoning. Try not to add new facts that change the legal analysis of the situation (e.g., the client snuck into the yard at night; or the client threw a rock at dog and then ran, rather than simply picking up the football and running away from the dog), but you are welcome to elaborate on and color in or characterize the facts provided above.

2.   Draft a short section employing rule-based reasoning which applies the Apex dog-bite rule to the facts of client's situation.

3.   Draft one or two paragraphs employing analogical reasoning using one or more of the cases (Cases 1, 2, 3) provided above.

III.   THE LIFE OF A CASE, STATE AND FEDERAL COURT SYSTEMS, AND JURISDICTION (*Legal Writing and Analysis*, Chapter 3)

A. The Life of a Case in Civil Litigation

QUESTIONS FOR DISCUSSION AND REVIEW

1. When a complaint is filed and served on defendant, what can the defendant do?

2. If a motion to dismiss is denied, what happens?

3. What is the response to a **reply** called? What is the response to this document called? Are you routinely able to file either one without special permission? What is that permission called?

4. Defendant filed a motion to dismiss and wants to notice up the motion for a hearing. Will defendant get a hearing? Why or why not?

5. What are the four major methods to discover information from your opponent in civil litigation? Explain how each works.

6. If someone is holding back documents and information from you in discovery, what do you do (after you tire of harassing them with incessant telephone calls)?

7. What are the two main elements asserted by the movant in support of every summary judgment motion?

8. When is an optimal time to file a summary judgment motion, and why?

9. What typically happens if a summary judgment motion is denied?

10. What is the primary reason for holding a trial? What is the difference between a bench trial and a jury trial?

11. If the jury enters a verdict against you, what options are open to you?

12. The loser in the trial court is called what on appeal?

13. In a typical civil case in this country, how many appeals are you entitled to as a matter of right?

14. What is a term that properly identifies the highest court in any jurisdiction? How would your case wind up in that court?

15. What happens if the appellate court reverses the lower court in a purely legal determination (<u>i.e.,</u> concerning what the law provides or how the law is supposed to work in the situation at hand)? What happens if the appellate court reverses on the basis of one or more procedural errors?

B. State and Federal Court Systems and the Hierarchy of Judicial Authority

QUESTIONS FOR DISCUSSION AND REVIEW

1. The <u>Supreme Court of Texas</u> can affirm or reverse the decisions of which courts and in what kinds of cases?

2. Can a judge ever overturn the decision of a justice?

3. What is the hierarchy of judicial authority above the <u>Albany County Court</u> in New York?

4. If you take an appeal from a decision of the <u>Illinois Circuit Court</u>, where might your appeal go?

5. If a state trial court of general jurisdiction in New Mexico is deciding an issue of New Mexico law, which courts' decisions potentially will be binding on this court:

    a.   United States Supreme Court

    b.   New York Supreme Court

    c.   New Mexico Court of Appeals

    d.   Alamogordo Municipal Court, New Mexico

    e.   Chaves County Probate Court, New Mexico

f.   United States District Court for the District of
New Mexico, Albuquerque Division?

6. If the Honorable Lester Ketterling is a District Judge of the District Court of North Dakota, Northeast Judicial District (a trial court of general jurisdiction), which courts' opinions is he likely to read most closely when he is researching how the courts have interpreted the statute Title 9, Chapter 9-06 of the North Dakota Century Code?

a.   Court of Criminal Appeals of Texas

b.   United States Court of Appeals for the Eighth
Circuit

c.   Bismarck Municipal Court, North Dakota

d.   District Court of North Dakota, South Central
Judicial District

e.   District Court of North Dakota, Northeast Judicial District

f.   Court of Appeals of North Dakota?

C. Jurisdiction

QUESTIONS FOR DISCUSSION AND REVIEW

1. If a person is building a house outside the zoning board's jurisdiction, what does that mean? Which use of the term jurisdiction is this referencing?

2. A court might have jurisdiction over an action but not have venue. How can that be?

3. If a person constantly does business in Florida, but never steps foot there, what methods might a Florida court use to exercise jurisdiction over this person?

4. Sue is an artist who sues her landlord in the Maine District Court, District III, Bangor, for taking pictures of her artwork and selling the photographs in violation of her copyright. Before she knows it, her case winds up in the United States District Court for the District of Maine, Bangor Office. What happened? Can she add a claim to her complaint seeking the value of a painting that the landlord crushed when he slammed open the door to her apartment?

5. Ralph has a beef with his old buddy Norton for stealing food out of his icebox. Ralph would like to sue him in North Carolina, where Ralph now lives in retirement, but Norton still lives in New York City. One day, while having a beer at a bar across the street from the local airport, Ralph sees Norton walk out of the airport and cross the street and walk into the bar. The two former neighbors embrace and Norton tells the tale of his plane losing a section of the rudder forcing them to make an emergency landing at the airport. Ralph wastes no time in serving Norton with the North Carolina court's summons and complaint that he had with him, suing him for his past mooching. Norton says "Thanks a lot, Ralphie boy!" and storms out, and flies home on the next plane out. Based on these facts, can the North Carolina court exercise jurisdiction over Norton? If Norton wants to sue Ralph back for swindling him out of money in a futile scheme to renovate a hotel in New Jersey, what can he do, and where can he do it?

6. Jane moved from Manchester, England to Ohio, and opened a coke processing plant near the Ohio River in Cincinnati. She put it into operation on May 12, and almost immediately released a huge cloud of noxious fumes that drifted over the river and caused injuries to people strolling in Walker Park in Dayton, Kentucky. Jane is so distraught, she closed down the plant that same day, and never reopened it. She immediately retired to Arizona and from then on has never left her retirement condo. Based on these facts, can the injured parties in Kentucky sue her in a Kentucky court? Where else might they sue her?

7. Clara's homemade roach killer recipe was so effective that all of her neighbors wanted to use it. She slapped some handwritten labels on some mason jars and filled them with the roach killer

and sold them to her friends and neighbors. One neighbor accidentally took a swig of the roach killer thinking it was the jar of corn whisky he had stashed under the sink, and suffered a serious injury. A friend tells Clara she better retain a lawyer that knows her way around federal law. Why did she give this advice?

8. Bobo is a citizen and resident of Cape Code, Massachusetts. He had his seaside newsstand destroyed by a crowd of tourists that swarmed the stand when it was rumored that Bobo had retrieved John F. Kennedy Jr.'s watch from the ocean and had it on display at the stand. Through diligent effort, Bobo determined that the tourists were citizens and residents of New York City, Boston, Philadelphia, Washington D.C., and Baltimore. Is it possible to sue all of them for negligence in one court? What about in a federal court?

IV. DETERMINING THE RULE FROM A SINGLE CASE OR OTHER AUTHORITY (*Legal Writing and Analysis,* Chapter 4)

WRITING PROBLEMS

1. Read the following case and determine the borrowed rules, the applied rules and the holding of the case. Discuss any dicta that you think is noteworthy. Please note—this case is fictional. Any resemblance to people you know is regrettable:

768 W.2d 223   September 17, 1985

Daisy Mae DuBois, Plaintiff	Counsel: Sylvester Chaser, Chaser & Ambulancer, P.C., Dogpatch, for Plaintiff.
v.	
Abner Morton Heel, Defendant	Willkie Cave, Pompous, Boring & Whiteshoe LLP, Dogpatch, for Defendant.
No. 84CV1299-MDM	
Circuit Court for Podunk County, State of Apex	Murphy, Judge:

Before this Court is plaintiff's motion pursuant to Local Rule 15 to separate and divide property in a common law marriage. The facts established at a one day trial on September 4, 1985, are as follows. Ms. DuBois ("plaintiff") and Mr. Heel ("defendant") have lived in the same house for seven years. They lease the house in which they cohabitate, and they stated on the lease that plaintiff and defendant were husband and wife. Both plaintiff and defendant signed the lease. The also signed loan documentation to purchase a 1978 Chevy pickup truck in August 1981 and a 1976 Harley Davidson motorcycle in March 1983. On each loan application they stated that plaintiff and defendant were husband and wife and both parties signed each loan. In 1980, defendant told a census taker that the plaintiff was his wife, that they were married for two years and that they lived together in the same household.

On November 22, 1984, defendant became enraged at plaintiff when she refused to let him pick and eat the skin off the Thanksgiving turkey. He threw his half-full beer can at her, which hit plaintiff and splashed beer on her clothing. A shouting match ensued, in which defendant proceeded to gather up all the empty beer cans out of the trash and pelt plaintiff with them until she fled the house. On the following Saturday, plaintiff at-tempted to return to the house to retrieve her clothing, but defendant "chased her out" by again throwing empty or partially empty beer cans at her. Plaintiff filed this suit on December 10, 1984.

Local Rule 15 states:

If two persons living in a common law marriage separate following an act of aggression or violence by the common law husband against the common law wife, the common law wife may sue in the circuit court for a division of any property the two acquired during their common law marriage.

Rules of the Circuit Ct. for Podunk County (1982 ed.), Rule 15.

In Apex, it has long been recognized that a common law marriage exists between two persons if they:

1. Cohabitate;

2. For at least one year;

3. Hold out the other person as a spouse;

4. Have the intent or agreement to be married.

Pogo v. Dawg, 43 W. 234, 236 (Apex 1923).

In the instant case, there is no question that plaintiff and defendant cohabitated for over a year; both parties admitted that they lived under the same roof for seven years. Not surprisingly, the parties differ as to whether they held each other out as a spouse and had the intent or agreed to be married. In such a case, the courts refer to the circumstances of each individual case.

It is sufficient if the defendant has at least twice held out the plaintiff as his spouse. Here, the defendant concedes that he described the plaintiff as his wife on the lease for their house, and on certain loan documentation. These two instances satisfy the third element. The fourth element, intent or agreement to be married, may be shown by a continuous, monogamous relationship of the husband with the wife. It is not necessary to prove either party's state of mind so long as it is shown that the two lived in a monogamous relationship for an appreciable period of time. Seven years is certainly an "appreciable period of time." However, in this case we have additional proof of the husband's state of mind when he went out of the way to tell a census taker that he was married for two years to the plaintiff. Nothing in the facts of the case indicate that

defendant had changed his mind about the plaintiff between 1980 and the date of their breakup.

Having determined that plaintiff and defendant lived in a common law marriage, we now turn to the portion of the rule requiring that their separation follow: "an act of aggression or violence by the common law husband against the common law wife." The threshold for this requirement is low; it is enough if any unwanted hostile act is attempted or undertaken by the husband against the wife. Certainly, defendant's two assaults and batteries against the person of the plaintiff are sufficient under this standard, however minor the damage inflicted may have been.

Plaintiff's motion for division of property under Local Rule 15 is granted. The property at issue, two vehicles, are of roughly equal value. Plaintiff has requested an award of the Harley Davidson motorcycle, and this request is granted. Therefore,

IT IS HEREBY ORDERED, ADJUDGED AND DECREED that plaintiff shall take from defendant the possession and ownership of the 1976 Harley Davidson motorcycle identified in the complaint in this matter.

V. DETERMINING THE APPLICABLE RULE: ANALYSIS OF MULTIPLE AUTHORITIES (*Legal Writing and Analysis*, Chapter 5)

QUESTIONS FOR DISCUSSION AND REVIEW

1. Bob is a student at Our Lady of the Lake University in Kit Carson County, Colorado. One night, he and three friends climbed the walls of the library and attempted to paint over the face of Jesus Christ depicted in the sixty foot high stained glass window on the front of the library. They wanted to replace the face of Christ with that of Tim Green, the star running back of the school who had just received the Heisman Trophy for that year. Just as they were getting started, one friend lost his balance and fell, but he was able to grasp the waistband of Bob's shorts. Unfortunately, as he slipped, he pulled Bob's shorts and underwear down to Bob's knees. As luck would have it, the Assistant Dean of Student Life, Msgr. O'Reilly, who periodically suffered from fits of insomnia, happened then to walk by the front of the library and saw Bob in all his glory swinging in front of the face of Christ. O'Reilly saw to it that Bob was charged with indecent exposure under <u>Colo. Rev. Stat. § 18-7-302</u> (1999), in a criminal case filed in the District Court for Kit Carson County. (O'Reilly did not notice that the boys also were engaged in vandalism.) Bob's father has sent your firm a $15,000 retainer, and asked you to look into Bob's defense of the crime. Rank the following authorities in order of their value to your analysis of the law that governs Bob's situation. Note that ties are possible for authorities that are roughly the same value to your analysis:

   a. <u>Smith</u> case (1990), affirmed the conviction of a gas station attendant who refused to close his fly while working at a gas station. He was prosecuted and convicted for indecent exposure under <u>Colo. Rev. Stat. § 18-7-302</u>. The case was issued by the Colorado Court of Appeals, Division Three, the court that hears appeals from the District Court for Kit Carson County.

b.   <u>Jones</u> case (1957), affirmed the order of punitive dismissal of an officer who got into a "contest" involving outdoor urination with some of his junior officers at the United States Air Base at Aviano, Italy. The officer was punitively dismissed for conduct unbecoming an officer under Article 133, Uniform Code of Military Justice, <u>10 U.S.C. §</u> <u>933</u>. The case was issued by the United States Supreme Court.

c.   <u>Colorado Revised Statutes Annotated, section 18-7-302</u>.

d.   <u>Rednape</u> case (1998), affirmed the conviction of a window-washer who exposed himself to federal employees while hanging 15 stories up on the face of a federal building in Denver. He was prosecuted under 18 U.S.C. § 380043 (the language of which essentially is the same as <u>Colo. Rev.</u> <u>Stat. § 18-7-302</u>, but requires the exposure to take place on federal property). This case was issued by the United States Court of Appeals for the Tenth Circuit, hearing an appeal from the United States District Court for the District of Colorado.

e.   Title 18 of the United States Code, section 380043.

f.   <u>Fletcher</u> case (1977), affirmed the lower court's decision involving an indigent man who was robbed and beaten and left to wander naked in Vail, Colorado. He was prosecuted and found not guilty under <u>Colo. Rev. Stat. § 18-</u> <u>7-302</u>. The case was issued by the Colorado Supreme Court.

g.   <u>Fuller</u> case (1994), affirmed the conviction of a woman who appeared topless in order to obtain necklaces of beads on the streets of Salina, Kansas, during a local Mardi Gras celebration. She was charged and convicted of the crime of common law indecent exposure. The case was issued by the Kansas Supreme Court.

h.   Chapter 43, subsection D, of Prosser's treatise on <u>Torts</u>, discussing tort liability for indecent exposure.

i.   Note, <u>Criminal Liability for Indecent Exposure in Colo-</u> <u>rado, Utah, and Idaho</u>, 97 Colum. L. Rev. 345 (1997).

j.   E. Allen Farnsworth, <u>Contractual Dysfunction and Indecent Exposure: Drafter's Liability for Debt Instruments under 15 U.S.C. § 3467</u>, 25 Md. J. Contemp. Legal Issues 56 (1997).

2. Your client Mary does a mean Elvis impersonation. She was performing at B.B. King's Blues Club in Memphis, when she was served with process and enjoined under <u>17 U.S.C. §§ 501</u>, <u>502</u>, from selling reprints of movie posters of Elvis at intermission. Apparently, the works were copyrighted and she had simply purchased five posters and then made multiple color copies of them at the local Kinkos. Mary thought that because Elvis was dead, anyone could use pictures of him for commercial gain or profit. She has been sued by Graceland Properties, Inc. for copyright infringement in the United States District Court for the Western District of Tennessee, Western Division. Rank the following authorities in order of their value to your analysis of the law that governs Mary's situation. Note that ties are possible for authorities that are roughly the same value to your analysis:

    a.   <u>Sun Records</u> case (1980), affirms a conviction for unfair competition under Tennessee law in a case involving the duplication and sale of copyrighted music recordings. The case was issued by the Court of Appeals of Tennessee, the court that hears appeals from the Circuit Court for Shelby County, Memphis, Tennessee.

    b.   <u>Lewis</u> case (1961), reverses judgment for plaintiff in copyright infringement case involving distribution of pirated recordings of Igor Stravinsky. The recordings were made by a college professor for use in lectures, and no commercial profit or gain was made by the professor from the recordings. The case was issued by the United States Supreme Court.

    c.   The U.S. Copyright Act of 1976, <u>17 U.S.C. § 101</u> *et seq.*

d.   <u>Cash</u> case (1998), affirms judgment for plaintiff in copyright infringement case in which defendant illegally taped country music star's concert and sold bootleg recordings over the Internet. The case was issued by the United States Court of Appeals for the Eighth Circuit.

e.   <u>Perkins</u> case (1997), affirming a judgment against plaintiff for liability under the Visual Artists Rights Act of 1990, <u>17 U.S.C. § 106A</u>, for mutilation of an artist's painting. The case was issued by the United States Court of Appeals for the Sixth Circuit.

f.   <u>Parker</u> case (1994), where defendant was held liable for copyright infringement and unfair trade practices when he copied plaintiff's designs for western casual wear so as to produce clothing that was sold through catalog sales. The case was issued by the United States District Court for the Western District of Tennessee, Eastern Division.

g.   Chapter 13, sections A-F, of Melville B. Nimmer's famous treatise, <u>Nimmer on Copyright</u> (1998), discussing injunctive relief for infringement of protected works of visual media.

h.   Melville B. Nimmer, <u>Sources of the American Copyright Tradition in Elizabethan England</u>, 57 Colum. L. Rev. 48 (1957).

i.   <u>18 C.J.S. Copyrights § 60</u> on copyright infringement. Corpus Juris Secundum is a legal encyclopedia.

WRITING PROBLEM

1. Read the following excerpts from cases and formulate through rule synthesis the applicable rule for common law marriage in Apex, followed by any sub-rules on specific elements of the overall rule:

Pogo v. Dawg, 43 W. 234, 236 (Apex 1923) [Apex Supreme Court - the court of last resort in Apex] stated:

> In Apex, it has long been recognized that a common law marriage exists between two persons if they: (1) cohabitate; (2) for at least one year; (3) hold out the other person as a spouse; and (4) have the intent or agreement to be married.

DuBois v. Heel, 768 W.2d 223, 224 (Apex Cir. Ct. 1985) [trial level court] adopted the above rule, and went on to state:

> [T]he parties differ as to whether they held each other out as a spouse and had the intent or agreed to be married. In such a case, the courts refer to the circumstances of each individual case. It is sufficient if the defendant has at least twice held out the plaintiff as his spouse. Here, the defendant concedes that he described the plaintiff as his wife on the lease for their house and on certain loan documentation. These two instances satisfy the third element. The fourth element, intent or agreement to be married, may be shown by a continuous, monogamous relationship of the husband with the wife. It is not necessary to prove either party's state of mind so long as it is shown that the two lived in a monogamous relationship for an appreciable period of time. Seven years certainly is an 'appreciable period of time.' However, in this case we have additional proof of the husband's state of mind when he went out [of] the way to tell a census taker that he was married for two years to the plaintiff. Nothing in the facts of the case indicate that defendant had changed his mind about the plaintiff between 1980 and the date of their breakup.

Long v. Short, 745 W.2d 123, 125 (Apex Ct. App. 1st Dist. 1979) [Apex intermediate level appellate court] does not adopt the Pogo rule. It states:

> In order to demonstrate the existence of a common law marriage, plaintiff must show: (1) objective evidence of intent to be husband and wife, and (2) subjective evidence

of intent to be husband and wife. Cohabitation, an appreciable length of cohabitation, and monogamy are regarded as objective evidence of intent to be married. A spouse's statements and representations concerning the status of the person he or she is living with are subjective evidence of intent to be married. It is a basic requirement of the claim that the couple must have commingled their finances — if the "wife" kept her paycheck and lived off of it by herself, and the husband did the same, there is no common law marriage.

Thin v. Stout, 812 W.2d 445, 448 (Apex Ct. App. 1st Dist. 1991) [Apex intermediate level appellate court]. Thin adopts the Pogo rule and cites DuBois, but the plaintiff-appellant ("wife") loses, even though the four criteria are met. In denying relief to the wife, the Thin court states:

> The husband and wife here were once legally and officially married, then divorced, and were subject to a divorce decree at the time that they started living together again. After the second time around went sour, the wife was thrown out, and then tried to go after half of the husband's property under the common law rule. This situation is not covered by the rules of common law marriage. A couple living under a divorce decree must abide by the terms of the decree, and neither spouse can avoid the decree by asserting a claim for division of property through common law marriage rules.

VI.   ORGANIZATION OF LEGAL WRITING (*Legal Writing and Analysis*, Chapter 6)

WRITING PROBLEMS

1. Identify the TREAT sections in the following writing sample. For example, Thesis on Main Issue; Application of Sub-Rule on Element (B); Sub-Sub-Thesis on Element (a). Where you have identified an Explanation section, indicate whether you think it is synthesized or unsynthesized.

Hints: There are three elements at issue—peaceful conduct, lawful presence, and provocation. One of these elements has a sub-rule with multiple elements, all of which are at issue. One of the sub-rules has a sub-sub-rule with two elements, both of which are at issue.

Don't worry about citation form — we have used a simple form that is not ALWD or Bluebook form simply to indicate the places where authority would be used.

We have simplified the Thesis headings to save space; actual thesis headings in legal writing should provide more information to support the thesis (the "because part," for example: "The dog's bite was disproportionate to the threat of injury because . . .").

Don't take the "law" we are writing here seriously. We are improvising on the law simply to demonstrate how the TREAT format works. We are not trying to teach you actual principles about dog-bite liability.

We have filled in the description of a few sections to help you get started. You must fill in the rest of the labels:

[Thesis on Main Issue:]

I.   DEFENDANT FORD IS LIABLE FOR PLAINTIFF SMITH'S DOG BITE INJURIES

[Rule on _____:]

In Texas, in order to prevail on a cause of action for injuries resulting from the attack of a dog, a plaintiff must prove: (A) defendant owned or harbored the dog; (B) plaintiff was peacefully conducting himself or herself at the time of the attack; (C) plaintiff was in a place where he or she had a lawful right to be; and (D) plaintiff did not provoke the dog into attacking. Timmy v. Lassie, 567 S.W.2d 123, 125 (Tex. 1995); Bobby v. Rin Tin Tin, 569 S.W.2d 789, 791-92 (Tex. App. 1997).

[Sub-Thesis on Element A:]

A. Defendant owned the dog.

[Roadmap disposing of Element A:]

Defendant Ford admits that he owned and harbored the dog that caused plaintiff Smith's injuries. Therefore, this element is not disputed in this case.

[Sub-Thesis on _____:]

B. Plaintiff was acting peacefully.

[Sub-Rule on Element B:]

To be conducting oneself peacefully, one must be engaging in a normal day-to-day activity or business and not behaving in a loud and boisterous behavior in close proximity to a strange dog. Bobby, 569 S.W.2d at 792.

[Check one: The following Explanation section is _____ Synthesized _____ Unsynthesized]

In Timmy, the plaintiff's claims were dismissed by the trial court for failure to state a claim, and this order was affirmed by the Court of Appeals, 562 S.W.2d 135 (Tex. App. 1993), and the Supreme Court. 567 S.W.2d at 125. Plaintiff Timmy had broken into the home of defendant by smashing a plate glass window, and had broken open several internal doors before encountering defendant's dog. The Supreme Court stated that "an illegal and violent destruction of property" violates the "peaceful conduct" rule. 567 S.W.2d at 124.

In Bobby, the Texas Court of Appeals affirmed the trial court's order of summary judgment against the plaintiff. 569 S.W.2d at 792. The plaintiff and several of his friends had broken into a house in order to throw an impromptu party at the absent homeowner's expense. The party was loud and raucous, and several neighbors called the police to complain about the noise. Plaintiff stumbled upon defendant's dog when he opened the door to the basement. The court denied recovery to plaintiff on the grounds that his conduct violated the peaceful conduct requirement because it was a criminal "breaking and entering" of the home and "a disturbance of the peace." Id.

In Mouse v. Pluto, 571 S.W.2d 13, 15 (Tex. App. 1998), the Court of Appeals again held that plaintiff's conduct must amount to a "civil breach of the peace" in order to fail the "peaceful conduct" requirement. Plaintiff Mouse and two of his friends had ridden their bicycles across the defendant's yard several times on a hot summer morning. Their action had disturbed defendant's dog a great deal, and eventually, the dog got loose and bit the plaintiff. Plaintiff prevailed at trial, and the Court of Appeals affirmed, stating that bike riding was a normal day-to-day activity for children, and was not sufficiently boisterous and noisy as to be a disturbance of the peace that would violate the rule. Id.

[Check one: The following Application section
_____ applies cases to the client's facts <u>or</u>
_____ applies principles about the law and the interpretation of the
rules derived from a synthesis of the authorities]

In the instant case, plaintiff Smith did nothing to breach the peace. She pushed open the door to defendant Ford's apartment; she did not break it down or go in by smashing a window. Plaintiff's action cannot be characterized as a criminal breaking and entering. Her presence in the apartment was quiet and unobtrusive. Therefore, plaintiff Smith will not be found to have violated the peaceful conduct element of the Dog Bite rule.

[Sub-Thesis on _____:]

C. Plaintiff had a Lawful Right to be in Defendant's Apartment.

[Sub-Rule on _____:]

In order to recover, plaintiff must show that she was not trespassing or exceeding the limits of an actual or implied license to be present at the site of the attack. Timmy, 567 S.W.2d at 125-26; Bobby, 569 S.W.2d at 792. Although this element appears to have two requirements, the "lawful presence" element is really a single requirement of "no trespassing," because "to be trespassing, a person must certainly have exceeded the limits of their license, if any," and "[i]f a person has exceeded the limits of their license, they are trespassing." Bobby, 569 S.W.2d at 792-93.

**[Check one: The following Explanation section is
____ Synthesized ____ Unsynthesized]**

Trespassing in Texas has never encompassed an accidental straying onto the property of another because of a mistake of fact. Compare Bears v. Goldilocks, 445 S.W.2d 988, 989 (Tex. 1973) (defendant's accidental entrance into plaintiffs' household because defendant believed it to be the home of her grandmother was held not to be a trespass), and Mouse, 571 S.W.2d at 15 (plaintiff did not trespass when he had been allowed to ride his bike over the edge of defendant's lawn on many occasions with defendant's knowledge without defendant stopping him and did not know he did not have permission to ride straight through defendant's front yard), and Sawyer v. Joe, 700 S.W.2d 348, 350 (Tex. Cir. Ct. Tamarac Cty. 1989) (accidental straying onto property in the dark is not trespassing), with Bobby, 569 S.W.2d at 793 (breaking into a house in order to throw an impromptu party was trespassing). See also Restatement (Second) of Torts § 7812 (1978) (no trespass from accidental straying onto property). Under criminal law, breaking and entering a premises will constitute a trespass while remaining on a premises under a mistaken belief of permission to remain will not. Compare People v. Butler, 543 S.W.2d 908 (Tex. 1988) (reentering premises after dark when occupants were sleeping was trespass), with People v. Maid, 565 S.W.2d 234 (Tex. App. 1994) (remaining in entry hallway after business hours at premises while waiting for a city bus that was late was not a trespass). It is the mistake of fact itself that grants to the person a limited license to be present, but only for so long as it is reasonable for the person to remain mistaken about their permission to be at the location. Bears, 345 S.W.2d at 989-90; Mouse, 571 S.W.2d at 15; Sawyer, 700 S.W.2d at 350. The rule from this line of cases has never been altered or amended in Texas. See Hansel & Gretel v. Hag, 889 F.2d 345, 347 (5th Cir. 1994) (discussing the viability of the Bears rule as applied in Mouse and Sawyer).

**[The following Application section uses _____
reasoning to apply one case's holding to the client's situation
because the case is so close to the client's facts]**

Smith's situation is identical to that of defendant Goldilocks in the Bears case. Smith was mistaken about the floor she had gotten off on and about the identity of the owner of the apartment she was entering. There were no markings outside the elevator door to indicate the floor number, and defendant's door had no markings on it that might have clued Smith in to her mistake. This case is controlled by Bears, and Smith is entitled to recover in spite of her accidental entrance into defendant's home.

[**Sub-Thesis on** _____:]

D. Plaintiff did not provoke Defendant's dog into attacking.

[**Sub-Rule on** _____:]

Under the Dog Bite rule in Texas, provocation means: (1) striking the dog, or (2) directly threatening the dog with physical harm; (3) so long as the dog's attack is not out of proportion to the provocation. Timmy, 567 S.W.2d at 125-26; Bobby, 569 S.W.2d at 792; Bears, 345 S.W.2d 988, 989-90.

[**Sub-Sub-Thesis on Element 1:**]

1. Plaintiff did not strike the dog.

[**Roadmap disposing of Element 1:**]

Striking requires physical contact with the dog. Id. It is undisputed that Smith did not strike the dog.

[**Sub-Sub-Thesis on** _____:]

2. Plaintiff did not threaten the dog.

[**Sub-Sub-Rule on** _____:]

Defendant has spent the most time attempting to refute plaintiff Smith's argument on the "threat" element of the rule on provocation. Defendant's effort is to no avail, because the definition of a "threat" to a dog under the law is: "a violent act or gesture directed against the dog that suggests that immediate physical harm to the dog is imminent." Timmy, 567 S.W.2d at 126; see also Bears, 345 S.W.2d at 990 ("plaintiff must threaten to cause severe and immediate harm to the dog itself").

[Explanation section (synthesized):]

No Texas court has ever denied recovery to a plaintiff on the ground that a threat provoked the dog where the plaintiff was not armed with a weapon. Compare Rubble v. Flintstone, 580 S.W.2d 23, 27 (Tex. App. 1983) (recovery denied where plaintiff threatened dog with a club), and Thatcher v. Sawyer, 455 S.W.2d 45, 47 (Tex. App. 1978) (recovery denied where plaintiff threatened dog with a rifle), with Dilbert v. Dogbert, 798 S.W.2d 123, 126 (Tex. 1990) (recovery allowed where plaintiff yelled and gestured at the dog but was unarmed), and Van Pelt v. Brown, 422 S.W.2d 234, 237 (Tex. App. 1972) (recovery allowed where plaintiff waved blanket at dog, but was otherwise unarmed).

The Texas Supreme Court in Dilbert established that a plaintiff must have some means of inflicting immediate harm on the dog other that simply being armed with his or her own fists and feet. 798 S.W.2d at 126-27. A plaintiff's threat to pummel the dog with his or her fists is insufficient to exonerate the dog-owner from liability for the dog's attack. Id.

[Application section applying principles derived from the case law and not cases themselves:]

Smith did not threaten the dog with a weapon. Her gesturing with one index finger at the dog cannot be viewed as a threat of imminent, violent harm to the dog. Therefore, Smith did not threaten the dog within the meaning of the Dog Bite rule.

[Sub-Sub-Thesis on _____:]

3. The Dog's Attack was Disproportionate to Smith's Actions.

[Sub-Sub-Rule on _____:]

"Proportionality" under the Dog Bite rule is defined as requiring that: (a) the nature of the attack and the (b) severity of the attack both must be in proportion to the injury inflicted or threatened by the plaintiff. Bobby, 569 S.W.2d at 792. Even if Smith were found to have threatened the dog, the dog's attack was disproportionate to any threat in terms of the attack's nature and severity.

[Sub-Sub-Sub-Thesis on Element (a):]

    a.   <u>The nature of the attack was dispropor-tionate to the injury threatened by Smith.</u>

[Sub-Sub-Sub-Rule on Element (a) and Explanation section (unsynthesized)]

The nature of the attack must be examined to see if the attack was overly vicious and out of proportion to the injury inflicted on or threatened against the dog by the plaintiff. Id. at 793. In Bobby, a dog was slapped on its snoot by the plaintiff, and the dog responded by biting the plaintiff on the face and neck. This response of biting the vital areas of the plaintiff's body was held to be disproportionate to the striking of the dog's face with an open hand. Id.

Although no other Texas case discusses this element, the Texas Supreme Court in Smithy v. Jonesy, 123 S.W.2d 345, 347 (Tex. 1965), surveyed the law of Texas, Iowa, Illinois, and Arkansas, and determined that if a dog is struck by the hand or foot of a plaintiff, the dog may only respond by biting the hand, arm or leg of the plaintiff in an effort to subdue the plaintiff; otherwise the attack is disproportional.

In the instant case, the dog responded to a hand gesture, not a slap, and responded by biting the face, neck and arm of the plaintiff. The dog did not attempt to subdue the plaintiff. The nature of this response was disproportionate to the action taken by plaintiff prior to the attack.

[Sub-Sub-Sub-Thesis on _____:]

        b.   <u>The severity of the attack was dispropor-</u>
                  <u>tionate to the injury threatened by Smith.</u>

[Sub-Sub-Sub-Rule on _____ and Explanation section (one case—no synthesis):]

Bobby establishes that the severity of the injury caused by dog's response to the plaintiff's action must be the same or less than the severity of the injury inflicted on the dog by the plaintiff. 569 S.W.2d at 792-93. In Bobby, a dog's biting of the plaintiff on his face and neck was held to be disproportionate to the striking of the dog's face with an open hand.

[Application section and Thesis Restated as Conclusion on Element (b)]

Plaintiff Smith inflicted no injury on the dog. Therefore it is clear that the dog's attack on Smith was disproportionately severe. Smith is fully entitled to recover damages for a disproportionately severe attack.

[Thesis on Main Issue Restated as Conclusion:]

As discussed above, all of the elements of the Texas Dog Bite rule are established by plaintiff Smith. Smith is entitled to recovery from defendant for the injuries inflicted on Smith by defendant's dog.

---

2.   Prepare an outline of the Theses, Sub-Theses, and Sub-Sub-Theses from the TREATs, Sub-TREATs and Sub-Sub-TREATs that would be required for the discussion of the legal issues described in the following fact pattern:

You have a client whose name is "Warren Buffet" and he lives in Nebraska. He is not, however, the billionaire investor Warren Buffet who also lives in Nebraska. One fine day, your client received a large dividend check from Worldwide Widgets made out and addressed to "Warren Buffet." The address was not the same as your client's residence, and your client was well aware that he did not own any shares of Worldwide Widgets, but he cashed the check and kept the money all the same. The next month, another check arrived, and your client cashed it and kept the money. Now, your client has received a harshly drafted letter and several phone calls from Worldwide Widgets' lawyer demanding the money be returned. Your client wants to know if he can keep the money.

The elements of the cause of action of Money Had and Received in Nebraska are:

1. Receipt of money;

2. by mistake;

3. under circumstances that render the retention of the money unjust.

    The rule has a separate sub-rule to determine each element:

    Sub-rule 1 - Money is "received" when:

    (a) currency, including (i) bank notes, (ii) bank drafts, (iii) wire transfer, (iv) bearer paper, (iii) other legal tender;
    (b) is transferred;
    (c) by one person or entity;
    (d) and accepted into the possession of a different person.

Sub-rule 2 - Mistake occurs when:

a) the transferor knew or should reasonably have known of the correct recipient;
(b) the money is transferred to an incorrect recipient;
(c) the transfer was brought about by the transferor; and
(d) neither the intended recipient nor the incorrect recipient caused or contributed to cause the mistaken transfer.

Sub-rule 3 - The recipient's retention of the money is unjust if:

(a) the money has enriched the recipient;
(b) under all the facts and circumstances of the case and the principles of equity, the retention of the funds by the incorrect recipient is improper.

3. Your firm's client, Jones, age 23, was driving a rental car when it was pulled over by the police for speeding. The police officers noticed a clear plastic bag containing a large quantity of a white powder stuffed in the map pouch behind the passenger seat. When questioned about the bag, Jones claimed that he never saw it before and he knew nothing about it, but he had had two passengers on his trip and they might have left it there. The bag turned out to contain two kilos of cocaine. Jones is on trial with his two passengers as codefendants in a conspiracy case in which the defendants are alleged to have distributed drugs and used firearms in connection with drug offenses. Jones maintains that he has never had anything to do with drugs or guns and was not part of the conspiracy. The prosecutors wish to introduce photographs of Jones taken in his high school production of "Scarface: the Musical," in which Jones played the title role. The photos depict Jones handling huge bags of drugs, firing submachine guns, and at one point plunging his face into a huge mound of cocaine. The prosecution claims that the pictures are relevant, because they show Jones had great familiarity with drugs, weapons, and drug

trafficking because of his "Scarface" performance. Your boss wants to exclude the photos on the grounds that the probative value of the photos is outweighed by the unfair prejudice to Jones that will occur if they are shown to the jury.

Federal Rule of Evidence 403 states in relevant part: "Although relevant, evidence may be excluded if its probative value is substantially outweighed by the danger of unfair prejudice." The Federal Rules of Evidence are the source of this rule, and they are applicable in this jurisdiction.

Your research has produced three cases from your jurisdiction that discuss and apply Fed. R. Evid. 403 that are potentially useful to this matter:

Case 1:   Prosecution sought to use photographs of a defendant in a drug conspiracy case posing with his small children next to piles of methamphetamine, and sometimes brandishing weapons next to the drugs. The photographs were held admissible, because the probative value of the photos in showing defendant's active participation in the conspiracy (rather than defendant's assertion that he was a casual drug user, not an active participant) outweighed any unfair prejudicial effect caused by the photographs in persuading the jury to find the defendant guilty of the crime.[4]

Case 2:   Prosecution was allowed to introduce multiple photographs of firearms, drugs, and drug paraphernalia seized from a site used by members of alleged drug conspiracy, including defendant, because the photos' probative value in showing the extent and nature of defendant's involvement in a far flung conspiracy to distribute drugs outweighed any unfair prejudicial effect of the use of the photos in persuading the jury to find the defendant guilty of the crime.[5]

---

4 Based on *United States v. Hester*, 140 F.3d 753, 759 (8th Cir. 1998).

5 Based on *United States v. Candelaria-Silva*, 162 F.3d 698, 704-05 (1st

Case 3:   In drug conspiracy case, graphic photographs of de-fendant's wife's face after defendant allegedly beat her were held inadmissible, because there was no proba-tive value in the photographs. No fact at issue in the drug conspiracy case was made more or less likely to be true by the introduction of the photographs, and the credibility of defendant's or his wife's testimony on any issue important to the case was not challenged or buttressed by evidence of the matters depicted in the photographs. The admission of the photographs pre-sented a risk of unfair prejudice to defendant because they might stir the jury's emotions against him.[6]

Case 4:   Photographs of apartments that were alleged to be "crack houses" located in the same building where defendant lived and which showed drugs and drug paraphernalia lying about were inadmissible in defen-dant's drug conspiracy trial. There was no evidence that defendant had ever stepped foot in any of the apartments depicted in the photographs, and there was a significant risk that the jury would mistakenly associate the things depicted in the photographs with defendant and prejudge him of the crime of which he was charged.[7]

A.   Draft a statement of facts (1-2 paragraphs) for Jones's motion to exclude the evidence that em-ploys narrative reasoning.   Mention the back-ground facts of the case and the facts concerning the photographs.

B.   Draft a Thesis heading, Rule section, and Expla-nation section using the above cases.

Cir. 1998); *United States v. Chambers*, 918 F.2d 1455 (9th Cir. 1990).

6 Based on *United States v. Hands*, 184 F.3d 1322 (11th Cir. 1999).

7 Loosely based on *United States v. Akers*, 702 F.2d 1145 (D.C. Cir. 1983).

C.   Draft an Application section, again using the above cases.

4. In Colorado, a person commits indecent exposure if he knowingly exposes his genitals to the view of any person under circumstances in which such conduct is likely to cause affront or alarm to the other person.

Bob is a student at Our Lady of the Lake University in Kit Carson County, Colorado. One night, he and three friends climbed the walls of the library and attempted to paint over the face of Jesus Christ depicted in the sixty foot high stained glass window on the front of the library. They wanted to replace the face of Christ with that of Tim Green, the star running back of the school who had just received the Heisman Trophy for that year. Just as they were getting started, one friend lost his balance and fell, but he was able to grasp the waistband of Bob's shorts. Unfortunately, as he slipped, he pulled Bob's shorts and underwear down to Bob's knees. As luck would have it, the Assistant Dean of Student Life, Msgr. O'Reilly, who periodically suffered from fits of insomnia, happened then to walk by the front of the library and saw Bob in all his glory swinging in front of the face of Christ. O'Reilly saw to it that Bob was charged with indecent exposure under <u>Colo. Rev. Stat. § 18-7-302</u> (1999), in a criminal case filed in the District Court for Kit Carson County. (O'Reilly did not notice that the boys also were engaged in vandalism.) Bob's father has sent your firm a $15,000 retainer, and asked you to look into Bob's defense of the crime.

A.   Using the facts above, draft a statement of facts from Bob's perspective in defense of the crime.

B.   Using the same facts, draft a statement of facts from the county prosecutor's perspective in support of conviction.

C.   Draft an explanation section employing explanatory synthesis that is based on three or more of the following authorities:

a. <u>Smith</u> case (1990), affirmed the conviction of a gas station attendant who refused to close his fly while working at a gas station. He was prosecuted and convicted for indecent exposure under <u>Colo. Rev. Stat. § 18-7-302</u>. The case was issued by the Colorado Court of Appeals, Division Three, the court that hears appeals from the District Court for Kit Carson County.

b. <u>Jones</u> case (1957), affirmed the order of punitive dismissal of an officer who got into a "contest" involving outdoor urination with some of his junior officers at the United States Air Base at Aviano, Italy. The officer was punitively dismissed for conduct unbecoming an officer under Article 133, Uniform Code of Military Justice, <u>10 U.S.C. § 933</u>. The case was issued by the United States Supreme Court.

c. <u>Colorado Revised Statutes Annotated, section 18-7-302</u>.

d. <u>Rednape</u> case (1998), affirmed the conviction of a window-washer who exposed himself to federal employees while hanging 15 stories up on the face of a federal building in Denver. He was prosecuted under 18 U.S.C. § 380043 (the language of which essentially is the same as <u>Colo. Rev. Stat. § 18-7-302</u>, but requires the exposure to take place on federal property). This case was issued by the United States Court of Appeals for the Tenth Circuit, hearing an appeal from the United States District Court for the District of Colorado.

e. Title 18 of the United States Code, section 380043.

f. <u>Fletcher</u> case (1977), affirmed the lower court's decision involving an indigent man who was robbed and beaten and left to wander naked in Vail, Colorado. He was prosecuted and found not guilty under <u>Colo. Rev. Stat. § 18-7-302</u>. The case was issued by the Colorado Supreme Court.

g. <u>Fuller</u> case (1994), affirmed the conviction of a woman who appeared topless in order to obtain necklaces of beads on the streets of Salina, Kansas, during a local Mardi Gras celebration. She was charged and convicted of the crime of common law indecent exposure. The case was issued by the Kansas Supreme Court.

h. Chapter 43, subsection D, of Prosser's treatise on <u>Torts</u>, discussing tort liability for indecent exposure.

i. Note, <u>Criminal Liability for Indecent Exposure in Colorado, Utah, and Idaho</u>, 97 Colum. L. Rev. 345 (1997).

j. E. Allen Farnsworth, <u>Contractual Dysfunction and Indecent Exposure: Drafter's Liability for Debt Instruments under 15 U.S.C. § 3467</u>, 25 Md. J. Contemp. Legal Issues 56 (1997).

Invent details for these authorities as necessary, but follow the format of a synthesized explanation section.

5. Federal law defines copyright infringement as the "unauthorized copying of a protected creative work." There is an exception to the rule for "fair use," and one such fair use is for "comment [or] criticism" and another fair use is use for "educational" purposes.

Your client Mary does a mean Elvis impersonation. She was performing at B.B. King's Blues Club in Memphis, when she was served with process and enjoined under <u>17 U.S.C. §§ 501</u>, <u>502</u>, from selling reprints of movie posters of Elvis at intermission. Apparently, the works were copyrighted and she had simply purchased five posters and then made multiple color copies of them at the local Kinkos. Mary thought that because Elvis was dead, anyone could use pictures of him for commercial gain or profit. She has been sued by Graceland Properties, Inc. for copyright infringement in the United States District Court for the Western District of Tennessee, Western Division.

A. Using the above facts, draft a statement of facts from Mary's perspective in defense of the lawsuit.

B. Using the same facts, draft a statement of facts from plaintiff Graceland Properties' perspective in support of liability.

C. Draft an explanation section employing explanatory synthesis that is based on three or more of the following authorities:

a. <u>Sun Records</u> case (1980), affirms a conviction for unfair competition under Tennessee law in a case involving the duplication and sale of copyrighted music recordings. The case was issued by the Court of Appeals of Tennessee, the court that hears appeals from the Circuit Court for Shelby County, Memphis, Tennessee.

b. <u>Lewis</u> case (1961), reverses judgment for plaintiff in copyright infringement case involving distribution of pirated recordings of Igor Stravinsky. The recordings were made by a college professor for use in lectures, and no commercial profit or gain was made by the professor from the recordings. The case was issued by the United States Supreme Court.

c. The U.S. Copyright Act of 1976, <u>17 U.S.C. § 101</u> *et seq.*

d. <u>Cash</u> case (1998), affirms judgment for plaintiff in copyright infringement case in which defendant illegally taped country music star's concert and sold bootleg recordings over the Internet. The case was issued by the United States Court of Appeals for the Eighth Circuit.

e. <u>Perkins</u> case (1997), affirming a judgment against plaintiff for liability under the Visual Artists Rights Act of 1990, <u>17 U.S.C. § 106A</u>, for mutilation of an artist's painting. The case was issued by the United States Court of Appeals for the Sixth Circuit.

f. <u>Parker</u> case (1994), where defendant was held liable for copyright infringement and unfair trade practices when he copied plaintiff's designs for western casual wear so as to produce clothing that was sold through catalog sales. The case was issued by the United States District Court for the Western District of Tennessee, Eastern Division.

g. Chapter 13, sections A-F, of Melville B. Nimmer's famous treatise, <u>Nimmer on Copyright</u> (1998), discussing injunctive relief for infringement of protected works of visual media.

h. Melville B. Nimmer, <u>Sources of the American Copyright Tradition in Elizabethan England</u>, 57 Colum. L. Rev. 48 (1957).

i. <u>18 C.J.S. Copyrights § 60</u> on copyright infringement. Corpus Juris Secundum is a legal encyclopedia.

Invent details for these authorities as necessary, but follow the format of a synthesized explanation section.

6. Synthesize the following discussion of case law. Wherever you find an unsynthesized presentation of cases convert it to a synthesized presentation using explanatory synthesis:

The question before us is whether this rule of liability, as applied to an action brought by a public official against critics of his official conduct, abridges the freedom of speech and of the press that is guaranteed by the First and Fourteenth Amendments.

Respondent relies heavily, as did the Alabama courts, on statements of this Court to the effect that the Constitution does not protect libelous publications. *Konigsberg v. State Bar of California*, 366 U.S. 36, 49, and n. 10, 81 S.Ct. 997, 6 L.Ed.2d 105; *Times Film Corp. v. City of Chicago*, 365 U.S. 43, 48, 81 S.Ct. 391, 5 L.Ed.2d 403; *Roth v. United States*, 354 U.S. 476, 486-487, 77 S.Ct. 1304, 1 L.Ed.2d 1498; *Beauharnais v. Illinois*, 343 U.S. 250, 266, 72 S.Ct. 725, 96 L.Ed. 919; *Pennekamp v. Florida*, 328 U.S. 331, 348-349, 66 S.Ct. 1029, 90 L.Ed. 1295; *Chaplinsky v. New Hamphire*, 315 U.S. 568, 572, 62 S.Ct. 766, 86 L.Ed. 1031; *Near v. Minnesota*, 283 U.S. 697, 715, 51 S.Ct. 625, 75 L.Ed. 1357.

Those statements do not foreclose our inquiry here. None of the cases sustained the use of libel laws to impose sanctions upon expression critical of the official conduct of public officials. The dictum in *Pennekamp v. Florida*, 328 U.S. 331, 348-349, 66 S.Ct. 1029, 1038, 90 L.Ed. 1295, that 'when the statements amount to defamation, a judge has such remedy in damages for libel as do other public servants,' implied no view as to what remedy might constitutionally be afforded to public officials. In *Beauharnais v. Illinois*, 343 U.S. 250, 72 S.Ct. 725, 96 L.Ed. 919, the Court sustained an Illinois criminal libel statute as applied to a publication held to be both defamatory of a racial group and 'liable to cause violence and disorder.' But the Court was careful to note that it 'retains and exercises authority to nullify action which encroaches on freedom of utterance under the guise of punishing libel'; for 'public men, are, as it were, public property,' and 'discussion 'cannot be denied and the right, as well as the duty, of criticism must not be stifled.' Id., at 263-264, 72 S.Ct. at 734, 96 L.Ed. 919 and n. 18. In the only previous case that did present the question of constitutional limitations upon the power to award damages for libel of a public official, the Court was equally divided and the question was not decided. *Schenectady Union Pub. Co. v. Sweeney*, 316 U.S. 642, 62 S.Ct. 1031, 86 L.Ed. 1727.

In deciding the question now, we are compelled by neither precedent nor policy to give any more weight to the epithet 'libel' than we have to other 'mere labels' of state law. *N.A.A.C.P. v. Button*, 371 U.S. 415, 429, 83 S.Ct. 328, 9 L.Ed.2d 405. Like insurrection, *Herndon v. Lowry*, 301 U.S. 242, 57 S.Ct. 732, 81 L.Ed. 1066, contempt, *Bridges v. California*, 314 U.S. 252, 62 S.Ct. 190, 86 L.Ed. 192; *Pennekamp v. Florida*, 328 U.S. 331, 66 S.Ct. 1029, 90 L.Ed. 1295, advocacy of unlawful acts, *De Jonge v. Oregon*, 299 U.S. 353, 57 S.Ct. 255, 81 L.Ed. 278, breach of the peace, *Edwards v. South Carolina*, 372 U.S. 229, 83 S.Ct. 680, 9 L.Ed.2d 697, obscenity, *Roth v. United States*, 354, U.S. 476, 77 S.Ct. 1304, 1 L.Ed.2d 1498, solicitation of legal business, *N.A.A.C.P. v. Button*, 371 U.S. 415, 83 S.Ct. 328, 9 L.Ed.2d 405, and the various other formulae for the repression of expression that have been challenged in this Court, libel can claim no talismanic immunity from constitutional limitations. It must be measured by standards that satisfy the First Amendment.

The general proposition that freedom of expression upon public questions is secured by the First Amendment has long been settled by our decisions. The constitutional safeguard, we have said, 'was fashioned to assure unfettered interchange of ideas for the bringing about of political and social changes desired by the people.' *Roth v. United States*, 354 U.S. 476, 484, 77 S.Ct. 1304, 1308, 1 L.Ed.2d 1498. 'The maintenance of the opportunity for free political discussion to the end that government may be responsive to the will of the people and that changes may be obtained by lawful means, an opportunity essential to the security of the Republic, is a fundamental principle of our constitutional system.' *Stromberg v. California*, 283 U.S. 359, 369, 51 S.Ct. 532, 536, 75 L.Ed. 1117. '(I)t is a prized American privilege to speak one's mind, although not always with perfect good taste, on all public institutions,' *Bridges v. California*, 314 U.S. 252, 270, 62 S.Ct.

190, 197, 86 L.Ed. 192, and this opportunity is to be afforded for 'vigorous advocacy' no less than 'abstract discussion.' *N.A.A.C.P. v. Button*, 371 U.S. 415, 429, 83 S.Ct. 328, 9 L.Ed.2d 405. The First Amendment, said Judge Learned Hand, 'presupposes that right conclusions are more likely to be gathered out of a multitude of tongues, than through any kind of authoritative selection. To many this is, and always will be, folly; but we have staked upon it our all.' *United States v. Associated Press*, 52 F.Supp. 362, 372 (D.C.S.D.N.Y.1943). . . .

Thus we consider this case against the background of a profound national commitment to the principle that debate on public issues should be uninhibited, robust, and wide-open, and that it may well include vehement, caustic, and sometimes unpleasantly sharp attacks on government and public officials. See *Terminiello v. Chicago*, 337 U.S. 1, 4, 69 S.Ct. 894, 93 L.Ed. 1131; *De Jonge v. Oregon*, 299 U.S. 353, 365, 57 S.Ct. 255, 81 L.Ed. 278. The present advertisement, as an expression of grievance and protest on one of the major public issues of our time, would seem clearly to qualify for the constitutional protection. The question is whether it forfeits that protection by the falsity of some of its factual statements and by its alleged defamation of respondent.

Authoritative interpretations of the First Amendment guarantees have consistently refused to recognize an exception for any test of truth-whether administered by judges, juries, or administrative officials-and especially one that puts the burden of proving truth on the speaker. Cf. *Speiser v. Randall*, 357 U.S. 513, 525-526, 78 S.Ct. 1332, 2 L.Ed.2d 1460. The constitutional protection does not turn upon 'the truth, popularity, or social utility of the ideas and beliefs which are offered.' *N.A.A.C.P. v. Button*, 371 U.S. 415, 445, 83 S.Ct. 328, 344, 9 L.Ed.2d 405. As Madison said, 'Some degree of abuse is inseparable from the proper use of every thing; and in no instance is this more true than in that of the press.' 4 Elliot's Debates on the Federal Constitution (1876), p. 571. . . .

That erroneous statement is inevitable in free debate, and that it must be protected if the freedoms of expression are to have the 'breathing space' that they 'need * * * to survive,' *N.A.A.C.P. v. Button*, 371 U.S. 415, 433, 83 S.Ct. 328, 338, 9 L.Ed.2d 405, was also recognized by the Court of Appeals for the District of Columbia Circuit in *Sweeney v. Patterson*, 76 U.S.App.D.C. 23, 24, 128 F.2d 457, 458 (1942), cert. denied, 317 U.S. 678, 63 S.Ct. 160, 87 L.Ed. 544. . . .

Injury to official reputation error affords no more warrant for repressing speech that would otherwise be free than does factual error. Where judicial officers are involved, this Court has held that concern for the dignity and reputation of the courts does not justify the punishment as criminal contempt of criticism of the judge or his decision. *Bridges v. California*, 314 U.S. 252, 62 S.Ct. 190, 86 L.Ed. 192. This is true even though the utterance contains 'half-truths' and 'misinformation.' *Pennekamp v. Florida*, 328 U.S. 331, 342, 343, n. 5, 345, 66 S.Ct. 1029, 90 L.Ed. 1295. Such repression can be justified, if at all, only by a clear and present danger of the obstruction of justice. See also *Craig v. Harney*, 331 U.S. 367, 67 S.Ct. 1249, 91 L.Ed. 1546; *Wood v. Georgia*, 370 U.S. 375, 82 S.Ct. 1364, 8 L.Ed.2d 569. If judges are to be treated as 'men of fortitude, able to thrive in a hardy climate,' *Craig v. Harney*, supra, 331 U.S., at 376, 67 S.Ct., at 1255, 91 L.Ed. 1546, surely the same must be true of other government officials, such as elected city commissioners. Criticism of their official conduct does not lose its constitutional protection merely because it is effective criticism and hence diminishes their official reputations. . . .

Excerpted from *N.Y. Times Co. v. Sullivan*, 376 U.S. 254, 268-74 (1964).

7. Synthesize the following discussion of case law. Wherever you find an unsynthesized presentation of cases convert it to a synthesized presentation using explanatory synthesis:

The Fourteenth Amendment forbade states to deny the citizen 'due process of law.' But its terms gave no notice to the people that its adoption would strip their local governments of power to deal with such problems of local peace and order as we have here. Nor was it hinted by this Court for over half a century that the Amendment might have any such effect. In 1922, with concurrence of the most liberty-alert Justices of all times-Holmes and

Brandeis-this Court declared flatly that the Constitution does not limit the power of the state over free speech. *Prudential Insurance Co. v. Cheek*, 259 U.S. 530, 543, 42 S.Ct. 516, 522, 66 L.Ed. 1044, 27 A.L.R. 27. In later years the Court shifted this dogma and decreed that the Constitution does this very thing and that state power is bound by the same limitation as Congress. *Gitlow v. New York*, 268 U.S. 652, 45 S.Ct. 625, 69 L.Ed. 1138. I have no quarrel with this history. See *West Virginia State Board of Education v. Barnette*, 319 U.S. 624, 63 S.Ct. 1178, 87 L.Ed. 1628, 147 A.L.R. 674. I recite the method by which the right to limit the state has been derived only from this Court's own assumption of the power, with never a submission of legislation or amendment into which the people could write any qualification to prevent abuse of this liberty, as bearing upon the restraint I consider as becoming in exercise of self-given and unappealable power.

It is significant that provisions adopted by the people with awareness that they applied to their own states have universally contained qualifying terms. The Constitution of Illinois is representative of the provisions put in nearly all state constitutions and reads (Art. II, s 4): 'Every person may freely speak, write and publish on all subjects, being responsible for the abuse of that liberty.' (Emphasis added.) That is what I think is meant by the cryptic phrase 'freedom of speech,' as used in the Federal Compact, and that is the rule I think we should apply to the states. . . .

Streets and parks maintained by the public cannot legally be denied to groups 'for the communication of ideas.' *Hague v. C.I.O.*, 307 U.S. 496, 59 S.Ct. 954, 83 L.Ed. 1423; *Jamison v. Texas*, 318 U.S. 413, 63 S.Ct. 669, 671, 87 L.Ed. 869. Cities may not protect their streets from activities which the law has always regarded subject to control, as nuisances. *Lovell v. Griffin*, 303 U.S. 444, 58 S.Ct. 666, 82 L.Ed. 949; *Schneider v. State*, 308 U.S. 147, 60 S.Ct. 146, 84 L.Ed. 155. Cities may not protect the streets or even homes of their inhabitants from the aggressions of organized bands operating in large numbers. *Douglas v. Jeannette*, 319 U.S. 157, 63 S.Ct. 877, 87 L.Ed. 1324. As in this case, the facts are set forth fully only in the dissent, 319 U.S. at page 166, 63 S.Ct. at page 882. See also *Martin v. Struthers*, 319 U.S. 141, 63 S.Ct. 862, 87 L.Ed. 1313. Neither a private party nor a public authority can invoke otherwise valid state laws against trespass to exclude from their property groups bent on disseminating propaganda. *Marsh v. Alabama*, 326 U.S. 501, 66 S.Ct. 276, 90 L.Ed. 265; *Tucker v. Texas*, 326 U.S. 517, 66 S.Ct. 274, 90 L.Ed. 274. Picketing is largely immunized from control on the ground that it is free speech, *Thornhill v. Alabama*, 310 U.S. 88, 60 S.Ct. 736, 84 L.Ed. 1093, and police may not regulate sound trucks and loudspeakers, *Saia v. New York*, 334 U.S. 558, 68 S.Ct. 1148, 92 L.Ed. 1574, though the Court finds them an evil that may be prohibited altogether. *Kovacs v. Cooper*, 336 U.S. 77, 69 S.Ct. 448. And one-third of the Court has gone further and declared that a position 'that the state may prevent any conduct which induces people to violate the law, or any advocacy of unlawful activity, cannot be squared with the First Amendment. * * *' and it is only we who can decide when the limit is passed. *Musser v. Utah*, 333 U.S. 95, 102, 68 S.Ct. 397, 400, 92 L.Ed. 562. Whatever the merits of any one of these decisions in isolation, and there were sound reasons for some of them, it cannot be denied that their cumulative effect has been a sharp handicap on municipal control of the streets and a dramatic encouragement of those who would use them in a battle of ideologies.

Excerpted from *Terminiello v. City of Chicago*, 337 U.S. 1, 28-31 (1949) (Jackson, J. dissenting).

VII.   THE OFFICE MEMORANDUM AND THE CLIENT LETTER (Legal Writing and Analysis, Chapter 7)

WRITING PROBLEMS

1. Change these issues (questions presented) to make them more helpful and meaningful to the reader. Be sure to include: (1) a concise statement of the issue; (2) that includes key facts and relevant elements of the law; and (3) reveals the relevant elements of the law by borrowing key language from the rules that govern the issue.

    a. Whether photographs of "crack houses" in defendant Smith's apartment building are admissible?

b.   Whether the photographs of defendant Heel standing with his baby in font of bags of drugs is more probative than prejudicial?

c.   Whether Warner provoked his neighbor's dog to attack when he retrieved his football from his neighbor's yard?

d.   Whether Warner's neighbor's dog's attack on Warner was disproportionate to the provocation of the dog?

2.   Change these conclusions (brief answers) to make them more helpful and meaningful to the reader. Be sure to include: (1) a concise summary of the relevant facts; (2) a summary of the relevant, disputed elements of the law; (3) a statement of the author's legal conclusions on the issue.

a.   The photographs of "crack houses" in defendant Smith's apartment building are inadmissible under Rule 403. There is nothing to link Smith to the "crack houses."

b.   Yes, the photographs of defendant Heel standing with his baby in font of bags of drugs are more probative than prejudicial and are admissible under Rule 403. The photographs show that Heel knew there were drugs around.

c.   Warner provoked his neighbor's dog to attack when he retrieved his football from his neighbor's yard. He ran across the yard where the dog could see him, and any self-respecting guard dog would pursue and attempt to deter such conduct.

d.   No, Warner's neighbor's dog's attack on Warner was not disproportionate to the provocation of the dog. The dog saw Warner as an intruder and had a right to protect the neighbor's property from a trespasser.

3.   Change these thesis headings adding factual or legal details to make them more helpful and meaningful to the reader (and remember to include the "because" part):

a. The photographs of "crack houses" are inadmissible.

b. Photographs of Heel standing with his baby in font of bags of drugs are admissible because they are more probative than prejudicial.

c. Provocation of the dog by Warner.

d. Warner's neighbor's dog's attack on Warner was not dispro-portionate to the provocation of the dog.

4. Draft a client letter to your client FOAM based on the following office memorandum:

MEMORANDUM

TO: Michael D. Murray

FROM: Student

DATE: October 14, 2004

RE: Friends of Alternative Marriage ("FOAM")/National Midnight Star v. FOAM (C1234/00001)

SUBJECT: Parody Defense in a Copyright Infringement Case

ISSUE

Is FOAM's use of copyrighted images in a poster advocating gay marriage, where FOAM transforms the appearance of the images but does not comment on the copyrighted expression in those images, parody un-der statute 17 U.S.C. § 107 on "fair use" of copyrighted works?

CONCLUSION

No. To qualify as parody under 17 U.S.C. § 107 the use must be transformative and the infringer must use the copyrighted work to comment, at least in part, upon the copyrighted expression in the work. FOAM used the copyrighted works in a transformative manner by superimposing images and text on top of the copyrighted originals. FOAM used the copyrighted material exclusively to comment upon the institution of marriage, not to comment upon the copyrighted expression. Therefore, FOAM's use of the pictures is not parody, and will not be fair use.

STATEMENT OF FACTS

FOAM, a non-profit organization advocating alternative marriage, used images copyrighted by NMS, a tabloid magazine, without NMS's permission. Two images were used, placed on a poster with quotes concerning the sanctity of marriage. The first was a photograph of Britney Spears' marriage license with a faint image of Mrs. Spears and some text superimposed by FOAM. The second was a picture of Mrs. Spears, her then husband, and another couple with the faces of a married celebrity couple superimposed upon the heads of the other couple. NMS has filed suit against FOAM for copyright infringement in the United States District Court for the Southern District of New York.

DISCUSSION

I. FOAM's use of the images is not a parody under statute 17 U.S.C. § 107.

The copyright code provides for fair uses of copyrighted works as follows:

The fair use of a copyrighted work...for purposes such as criticism... is not an infringement of copyright. In determining whether the

use made of a work in any particular case is a fair use the factors to be considered shall include--
(1) the purpose and character of the use, including whether such use is of a commercial nature or is for nonprofit educational purposes;
(2) the nature of the copyrighted work;
(3) the amount and substantiality of the portion used in relation to the copyrighted work as a whole; and
(4) the effect of the use upon the potential market for or value of the copyrighted work.

17 U.S.C. § 107.

Parody is regarded as a form of criticism. Seuss 1400. The rules do not require rigid application if it would stifle the creativity the law is designed to foster. Campbell 1170.

The second part of element one, commercial nature, and elements two, three, and four are not addressed below. FOAM has non-commercial status as a non-profit. The copyrightable nature of NMS's works is not in dispute and FOAM used the works in their entirety. The potential market for these copyrighted works is unknown pending further research.

A. The purpose and character of FOAM's use of the pictures is not parody under statute 17 U.S.C. § 107.

"The heart of any parodist's claim to quote is...the use of some elements of a prior author's composition to...at least in part, comment on that author's works." Campbell 1172. The new work must be transformative. Campbell 1171.

1. FOAM's use of the copyrighted works did not comment on the copyrighted work.

The threshold question when fair use is raised in defense of parody is whether a parodic character may be reasonably perceived. See Campbell at 1173 (contrast between words of infringing song and words of original reasonably perceived as parody); Leibovitz at 115 (male head on pregnant body reasonably perceived to comment on original's praise of pregnant form). The infringing work must comment, at least in part, upon the style or substance of the artists' expression. See Campbell at 1174 (infringing work used opening lines of song to mock naiveté of expression in original); Leibovitz at 115 (male head in place of female head mocks pretentiousness expressed in original work); Steinberg at 715 (copy of artist's style without intent to comment upon artist's style was not a parody).

Parodic use of NMS' copyrighted photographs must address the copyrighted expression in these photographs, not the factual content. The copyrightable elements in a photograph may include, but are not limited to, posing the subjects, lighting, angle, selection of film and camera, and evoking the desired expression. Rogers, 307 FOAM used these works, as indicated by the surrounding quotations, to encourage an alternative view of marriage. This use relied upon the factual content in the pictures to draw attention and suggest certain ideas about marriage. The changes FOAM made to the copyrighted works do not address the copyrighted expression unique to the work.

2. FOAM's use of the copyrighted works was transformative

The new work of the alleged infringer should add something new, with a further purpose or different character, altering the first with new expression, meaning, or message, such that it can be described as transformative. Campbell at 1171.

"Transformative" requires the addition of something distinct from the style and substance of the copyrighted work such that the infringing work is not merely derivative of the original. See Leibovitz at 114 (copy of a picture of a woman but for the addition of a man's head is transformative); Seuss at 1401 (use of Seuss's style alone is not transformative); see Koons at 311 (sculpture, a nearly exact three dimensional copy of a copyrighted picture, is derivative).

FOAM's use of the work does add something new and distinct to the works: two celebrity heads superimposed on the Spears wedding picture and an image of Spears combined with text superimposed over the top of the wedding certificate. FOAM's use was transformative.

FOAM's use of these copyrighted images without commenting upon the copyrighted expression in the images is not parody, and thus is not fair use.

_____

5. You represent Abraham Baum, the plaintiff in a suit brought pursuant to New York Civil Rights Law §§ 50-51 against York Media Holdings, LLC, for violation of Mr. Baum's right of privacy. Draft a client letter to Mr. Baum explaining the following order of the court in the litigation:

UNITED STATES DISTRICT COURT
SOUTHERN DISTRICT OF NEW YORK
SOUTHERN DIVISION

ABRAHAM BAUM,   )
)
          Plaintiff,   )
)
     v.   )   NO. 09-CIV-123 (PKL)
)
YORK MEDIA HOLDINGS,)
LLC, D/B/A YORK   )
MAGAZINE,   )
          Defendant.   )

ORDER AND JUDGMENT

PETER K. LEISURE, J.

The underlying action, brought under N.Y. Civil Rights Law § 51, concerns defendant's use of a photograph of plaintiff, concededly without his consent. The motion before the court brought by defendant York Media Holdings, LLC ("YMH"), is for summary judgment seeking dismissal of the complaint.

DISCUSSION

YMH claims that the challenged photograph was initially used in the context of and as an illustration of a newsworthy article in YMH's York Magazine publication ("the Magazine") and therefore is exempt from the application of New York State privacy laws because it is protected free speech by a member of the press under the United States and New York State Constitutions. All subsequent uses of this image, it is asserted, were undertaken to advertise the initial use in incidental or ancillary secondary uses, or were independently justified as First Amendment protected artistic expression.

In this motion, certain facts are not in dispute or are stipulated to:

Plaintiff Baum ("Baum") is an Orthodox Hasidic Jew and a member of the Klausenberg Sect, a sect that was almost completely destroyed during the Holocaust. He holds a deep religious conviction that the use of his image for commercial and public purposes violates his religion. In particular he believes that each of YMH's uses of his image violates the Second Commandment prohibition (from the Book of Exodus) against creation and worship of graven images.

In December 2008, a photographer working for YMH took a photograph of Baum as he was leaving his place of business and walking on a public sidewalk on a public street in New York City. Baum was unaware that the photographer had taken his photograph.

YMH used this photograph on the cover of its publication, the Magazine, in the December 9, 2008, issue of the Magazine. This use is shown in Exhibit 1 to the Complaint in this matter. The December 9, 2008, issue of the Magazine contained a story concerning the effect of the 2008 economic climate on the diamond district and diamond sales and gem cutting industry in New York City. Baum owns a diamond and gem cutting business and is employed in the diamond district and in the diamond and gem cutting industry.

YMH further used Baum's photograph as depicted on the cover of the December 9, 2008, issue of the Magazine in two subscription page advertisements for its York Magazine publication that ran in the December 29, 2008, issue of the magazine and the January 5, 2009, issue of the magazine. These uses are shown in Exhibits 2 and 3 attached to the Complaint.

YMH further used the image and likeness of Baum by making a cartoon of Baum's face and putting it on a cartoon body and identifying Baum by his first name ("Abe") in the subscription page advertisement shown in Exhibit 3 attached to the Complaint.

YMH did not seek or obtain consent to photograph Baum nor did it seek or obtain consent to use any photograph or image or likeness or the first name of Baum accompanying any image or likeness of Baum in any advertisement or for any use whatsoever.

The photographic image and the caricature of Baum as presented and depicted in Exhibits 1, 2, and 3 to the Complaint are readily identifiable as reflecting the image and likeness of plaintiff Baum.

YMH's publication York Magazine is a biweekly periodical publication of general and widespread circulation. It is read by tens of thousands of persons in and out of New York State, but particularly, it is read by persons in the area of New York City where Baum lives, works, and resides. Furthermore, the advertisements shown in Complaint, Exhibits 2 and 3 were displayed throughout the boroughs of New York on billboards and on the sides of public transportation buses and in advertising placards in the New York City Subway system.

When plaintiff first discovered the photograph of his image in early December 2008, he immediately contacted defendants regarding the use. YMH responded that the photographs were not being used for either "advertising" or "trade" and that it believed it was within its legal rights to continue use the photograph of plaintiff in the manner it had been using them. This action ensued.

N.Y. Civil Rights Law §§ 50 and 51 prohibit the unconsented use of identity within the State of New York "for advertising purposes or for the purposes of trade." The rights contained in these statutory sections are the exclusive remedies allowed in New York State for an unauthorized use of one's likeness. *Howell v. Post*, 81 N.Y.2d 115 (1993). Right of privacy laws are intended to defend the average person from unwanted public exposure and the potential emotional damage thereby inflected. Weisfogel, *Fine Arts v. Uncertain Protection: The New York Right of Privacy Statute and the First Amendment*, 20 Columbia-VLA J.L. & Arts 91 (1995). New York's Privacy laws were enacted to strike a balance between the right to privacy, on the one hand, and the right to First Amendment free speech and free press on the other. *Arrington v. New York Times*, 55 N.Y.2d 433 (1982).

The elements of a privacy claim under Civil Rights Law §§ 50 and 51 are: (1) use of plaintiff's name, portrait, picture or voice, (2) for advertising purposes or for trade, (3) without consent, and (4) within the State of New York. *Hoepker v. Kruger*, 200 F.Supp.2d 340 (SDNY 2002). YMH concedes facts that establish elements 1, 3 and 4 of a privacy cause of action. It claims, however, that as a matter of law, the photograph of Baum was not used for "advertising" or "trade" purposes. YMH claims that the photograph of Baum was used in a "newsworthy" way in the context of the reporting of a news story and that this type of use is expressly not included within the privacy protections under New York's statute. It further contends that the publication of newsworthy photos and illustrations of newsworthy stories cannot constitutionally be within the protection of New York's privacy laws because it is constitutionally protected speech. U.S. Const. amend. I; N.Y. Const. art. I, § 8.

Baum denies that the photograph was used in a proper manner to illustrate a news story. He argues that YMH's intended purpose was to pick a random but interesting-looking image of a person found on the street in the general vacinity of a diamond and gem business and to exploit that image to attact attention to the cover of its magazine and sell more magazines through the initial use and the two subsequent uses of the image in commercial subscription advertisements in the Magazine. Baum claims that each use of his photograph constitutes a commercial use in trade or advertising that is actionable under the privacy laws.

Baum urges that privacy cases require a balancing of competing constitutional interests. Baum argues that freedom of expression is not an absolute guaranty, but requires a trier of fact to weigh Baum's constitutional rights to privacy and his right to practice his religion against YMH's competing interests.

The N.Y. Court of Appeals has repeatedly held that the New York statutory right of privacy restricts the use of one's likeliness against use for advertising and trade only and nothing more. It is a strictly construed statute enacted with sensitivity to the potentially competing values of privacy protection versus free speech. *Messenger v. Gruner*, 94 N.Y.2d 436 (2000); *Finger v. Omni Publs. Int.*, 77 N.Y.2d 138 (1990); *Arrington v. New York Times*, 55 N.Y.2d 433 (1982).

There are recognized categories of protected uses that are not actionable under Civil Rights Law §§ 50 and 51. The most widely recognized protected category is for matters that are "newsworthy." *Messenger v. Gruner, supra.* The courts also recognize that as long as the primary purpose of the use is newsworthy, incidental or ancillary commercial use of the image does not otherwise turn a protected use into an unprotected use. *Arrington v. New York Times, supra*; *Altbach v. Kulon*, 302 A.D.2d 655 (3rd Dept. 2003). Thus, for example, use of a likeness in connection with advertising or selling newspaper subscriptions does not convert an excepted use into an actionable use under the New York State privacy laws. *Messenger v. Gruner, supra*; *Velez v. VV Pub. Cap*, 135 A.D.2d 47 (1st Dept. 1988), leave to app. den'd, 72 N.Y.2d 808 (1988). Moreover, a profit generating motive will not convert an otherwise newsworthy use of someone's likeness into one that is used for advertising or trade purposes. *Dworkin v. Hustler Magazine*, Inc., 867 F.2d 1188 (9th Cir.), cert. denied, 110 S.Ct. 59 (1989).

The Court is satisfied that the initial use of Baum's image by YMH on the cover of the Magazine was an appropriate and protected newsworthy use of the image in conjunction with a news story that ran in the same issue of the Magazine. Baum works in and owns a business in the diamond and gem industry in New York City and was photographed on a public street leaving his diamond and gem business. The fact that Baum is no celebrity and is not the singular "face of the New York City diamond and gem industry," as repeatedly asserted by Baum, does not change the fact that he has a connection and association with the diamond and gem industry that is sufficient to allow the use of his image to illustrate a news story on that industry, and the use was not simply "an advertisement in disguise." *See Rogers v. Grimaldi*, 875 F.2d 994 (2d Cir. 1989); *Parks v. LaFace Records*, 329 F.3d 437 (6th Cir. 2003).

Nor is the second use of the image of Baum a violation of Baum's privacy rights. As long as the primary purpose of the use was newsworthy, incidental or ancillary commercial use of the image does not otherwise turn a protected use into an unprotected use. *Arrington v. New York Times, supra*; *Altbach v. Kulon*, 302 A.D.2d 655 (3rd Dept. 2003). Thus, for example, use of a likeness in connection with advertising or selling news media subscriptions does not convert an excepted use into an actionable use under the New York State privacy laws. *Messenger v. Gruner, supra*; *Velez v. VV Pub. Cap*, 135 A.D.2d 47 (1st Dept. 1988), leave to app. den'd, 72 N.Y.2d 808 (1988). Uses such as the reproduction of a magazine cover in a subsequent advertisement to sell subscriptions of the same magazine are not actionable even if the person depicted on the cover complains and refuses to consent to the second use. *See Namath v. Sports Illustrated*, 371 N.Y.S.2d 10 (App. Div. 1st Dept. 1975), aff'd, 352 N.E.2d 584 (N.Y. 1976).

The third use of Baum's image in cartoon form gives the Court the most pause. YMH asserts that this is just one more incidental or ancillary use of Baum's image. I do not agree. The consensus of the case law in this area requires the use of the image to advertise the quality and nature of the <u>contents</u> of the publication. The modified cartoon image of Baum did not appear in the Magazine prior to its use in advertising for subscription sales in the January 5, 2009, issue of the Magazine. Thus, the advertisement was not showing any "contents" of the Magazine at all, it was just showing a newly doctored version of an image that did appear earlier on the cover of the Magazine.

Perhaps in recognition of this fact, YMH has raised the alternative defense to its use of the cartoon image that the use is "artistic" in nature and is sufficiently related to the earlier protected uses but transformed in an artistic way that it still is exempted from action under the N.Y. Civil Rights Law §§ 50 and 51. I turn to this argument now.

In recent years, some New York courts have addressed the issue whether an artistic use of an image is a use exempted from action under New York States Privacy Laws. *Altbach v. Kulon*, 302 A.D.2d 655 (3rd Dept. 2003); *Simeonov v. Tiegs*, 159 Misc.2d 54 (N.Y. Civ. Ct. 1993); *Hoepker v. Kruger*, 200 F.Supp.2d 340 (SDNY 2002). They have consistently found "art" to be constitutionally protected free speech, that is so exempt. The Court agrees.

Even while recognizing "art" as potentially exempted use removed from the reach of New York's privacy laws, the problem of sorting out what allegedly artistic expressions may or may not legally receive the benefits of this protection remains a difficult one. Some states for example, limit art to transformative and not duplicative likenesses. See, e.g., *Comedy III Productions, Inc. v. Gary Saderup, Inc.*, 25 Cal.4th 387 (2001), cert. denied, 534 U.S. 1078 (2002) [only transformative art was entitled to First Amendment protection in California]. Other states have limited exempted use to original works of fine art, but not to distribution of reproductions. *Martin Luther King, Jr. Center for Social Change, Inc. v. American Heritage Products, Inc.*, 250 Ga.135, 296 S.E.2d 697 (1982).

New York has been fairly liberal in its protection of what constitutes art. *Altbach v. Kulon, supra*; *Simeonov v. Tiegs, supra*; *Hoepker v. Kruger, supra*. In *Hoepker v. Kruger*, the court recognized that art can be sold, at least in limited editions, and still retain its artistic character. This analysis recognizes that First Amendment protection of art is not limited to only starving artists. The analysis in *Hoepker* is consistent with the primary purpose and incidental purpose doctrines, that have developed in connection with the newsworthy exemptions to privacy protections. A profit motive in itself does not necessarily compel a conclusion that art has been used for trade purposes. *DiGregorio v. CBS, Inc.*, 123 Misc.2d 491 (Sup Ct N.Y. Co 1984).

In its moving papers, YMH has made a prima facie showing that the cartoon image of Baum is "art." This is not a subjective determination, and cannot be based upon the personal preferences of either party or the court. YMH has demonstrated that the image is virtually the same as the image used in the earlier, protected uses on the cover and in the initial subscription advertisement; this is obvious just by looking at the cartoon. To the extent it is different, it is only because the image has been transformed in an artistic way, which further supports protection from suit under section 51 because artistic transformation is a form of speech that is encouraged and protected by the First Amendment freedom of expression public policy.

Baum complains that YMH's use of his image is different because of his religious beliefs and the need to protect them as supported by the public policy underlying the free exercise clause of the First Amendment and the general constitutional protections of privacy derived from the prenumbra of the Bill of Rights of the U.S. Constitution. The facts of this case, in and of themselves, however, do not otherwise convert news or art or other protected expression into something used in trade. They do not raise a sufficient factual basis to challenge YMH's prima facie showing that the photograph was used for newsworthy purposes and to advertise these newsworthy uses, and that the cartoon use further is protected as art.

The free exercise clause, however important to our country and the values upon which it was founded, restricts state action. *Zelman v. Simmon-Harris*, 122 S.Ct. 2460 (2002). There is no state action complained of in this case, only the private actions of defendants. Thus, this situation is distinguishable from circumstances where the government required a photograph that was claimed to be a violation of a fundamental religions belief. See *Quarnes v. Peterson*, 728 F.2d 1121 (9th Cir. 1984). The issues raised by Baum do not rise to constitutional consideration.

Clearly, Baum finds the use of the photograph bearing his likeness deeply and spiritually offensive. The sincerity of his beliefs is not questioned by YMH or this Court. While sensitive to Baum's distress, it is not redressable in the courts of civil law. In this regard, the courts have uniformly upheld Constitutional First Amendment protections, even in the face of a deeply offensive use of someone's likeness. Thus, in *Arrington*, supra, the Court of Appeals recognized that an African American man's image was being used in a manner that conveyed viewpoints that were offensive to him. It nonetheless found the use of the image protected. In *Costlow v. Cusimano*, 34 A.D.2d 196 (4th Dept.) the court held that the parents of children who died by suffocation when they trapped themselves in a refrigerator could not assert a privacy claim to prevent defendant from publishing an article with photographs of the premises and the deceased children, because the article was "newsworthy." These examples illustrate the extent to which the constitutional exceptions to privacy will be upheld, notwithstanding that the speech or art may have unintended devastating consequences on the subject, or may even be repugnant. They are, as the Court of Appeals recognized in *Arrington*, the price every person must be prepared to pay for in a society in which information and opinion flow freely. 55 N.Y.2d at 442.

The Court, therefore, finds that Baum has failed to state a cause of action under New York Civil Rights Law § 51. Summary judgment is granted on such basis.

CONCLUSION

In accordance with the aforementioned, it is hereby:

ORDERED that defendant, YMH's motion for summary judgment dismissing the complaint is granted in its entirety; and it is further

ORDERED that the clerk is directed to enter a judgment in favor of YMH dismissing the complaint, with prejudice.

Any relief request not expressly granted herein is denied.

This shall constitute the decision and order of the Court.

Date: February 6, 2009

VIII. EDITING AND FINE TUNING YOUR WRITING
(Legal Writing and Analysis, Chapter 8)

WRITING PROBLEMS

1. Edit the following office memorandum. Pay attention to grammar, legal writing style, organization (use of TREAT format and explanatory synthesis), and coherence more than the legal discussion. You may want to make one pass through the memorandum just for superficial problems (typos, grammar errors, spelling errors, legal writing style errors), a second pass for major structural problems (organization and use of the TREAT format and explanatory synthesis), and one last pass for smaller-scale substantive problems (word choice, bad sentences, improper usage issues, transitions, coherence, overall readability). Do not evaluate the citations — this memo was written with abbreviated citation forms pursuant to the instructions for the assignment. Note at least ten edits or changes you would make to the memorandum.

MEMORANDUM

TO: Michael D. Murray, Carol Ng Book

FROM: Student

DATE: September 25, 2006

RE: *Advocates of Alternative Marriage/Zip Mag v. AAM*
               (C124/00001)

SUBJECT: Use of Parody Defense in Copyright Infringement Case

ISSUE

Is Advocates of Alternative Marriage (AAM) liable for their unauthorized reproductions of Zip Mag's copyrighted images of public figures in full for the purposes of noncommercial advertising?

CONCLUSION

Yes. AAM will be liable to Zip Mag for copying Zip Mag's images because, though they altered the images, they did not criticize or comment on them and their use was not sufficiently transformative.

STATEMENT OF FACTS

As part of an effort to support their political cause, AAM reproduced several of Zip Mag's copyrighted images to make fundraising posters without Zip Mag's permission. AAM modified the images by splicing more of Zip Mag's copyrighted images onto the poster and adding original captions. AAM got sued.

DISCUSSION

I. AAM will be liable for its use of Zip Mag's copyrighted images because their reproductions do not qualify for fair use as parodies.

The factors that must be considered to determine whether or not a reproduction of a copyrighted work is fair use are:

> (1) the purpose and character of the use, including whether such use is of a commercial nature or is for nonprofit educational purposes; (2) the nature of the copyrighted work; (3) the amount and substantiality of the portion used in relation to the copyrighted work as a whole; and (4) the effect of the use upon the potential market for or value of the copyrighted work.

17 U.S.C. § 107. These "factors are to be explored and weighed together." Campbell at 1166, Leibovitz at 112. The factors are meant to be "guidelines for 'balancing the equities,' not . . . 'definitive or determinative' tests." Dr. Seuss at 1399. However, the factors are not necessarily to be weighed equally; for example, "the more transformative the new work, the less will be the significance of other factors, like commercialism, that may weigh against a finding of fair use." Campbell at 1171. Also, "the fourth factor, effect on the potential market for, or value of, the original, [may be] 'the single most important element of fair use.'" Leibovitz at 113.

A. AAM's full reproductions of Zip Mag's copyrighted images were for noncommercial use, and may not have affected the market value of the original work.

AAM is a nonprofit organization and their use of the images for fundraising purposes was a noncommercial use. Zip Mag's images are publicly known, expressive works and are copyrightable. AAM reproduced the images in their entirety, modifying them with portions of other

Zip Mag copyrighted images, but even extensive copying may still be fair use. <u>Leibovitz</u> at 116, <u>Rogers</u> at 311. The effect on the market for the original work is undetermined, but it is sensible to conclude that the reproductions would be unlikely to affect the value of the originals. <u>Campbell</u> at 1177.

> **B. AAM's fundraising posters do not qualify for fair use as parodies because they do not criticize or comment on the original works and they are not sufficiently transformative.**

A reproduction may be fair use even if it uses significant amounts of the original, as long as it is sufficiently transformative. <u>See Campbell</u> (it was not excessive for a rap group to reproduce the "heart" of another artist's song in their parody); <u>Leibovitz</u> (the extensive copying of an original photograph beyond what was necessary to "conjure up" the original did not weigh against fair use). A parody by its nature as a transformative work is unlikely to serve as a market substitute for the original. <u>See Campbell</u> (a rap parody of a rock ballad could not be presumed to affect the market value of the original).

> **1. AAM's fundraising posters do not criticize or comment on the original works because their focus is on more general topics.**

Copyrighted works may be reproduced under certain circumstances. "The fair use of a copyrighted work . . . for purposes such as criticism [and] comment . . . is not an infringement of copyright." 17 U.S.C. § 107.

To qualify for fair use, the original work must be the object of the commentary or criticism. <u>See Steinberg</u> (parodying a general idea or view does not justify copying an artistic expression of that idea). Indeed, satire, which ridicules more general themes, does not require the reproduction of a copyrighted work in order to make its point, unlike parody. See Campbell (if the new work does not comment on or criticize the original it is not a parody, but a satire and requires further justification for the use); Dr. Seuss (the use of a work to comment on something unrelated to the original was not fair use).

AAM's first poster reproduced Britney Spears' marriage certificate, adding a picture of Spears to the background and text that reads "*GOOD FOR 55 HOURS ONLY." This message clearly criticizes Spears and comments on her short-lived first marriage, but does not make Zip's work the object of its attention. The second poster reproduced a wedding picture of Spears and husband Jason with the faces of Jennifer Lopez and Marc Antony superimposed over the bodies of an unidentified couple. To this picture AAM added a caption reading, "BY ALL MEANS – STOP GAY MARRIAGE/DON'T LET IT MAKE MARRIAGE LESS SACRED." Again, this criticism is focused on the chaotic love lives of the named celebrities and on the political position opposing homosexual marriage.

AAM's posters did comment on society's views on marriage and criticized the celebrity in the pictures as well as the political position opposing homosexual marriage. However, to make a general criticism that could be made without copying the original work does not justify the reproduction of that work. Neither of AAM's reproductions qualify as parodies because they did not comment on or criticize the copied works, but focused on the vices and follies of celebrities and the apparent hypocrisy of a political stance.

2. AAM's fundraising posters are not transformative because they do not add to the original in a way that creates something new.

A transformative work "adds something new, with a further purpose or different character, altering the first with new expression, meaning, or message." Campbell at 1171. Although "transformative use is not absolutely necessary for a finding of fair use, . . . the more transformative the new work, the less will be the significance of other factors." <u>Campbell</u> at 1171. While "even 100 percent copying [may] not preclude a fair use finding", the full reproduction "may reveal a dearth of transformative character or purpose." <u>Rogers</u> at 311; <u>Campbell</u> at 1176.

A work is not sufficiently transformative if it copies the original without becoming a new expression itself. <u>See Rogers</u> (an artist's reproduction of a photograph as a statue, while different, was not fair use because the artist copied the original's expression). In addition, even the use of parts of an original work will bar a fair use finding. <u>See Steinberg</u> (a substantial similarity to another work is enough to infringe copyright).

AAM's reproducing of Zip Mag's images in their entirety is a large factor in the evaluation of the extent to which it is transformative. AAM did not transform Zip Mag's images, but merely spliced several of their images together and added a caption. This is not transformative as much as it is using Zip Mag's work in full and adding a slogan to convey a political message. While different, AAM's posters are still substantially similar to the original works and are not a new expression.

AAM's fundraising posters are not transformative works because they are substantially similar to the originals without becoming new expressions.

AAM will be liable to Zip Mag for the use of their copyrighted images because their reproductions do not qualify as parodies because they do not criticize or comment on the original works and they are not sufficiently transformative. However, because the criticism was partially directed at celebrities, it could be argued that this criticism could not have been made without the use of some copyrighted images. This argument brings to light an unexamined area of the fair use of images of public figures. To hinder the ability of others to parody celebrities in photograph by making them liable to the photographers could stifle an area of creativity, defeating one of the purposes of copyright law. As noted in <u>Campbell</u>, "the goal of copyright [is] to promote science and the arts."

---

2. Edit the following office memorandum. Pay attention to grammar, legal writing style, organization (use of TREAT format and explanatory synthesis), and coherence more than the legal discussion. You may want to make one pass through the memorandum just for superficial problems (typos, grammar errors, spelling errors, legal writing style errors), a second pass for major structural problems (organization and use of the TREAT format and explanatory synthesis), and one last pass for smaller-scale substantive problems (word choice, bad sentences, improper usage issues, transitions, coherence, overall readability). Note at least ten edits or changes you would make to the memorandum.

MEMORANDUM

TO: Michael D. Murray

FROM: Student

DATE: November 14, 2007

RE: Victor Chandelbise/Products Claim (C68901/89012)

SUBJECT: Possible suit arising from death of wife

ISSUES

1. Whether Victor Chandelbise (Mr. C) may bring a legitimate products liability suit against the health care provider Homenides de Histangua Hospital (HHH) and Dr. Finache (as surgeon) for strict liability for failure to warn as a health care provider.

2. Whether Dr. Finache will be liable for product liability for strict liability for failure to warn, when he implanted a mechanical heart valve of his design and manufacture into a patient (after a warning of potential dangers and potential clicking noise from the valve did not cause the patient to decline reception of the valve) and it does not appeared to have malfunctioned, but the patient died of panic-induced heart failure after she noticed the valve clicking and viewed a program describing the death of six others with the same valve after they heard enhanced clicking.

CONCLUSIONS

1. No, Mr. C may not bring a products liability suit against HHH and Dr. Finache (as surgeon) for strict liability for failure to warn. As health care providers, hospitals are excepted from strict liability for failure to warn suits under Missouri law.

2. No, Dr. Finache, as manufacturer of the valve, will not be liable for product liability for strict liability for failure to warn because the mechanical heart valve did not malfunction and was therefore not defective. Consequently, the case against Dr. Finache fails to meet two of the five elements required by Missouri law to bring a strict liability for failure to warn case.

STATEMENT OF FACTS

Yvonne Chandelbise (Mrs. C), the plaintiff's deceased wife, suffered from end-stage degradation of heart muscle tissue. After trying other treatments that did not work, Yvonne was referred to Dr. Finache of HHH. Dr. Finache was the inventor and manufacturer of the Keltic VII artificial heart.

Before receiving the Keltic VII, Mrs. C met with Dr. Finache and was warned that she would be only the thirteenth person to receive the mechanical valve, and was warned of the risks associated with experimental procedures with little track record. Mrs. C was also informed at this time that the valve would click. She elected to receive the valve and, on March 17, 2007, the valve was surgically implanted. The surgery was a success.

As of April 12, 2007, Mrs. C claimed to be pleased with the Keltic VII. Over the summer Yvonne noticed that the valve's clicking was getting louder, but was told by Dr. Finache that there was no problem. According to her husband, Mrs. C led an improved life until September 13, 2007. On September 13, she viewed a Spinline program on television that detailed the deaths of other Keltic VII recipients after their valves' clicking became louder. Mrs. C panicked and subsequently died of a massive myocardial infarction in her left ventricle. After her death, two separate tests confirmed that, although clicking loudly, her Keltic VII had been functioning properly and had not broken apart or caused her heart attack. This case will be brought in the Missouri Circuit Court for St. Louis County.

DISCUSSION

I. HHH CANNOT BE SUED FOR STRICT LIABILITY FOR FAILURE TO WARN BECAUSE, UNDER MISSOURI LAW, HEALTH CARE PROVIDERS ARE NOT LIABLE FOR STRICT LIABILITY CLAIMS.

Missouri law dictates that: "The provisions of. . . 537.760 [products liability]. . . shall not apply to actions under sections 538.205 to 538.230." Mo. Rev. Stat. §538.300 (1987).

The Missouri Supreme Court has applied § 538.300 to case law: "Further buttressing the conclusion that strict liability is not applicable to health care providers is sec. 538.300. . . provid[ing] that the provisions. . . relating to products liability actions, are not applicable to actions against health care providers." *Budding v. SSM Healthcare Syst.*, 19 S.W.3d 678, 681 (Mo. 2000).

In this case, HHH is a health care provider as defined by Missouri statute which defines "Health care provider" as: ". . . any physician, hospital, etc." Mo. Rev. Stat. § 538.205 (1987) Therefore, the hospital cannot be sued for products liability.

HHH and Dr. Finache (as the surgeon) cannot be sued for strict liability for failure to warn because, under Missouri law, health care providers are not liable for strict liability claims.

II. DR. FINACHE WILL NOT BE LIABLE FOR A PRODUCTS LIABILITY SUIT FOR STRICT LIABILITY FOR FAILURE TO WARN, SINCE CHANDELBISE CANNOT MAKE OUT THE DEFECTIVE AND CAUSATION ELEMENTS OF A STRICT LIABILITY PRODUCT LIABILITY CASE.

Missouri Revised Statute § 537.760 states that a

" '. . . products liability claim' means a claim in which the plaintiff seeks relief in the form of damages on a theory that defendant is strictly liable for such damages because:

> 1. the defendant, wherever situated in the chain of commerce, transferred a product in the course of his business; and
>
> 2. the product was used in a manner reasonably anticipated; and
>
> 3. . . .
>
> > b   the product was then unreasonably dangerous when put to a reasonably anticipated use without knowledge of its characteristics, and the plaintiff was damaged as a direct result of the product being sold without an adequate warning"

The Missouri Supreme Court has broken products liability claims into five elements:

(1) defendant sold the product in question in the course of defendant's business; (2) the product was unreasonably dangerous at the time of sale when used as reasonably anticipated without knowledge of its characteristics; (3) the defendant did not give adequate warning of the danger; (4) the product was used in a reasonably anticipated manner; and (5) plaintiff was damaged as a direct result of the product being sold without an adequate warning.

Tune v. Synergy Gas Corp. 883 S.W.2d 10, 13 (Mo. 1994).

For this case, only elements two and five need to be determined. Element one (sale) is met because Dr. Finache sold or provided the valve to Mrs. C in the normal course of his business. Element three (warning) is met because Dr. Finache warned of the potential clicking noise of the valve. Element four (reasonable use) is met because Mrs. C received the mechanical heart valve in the normal manner and used it as was intended. Mr. C's ability to state a strict liability case against Dr. Finache is contingent upon meeting elements two and five.

A. Mrs. C's mechanical heart valve was not defective, because she had previously been warned of the clicking and the heart valve did not malfunction.

Missouri case law states: ". . . the doctrine of strict liability. . . is not applicable unless there is a product failure or malfunction." *Spuhl v. Shiley, Inc.* 795 S.W.2d 573, 580 (Mo. Ct. App. Eastern District 1990)

The *Spuhl* court relies on the following definition of defective: "A product is in a 'defective condition' where the condition is one not contemplated by the ultimate consumer. . . ." *Spuhl,* 795 S.W.2d at 580(citing Restatement (Second) of Torts § 402A(1)).

The controlling Missouri case law consistently holds that actual malfunction must be proven in order to recover under strict liability: Compare *Spuhl*, 795 S.W.2d 573(court denied plaintiff damages under strict liability and negligent failure to warn, when plaintiff feared that his mechanical heart valves would fail, but the valves did not actually malfunction) and *Mothershead v. Greenbriar Country Club*, 994 S.W.2d 80 (Mo. Ct. App. 1999)(court denied plaintiff injured in sled accident recovery of damages against sled manufacturer, when there was no proof that the sled had actually malfunctioned) with *Hill v. Air Shields, Inc.*, 721 S.W.2d 112 (Mo. Ct. App. E.D. 1986)(excessive exposure to oxygen due to incubator malfunction resulted in blindness to infant plaintiff) and *Yocum v. Piper Aircraft Corp.*, 738 S.W.2d 145 (Mo. Ct. App. E.D. 1987) (defective stabilator trim tab system in airplane caused plaintiff's death).

In cases dealing with mechanical heart valves, various courts have agreed that recovery for strict liability and failure to warn claims must be precipitated be actual product malfunction: *Spuhl*, 795 S.W.2d 573(court denied strict liability damages based on fear that mechanical valve would fail, when it had not actually malfunctioned); *Pfizer, Inc. v. Farsian*, 682 So.2d 405 (Ala. 1996)(court denied damages for injury based on the risk that valve may one day fail, but had not actually malfunctioned); *Angus v. Shiley Inc.*, 989 F.2d 142 (3d Cir.1993), (court denied damages based on fear of valve failure due to alleged failure to warn, when no malfunction had actually taken place); *Brinkman v. Shiley, Inc.*, 732 F.Supp. 33 (M.D.Pa.), affirmed, 902 F.2d 1558 (3d Cir.1989), (court dismissed claims of negligence and strict liability stemming from heart valve implants, when valves had not actually malfunctioned); *Lauterbach v. Shiley, Inc.*, 1991 U.S. Dist. LEXIS 21782 (D. Tex. 1991) (court denied recovery of damages for failure to warn, when mechanical heart valve had failed in other patients but not plaintiff); *Walus v. Pfizer, Inc.*, 812 F. Supp. 41 (D.N.J. 1993)(court stated that plaintiffs had no valid cause of action against manufacturer of valve, when plaintiff's valve had not actually malfunctioned).

In this case, Mrs. C's heart valve did not appear to malfunction. In *Spuhl,* the plaintiff brought a strict liability suit against the manufacturer of his mechanical heart valves, citing emotional distress due to alleged defects in the valves. The court held that, to bring a strict liability suit, the product must have actually malfunctioned. Since *Spuhl* is a controlling authority, Mr. C would have to demonstrate that Mrs. C's Keltic VII actually malfunctioned. Citing fear of malfunction or malfunction in other patients is not sufficient to satisfy the defect element of a strict liability suit.

Mrs. C's mechanical heart valve was not defective, because she had previously been warned of the clicking and the heart valve did not malfunction.

B. Missouri case law precludes Mr. C from claiming the causation element of strict liability, because him and his wife were warned of her mechanical heart's potential dangers and that warning did not cause her to refuse implantation of the mechanical heart.

The Missouri Supreme Court has articulated two sub-elements of the causation element for strict liability cases: "(1) the product for which there was no warning must have caused plaintiff's injuries, and (2) the plaintiff must show that a warning would have altered the behavior of those involved in the accident." (*Tune v. Synergy Gas Corp.* 883 S.W.2d 10, 14 (Mo. 1994))

Further, the Chandelbises would not be able to recover on a theory of emotional distress, as the court in *Spuhl* states: "Recovery for emotional distress without physical injury or impact should be governed by the application of general tort principles. . . ." *Spuhl,* 795 S.W.2d at 580.

Heart valve cases from Missouri and from around the country support the inability to claim emotional damages under strict liability without actual product malfunction: *Spuhl,* 795 S.W.2d 573(court denied recovery for emotional distress under strict liability when no actual malfunction and subsequent physical injury occurred); *Pfizer, Inc. v. Farsian,* 682 So.2d 405 (Ala.1996) (court denied damages claimed based on plaintiff's fear that mechanical valve would fail in the future); *Angus v. Shiley Inc.,* 989 F.2d 142 (3d Cir.1993) (court denied recovery of damages for severe mental anguish and chronic fear of heart valve failure when no actual malfunction had occurred); *Brinkman v. Shiley, Inc.,* 732 F.Supp. 33 (M.D.Pa. 1989)(court dismissed plaintiff's claims of emotional distress since no physical harm was suffered from valve); *Lauterbach v. Shiley, Inc.,* 1991 U.S. Dist. LEXIS 21782 (D. Tex. 1991) (court denied recovery of damages for fear of future malfunction of valve); *Walus v. Pfizer, Inc.,* 812 F. Supp. 41 (D.N.J. 1993)(court stated that plaintiffs had no valid cause of action against manufacturer of valve, when valve had not actually malfunctioned but plaintiff feared it might).

In this case, Mr. and Mrs. C were both warned of the potential clicking of the heart valve and elected to go through with the surgical implantation.

Missouri case law precludes Mr. C from claiming the causation element of strict liability, because him and his wife were warned of her mechanical heart's potential dangers and that warning did not cause her to refuse implantation of the mechanical heart.

Mr. C is unable to fulfill the second of five required elements for products liability claims, because he cannot demonstrate that the mechanical heart valve malfunctioned so as to be deemed defective. Further, Mr. C is unable to meet the fifth of the five elements since him and his wife were warned by Dr. Finache of the potential clicking of the mechanical valve and elected to receive the valve anyway. Since Mr. C cannot fulfill two of the five required elements for a strict liability claim in Missouri, he will be unable to successfully bring suit against Dr. Finache for strict liability for failure to warn.

IX.   LEGAL CITATION (Legal Writing and Analysis, Chapter 9)

CITATION EXERCISES

Identify what is wrong (if anything) with the following citations. For your information, we have indicated the number of errors for each citation. Remember: spacing counts!

SERIES 1

1.   <u>Brownstein v. Morris</u>, 203 N.Y.S.2d 465 (N.Y. App. Div. 4th Dep't 1990). [1 error]

2.   The applicable standard is gross negligence. <u>Smith v. Jones</u>, 918 S.W. 2d 222, 224 (Mo. 1997). [1 error]

3.   The evidentiary standard is one of gross negligence. Missouri Rev. Stat. §232.12 (1986); See <u>Smith v. Jones</u>, 218 S.W.3d 222, 224 (Mo. 2005); <u>Huffy v. Carmichael</u>, 846 S.W.2d 333, 345 (Mo. 1987). [4 errors]

4.   The Illinois Dog Bite Statute, 510 Ill. Comp. Stats. section 5/16 (Smith Hurd 1996); defines a dog-owner's liability for a dog bite. [3 errors]

5.   Dog bite liability requires a lack of provocation, <u>See</u> Ky. Rev. Stat. Ann. §§ 123 (1996); <u>Norton v. Cramden</u>, 354 Ky. 268, 270 (1946); <u>Eckert v. Triesberger</u>, 210 Ky. App. Rptr. 207 (Ky. App. 1965), but provocation can be offset if the dog is a hunting dog, Eckert, <u>Id.</u>, or a dog trained to kill. <u>Norton</u>, <u>Id.</u> [8 errors]

6. The <u>Erie</u> doctrine confuses the issue of choice of law. <u>Mast v. John</u>, 75 Iowa 23, 24 (1988); <u>see also</u> <u>Hill v. Willy</u>, 866 P. 2d 433, 444 (OK. 1978) (discussing fact that <u>Erie</u> confuses most issues of conflict of laws, including forum selection.).   [4 errors]

7. Car dealers must take reasonable care not to deceive buyers. <u>cf.</u> <u>Cloff v. Decchor</u>, 239 So. E. 2d 235, 237 (S.C. Ct. App. 1st Dist.) (jeweler required to take reasonable care not to deceive customer); <u>Uy v. Hale Bopp Comet Company</u>, 236 Ga. 457, 459 (1973) (similar).   [5 errors]

8. If the shoe fits, a person will wear it. <u>Compare</u> <u>Non v. Den</u>, 432 Vt. 234, 236 (1990) (shoe fit, it was worn); <u>and</u> <u>Ricky v. Mertz</u>, 365 Vt. 245, 249 (1982) (shoe fit, it was worn); <u>with</u> <u>Soby v. Sagy</u>, 953 Vt. 988, 991 (1997) (shoe did not fit, it was not worn); <u>and</u> <u>Hujey v. Quacker</u>, 289 Vt. 656, 659 (1978) (per curiam) (shoe did not fit, it was not worn).   [1 error]

9. The following paragraphs appear in the document:

    Red is used for anger. <u>Rea v. Olena</u>, 123 U.S. 234, 238 (1923). Blue is for peace. <u>Id.</u> Purple is for sorrow. <u>Id.</u> at 239.

    When writing, try to be colorful. <u>Rea</u>, <u>supra</u>, 123 U.S. at 239. It is the best practice in Missouri, because statutes require it. Mo. Rev. Stat. § 212.2, 212.6, 254.2. However, it cannot overcome a procedural defect. <u>Id.</u> § 212.2 *et seq.*   [3 errors]

10. The <u>Erie</u> doctrine confuses the issue of choice of law. <u>Masters, Inc. v. Johns</u>, 55 N.W. 23, 24 (Minn. 1917); <u>see also</u> <u>Hill v. Williams</u>, 766 N.W. 433, 444 (Minn. 1918). It also confuses conflict of laws, <u>id.</u>, including the law of forum selection. <u>See</u> <u>Masters, Inc.</u>, <u>id.</u> at 25.   [2 errors]

11. <u>Mr. Roger Smith v. Mr. Jones' Washing Mach. Co., Incorporated</u>, 12 S.W.2d 13 (Tenn. 1937).   [2 errors]

12. <u>State of Missouri in the relation of Jay Nixon, Attorney General v. American Tobacco Indus., Inc.</u>, 980 S.W.2d 233 (Mo. 1998). [2 errors]

13. <u>Presy v. Weckston</u>, 833 S.W.2d 222, 223, 224, 233-35 (TX. 1996). [1 error]

14. Which of the following is incorrect:

    N.Y. Gen. Constr. Law § 456 (McKinney 1989)

    N.Y. Mun. Home Rule Law 77(a) (Consol. 1990)

    N.Y. C.P.L.R. 8209 (Gould 1991)

15. <u>Roget v. Hammond</u>, 488 F.2d 745, 766 (2d Cir. 1958), <u>certiorari denied</u>, 354 N.Y. 347 (1958). [3 errors]

16. Certain <u>non-majority opinions</u> were criticized. <u>Tex v. Texas Horn Co.</u>, 357 Ark. 456, 468 (1948) (Simpson, J., dissenting) (emphasis supplied) (arguing for new rule in Arkansas). [Are there any errors?]

17. <u>Idaho Const.</u>, art. 2, cl. 1 [2 errors]

18. 3 Murray, <u>How to Write the Best Brief in the World and other Moot Points</u>, 23-24 (Random House 1999). [3 errors]

19. <u>Restatement (Second) of Conflicts of Law</u>, sec. 23 (ALI 1966) [3 errors]

20. C.H. DeSanctis, "The Real Life of Lawyers: No Fun, No Rest," 24 Harvard L. Rev. 245-46. [5 errors]

SERIES 2

1. Which citation is correct?

> Mr. Carne Asada v. Ms. Chili Relleno, 123 F.2d 34 (7th
> Cir. 1900)

> Asada v. Relleno, 123 F.2d 34 (7th Cir. 1900)

2. Which citation is correct?

> All you need is love, Ono v. Lennon, 34 N.E.2d 23, 24
> (N.Y. 1979), love is all you need. Starr v. McCartney, 44
> N.E.2d 55, 56 (N.Y. 1982).

> All you need is love; Ono v. Lennon, 34 N.E.2d 23, 24
> (N.Y. 1979); love is all you need. Starr v. McCartney, 44
> N.E.2d 55, 56 (N.Y. 1982).

3. Which citation is correct?

> You may say I'm a dreamer, See Ono v. Lennon, 34 N.E.2d
> 23, 24 (N.Y. 1979), but I'm not the only one. See Starr v.
> McCartney, 44 N.E.2d 55, 56 (N.Y. 1982).

> You may say I'm a dreamer, see Ono v. Lennon, 34 N.E.2d
> 23, 24 (N.Y. 1979), but I'm not the only one. See Starr v.
> McCartney, 44 N.E.2d 55, 56 (N.Y. 1982).

4. Which citation is correct?

> Monkeys and gorillas are primates. Stanley v. Neutron,
> 112 S.W.3d 123, 124 (Mo. Ct. App. E. Dist. 1990), quot-
> ing Clemens v. Scott, 11 S.W.3d 32, 33 (Mo. 1990).

> Monkeys and gorillas are primates. Stanley v. Neutron,
> 112 S.W.3d 123, 124 (Mo. Ct. App. E. Dist. 1990), quot-
> ing Clemens v. Scott, 11 S.W.3d 32, 33 (Mo. 1990).

Monkeys and gorillas are primates. <u>Stanley v. Neutron</u>, 112 S.W.3d 123, 124 (Mo. Ct. App. E. Dist. 1990) (quoting <u>Clemens v. Scott</u>, 11 S.W.3d 32, 33 (Mo. 1990)).

5. Which of the following are proper introductory phrases?

<u>See, e.g.</u>,
<u>Id.</u>
<u>Contra</u>
<u>See generally</u>
<u>See in addition</u>
<u>E.g.</u>,
<u>Egad</u>
<u>See also</u>
<u>[no signal]</u>
<u>But see</u>
<u>Accordingly</u>
<u>Compare</u> . . . <u>and</u> . . . <u>with</u> . . . <u>and</u>
<u>Cf.</u>
<u>Cg.</u>
<u>supra</u>

6. Which of the following cites to constitutions, statutes, and secondary sources are correct?

Mo. Rev. Stat. § 367.123 (1999)

510 Ill. Comp. Stat. 5/16 (1996)

Ind. Code § 72.3 (2001)

U.S. Const. art. II, § 1, cl. 2

U.S. Const. amend. XIV

21 Charles Alan Wright & Arthur R. Miller, Federal Practice and Procedure § 1006 (2d ed. 1987)

Restatement (Second) of Torts § 14 (1979)

H.R. 3055, 94th Cong. § 2 (1976)

Fed. R. Evid. 401

Samuel D. Warren, The Right of Privacy, 4 Harv. L. Rev. 193, 195 (1890)

Vicki Hearne, Wise Men and Elephants, N.Y. Times, Feb. 21, 1993, § 7, at 28

Lynn Hirsch, The Misfit, Vanity Fair, Apr. 1991, at 158

7. Which of the following are proper abbreviations?

S.D.N.Y.

Mo. Ct. App.

F.Supp.2d

cert. denied

Ill. Ct. App.

Ala.   (for Alabama)

Alaska (for Alaska)

appeal filed (for appeal filed)

certiorari dismissed

F. 3d

U.S. v. Jones

(U.S. Dist. Ct. E.D. Mo. 1990)

Cal.App.3d

Organ. of American States

W.D.N.C.

Colum. J. Transnat'l L.

Harv. Int'l L.J.

SERIES 3

1. What, if anything, is wrong with each of the following citations:

    Dog v. Cat, 17 F.Supp.2d 14 (7th Cir. 2001)
    Dog v. Cat, 17 F. Supp. 2d 14 (7th Cir. 2001)
    Dog v. Cat, 17 F. Supp. 2d 14 (N.D. Illinois 2001)
    Dog v. Cat, 17 F. Supp. 2d 14 (N.D. Ill. E.D. 2001)
    Dog v. Cat, 17 F. Supp. 2d 14 (N.D. Ill. 2001)

2. What, if anything, is wrong with each of the following short form citations:

    Long form: *Dog v. Cat*, 17 F. Supp. 2d 14 (W.D. Tenn. 2003)
    Dog v. Cat, 17 F. Supp. 2d 14
    Dog v. Cat, 17 F. Supp. 2d at 18
    Dog, 17 F. Supp. 2d 14 at 18
    Dog, 17 F. Supp. 2d 14, 18
    Dog, 17 F. Supp. 2d at 18
    Id.
    Id. at 18

3. What, if anything, is wrong with each of the following citations:

    Dog v. Cat, 917 F. 2d 14 (7th Cir. 2001) (Justice Cooper)
    Dog v. Cat, 917 F. 2d 14 (7th Cir. 2001) (Judge Cooper)

Dog v. Cat, 917 F.2d 14 (7th Cir. 2001) (Judge Cooper)
Dog v. Cat, 917 F.2d 14 (7th Cir. 2001) (Hon. Cooper)
Dog v. Cat, 917 F.2d 14 (7th Cir. 2001) (Cooper, J.)

4. What, if anything, is wrong with each of the following citations:

Cop v. Robber 17 Cal.2d 14 (Cal. 2001)
Cop v. Robber 17 Cal. 2d 14 (Cal. 2001)
Cop v. Robber,17 Cal. 2d 14 (Cal. 2001)
Cop v. Robber,17 Cal.2d 14 (Cal. 2001)
Cop v. Robber,17 Cal. 2d 14 (2001)

5. What, if anything, is wrong with each of the following citations

Cop v. Robber 88 S. Ct. 414 (U.S. 1988)
Cop v. Robber 88 S. Ct. 414 (1988)
Cop v. Robber, 88 S. Ct. 414 (1988)
Cop v. Robber, 88 S.Ct. 414 (1988)
Cop v. Robber, 525 U.S. 875 (1988)

6. What, if anything, is wrong with each of the following citations:

17 U.S.C.S. 107 (1976)
17 U.S.C.S. §107
17 U.S.C.S. § 107 (1976)
17 U.S.C.A. § 107 (1976)
17 U.S.C. § 107 (1976)

7. What, if anything, is wrong with each of the following citations:

765 Ill.Stat. § 1075/5 (1998)
765 Ill. Stat. § 1075/5 (1998)
765 Ill.Comp.Stat. § 1075/5 (1998)
765 Ill. Comp. Stat. § 1075/5 (1998)
765 Ill. Comp. Stat. 1075/5 (1998)

8. What, if anything, is wrong with each of the following statutory short forms:

> Long form: Mo. Rev. Stat. § 1075.23 (1998)
> Mo. Rev. Stat. § 1075.23
> Mo. Rev. Stat. §§ 1075.23, 1075.24
> Id.
> Id. § 1075.24

9. What, if anything, is wrong with each of the following citations:

> United States Const., Fourteenth Am.
> U.S. Const., 14th Am.
> U.S. Const., Amend. 14
> U.S. Const., amend. XIV
> U.S. Const. amend. XIV

10. What, if anything, is wrong with each of the following citations:

> Murray, Explanatory Synthesis, 14 Colum.L.Rev. 24, 25 (1914)
> Michael D. Murray, Explanatory Synthesis, 14 Colum.L.Rev. 24, 25 (1914)
> Michael D. Murray, <u>Explanatory Synthesis</u>, 14 Colum.L.Rev. 24, 25 (1914)
> Michael D. Murray, <u>Explanatory Synthesis</u> 14 Colum. L. Rev. 24, 25 (1914)
> Michael D. Murray, <u>Explanatory Synthesis</u>, 14 Colum. L. Rev. 24, 25 (1914)

11. What, if anything, is wrong with each of the following citations:

> Amer. Law Inst., <u>The Restatement (Second) of Torts</u>, § 14
> <u>The Restatement (Second) of Torts</u>, § 14
> <u>Restatement (Second) of Torts</u>, § 14 (1967)
> Restatement (Second) of Torts, § 14 (1967)
> Restatement (Second) of Torts § 14 (1967)

12. What, if anything, is wrong with each of the following citations:

House Resolution 3055, 94th Congress, section 2 (1976)
House Res. 3055, 94th Congress, § 2 (1976)
H. Res. 3055, 94th Congress § 2 (1976)
H. Res. 3055, 94th Cong. § 2 (1976)
H.R. 3055, 94th Cong. § 2 (1976)

13. What, if anything, is wrong with each of the following citations:

Senate Report No. 89-910, at page 4 (1965)
Senate Report No. 89-910, at p. 4 (1965)
Senate Report No. 89-910, at 4 (1965)
Sen. Report No. 89-910, at 4 (1965)
S. Rep. No. 89-910, at 4 (1965)

14. What does it report?

S.W. S.W.2d S.W.3d

F.R.D.

Ill. Dec.

Idaho

U.S.

Misc. Misc. 2d

F. F.2d F.3d

Ill. Ill. 2d Ill. 3d

Cal. App.   Cal. App. 2d

X.   PREPARING A CASE BRIEF OR CASE ANALYSIS FOR CLASS (Legal Writing and Analysis, Appendix A)

CASE BRIEFING EXERCISE

Write a case brief of the following judicial opinion:

Jo Ann NELSON, by her father and next friend,
Eric D. Nelson, Plaintiff-Appellant,

v.

George N. LEWIS, Defendant-Appellee.

No. 75--432.
Appellate Court of Illinois, Fifth District.
March 3, 1976.

Plaintiff, by her father and next friend, brought action under dog bite statute for injuries inflicted upon her by defendant's dog. The Circuit Court, St. Clair County, Robert L. Gagen, J., rendered judgment in favor of defendant, and plaintiff appealed. The Appellate Court, Karns, P.J., held that "provocation" within meaning of dog bite statute means either intentional or unintentional provocation, that defendant's dog was provoked by plaintiff's unintentional acts and did not viciously react to those acts, and that thus plaintiff was precluded from recovering.

Affirmed.

Fleming & Fleming, O'Fallon, for plaintiff-appellant.

Brady, Donovan & Hatch, By Vincent J. Hatch, Belleville, for defendant-appellee.

KARNS, Presiding Justice.

Plaintiff, by her father and next friend, brought an action under the Illinois "dog-bite" statute (Ill.Rev.Stat.1973, ch. 8, par. 366) for injuries inflicted upon her by defendant's dog. From judgment entered on a jury verdict for the defendant, she appeals.

On the date of her injury, plaintiff Jo Ann Nelson, a two and a half year old, was playing "crack-the-whip" in defendant's backyard with his daughter and other children. Jo Ann was on the end of the "whip." The testimony shows that after she had been thrown off the whip, Jo Ann fell or stepped on the dog's tail while the dog was chewing a bone. The dog, a large Dalmatian, reacted by scratching the plaintiff in her left eye. There was no evidence that plaintiff or anyone else had teased or aggravated the dog before the incident, nor was there evidence that the dog had ever scratched, bitten, or attacked anyone else. According to its owner, the dog had not appeared agitated either before or after the incident. As a result of her injuries, Jo Ann incurred permanent damage to a tear duct in her left eye. It was established that Jo Ann's left eye will overflow with tears more frequently and as a result of less irritation than normal, but that her vision in the eye was not affected.

[1] Our statute pertaining to liability of an owner of a dog attacking or injurying {sic} persons provides:

> If a dog or other animal without provocation, attacks or injures any person who is peacefully conducting himself in any place where he may lawfully be, the owner of such dog or other animal is liable in damages to such person for the full amount of the injury sustained. Ill. Rev. Stat. 1973, ch. 8, par. 366.

Under this statute there are four elements that must be proved: injury caused by a dog owned or harbored by the defendant; lack of provocation; peaceable conduct of the person injured; and the presence of the person injured in a place where he has a legal right to be. Siewerth v. Charleston, 89 Ill.App.2d 64, 231 N.E.2d 644 (1967); Messa v. Sullivan, 61 Ill.App.2d 386, 209 N.E.2d 872 (1965); Beckert v. Risberg, 50 Ill. App.2d 100, 199 N.E.2d 811 (1964) Rev'd on other grounds 33 Ill.2d 44, 210 N.E.2d 207 (1965). There is no dispute but that the dog caused the plaintiff's injury; the defendant owned the dog; the plaintiff's conduct was peaceable; and she was injured in a place where she had a legal right to be. The issue presented is whether plaintiff's unintentional act constitutes "provocation" within the meaning of the statute.

[2] It appears that this issue has not been passed upon by an Illinois court. The statute does not distinguish between intentional and

unintentional acts of provocation and thus, defendant argues, an unintentional act, so long as it provokes an animal or dog, may constitute provocation. Defendant's position, that the mental state of the actor who provokes a dog is irrelevant is consistent with the commonly understood meaning of provocation. Provocation is defined as an act or process of provoking, stimulation or incitement. Webster's Third New International Dictionary. Thus it would appear that an unintentional act can constitute provocation within the plain meaning of the statute.

Only three reported decisions have considered the question of provocation within the meaning of this statute. In Siewerth v. Charleston, supra, the court held there was provocation where the injured boy and his companion kicked a dog three times. The argument was there raised that provocation meant only an intentional act, but the court did not pass upon this contention as it found the injured boy's acts in kicking the dog clearly intentional and provoking. In Messa v. Sullivan, supra, the court found no provocation on the part of the plaintiff where she walked into a hallway patrolled by a watch dog that attacked her on sight. The court held the acts of the plaintiff did not constitute provocation within the intent of the statute and that plaintiff had a right to be on the defendant's premises.

While plaintiff argues that in Messa the plaintiff did not intend to provoke the dog and there was no provocation found, it appears that the court's holding was based on a determination that plaintiff's actions and conduct were not of a provoking nature, not on any determination of the intent with which plaintiff's acts were done. The court stated that it did not believe "provocation" within the meaning of the statute was intended to apply to a situation where a vicious dog interpreted a visitor's nonthreatening movements as hostile actions calling for attack. Similarly in Steichman v. Hurst, 2 Ill.App.3d 415, 275 N.E.2d 679 (1971), it was held that the acts of a postal carrier in spraying the defendant's dog with a repellant was not provocation. Although language in the decision might be read to mean that absence of intent by the plaintiff to provoke is material, we do not believe that this is an accurate reading of the opinion. In Steichman the letter carrier had previous difficulties with defendant's dog and had made several efforts to avoid the dog on the day she was attacked. The court characterized her conduct as "reasonable measures for self protection evoked by the dog's actions and deterring him only momentarily." Thus, the plaintiff's acts, although intentional, did not amount to an incitement or provocation of the dog, triggering the attack.

[3] In the present case, it was admitted that the plaintiff jumped or fell on the dog's tail; that the dog was of a peaceful and quiet temperament; and that the dog was gnawing on a bone when the incident occurred. Under these circumstances, we believe that the dalmatian was provoked, although the provocation was not intentional.

Plaintiff argues that since her act was unintentional, or that because she was of an age at which she could not be charged with scienter, she did not provoke the dog within the meaning of the act. Although her counsel presents a strong argument for interpreting the instant statute to impose essentially strict liability upon a dog owner for injuries caused to a child of tender years, we cannot agree that the public policy of this State compels the adoption of such a standard.

[4] At common law in Illinois, one injured by a dog could recover from the owner only if he could prove that the dog had manifested a disposition "to bite mankind" and that the dog's keeper or owner had notice of this disposition. Chicago and Alton Railroad Co. v. Kuckkuck, 197 Ill. 304, 64 N.E. 358 (1902); Domm v. Hollenbeck, 259 Ill. 382, 102 N.E. 782 (1913); Klatz v. Pfeffer, 333 Ill. 90, 164 N.E. 224 (1928). He could not recover for an injury resulting from his own contributory negligence either by knowingly exposing himself to the dangerous dog (Chicago and Alton Railroad Co. v. Kuckkuck, supra) or by provoking the dog. Keightlinger v. Egan, 65 Ill. 235 (1872). A dog owner's liability rested upon negligence, and he could be liable only if he harbored a "vicious" dog. Thus, one injured by a dog bore a substantial burden of proof.

[5][6][7][8] The instant statute, and its immediate predecessor, substantially eased this burden imposed by the common law. It eliminates the requisite proof that the dog was vicious towards humans and that the owner knew of this disposition, and made irrelevant questions of the injured person's contributory negligence (other than provocation). Beckert v. Risberg, 33 Ill.2d 44, 210 N.E.2d 207 (1965). We do not believe, however, that it was meant to impose strict liability on dog owners for all injuries caused by dogs, except those intentionally provoked. Instead this act was apparently drawn to eliminate as much as possible any inquiry into subjective considerations. Whether the injured person was attacked or injured while conducting himself in a peaceful manner in a place where he could lawfully be are all matters which require no inquiry into a person's intent. We believe that the determination of "provocation" should

also be made independently of such considerations. A determination of provocation does not require consideration of the degree of wilfullness which motivates the provoking cause. Had the legislature intended only intentional provocation to be a bar to recovery we think it would have so specified. Its conclusion apparently was that an owner or keeper of a dog who would attack or injure someone without provocation should be liable. This implies that the intent of the plaintiff is immaterial. Nor do we think that the plaintiff's status as a child of tender years should relieve her of all responsibility for a provoking act. Our Supreme Court in Beckert v. Risberg, 33 Ill.2d 44, 210 N.E.2d 207 (1965), sanctioned a jury instruction in the language of the statute where the plaintiff was a three year old boy. Although the court did not specifically address the issue, it appears by implication that a young child is not exempted from responsibility for his or her acts which provoke a dog under this statute.

We have been referred to decisions from other jurisdictions which permit an injured person to recover for unintentional acts which "provoke" a dog. Two of these cases, however, were decided on common law negligence theories, the courts concluding that these unintentional acts did not constitute contributory negligence. Smith v. Pelah, 2 Strange 1264, 93 Eng.Rep. 1171 (1795); Fake v. Addicks, 45 Minn. 37, 47 N.W. 450 (1890). Another case applied a statute which provided for strict liability for injuries inflicted by a dog unless the injury was voluntarily brought on by plaintiff with full knowledge of the probable consequences. Wojewoda v. Rybarczyk, 246 Mich. 641, 225 N.W. 555 (1929). These decisions are inapposite in that while they arise from similar factual situations they were decided upon legal theories which placed emphasis upon the injured person's scienter.

[9] Although we believe that the instant statute does not impose liability upon a dog owner whose animal merely reacts to an unintentionally provocative act, the present appeal does not involve a vicious attack which was out of all proportion to the unintentional acts involved. E.g. Messa v. Sullivan, supra. The dalmatian here apparently only struck and scratched plaintiff with a forepaw in response to the plaintiff's stepping or falling on its tail while it was gnawing on a bone, an act which scarcely can be described as vicious. Therefore we hold that "provocation" within the meaning of the instant statute means either intentional or unintentional provocation; that the defendant's dog was provoked by the plaintiff's unintentional acts and did not viciously react to these acts; and that no reversible error was committed in the trial court.

For the foregoing reasons, the judgment of the Circuit Court of St. Clair County is affirmed.

AFFIRMED.

JONES and GEORGE J. MORAN, JJ., concur.

———————————————————

Part III

Research and Writing
Problems and Exercises
in Legal Research Methods

I.   INTRODUCTION TO LEGAL RESEARCH (*Legal Research Methods*, Chapter 1)

RESEARCH REVIEW

1. Explain two reasons why you might use *Shepard's Citations* in the course of researching a legal issue.

2. Explain the difference between primary sources and secondary sources. List one example of each type of source.

3. Explain two benefits of using the United States Code Annotated instead of the United States Code to conduct federal statutory research.

4. Explain why you would not quote a headnote from a case in an office memorandum.

5. Write a case citation using correct Bluebook form based on the following information:

   Paula Corbin Jones, Plaintiff, sued William Jefferson Clinton, Defendant. This case was decided by the United States Court of Appeals for the Fourth Circuit on July 29, 1999. It appears in volume 159, page 821, of the Federal Reporter, Third Series.

6. List all of the possible reporters in which you might find a case decided by the Supreme Court of Illinois.

II.   RESEARCHING STATUTES AND CONSTITUTIONS
(*Legal Research Methods*, Chapter 2)

RESEARCH EXERCISES

1. Where do you find the official, "proof positive" version of U.S. laws that have not been codified and reenacted? Where is the official text of the laws that have been codified and reenacted?

2. Find 63 Stat. 1166. Is this a public or a private law? What is the proper citation to this law? What happened to Eiko Nakamura?

3. When was P.L.103-322 passed?

4. What effect did Public Law 103-322 § 330016 have on United States Code, Title 18?

5. What was the penalty for counterfeiting under 1 Stat. 115 § 14?

6. In what volumes of the U.S.C.A. do you find the Constitution of the United States of America? What case is cited in a subsection dealing with obscenity and sunbathing?

7. Your client accidentally set an American flag on fire at a Fourth of July parade. Several law enforcement officials witnessed the event and took down his name, address and telephone number. Client fears that he may be subject to a fine or other penalty for desecration or destruction of the flag. Using the General Index to the United States Code Annotated (soft cover volumes), see if you can find entries for desecration of the flag and for penalties associated therewith. What headings and subheadings of the index do you find, and what sections of the code are you referred to? Does one of those sections concern respect for the flag?

8. Under the section(s) of the code found above, is it considered properly respectful of the flag to use it as bedding or drapery in your home, especially if you festoon the flag in the process? What is the public law number of the act that created this section, and what is the date of enactment? Referring to the provision on fines and penalties that you found above, what is the criminal penalty (maximum fine or prison time) for desecration of the flag?

9. Your client has seen a rhinoceros tusk offered for sale on eBay. Client has recently learned that rhinoceros are endangered species, and she wonders if there are laws concerning the handling of rhinoceros parts. Using the General Index to the United States Code Annotated, is there a section (or a string of sections) of the United States Code concerning rhinoceros conservation? (Give the index heading and subheading and the code section(s)). What is the name of this title of the United States Code?

10. In section 1540(b) of the title of the United States Code found in response to question 9 above, what is the criminal penalty (maximum fine or prison time) for knowing violations of that chapter? What subsection to section 1540 of this title has been added in the time period of 2000 to 2005? Give the letter and title of the subsection.

III.   RESEARCHING CASE LAW (*Legal Research Methods,* Chapter 3)

RESEARCH EXERCISES

Research the answers to the following questions. In addition to writing down the answers, you should also write down the steps you undertook to answer the question. This should help you (and your professor) figure out where you went wrong if you get the wrong answer.

WEST DIGEST SYSTEM EXERCISES

SERIES 1

1. What digest topic is categorized under key number 281?

2. If your case involves Indiana law, in what digest should you begin to search for Indiana cases? Does this digest report federal cases associated with Indiana from the United States Supreme Court, the U.S. Court of Appeals for the 6th Circuit, and the U.S. District Courts located in Indiana? If this digest was unavailable, in what other digest series could you find Indiana cases? If you wanted to find additional federal cases outside of the 6th Circuit as persuasive authority, in what other digest series should you search?

3. On the 4th of July, a child in Georgia was given some sparklers and firecrackers to play with by his father. He went off, unattended, to play with them near a neighbor's corn field and accidentally set the field on fire. According to the South Eastern Digest 2d, may the owner of the field in Georgia state a cause of action against the child's father for his child's use of common fireworks? Which 1965 Georgia case had facts that sound a lot like this client's facts? What Georgia Code sections are cited in the digest with this case? Under what digest topic and key number did you find this case?

4. An Iowa youth, Frank Benjamin, was fascinated by an exhibit he saw at a local science center involving kite string and lightning. He decided to experiment with a kite of his own. Soon after take-off, however, his kite became entangled in a much more terrestrial power source, the high tension power lines hanging over a field where children often fly kites. Frank is harmed and his parents want to sue. According to the North Western Digest 2d, which 1992 Iowa case discussed the duty of care required of a power company for lines installed in places where people are likely to come in close proximity to them? Under what digest topic and key number did you find this case?

5. According to the Pacific Digest (volumes beginning 101 P.2d), is it grounds for divorce in Kansas to fail to talk to your wife when you are tired, even if she considers it to be extremely cruel? Which

1947 Kansas case addressed this issue? Under what digest topic and key number did you find this case?

6. A client in Mississippi opened an ice cold refreshing Banjo Beer® and gulped down two swallows before he noticed a foreign object in his mouth. He discovered it to be a dead cockroach. Your boss thinks she read a Mississippi case from the mid-1950's to mid-1960's that involved a roach in a beverage and discussed the injuries associated with such an incident. In which edition of the Decennial Digest (9th, 10th, etc.) might you find this case? Which case is she remembering (make sure it is a roach case)? Under what digest topic and key number did you find this case?

SERIES 2

Series 2, Exercises 1–5 may be answered using West's Tenth Decennial Digest or by using Westlaw or Lexis with the proper date restriction (1986 to 1996).

1. Your little brother, Jim, fell off a park bench while playing tag with one of his friends. Your parents are planning on suing the city. In what California case from 1986 to 1996 was the city immune from suit for injuries sustained in a city park caused from tree rope swinging?

2. Your son, Bill, decides to have a 4th of July party—same as every other year. During the firework display that he and his friends decide to put on for the neighborhood, the next-door neighbor's young daughter gets burned by one of the bottle rockets. What New York case from 1986-1996 has facts that are very similar to this situation?

3. You are reading a Patricia Cornwell novel and become curious about fingerprinting and its uses to identify criminals. What case from 1986-1996 involved a crook who was identified by his palm print on a money order?

4. You and your fiancé have a huge fight. You think this might be the big one—you guys probably are not going to last. However, you

like the ring he gave you. What cases from 1986-1996 establish engagement rings as conditional gifts? What is the condition?

5. Tim is out golfing and accidentally slices a shot into the woods. Unknown to him, there is a homeless man sleeping in a tree who is struck by Tim's golf ball causing serious injuries to the homeless man's head. The homeless man thinks he could get some money by suing Tim. According to what 1993 federal case arising in Kansas is Tim not strictly liable for the man's injuries?

6. Your cousin, Larry, and his wife sought a divorce. Full custody of their six children was given to Larry's wife. Where does the Massachusetts Digest discuss child support? What Massachusetts Supreme Court case from 1991 involves a duty to pay child support?

7. Is the death penalty legal in your state? What West headnote numbers discuss the legality of the death penalty?

8. What 1992 Texas case is cited under headnote Criminal Law 1206.1(2) in the Texas Digest 2d?

9. Your friend, Sally, just turned 16 and thinks she is in love. She and her new crush have decided to get married. According to the West Virginia Digest, can Sally get married in West Virginia at 16? What West Virginia authority established the age limitations on marriage in West Virginia?

10. Robby is in Daytona on vacation staying at the Sun and Beach Hotel. Early one morning he is running through the lobby to get to the beach and catch some rays when he slipped on the wet floor and hit his head. His parents are furious with the hotel and now they have come to you seeking a legal remedy. What case in the West's Illinois Digest discusses a hotel manager's liability when a guest fell due to "defective flooring"?

AMERICAN LAW REPORTS (ALR) EXERCISES

SERIES 1

1. You represent Kelly Berra. Better known to her adoring fans as Yeh-Yeh Apple. She is a New Orleans native, but internationally famous for her Latin dance performances. Ms. Apple headed down to Colombia, South America this spring for a six-week national tour. She performed in hotel lounges and bars. The tour seemed to be a great success until one fateful April evening outside Cartagena. While Ms. Apple was performing at the Hotel Allende's pool side cantina, a small contingent of leftist guerillas laid siege to the entire hotel district. The rebels cut power and water supplies to the entire area and set up a perimeter with machine gun posts. The government responded quickly to this embarrassing incident. After two days of fierce battle with government forces, the rebels were turned back and the guests were able to leave their hotels. Ms. Apple headed straight for the hotel where she was staying to find that it had been used as the rebel's base camp. All of her belongings had been destroyed during the siege. Deeply troubled by her sudden bad luck, Ms. Apple hired transportation to the airport and caught the first flight back to New Orleans. She arrived disheveled, carrying only her gig bag. She was in a state of nervous shock after her traumatic experience. Upon arrival, a group of uniformed U.S. Customs agents approached her and detained her for three hours for questioning and search by drug sniffing dogs. Ms. Apple, who considers herself an honest, law-abiding citizen, wonders why she was suspected of being a drug courier. She wants you to explain the Customs Service's profiling system. Use only the ALR in answering the following questions: What article provides information on this subject? Who wrote this article? What Louisiana case is cited in this article?

2. Lori Vamos is a school bus driver in Santa Fe, New Mexico. The town has a large number of railroad tracks running through it. School bus drivers are required to stop at each crossing and look both ways before crossing the tracks. Lori always stopped at these crossings in the past, especially after a near-miss in 1984 caught the entire town's attention. Unfortunately, Lori is about to suffer her first attack of "Sudden Adult Onset Narcolepsy" ("SAON").

There is a test for SAON, but the Laredo Public School Authority ("Authority") feels that the test is too expensive since fewer than 1 in 70,000 people suffer from the disease. The Authority also believes that it would not be liable if there was a crash caused by their failure to test for SAON. What ALR article would provide information on the issue of the Authority's liability in this situation?

3. Gary Sparks wants to open a new business called Mega-Fireworks Blowout. Gary has retained your firm to organize his business and to give him advice on the applicable state laws dealing with fireworks. What ALR 5th articles are there on local laws regulating fireworks? How many North Carolina statutes are listed in the ALR 5th article dealing with state fireworks laws?

4. The Cardiac Jogging Society ("CJS") is a group of 20 heart attack survivors who spend each Saturday jogging through the city park as part of their rehabilitation regime. Although all of them are in fairly good shape, they are under standing orders to avoid being startled by sudden loud noises or dangerous situations. Most of the members are in their early 60's. Byron Grave has just opened his dog walking service called Pexercise. As part of the Pexercise program, dogs are classed as to size and temperament and assigned to a trained Pexercise Guide™ who takes the dogs on their assigned route. Byron himself handles the dogs requiring the most expertise. He affectionately calls this group the A-Team. The 15 members of the A-Team are all 100 pounds or larger and include such breeds as German Shepherds, Great Danes, Giant Schnauzers, and Black Labs. On Friday, the A-Team was moving up the park bike trail in an orderly fashion when the CJS came suddenly around a steep bend in the trail, startling the members of both groups. Pandemonium broke out as the dogs began tangling their leashes around Byron and each other. One dog lightly nipped a CJS member on the calf. Two CJS members were taken to the emergency room with chest pains. Byron would like to know which ALR 4th articles are apposite to these facts. Is there a Wisconsin case discussing the owner's knowledge of their dog's viciousness before they can be held liable? What is its citation?

SERIES 2

1. You are sitting at your favorite restaurant when your sister begins choking on her chicken marsala. You are waiting for someone to help her when you remember you are certified in first aid and CPR. You save your sister. Two weeks later you are telling your heroic story to a friend and she asks about the duty of the restaurant or its employees in helping a choking customer. What article in the ALR 5th covers this topic? According to this article, how many people choke on food each year in the United States? What is the duty of the restaurant, or its employees, to a choking patron and what case established this level of duty?

2. Your aunt, Isabella, is a famous Italian chef. She uses olive oil in everything—it's her secret ingredient. You are in the law library one day and decide to look up more about olive oil and any legal history it might have. What ALR Fed article discusses olive oil? What case is featured in the ALR Fed article on olive oil?

3. Your favorite home improver, Bob Villa, is doing a show on removing lead-based paint in residential settings. Before the show, you want to get a good background on this topic. What ALR Fed article discusses the removal of lead-based paint and its cause of lead poisoning? What 1995 New York case is featured in the ALR Fed article on this topic?

SHEPARD'S CITATION EXERCISES

Use Shepard's Citations to find the answers to the following questions. If the answers call for a case, give a full citation (style, citation, court, and date) for each case. If possible, do the exercises using the Shepard's print volumes first, then check your answers on Shepard's Online.

1. What year 2000 cases have cited 45 S.E. 747? Cite each case.

2. What dissenting opinion cited 45 S.E. 466 Case 2? Cite the opinion.

3. What did 515 S.E.2d 565 do to the case at 470 S.E.2d 114?

4. What effect did 139 S.E.2d 898 have on 144 S.E. 547?

5. Your facts are similar to 494 S.E.2d 870. The holding is favorable to your client. Should you rely on this case?

6. You are downcast and forlorn. Your client is doomed! Her facts are on all fours with 379 S.E.2d 271. Is all lost?

7. Is 358 S.E.2d 160 still good law?

8. Have any federal cases cited Mo. Rev. Stat. § 351.633? If so, cite the first two cases.

9. Did 720 A.2d 164 do anything to 602 A.2d 387?

10. What was the disposition of the case reported at 735 A.2d 9?

11. Did any Utah or Wisconsin cases cite 94 A.2d 34? If so, cite one case from each state.

12. What was the disposition of the case reported at 704 A.2d 81?

REPORTERS RESEARCH EXERCISES

SERIES 1

1. Who is the defendant(s) in the case cited at 221 F. 229? In what court does this case take place?

2. Properly cite the case cited in volume 771 of the Federal Reporter 2d Series p. 920?

3. In which case of the 181st volume of the Federal Reporter 3d Series has the Richland Parish Hospital as a party? Is the opinion of this case published?

4. Who was the district court judge in the case found on p. 337 of the 955th volume of the Federal Supplement? What is the style of this case?

5. What case is found on p. 1026 of the 867th volume of the Federal Supplement? Who are the intervening defendants?

6. Who was the appellant in the case located on p. 497 of volume 528 of the So. 2d?

7. On what page starts the case Autry v. Bryan in the 297th volume of S.E.2d? What day was the case decided? In what court was the case?

8. What judge wrote the opinion on p. 291 of the 505th volume of the P.2d? Who represented the Bauwens?

9. Of what was the appellant in the case cited 706 S.W.2d 664 found guilty?

10. What case is cited in the 665th volume of N.E.2d on p. 685? What parallel cite is given?

SERIES 2

1. Who represented Bessie McAfee in the case reported at 249 S.W.2d 822?

2. What is the style of the case reported at 389 U.S. 128? What are the parallel cites in the Supreme Court Reporter and in the Lawyers Edition reporter?

3. What New Jersey plumbing company is mentioned by name at page 696 in the 681st volume of the regional reporter that reports New Jersey cases?

4. On what page of the 115th volume of the N.W. reporter is the case involving Webster City Steel Radiator Company?

5. Find and properly cite the case styled South County Sand & Gravel Co., Inc. v. Town of South Kingstown, in the reporter which reports the decisions of the Federal Courts of Appeals.

6. What court rendered the decision in the case reported at 598 A.2d 580?

7. Which judge wrote the opinion at 598 A.2d 580?

8. Who represented Mary A. Ziehm in the Maine case reported at Volume 433, Page 725 in the regional reporter that includes Maine decisions?

9. Read the case at 201 P. 522. How old was Carney Varner when he testified in that case?

10. In Walker v. State, 153 P. 209 (Okla. Crim. App. 1915), where did Bessie Burgess believe she would go if she told a story and was a bad girl?

11. In Walker v. State, 153 P. 209 (Okla. Crim. App. 1915), on what grounds did the Court find that the court below erred in refusing the defendant's request for a physical examination?

12. How does the Maryland Court of Appeals characterize the Maryland Rules of Procedure in Stewart v. State, 638 A.2d 754 (Md. 1994)?

13. What piece of machinery injured young Mr. Goza in 172 S.W. 825?

14. How did Texas Lawyer McKinney claim he came upon the stolen property found in his possession in McKinney v. State reported in volume 627 of the Texas regional reporter?

15. What did Samuel Robinson's attorney tell him would happen if he exercised his Constitutional right to a jury trial in People v. Robinson, 5 Ill. App. 3d 1065?

SERIES 3

1. Who is the first named defendant in the case cited at 221 F. 229? What court issued this opinion?

2. In which case of the 181st volume of the Federal Reporter, Third Series is the Richland Parish Hospital listed as a party? Is the opinion of this case published? Was this case affirmed or reversed?

3. Which district court judge wrote the opinion in the case found on p. 337 of the 955th volume of the Federal Supplement? Who represented the plaintiff, John Barone? What date was ordered by the court for a pretrial conference in the case?

4. On what page of the 297th volume of the South Eastern Reporter, Second Series does the case <u>Autry v. Bryan</u> begin? On what date was the case decided? In what court was the case decided? How many justices signed off on the opinion?

5. Using the key number digest in the back of the 665th volume of N.E.2d, what case on consumer protection is reported in the volume? What parallel cites for this case are given? On what date was rehearing denied in the case?

IV.   RESEARCHING FEDERAL REGULATORY AND ADMINISTRATIVE LAW (*Legal Research Methods*, Chapter 4)

RESEARCH EXERCISES

Your firm's biggest client is Acme Medical Assoc. ("AMA"), a clinical medical testing firm. AMA president Clara Beaker would like to know how the federal government defines a nephelometer. Answer the following questions using ONLY the Code of Federal Regulations, LSA pamphlets, and the Federal Register.

1. What C.F.R. part discusses clinical chemistry and toxicology devices?

2. What C.F.R. subpart defines a "nephelometer"? What subpart classifies it?

3. Has this regulation been updated during the year 2000?

    Answer the following questions ONLY if you found that the regulation has been updated in the year 2000.

4. Where was it updated in the Federal Register?

5. What did the update consist of?

V.   RESEARCHING SECONDARY SOURCES OF THE LAW: ENCYCLOPEDIAS, TREATISES, LAW REVIEWS, AND PERIODICALS (*Legal Research Methods*, Chapter 5)

RESEARCH EXERCISES

Research the answers to the following questions. In addition to writing down the answers, you should also write down the steps you undertook to answer the question.

ENCYCLOPEDIA RESEARCH EXERCISE

Use the legal encyclopedias indicated in each exercise to answer the questions found therein:

SERIES 1

1. Where does the American Jurisprudence discuss fireworks and the sale to minors? What state prohibits the sale of fireworks to children under 12?

2. Your brother, Russ, wants to get married, but he does not want to hassle with a wedding ceremony or the justice of the peace. He wants to know if mere cohabitation is enough to establish

a common-law marriage? Where is this topic discussed in the American Jurisprudence?

3. Your next door neighbor's dog is barking and keeping you up all night long. Where does the American Jurisprudence discuss dog barking being a nuisance? What New York case is cited as exempting dog barking as a nuisance?

4. Susan's son has just been qualified to enter into his school's gifted and talented program. Susan wants you to find out more about public school's gifted programs. What Pennsylvania case, cited in the Corpus Juris Secundum (CJS), discusses mandatory gifted school programs for public school children?

5. In the CJS, what Texas case discusses the drug Dolophine?

6. What is the CJS definition of a pool table? What case is cited for the definition?

SERIES 2

1. After watching a stirring episode of "Law and Order: Traffic Safety Unit," you are inspired to find out what all this *Miranda* warning stuff is about. Cite the Corpus Juris Secundum article and American Jurisprudence sections that describe the warnings police are required to give to the newly arrested.

2. The SleepyTime Motel outside Lazy Eye, Nevada is home to a surprising assortment of drifters from all over the United States. Many of these folks are only passing through, but they stop for the restaurant at the SleepyTime. The specialty dish is a honey cake with fresh coffee. The honey cake is made with real desert flower honey from the motel's own hives. These are located some 40 yards from the motel buildings, on a bluff overlooking a spectacular valley. Your client is Paul Oswald, a mucilage sales representative from Shoboshko, Wisconsin. He loves the smell of the desert in the morning and the honey cake has brought him to stay at the SleepyTime many times in the past. After a restful night, Paul decides to take in the sunrise over the valley before a

fresh baked honey cake breakfast. If he had stopped for breakfast first he might have noticed the Lazy Eye Herald's cover story on the recent spate of livestock deaths due to an infestation of swarming killer bees. As it is, he is quietly standing on the bluff near the hives when a strange haze descends over the sun. Yes, Paul is one of the few people to see a squadron of killer bees in attack formation and live to tell the tale. Not realizing the gravity of the situation, Paul stares transfixed at the swirling mass of homicidal insects. Just in time, the spell is broken and Paul begins to sprint for the safety of the SleepyTime lobby. Paul is stung several dozen times before the motel maintenance personnel are able to spray him off with a hose. The SleepyTime management gives Paul a free night stay and a honey cake special, but he is still upset about his ordeal. What section of American Jurisprudence discusses a similar case? What case discusses a hotel guest bit by a rat?

3. Your old high school buddy Daryl has always had an exciting life. Daryl travels the world as a cameraman with SBNN (Sound Bite News Network). He got a special present from a group of survivalists in eastern Oklahoma, "So he'd be ready when the U.N. black helicopters descend upon the Americas." The gift is a chrome plated .45 caliber pistol. Unfortunately, Daryl was in such a hurry to get back into an urban area for a Koffeebuc's Kappucino and some sanity that he simply shoved the handgun under the seat of his car. Speeding along a two lane suburban road, Daryl is pulled over by a local police officer. Daryl is asked to submit to a search of the car and he consents, forgetting about the firearm under his seat. Daryl is released on bond after being arraigned for possession of a concealed weapon. He asks you to research this issue for him, and to tell him if Oklahoma has any exceptions to the law against possession of concealed weapons. Using only the Corpus Juris Secundum, answer the following questions: What section of the CJS discusses concealed weapons? Is there an exception apposite to these facts? Are there any Oklahoma cases cited in this section?

4. One day Cindy Davis comes into your office looking for representation. She is a master Saab mechanic. Her expertise makes her a valuable employee for many dealerships and repair shops. Ms. Davis is happy at her current job, but the shop owner chain smokes. Ms. Davis believes that the second hand smoke is harming her

health. What Corpus Juris Secundum article discusses this issue? What American Jurisprudence section is the most relevant to this issue?

5. Your client is an artist who submitted several paintings of nudes to a juried art exhibit sponsored by the City of Peoria, Illinois. Her paintings were rejected as "inappropriate" even though your client thinks they are far from obscene. Using Corpus Juris Secundum, what topic should you look under for guidance on the standards used to evaluate the city's decision? Under this topic, to what interest must the art appeal in order to be considered obscene? What U.S. Supreme Court case involving a west coast state lends its name to the test used to make the evaluation? What pre-1978 case discusses a Mississippi statute that was held to be invalid for overbreadth? What post-1978 U.S. Supreme Court case involving and arising in a midwest corn belt state discusses the concept that "most prudish or most tolerant" viewpoints are irrelevant in the determination?

TREATISE RESEARCH EXERCISES

Use the treatises indicated below to answer the following questions:

SERIES 1

Wright & Miller, Federal Practice and Procedure:

1. What section of Wright & Miller's Federal Practice and Procedure covers Internet jurisdiction over nonresident defendants? In this section of Wright & Miller, what is the name of the 1997 Western District of Pennsylvania case involving a cigarette lighter manufacturer that the authors think is "the most influential judicial opinion thus far" on the topic of Internet jurisdiction? What kind of scale is used to evaluate categories of websites? According to the notes here, in what section of Wright & Miller, Federal Practice and Procedure would be learn more about this scale?

Farnsworth on Contracts:

2. According to Farnsworth on Contracts, how can one terminate the power of acceptance?

3. What Illinois case, cited in Farnsworth on Contracts, explains further the idea of lapse of the offer?

Williston on Contracts:

4. What does Williston say is the difference between usage and custom?

5. What Massachusetts case distinguished usage and custom?

Murray on Contracts:

6. What is the difference, according to Murray on Contracts, between a unilateral and a bilateral contract?

7. According to Murray on Contracts, what are the two tests of unconscionability?

Nimmer on Copyright:

8. What does Nimmer on Copyright say about the definition of "musical works" (altered)?

9. Your great uncle was a fine musician and composer. After his death, a nearly complete score for a symphony was discovered in his piano bench. You wonder if he or his estate could claim any rights in the work. What section of Nimmer on Copyright discusses posthumous rights? What famous composer's case is discussed at great length in this section? What is the style of this composer's case? Was the trial court's opinion in this case reversed?

10. How does Nimmer define "derivative work" for copyright purposes?

Couch on Insurance 3d:

11. According to § 35:4 of Couch on Insurance, who may object to breach of Prohibitory Clause?

12. What topic is covered in § 42:1 of Couch on Insurance? When does the husband have an insurable interest in his wife's property?

Restatement (Second) of Contracts:

13. According to Restatement (Second) of Contracts, what parties are required for the forming of a contract?

14. What topic is covered in Restatement (Second) of Contracts § 149? What happens when the second contract is unenforceable under the Statute of Frauds?

Restatement (Second) of Torts:

15. According to Restatement 2d on Torts, how can one commit conversion?

16. According to Restatement 2d on Torts, what are the minimum skills required of a dentist?

Restatement (Second) of Agency:

17. According to Restatement 2d on Agency, what is an escrow holder?

18. What is the liability, according to Restatement 2d on Agency, of an agent to another in assault?

SERIES 2

1. You are on a float trip down the Kokosing River in Ohio with a group of law students. One of your party trips over a rock and

hurts his arm. Luckily, your mother forced you to join the "Young Explorers" when you were in grade school. You quickly convert a nearby sapling into a makeshift splint and, using vines, begin tying your fallen comrade's arm down, hopefully, setting the bone in the process. The other students are muttering something about liability and a roller skating rink case. Does the Second Restatement of Torts § 892D have any bearing on this problem?

2. Your cousin has negotiated a million-dollar deal to purchase a piece of real property commonly known as The Brooklyn Bridge, with an option to purchase the Lincoln Tunnel for a fixed price within two years thereafter. He wants to get out of the sale agreement. The agreement is completely oral. The sale is set to close in a few days. You ask around and you think that the statute of frauds could be useful for getting out of the contract. Since you don't have an expert understanding of the statute of frauds, you decide to consult a treatise, Corbin on Contracts. Which volume and section of Corbin on Contracts talks about the statute of frauds? How is the statute of frauds raised in litigation?

3. You are a Magistrate Judge in the Western District of Washington. You are presiding over a misdemeanor drug trial. There sits the accused, your childhood nemesis. Back in grade school Joseph Escargot was known as "Little Joey," and you find out that he still carries this nickname because it is listed as an alias on the indictment. He has diversified his criminal activities since starting out in the playground extortion field many years ago. You suppress a gleeful grin at the thought of presiding over his downfall, and are even happier to realize that Little Joey does not even recognize you. Because your internal ethics meter is making a loud racket, you decide to consult Moore's Federal Practice, just to check if there are any problems of bias in your presiding over this matter. Of what magnitude is the disqualification of a biased federal judge? What section answers this question?

4. Your friend, let's call him "Lobert" so as to disguise his real name, went down to Cancun with his (former) girlfriend for spring break last year. Lobert brought a disposable camera with him. During the trip much fun was had by all. After a wild evening at the cantina, Lobert took some rather risque' photographs of his girlfriend.

After returning home, Lobert dropped the film off at Stuff-Mart for processing. When he received the prints, Lobert was surprised to find that some of the photos had been removed and replaced with a notice that Stuff-Mart has a strict policy against developing pictures unsuitable for family enjoyment. Lobert is disappointed but thinks nothing of it. Several weeks later he notices that his girlfriend is being stared at by an unusual number of people when they go out in public. Soon people are openly laughing at her, and she is even harassed in school. She transferred to another school at great expense and humiliation.[8] The couple broke up, and Lobert's girlfriend seeks a legal remedy against Stuff-Mart for invasion of privacy. Use Prosser and Keeton's Torts treatise to answer the following questions: What section of the treatise discusses the tort doctrine of invasion of privacy? How many torts are associated with violations of privacy rights? What privacy action should Lobert's girlfriend consider bringing against Stuff-Mart? What are the elements that Lobert's girlfriend will need to prove in order to prevail in her action against Stuff-Mart?

LAW REVIEW ARTICLES RESEARCH EXERCISES

SERIES 1

1. Using the Index to Legal Periodicals & Books volume dated September 2001-August 2002 or the Journals and Law Reviews database on Westlaw, what is the title of the article written by Lori F. Damrosch in 2002? What is the citation given for this article?

2. Using the same index volume (Sept. 2001-Aug. 2002) or the Journals and Law Reviews database on Westlaw, what is the title of the article on Appellate Advocacy that involves a fish? Who is the author of this article? What is the citation given for this article? Looking at this "fishy" article in the actual bound volume for this law review, to whom is the author indebted for the vignette he quotes on the first page of the article?

---

8 This is based on a real case. *Lake v. Wal-Mart Stores, Inc.*, 582 N.W.2d 231 (Minn. 1998).

3. What is the title of the article published at 68 Mich. L. Rev. 389? Who wrote this article?

4. What page in volume 29 of the New England Law Review does the article, "Criminal Law's Greatest Mystery Thriller: Corporate Guilt Through Collective Knowledge" begin on?

5. What article is cited as 9 Ohio North. L. Rev. 369? Who is Marshall B. Kapp?

6. Who is the editor-in-chief of volume 33 of the University of Michigan Journal of Law Reform?

7. What article did Robert J. Rabin write in 30 Syracuse L. Rev.?

8. What law review article did Kevin Urick write in 1988?

9. How many articles did Jethro Busch write in 1999?

10. What law review article did Jesse Goldner write in 1993?

SERIES 2

Use the Index to Legal Periodicals, Shepard's, and the law reviews in your library or an online law review database to answer the following questions:

1. What Supreme Court cases are cited on page 399 of Volume 73 of the Michigan Law Review (just give the volume and page number from the reporter)?

2. What federal appellate case cited the article Breach of Confidence, 82 Colum. L. Rev. 1426?

3. Who wrote the 1997 Journal of Taxation article on the generation skipping transfer tax?

4. What article(s) did Adrian Hunt author in 1998?

5. What law review article did Jesse Goldner write in 1998? If there are more than one, give the first. Cite the article in Bluebook format.

VI. RESEARCHING LEGISLATIVE HISTORY (*Legal Research Methods*, **Chapter 6**)

RESEARCH EXERCISES

Federal Legislative History

1. Your firm represents Teluwhat!™, a consortium of startup telecommunications companies scattered throughout the United States. The member companies' operations center primarily on the provision of low cost telephone and datacom service for small businesses and residential and consumer markets. Most of the member companies have been formed in the past two years. They are very concerned about the impact of FBI wiretapping requirements on their business. Multiple law enforcement wiretap requests have been coming to the consortium members every day. It is requiring a large investment of time and money to satisfy all of these requests. The FBI claims that they have the right to ask for these lawful requests whenever they want under 47 U.S.C. § 1001. The partner for whom you work has asked you to compile a legislative history on this law. Answer the following questions about this legislation:

   What is the short title of this legislation? What is its public law number? What was its original bill number?

2. Obtain a copy of the CIS/INDEX legislative history abstract for this bill. In the summary, what provisions did the house report recommend be added to the bill with regard to cellular phone service?

3. Did the listed Report(s) recommend passage of the bill?

4. What **House** Report(s) were prepared on this legislation during the 103rd Congress?

    Using Westlaw, find and print a copy of the House Report(s) listed in your answer to question 4. Use the printout(s) to answer the following questions:

5. How many hearings were held during the 103rd Congress about this legislation? What were the dates of those hearings? Which committees were the hearings held before?

6. Who is (was) Roy Neel? What does RBOC stand for?

7. What was the major problem that the legislation was designed to remedy?

8. According to the report(s), was it Congress' intent to have this legislation cover the activities of Internet Service Providers?

    Locate and view a copy of Louis J. Freeh's, March 18, 1994 testimony to Congress using Westlaw. You do not need to print this document. Answer the following question using only the first paragraph:

9. What does Mr. Freeh identify as the source of a major threat to effective law enforcement?

VII.   RESEARCHING COURT RULES, LOCAL RULES, AND SUBJECT-SPECIFIC RESOURCES (*Legal Research Methods*, Chapter 7)

RESEARCH EXERCISES

Court Rules and Local Rules

1. What federal procedural rule governs the timeliness of an appeal?

2. What issue is addressed by the Federal District Court for the Northern District of Texas' local rule 53.1?

3. On what days is the U.S. District Court for the District of Utah open until 5:00pm?

Loose Leaf Services

4. BNA's Health Law & Business, loose-leaf series contains a sample confidentiality agreement. What is the page number for this agreement? What is the first word of the second numbered paragraph of that agreement?

5. What paragraph number is medical service contract depreciation indexed under in CCH's Standard Federal Tax Reporter series for the year 2005? What page number is that paragraph number on?

Part IV

Research and Writing Problems and Excercises in Advanced Legal Writing and Oral Advocacy; Trials, Appeals, and Moot Court

I.   **ADVERSARIAL LEGAL WRITING (*Advanced Legal Writing and Oral Advocacy: Trials, Appeals, and Moot Court*, Chapter 1)**

WRITING PROBLEM

1. Choose one of the following topics:

Your favorite/ least favorite movie or TV show or play

Your favorite/ least favorite entertainer or sports figure

Your favorite/ least favorite sport or sporting event

Your favorite/ least favorite form of poker or parlor game or casino game (e.g., Texas Hold-em Poker)

Your favorite/ least favorite politician or presidential candidate

Your favorite/ least favorite pet or animal

Baseball records set in the 1990's and 2000's

Your favorite/ least favorite work of art or style (school, genre, etc.) of art

Pete Rose's potential admission to the Baseball Hall of Fame

Media coverage of celebrity trials (Michael Jackson, Martha Stewart, etc.)

Senate hearings to evaluate U.S. Supreme Court judicial candidates

Draft a short, two-page essay in two parts: In Part I of your paper, write an objective, fair, and balanced description of the subject of your discussion in no more than 1-2 paragraphs, double-spaced. What are the merits and demerits, pros and cons of the subject of your discussion? Then, in Part II, write a persuasive, argumentative account (again in no more than 1-2 paragraphs, double-spaced) trying to convince the reader that your take on the subject is correct and the reader should adopt it; *e.g.*, persuading the reader that X is the least (or most) desirable Y around. Advocate and argue for your position. There should be a distinct difference between Part II (argumentative advocacy) and Part I (objective and predictive legal writing).

II.   PRETRIAL MOTIONS (*Advanced Legal Writing and Oral Advocacy: Trials, Appeals, and Moot Court*, Chapter 2)

WRITING PROBLEMS

1. Evaluate the following introductions to pretrial motions. Name three things that each one does well and two to three things that you would change about each one:

a. Newsflash Creative Media v. Black

MEMORANDUM IN SUPPORT OF
DEFENDANT'S MOTION TO DISMISS
FOR LACK OF PERSONAL JURISDICTION

Defendant Arnold Black moves this Court pursuant to Fed. R. Civ. P. 12(b)(2) to dismiss the complaint brought by Newsflash Creative Media ("NCM") for lack of personal jurisdiction.

INTRODUCTION

NCM is suing Arnold Black for a declaratory judgment sanctioning its exploitation of Black's image for T-shirt sales. NCM brings this action preemptively in response to Black's cease and desist request in an attempt to force Black to forego his responsibilities as Governor of California and defend himself in a distant forum.

Personal jurisdiction over the defendant Black is improper because the Due Process Clause requires minimum contacts with the forum state and Black has never conducted business in Tennessee, has only visited the state twice in twenty-six years, and was in the state for a mere two days during his latest visit. In addition, jurisdiction over Black in Tennessee would be unreasonable because the burden on Black to defend a lawsuit in a distant forum and forego his responsibilities as Governor outweigh the interests of NCM and the State of Tennessee in resolving the present case in Tennessee.

b. Newsflash Creative Media v. Black

MEMORANDUM IN SUPPORT OF
DEFENDANT'S MOTION TO DISMISS FOR
LACK OF PERSONAL JURISDICTION

Defendant Arnold Black ("Black") moves this Court pursuant to Fed. R. Civ. P. 12(b)(2), to dismiss the complaint for lack of personal jurisdiction.

INTRODUCTION

Newsflash Creative Media ("Newsflash") is suing Black to demolish his right of publicity. Newsflash must believe that they can exploit someone's image, and then force that person to come to them to defend that image.

Black moves to dismiss the complaint for lack of personal jurisdiction. Black has briefly visited Tennessee twice in his life: once in 1980 to pose for a calendar to raise funds for St. Jude's Research Hospital and once on October 3 and 4, 2006, for political fundraising events. This lawsuit only tangentially relates to the last visit in October 2006. Black has no other personal or professional contacts in or with Tennessee. Therefore, Black has not purposefully availed himself of the privilege of conducting activities in Tennessee. Black's contacts with Tennessee do not satisfy the minimum contacts and fair and substantial justice requirements of the Tennessee Long-Arm statute, Tenn. Code Ann. § 20-2-214 (1994), and the federal Due Process Clause, U.S. Const. amend. XIV, § 1.

c. Newsflash Creative Media v. Black

**PLAINTIFF'S RESPONSE TO
DEFENDANT ARNOLD BLACK'S
FED. R. CIV. P. 12(b)(2) MOTION TO DISMISS
FOR LACK OF PERSONAL JURISDICTION**

INTRODUCTION

Defendant Arnold Black ("Black") is attempting to silence his political opponents and escape the consequences of his actions. In 2006, Black, the Republican governor of California, purposefully availed himself of the privilege of conducting business in Tennessee when he conducted a cross-state political fundraising drive here. Plaintiff Newsflash Creative Media ("Newsflash"), an independent graphic design firm, sought to engage in political commentary and encourage discourse through the creation of several humorous t-shirts that referenced Black's career as an action star. Black became enraged, demanded that Newsflash stop exercising their right to free expression on the shirts, and threatened a financially burdensome lawsuit against Newsflash. The current action arose as a direct result of that interaction. Personal jurisdiction over Black is reasonable and satisfies the due process requirements of both the Tennessee long-arm statutes and the United States Constitution, and Black should not be allowed to escape the consequences of his actions by refusing to face his critics in Tennessee.

d. Newsflash Creative Media v. Black

PLAINTIFF'S MEMORANDUM IN OPPOSITION TO DEFENDANT'S FED. R. CIV. P. 12(b)(2) MOTION TO DISMISS FOR LACK OF PERSONAL JURISDICTION

INTRODUCTION

Personal jurisdiction is proper, as Defendant Arnold Black ("Black") purposefully engaged in activities directed toward the forum state by fundraising for Republican party candidates up for election in the state of Tennessee---an activity with real and tangible political and economic impact on the citizens of that state. Plaintiff Newsflash Creative Media ("Newsflash") responded with political commentary printed on T-shirts, the subject of which was Black's visit to Tennessee, commentary which Black attempted to silence through threats of litigation.

Black now objects to the ramifications of his involvement with the state, and seeks to dismiss so that he might reap the benefits of bringing his influence to bear on the citizens of Tennessee without allowing them legal recourse. Although stating he has insufficient contact with the forum, Black admitted in his cease and desist letter to Newsflash that he could invoke benefits and protections of both California and Tennessee law in his own defense. Under controlling authority of the state and federal law, Tennessee may exert jurisdiction over an individual who acts purposefully to cause consequence in the state and would avail himself of the benefits of operating within its borders.

2. Evaluate the following statements of facts to pretrial motions. Name three things that each one does well and two to three things that you would change about each one:

a. Newsflash Creative Media v. Black

STATEMENT OF FACTS

Black first traveled Tennessee for charity in 1980 to pose for a country music calendar designed to raise money for St. Jude's Research Hospital. See Declaration of Arnold Black dated Dec. 12, 2006, at ¶ 3 ("Black Dec."). Black was reimbursed for travel expenses but received no benefit from his visit. Id. ¶ 4.

Black's second visit to Tennessee occurred on October 3 and 4, 2006, when Black appeared at fundraisers for personal friends who were candidates for public office. Id. ¶ 3. Black received no compensation for his 2006 visit. Id. ¶ 4. Black has no other personal or professional contacts with Tennessee and has never conducted business in the state. Id.

On October 3, 2006, NCM, without Black's knowledge or consent, began producing and selling T-shirts bearing Black's image. See Declaration of Peter Max dated Dec. 22, 2006, at ¶ 5 ("Max Dec."). NCM has sold 8,000 T-shirts, totaling $160,000 in sales, through their exploitation of Black's likeness. Id. ¶ 7.

A letter requesting that NCM halt any further misuse of Black's image was drafted and sent on October 15, 2006. See Complaint, Exhibit 2. Rather than cooperate with Black, NCM preemptively brought the present suit.

b. Newsflash Creative Media v. Black

STATEMENT OF FACTS

Black is a citizen of California residing in Brentwood, California, and his principal place of career and personal business is Los Angeles, California. See Declaration of Arnold Black dated Dec. 12, 2006, ¶¶ 1-2 ("Black Dec."). Black is currently serving the State of California as its governor. See Black Dec. ¶ 2. This high office, along with Black's acting career, has made him a well-known figure. See id. ¶ 5. Other than two brief visits for fundraising, Black has no other personal or professional contacts in Tennessee. See id. ¶¶ 3-4. Black's first visit to Tennessee was in 1980 for a fundraising event for St. Jude's Research Hospital. See id. ¶ 3. For this trip, Black's only compensation was a reimbursement for travel expenses. See id. ¶ 4. Black's second visit to Tennessee was on October 3 and 4, 2006, to raise funds for friends' political campaigns. See id. ¶ 3. For this brief visit, Black received no compensation or benefits. See id. ¶ 4.

Upon hearing of Black's upcoming second visit, Newsflash, a corporation located in Memphis, Tennessee, decided to reap its own unauthorized rewards from Black's recognition value. See Complaint, ¶ 5. Newsflash designed T-shirts using Black's image. Id. Exhibit 1. Newsflash then sold 8,000 of those T-shirts at $20 apiece, thus taking in $160,000 by using Black's image. See id., ¶ 5. Black noticed these T-shirts during the visit. See Declaration of Peter Max dated Dec. 22, 2006, ¶ 9 ("Max Dec."). Upset about the exploitation of his name and image, Black sent a letter to Newsflash requesting that they stop selling the T-shirts and recover any already sold. See Max Dec. ¶ 9; Complaint, Exhibit 2.

c. Newsflash Creative Media v. Black

STATEMENT OF FACTS

In the midst of a contentious national election season, Black, an international movie star and the Republican governor of California, responded to requests from Tennessee Republicans by conducting a multi-stop campaign drive across Tennessee. Declaration of Arnold Black dated Dec. 12, 2006, at ¶¶ 2, 3 ("Black Dec."). During that trip, Black used his celebrity status to raise over $2 million for friends and fellow Republicans in Tennessee. Declaration of Peter Max dated Dec. 22, 2006, at ¶ 3 ("Max Dec."). In response, Newsflash designed several t-shirts featuring publicity photos from Black's movies to comment on the propriety of a star of violent action films appearing on behalf of Tennessee candidates. Max Dec. at ¶ 7; Complaint, Exhibit 1. Upon seeing the shirts, Black became furious and sent a threatening letter to Newsflash in Memphis, promising to file suit. Complaint, Exhibit 2. The lawsuit threatened by Black would by financially devastating for Newsflash, Max Dec. at ¶ 10, so Newsflash filed a complaint asking this Court to issue a declaratory judgment upholding their right to engage in politically relevant discourse through the t-shirts. See Complaint.

d. Newsflash Creative Media v. Black

STATEMENT OF FACTS

On October 2, 2006, Black, a celebrity-turned-politician in the public eye for nearly two decades, announced on national television that he would visit Tennessee the next day (Complaint ¶ 5). On October 3, 2006, and October 4, 2006, Black attended fundraising campaigns in two Tennessee cities, Memphis and Nashville, to leverage his celebrity on behalf of his political party (see Declaration of Arnold Black dated December 12, 2006, ¶ 3 (attached hereto as exhibit 1) ("Black Decl.")). He successfully raised two million dollars in support of the Republican party's candidates in Tennessee (Complaint ¶ 5).

On October 3, 2006, as a political statement, Newsflash, a graphic design company owned and managed by two artists, responded to his visit by printing and selling T-shirts with the star's image and commentary on the his involvement with Republican candidates in view of his violent movie roles. Id. The T-shirts, sold in the two cities Black had visited, allowed Newsflash to generate just four percent of the sum for the Democratic party that Black's efforts raised for the Republican party. Id.

On October 15, 2006, Black sent a facsimile and letter via U.S. mail in response to Newsflash's T-shirt message, threatening a lawsuit within eleven days if they did not comply with his wishes to cease voicing their political opinion by destroying any existing T-shirts containing their message and by halting production and sales of the T-shirts (see Black's letter to Plaintiff dated October 15, 2006, ¶ 1 (attached hereto as exhibit 2) ("Letter")). His motion to dismiss for lack of personal jurisdiction is in response to Newsflash's request for declaratory judgment under the Tennessee Personal Rights Protection Act (Complaint ¶¶ 7, 9).

3. Evaluate the following argument sections from pretrial motions. Look carefully at the thesis headings, the rule sections, the explanation sections (including their use or non-use of explanatory synthesis), the application sections, and the theses restated as conclusions. Name five things that each argument section does well and three to five things that you would change about each:

a. **Newsflash Creative Media v. Black**

ARGUMENT

I. THE ACTION MUST BE DISMISSED FOR LACK OF PERSONAL JURISDICTION BECAUSE DEFENDANT BLACK DID NOT HAVE SUFFICIENT CONTACTS WITH TENNESSEE.

Defendant Black brings a motion to dismiss NCM's action for "lack of jurisdiction over the person" under Fed. R. Civ. P. 12(b)(2). Tennessee law states:

> (a) Persons who are nonresidents of Tennessee and residents of Tennessee who are outside the state and cannot be personally served with process within the state are subject to the jurisdiction of the courts of this state as to any action or claim for relief arising from: . . . (2) Any tortious act or omission within this state; . . . [or] (6) Any basis not inconsistent with the constitution of this state or of the United States.

Tenn. Code. Ann. § 20-2-214 (2006); Tenn. Code. Ann. § 20-2-223 (2006); Tenn. Code. Ann. § 20-2-225 (2006). According to U.S. Const. amend. XIV § 1, "a person may not be deprived of life, liberty, or property without due process of the law." Therefore, the limits of Tennessee jurisdictional law are conterminous with the limits of federal due process. J.I. Case Corp. v. Williams, 832 S.W.2d 530, 531 (Tenn. 1992).

Due process requires that a defendant not present within the forum state "have certain minimum contacts with it such that the maintenance of the suit does not offend 'traditional notions of fair play and substantial justice.'" Burger King Corp. v. Rudzewicz, 471 U.S. 462, 474 (1985); Int'l Shoe Co. v. Washington, 326 U.S. 310, 317 (1945); J.I. Case Corp., 832 S.W.2d at 531. In the present case, there is no indication that NCM seeks an exercise of general jurisdiction so analysis will focus on the lack of specific jurisdiction.

The Sixth Circuit has developed a three-part test for determining whether a court may exercise jurisdiction consistently with due process:

> (1) the defendant must purposefully avail himself of the privilege of acting in the forum state or causing a consequence in the forum state; (2) the cause of action must arise from the defendant's activities there; and (3) the acts of the defendant or consequences caused by the defendant must have a substantial enough connection with the forum state to make the exercise of jurisdiction over the defendant reasonable.

Youn v. Track, Inc., 324 F.3d 409, 418 (6th Cir. 2003); Southern Mach. Co. v. Mohasco Industries, Inc., 401 F.2d 374, 381 (6th Cir. 1968). Each prong of the test will be addressed in the order specified above.

A. Defendant Black did not purposefully avail himself of the privilege of acting in Tennessee because his contacts with the state were random and fortuitous.

The purposeful availment test is not met by "random, fortuitous, or attenuated contacts," but by a "connection with the forum state . . . such that he should reasonably anticipate being haled into court there." Burger King Corp., 471 U.S. at 474-5; World-Wide Volkswagen Corp., 444 U.S. at 297-8; Calphalon Corp. v. Rowlette, 228 F.3d 718, 722 (6th Cir. 2000).

The contacts with the forum state must be substantial and continuous. Compare Burger King Corp., 471 U.S. at 478 (contacts sufficient because of extensive long-term agreement with corporation based in forum), with Calphalon Corp., 228 F.3d at 722 (seventeen month-long contract with corporation in forum insufficient contacts without continuous and substantial consequences in state). Contacts from which no direct benefit was derived will not form a basis for personal availment. Compare

World-Wide Volkswagen Corp., 444 U.S. at 299 (no jurisdiction because benefits derived from collateral relation with forum state), with Fortis Corp. Ins. v. Viken Ship Mgmt., 450 F.3d 214, 220 (6th Cir. 2006) (jurisdiction affirmed because benefits derived from forum state through doing business with corporation in state).

Although Black did twice visit Tennessee, he did not form any substantial or continuous contacts. Black did not establish any continuous or ongoing connections with Tennessee, and has done no business in Tennessee invoking the protection of Tennessee law. Black could not have reasonably anticipated being subjected to Tennessee jurisdiction based on his appearances in the state as a volunteer for fundraising purposes. Further, Black's film career cannot serve as a basis of minimum contacts because his career was based in California and had only collateral relation to Tennessee. Therefore, Black did not purposely avail himself of the privilege of acting in Tennessee to the extent necessary for jurisdiction to be proper.

---

b. Newsflash Creative Media v. Black

ARGUMENT

I. THE ACTION MUST BE DISMISSED FOR LACK OF PERSONAL JURISDICTION BECAUSE, BASED ON HIS CONTACT WITH THE STATE, BLACK NEITHER PURPOSEFULLY AVAILED HIMSELF TO, NOR WOULD IT BE REASONABLE TO SUBJECT HIM TO, TENNESSEE JURISDICTION.

According to Fed. R. Civ. P. 12(b)(2), a defendant may make a motion to dismiss based on "...lack of jurisdiction over the person." Because this diversity case has been brought before the United States District Court, Western District of Tennessee, Tennessee personal jurisdiction laws are applied. S. Mach. Co. v. Mohasco Indus., Inc., 401 F.2d 374, 376 (6th Cir. 1968). Also, because general jurisdiction is not at issue in this action, the analysis will focus only on specific jurisdiction.

In the parts applicable to this action, the Tennessee Long-Arm statute provides that:

> (a) Persons who are nonresidents of Tennessee...and cannot be personally served with process within the state are subject to the jurisdiction of the courts of this state as to any action or claim for relief arising from:
>> (1) The transaction of any business within the state;
>> (2) Any tortious act or omission within this state;
>> . . .
>> (6) Any basis not inconsistent with the constitution of this state or of the United States . . . .

Tenn. Code Ann. § 20-2-214 (1994).

The Tennessee Long-Arm statute is coterminous with the Due Process Clause of the United States Constitution. Masada Inv. Corp. v. Allen, 697 S.W.2d 332, 334 (Tenn. 1985); Intera Corp. v. Henderson, 428 F.3d 605, 616 (6th Cir. 2005). In pertinent part, U.S. Const. amend. XIV states that a person may not be deprived "...of life, liberty, or property, without due process of law..." The Due Process Clause has been interpreted to require minimum contacts with the forum state such that traditional notions of fair play and substantial justice are not offended. Int'l Shoe Co. v. Wash., 326 U.S. 310, 316 (1945).

Through International Shoe and its progeny, the United States Court of Appeals for the Sixth Circuit has developed a three-prong personal jurisdiction test requiring that the defendant purposefully avails himself of the privilege of acting in the forum state or causing a consequence in the forum state; that the cause of action arises out of the defendant's activities in the forum state; and that there be a substantial connection between the defendant and the forum state, such that exercise of personal jurisdiction is reasonable. Mohasco, 401 F.2d at 381.

A. The court does not have jurisdiction over Black because the frequency and type of his contacts with the state do not amount to purposeful availment.

To establish purposeful availment, contacts with the forum state must not be random, fortuitous or attenuated. Burger King Corp. v. Rudzewicz, 471 U.S. 462, 475 (1985). The unilateral activity of those who claim some relationship with a nonresident defendant cannot satisfy the requirement of contact with the forum State. Hanson v. Denckla, 357 U.S. 235, 253 (1958).

Contacts with the forum state must be systematic and continuous for there to be purposeful availment. Compare Kerry Steel, Inc. v. Paragon Indus., 106 F.3d 147, 151 (6th Cir. 1997)(defendant's single, one-time contract with a Michigan company was not enough for purposeful availment to Michigan jurisdiction), with Burger King, 471 U.S. at 482 (defendant's intentions to establish and continue a twenty-year business relationship with plaintiff was purposeful availment by defendant). A plaintiff's unilateral activity that produces some relationship with the defendant is not enough for purposeful availment. Compare Kerry Steel, 106 F.3d at 151 (no purposeful availment where an out-of-state defendant was approached by in-state plaintiff for business), with Burger King, 471 U.S. at 480-482 (there was purposeful availment where defendant had a continuous back-and-forth relationship with plaintiff because that relationship was more than just unilateral activity).

Black has not maintained personal or professional contacts with the State of Tennessee. Black has briefly visited the state twice in the last twenty-six years, and he did not receive any kind of compensation or benefit for the 2006 visit in question. This is not the type of systematic or continuous contacts that the courts have deemed to be purposeful availment. Also, Newsflash's making T-shirts without Black's knowledge or approval is exactly the kind of unilateral activity from which the courts have found no purposeful availment. Therefore, the court does not have jurisdiction over Black because he does not have the minimum contacts necessary for the purposeful availment prong.

c. Newsflash Creative Media v. Black

ARGUMENT

I. PERSONAL JURISDICTION EXISTS OVER BLACK IN TENNESSEE BECAUSE BLACK PURPOSELY AVAILED HIMSELF OF THE PRIVILEGE OF ACTING IN TENNESSEE, THIS ACTION AROSE DIRECTLY FROM THOSE ACTIONS, AND IT IS REASONABLE TO EXERCISE JURISDICTION IN TENNESSEE.

Defendant alleges "lack of jurisdiction over the person." Fed. R. Civ. P. 12(b)(6). This case is brought in diversity in the Western District of Tennessee, and therefore Tennessee law applies. Erie R.R. Co. v. Tompkins, 304 U.S. 64 (1938). Tennessee statute specifies in pertinent part, "Persons who are nonresidents of Tennessee . . . are subject to the jurisdiction of the courts of this state as to any action or claim for relief arising from . . . (6) Any basis not inconsistent with the constitution of this state or of the United States[.]" Tenn. Code Ann. § 20-2-214 (2004). Tennessee jurisdiction therefore extends to the limits imposed by U.S. Const. amend. XIV, which states, "a person may not be deprived of life, liberty, or property without due process of law." Masada Inv. Corp. v. Allen, 697 S.W.2d 332 (Tenn. 1985).

Plaintiff makes no claim of general jurisdiction over Black, and therefore this memorandum will address this Court's specific jurisdiction. Specific jurisdiction requires that sufficient "minimum contacts" exist between the defendant and the state, and that the exercise of jurisdiction comports with traditional notions of "fair play" and "substantial justice." Int'l Shoe Co. v. Washington, 326 U.S. 310 (1945). Specifically, the Sixth Circuit has held that three criteria must be met:

> First, the defendant must purposely avail himself of the privilege of acting in the forum state or causing a consequence in the forum state. Second, the cause of action must arise from the defendant's activities there. Finally, the acts of the defendant or consequences caused by the defendant must have a substantial enough connection

with the forum state to make the exercise of jurisdiction over the defendant reasonable.

So. Mach. Co. v. Mohasco Indus., 401 F.2d 374 (6th Cir. 1968).

A. Black purposefully availed himself of the privilege of acting in Tennessee.

The purposeful availment criterion is considered the "sine qua non" of personal jurisdiction in the Sixth Circuit. So. Mach. Co., 401 F.2d at 381-82. The criterion is satisfied if the defendant's contacts with the forum state are not "random," "fortuitous," or "attenuated," Burger King Corp. v. Rudzewicz, 471 U.S. 462, 475 (1985) (citing Keeton v. Hustler Magazine, Inc., 465 U.S. 770, 774 (1984)), but instead are of a nature such that the defendant "may reasonably anticipate being haled into court there." World-Wide Volkswagen Corp. v. Woodson, 444 U.S. 286, 297 (1980).

Even a single act by the defendant may be sufficient to establish jurisdiction under this criterion. See Calder v. Jones, 465 U.S. 783 (1984) (Florida journalist subject to personal jurisdiction in California on basis of single defamatory article about state resident); Burger King, 471 U.S. at 475 (single act may be sufficient to establish personal jurisdiction, although defendant's contacts exceeded single act); Neal v. Janssen, 270 F.3d at 331 (6th Cir. 2001) (single act of communication with resident plaintiff by nonresident defendant can be sufficient to justify exercise of personal jurisdiction). Contacts that specifically solicit or attempt to influence forum residents generally satisfy this criterion. See McGee v. Int'l Life Ins. Co., 355 U.S. 220 (1957) (jurisdiction appropriate over nonresident insurance company who specifically solicited resident's business); Keeton, 465 U.S. at 781 (finding defendant publisher had "deliberately exploited" forum state's market and therefore had purposefully availed itself of state); but see World-Wide Volkswagen, 444 U.S. 286 (jurisdiction inappropriate when defendant's contacts did not deliberately solicit business in forum state).

Black had multiple meaningful interactions in multiple parts of Tennessee. His campaign fundraisers were specifically targeted at the voters of Tennessee and calculated to influence the outcome of an important state election. Nothing about his visit was fortuitous or random; Black deliberately exploited his celebrity status in Tennessee to raise money for Republican candidates. Therefore, Black purposefully availed himself of the privilege of doing business in Tennessee, and he should have reasonably anticipated being haled into court here.

-----

d. Newsflash Creative Media v. Black

ARGUMENT

I.   THE TENNESSEE "LONG-ARM" STATUTE CONVEYS PERSONAL JURISDICTION OVER THE DEFENDANT BECAUSE HIS ACTIVITIES WERE DIRECTED AT AND CAUSED CONSEQUENCE TO THE STATE AND ITS CITIZENS

Under Tennessee law, non-residents of the state of Tennessee are "subject to the jurisdiction of the courts of this state as to any action or claim for relief arising from...(1) The transaction of any business within the state; (2) Any tortious act or omission within this state; . . . (6) Any basis not inconsistent with the constitution of this state or of the United States." Tenn. Code Ann. § 20-2-214 (2006). If jurisdiction can be based upon (6), then "it is unnecessary to discuss the applicability of sections (1) [and] (2)." Masada Inv. Corp. v. Allen, 697 S.W.2d 332, 335 (Tenn. 1985).

The due process clause allows that no state shall deprive "any person of life, liberty, or property without due process of law." U.S. Const. amend. XIV. Therefore, the application of the long-arm statute is coterminous with the limits of federal due process. See Masada, 697 S.W.2d 332, 334 (Tenn. 1985). Nicholstone Book Bindery, Inc. v. Chelsea House Publishers, 621 S.W.2d 560, 562 (Tenn. 1981).

Under federal law, due process permits a state to assert personal jurisdiction over a non-resident defendant when the defendant has sufficient "minimum contacts" with the state, as "fair play" and "substantial justice" permit. Int'l Shoe Co. v. Washington, 326 U.S. 310, 316 (1945).

Jurisdiction may be general or specific; there is no assertion of general jurisdiction in this case, but the facts strongly support specific jurisdiction.

The Sixth Circuit established a three-prong test to determine when applying personal jurisdiction comports with due process.

> First, the defendant must purposefully avail himself of the privilege of acting in the forum state or causing a consequence in the forum state. Second, the cause of action must arise from the defendant's activities there. Finally, the acts of the defendant or consequences caused by the defendant must have a substantial enough connection with the forum state to make the exercise of jurisdiction over the defendant reasonable.

S. Mach. Co. v. Mohasco Ind. Inc., 401 F.2d 374, 381 (6th Cir. 1968). Each prong of the test is evaluated here in turn.

A. By actively engaging in fundraising activities for state-wide elections, Black purposefully availed himself of the privileges of operating within the forum state, Tennessee.

Due process requires an act of purposeful availment, one that "invokes the benefits and protections of [the forum state's] laws." Hanson v. Denckla, 357 U.S. 235, 253 (1958). The "focus is on the quality rather than the duration" of the act or contacts, and physical presence is not required. See Neal v. Janssen, 270 F.3d 328, 332 (6th Cir. 2001); LAK, Inc. v. Deer Creek Enter., 885 F.2d 1293, 1301 (6th Cir. 1989).

When an individual has initiated an action resulting in a consequence felt within the forum state, the purposeful availment prong of the test is satisfied. Compare Calder v. Jones, 465 U.S. 783, 788 (1984) (non-resident defendant initiated action into forum state by libeling celebrity and her activities within the forum, jurisdiction proper), and Masada, 697 S.W.2d 332, 335 (Tenn. 1985) (non-resident attorney services for real estate deal in forum, jurisdiction proper), with Reynolds v. Int'l Amateur Athletic Fed'n, 23 F.3d 1110, 1116 (6th Cir. 1994) (defamation suit based on activities outside forum, jurisdiction not proper).

The political nature of Black's activities, even with a result of a considerably lesser value than two million dollars, tangibly impacts the forum state. Black initiated debate in the Tennessee political forum by traveling to the state and actively taking part in fundraising, a debate which Newsflash merely joined once it had already begun. Although Black's forum-related actions are infrequent in occurrence, the economic consequences alone are sufficient to constitute "purposeful availment" of the benefits afforded an actor within the state.

4.　Research and draft a memorandum in support of motion to transfer venue or a memorandum in opposition to motion to transfer venue depending on whichever side you are assigned or choose to represent.

MEMORANDUM

TO:　　　　　Junior Associate

FROM:　　　　Senior Partner

DATE:　　　　January 18, 2008

RE:　　　　　<u>Grumbacher v. Elwood "Lion" Forest</u>

SUBJECT:　　Motion to Transfer Venue

Defendant Elwood "Lion" Forest is the most famous Native American golfer on the PGA tour. Since his bursting onto the scene in 1999, after winning four consecutive PGA Amateur titles, he has continued to excel, winning ten of the "major" tournaments in the last seven years, and winning the same major (the British Open) in three consecutive years, 2003, 2004, and 2005. He has received an enormous amount of attention from the United States and world press. In the last three years, he has been on the cover of over 180 newspapers and more than 250 sports and news magazines. He has received close to $90 million in product endorsement contracts in 2007, including a deal with TropoOrangie Products for $45 million that put his face on the label of orange juice cartons the world over.

Plaintiff Newton Grumbacher is an artist living in Chicago, Illinois. His medium is oil paint, and he paints outdoors as much as possible. Once, he attended a PGA event at Kemper Lakes Course in Deerfield, Illinois, and saw Lion Forest in action. He sketched the golfer making several shots, and went back to his studio and completed a painting of the golfer in the midst of one of his signature shots. Friends of the artist thought the painting was fantastic, and they encouraged Grumbacher to make some prints of the painting. Grumbacher created a limited series of 200 prints which he began to sell for $600/each. He also created a line of coffee mugs ($8) and golf towels ($10). All the prints, mugs and towels have the same image on them, the painting of Lion Forest with the Artists' name emblazoned across the bottom of the picture

Lion Forest saw one of the golf towels at an event, and became furious. He immediately had his lawyers draft up a threatening cease and desist letter to Grumbacher. (Complaint, exhibit 1). The letter demanded that Grumbacher cease the distribution or sale of any prints, mugs, towels, or any other article that features the likeness of Lion Forest produced without the consent of Mr. Forest, and retrieve and destroy all existing examples of such items, within 10 days, or Mr. Forest would sue Mr. Grumbacher under Illinois and Federal law for violation of Mr. Forest's right of publicity.

Grumbacher, being no stranger to controversy, got the jump on Mr. Forest and sued him in the Northern District of Illinois for declaratory judgment under Federal False Designation of Origin Act, 15 U.S.C. § 1125 and the Illinois Right of Publicity Act, 765 Ill. Comp. Stat. 1075/30 et seq.

Our first task is draft a court brief (Memorandum in Support/Opposition) regarding the Motion to Transfer Venue filed by Defendant Forest. See attached court file. Use the declarations in the court file when you are drafting your memorandum.

UNITED STATES DISTRICT COURT
NORTHERN DISTRICT OF ILLINOIS
EASTERN DIVISION

NEWTON W. GRUMBACHER,	)	
	)	
Plaintiff,	)	No. 02-C-9345
	)	(Judge Ruben Castillo)
	)	
ELWOOD FOREST, A/K/A "LION"	)	
FOREST,	)	JURY TRIAL
	)	DEMANDED
	)	
Defendant.	)	

COMPLAINT

NOW COMES Plaintiff Newton W. Grumbacher ("Plaintiff"), and for his complaint against Defendant Elwood Forest, also known as the professional golfer "Lion" Forest ("Defendant"), states as follows:

PARTIES

1. Plaintiff is a citizen and resident of the City of Chicago, Cook County, State of Illinois. He is domiciled in the State of Illinois.

2. Defendant Lion Forest is a citizen and resident of the State of Florida, and is domiciled in West Palm Beach, Florida.

JURISDICTION AND VENUE

3. This Court has subject matter jurisdiction over this action under 28 U.S.C. § 1332(a)(1) in that Plaintiff and Defendant have diverse citizenship, and the matter involves over $75,000 in controversy.

4. This Court further has subject matter jurisdiction over this action under 28 U.S.C. § 1331, in that the action arises under federal law, the Federal False Designation of Origin Act, 15 U.S.C. § 1125. This court has supplemental jurisdiction over the portion of the claim that involves the Illinois Right of Publicity Act, 765 Ill. Comp. Stat. 1075/30 et seq.

5. Venue is proper in this district pursuant to 28 U.S.C. § 1391(a)(2) because a substantial part of the events or omissions giving rise to the claims occurred in this district.

COUNT I - DECLARATORY JUDGMENT

6. On June 2, 2007, Plaintiff saw Defendant in person participating in a golf tournament at Kemper Lakes Country Club in Deerfield, Illinois.

7. On that date, Plaintiff made five sketches of Defendant playing golf. Later, he used these sketches to produce an oil on canvas painting which depicts Defendant playing golf.

8. The painting is an artistic creation and a work of art, embodying ideas and images, and reflecting Plaintiff's artistic interpretation and skill. Thus, Plaintiff's painting is protected under state and federal law, including the Federal False Designation of Origin Act, 15 U.S.C. § 1125, and the Illinois Right of Publicity Act, 765 Ill. Comp. Stat. 1075/30 et seq., from claims of infringement or violation of Defendant's rights of publicity.

9. Defendant is a famous public figure. He is one of the most famous golfers currently active on the PGA circuit. His name and image are well know all across the world. Defendant excels at his sport, winning ten of the major tournaments in seven years, and winning the same major

(the British Open) in three consecutive years, 2003, 2004, and 2005. He has received an enormous amount of attention from the United States and world press. In the last three years, he has been on the cover of over180 newspapers and more than 250 sports and news magazines. He has received close to $90 million in product endorsement contracts in 2007, including a deal with TropoOrangie Products for $45 million that put his face on the label of orange juice cartons the world over. Defendant is a subject worthy of news attention and depiction. Thus, Plaintiff's painting is protected under state and federal law, including the Federal False Designation of Origin Act, 15 U.S.C. § 1125, and the Illinois Right of Publicity Act, 765 Ill. Comp. Stat. 1075/30 et seq., from claims of infringement or violation of Defendant's rights of publicity.

10. Plaintiff has made derivative works of his painting, including a limited edition of 200 high quality, serigraph transfer, individually numbered and signed prints of the painting, worth at least $600 each. Plaintiff has also produced coffee mugs and golf towels bearing the same image of the painting. The image of the painting is modified so as to add the artist's last name on each of the prints, mugs and towels.

11. In that the original painting is protected under state and federal law, including the Federal False Designation of Origin Act, 15 U.S.C. § 1125, and the Illinois Right of Publicity Act, 765 Ill. Comp. Stat. 1075/30 et seq., from claims of infringement or violation of Defendant's rights of publicity, each derivative work produced by the same artist is also protected from claims of infringement or violation of Defendant's rights of publicity.

12. On December 1, 2007, Defendant sent by facsimile transmission and U.S. Mail the letter attached hereto as Exhibit 1, threatening Plaintiff and demanding that Plaintiff cease and desist production, distribution and sale of all prints, mugs, towels, and any other "derivative works" of the painting without the consent of Defendant. The letter also calls for Plaintiff to destroy the original painting of Defendant and all

prints, mugs, towels, and other "derivative works" of the painting now and in the future possession of Plaintiff. The letter threatened a lawsuit within ten days of the letter if its terms were not followed.

13. An actual case and controversy exists between Plaintiff and Defendant based on the letter and the threats of legal action concerning Plaintiff's art contained therein.

WHEREFORE, Plaintiff requests the Court to order a declaratory judgment in favor of Plaintiff and against Defendant, ordering and decreeing that Plaintiff has the right to produce, sell, and distribute the painting of Defendant and prints, mugs, and towels bearing the image depicted in the original painting, and to award Plaintiff such further and other relief as the Court deems proper in the circumstances.

JURY TRIAL DEMANDED.

SMITH, MAPLE, & RUSH, P.C.

By:_____

Andres Smith
Ill. Bar No. 6157980
111 South Michigan Avenue
Chicago, Illinois, 60603-6110
Phone: 800-555-ARTY
Fax: 800-555-SU4U

Attorneys for Plaintiff
Newton W. Grumbacher

Filed: December 8, 2007

E. Lion Forest

18 Golfview Road
West Palm Beach, Florida 33406

December 1, 2007

By Facsimile and Mail:

Mr. Newton W. Grumbacher
234 Warsaw Street
Chicago IL 60609

Dear Sir:

I have engaged the law firm of Rogers, Alben, & Dana to investigate your unauthorized production, sale, and distribution of items bearing my image and likeness without my authorization. This is a violation of my rights under Illinois and federal law. I never authorized you or anyone else associated with you to produce, distribute or sell any item or derivative work that bears my image and likeness. You have produced no less than one oil painting, 200 (more or less) serigraph reprints of the oil painting, and numerous other derivative works, including but not limited to coffee mugs and towels. Please accept this as my demand that you cease production, distribution and sale or all items described above. Please take all necessary means to collect back any items whose sale is not yet final. And, within ten (10) days of the date of this letter, please provide proof to me at the above address of the destruction of all items described in this letter, including one oil painting, 200 (more or less) serigraph reprints of the oil painting, and numerous other derivative works, including but not limited to coffee mugs and towels, all of which bear my image and likeness.

If you fail to comply with the demands of this letter, within eleven (11) days of the date of this letter, I will initiate suit against you for injunctive relief, statutory and civil damages, in a court of law.

Sincerely,
E. Lion Forest

UNITED STATES DISTRICT COURT
NORTHERN DISTRICT OF ILLINOIS
EASTERN DIVISION

NEWTON W. GRUMBACHER,	)	
	)	
Plaintiff,	)	No. 00-C-9345
	)	Judge Ruben Castillo
	)	
ELWOOD FOREST, A/K/A "LION"	)	
FOREST,	)	
	)	
Defendant.	)	

MOTION TO TRANSFER VENUE

NOW COMES defendant Elwood "Lion" Forest (Defendant), and moves this Court pursuant to 28 U.S.C. § 1404, to transfer this action to the United States District Court for the Southern District of Florida, West Palm Beach Division. In support of this motion, Defendant states:

Defendant recognizes that venue is appropriate in this district because a portion of the events of this case did occur in this district. Nevertheless, as described in the attached Declarations of Elwood Forest and Scott Skiptracer, this action should be transferred for the convenience of the parties and witnesses and in the interest of justice. Venue is appropriate in the United States District Court for the Southern District of Florida, West Palm Beach Division because defendant resides there.

WHEREFORE, Defendant Elwood Forest prays the Court will transfer this action to the United States District Court for the Southern District of Florida, West Palm Beach Division and award Defendant costs and expenses and such further and other relief as the Court deems appropriate in this matter.

Respectfully Submitted,

ROGERS, ALBEN, & DANA

By:_____

Randal Alben
Ill. Bar No. 5322445
1010 Wacker, Suite 200
Chicago, IL 60602
Phone: (312) 555-9900
Fax: (312) 555-9901

Attorneys for Defendant E. Lion Forest

UNITED STATES DISTRICT COURT
NORTHERN DISTRICT OF ILLINOIS
EASTERN DIVISION

NEWTON W. GRUMBACHER,	)	
	)	
Plaintiff,	)	No. 00-C-9345
	)	Judge Ruben Castillo
	)	
ELWOOD FOREST, A/K/A "LION"	)	
FOREST,	)	
	)	
Defendant.	)	

DECLARATION OF ELWOOD FOREST

I, Elwood "Lion" Forest, of lawful age, do swear under penalty of perjury of the laws of the United States and the State of Illinois that I have first hand information concerning the following and the following information is true and correct:

1. I am 29 years old. I am a citizen and resident of Florida. I reside at 18 Golfview Road, West Palm Beach, Florida 33406.

2. My career and my own personal business and promotional activities are based in West Palm Beach, Florida. All of the witnesses to my personal affairs, promotions and publicity — including my agent, Guy Smith, my personal manager, Bea Jones, and my accountant and financial planner, Bill Murphy — are residents of the West Palm Beach area. None of these witnesses are amenable to process in the United States District Court for the Northern District of Illinois. All of the documents, exhibits, and other evidence of my fame, advertising, and promotional activities are located at 18 Golfview Road, West Palm Beach, Florida.

3. As a professional golfer, I travel a great deal, and on occasion I have traveled to the Northern District of Illinois for tournaments. I have only been in the Northern District of Illinois four times in the last seven years, having attended the last three Kemper Lakes Skins tournaments at Kemper Lakes Country Club in Deerfield, Illinois, and once attended the TropoOrangie Pro Am tournament at Tamarack Golf Club in Northern Illinois. Other than these short, six day appearances, I have had no connection whatsoever to the Northern District of Illinois.

4. I have no advertising or promotional agreement with any corporation that is incorporated in or has its principle place of business in the State of Illinois.

FURTHER DECLARANT SAYETH NAUGHT.

Sworn to under penalty of perjury on this 29th day of December 2007.

_____

Elwood "Lion" Forest

_____

UNITED STATES DISTRICT COURT
NORTHERN DISTRICT OF ILLINOIS
EASTERN DIVISION

NEWTON W. GRUMBACHER,	)	
	)	
Plaintiff,	)	No. 00-C-9345
	)	Judge Ruben Castillo
	)	
ELWOOD FOREST, A/K/A "LION"	)	
FOREST,	)	
	)	
Defendant.	)	

DECLARATION OF SCOTT SKIPTRACER

I, Scott Skiptracer, of lawful age, do swear under penalty of perjury of the laws of the United States and the State of Illinois that I have first hand information concerning the following and the following information is true and correct:

1. I am 38 years old. I am a citizen and resident of Chicago, Illinois.

2. I am a duly licensed and authorized private investigator and process server in the State of Illinois. I am licensed and authorized to do business in Cook County, City of Chicago, and Lake County, Illinois.

3. I was engaged by Defendant Forest to gather information regarding the above captioned matter.

4. Plaintiff Grumbacher is a citizen and resident of Chicago, Illinois whose maintains a household at 234 Warsaw Street, Chicago IL 60609. He maintains a studio and work space at 427 Addison, Chicago IL 60609. It is believed that the articles—serigraph prints, golf towels, and mugs bearing the unauthorized image of defendant and described in the complaint—were created at this studio and workspace. I observed a quantity of the described towels and mugs in the studio and workspace on December 28, 2007.

5. Plaintiff also maintains a semi-permanent residence in Greenacres, Florida in the vicinity of West Palm Beach, Florida. He has a small apartment above the garage of the home in Greenacres belonging to his aunt, Viridian Green. Neighbors reported to me that Plaintiff makes annual visits to this apartment, sometimes staying for up to two months in the winter.

6. Plaintiff has an ongoing relationship with the Coral View Gallery in Palm Springs, Florida, which is the close vicinity of West Palm Beach, Florida, and he has an ongoing relationship with the Marino Gallery in Miami, Florida, located in the jurisdiction of the United States District Court for the Southern District of Florida.

7. According to the 2006 General Service Administration Statistics on Federal Courts (Feb. 2007), the average time from filing to trial for a civil action in the United States District Court for the Southern District of Florida, West Palm Beach Division is 12 months whereas the average time from filing to trial for a civil action in the United States District Court for the Northern District of Illinois, Eastern Division is eighteen months to twenty four months.

FURTHER DECLARANT SAYETH NAUGHT.

Sworn to under penalty of perjury on this 12th day of January 2008.

_____

Scott Skiptracer

_____

UNITED STATES DISTRICT COURT
NORTHERN DISTRICT OF ILLINOIS
EASTERN DIVISION

NEWTON W. GRUMBACHER,   )
)
             Plaintiff,   )   No. 00-C-9345
)   Judge Ruben Castillo
)
ELWOOD FOREST, A/K/A "LION")
FOREST,   )
)
             Defendant.   )

DECLARATION OF NEWTON GRUMBACHER

I, Newton Grumbacher, of lawful age, do swear under penalty of perjury of the laws of the United States and the State of Illinois that I have first hand information concerning the following and the following information is true and correct:

1. I am 40 years old. I am a citizen and resident of Chicago, Illinois. My permanent residence is located at 234 Warsaw Street, Chicago IL 60609. I have a studio and work space at 427 Addison, Chicago IL 60609. All of the works of art described in the complaint—the original painting of defendant and the original works of art in the form of

serigraphs, art towels, and ceramic art pieces—were created and are located at my home address or my studio in Chicago, Illinois. None of the articles described in the complaint were created in the State of Florida or are located in the State of Florida.

2. From time to time I vacation in Greenacres, Florida, never more than twice a year, and usually for only two weeks at a time. None of the art involved in this matter was conceived or created in Florida. I maintain an ongoing relationship with the Coral View Gallery in Palm Springs, Florida, and the Marino Gallery in Miami, Florida, but none of the art works involved in this action and described in the complaint have ever been displayed or otherwise shown or ever even located in the State of Florida.

3. All of my witnesses, including my secretary, Carol Lander, and my studio assistant, Al Moore, have their permanent residence in Chicago and are not amenable to process in the United States District Court for the Southern District of Florida.

FURTHER DECLARANT SAYETH NAUGHT.

Sworn to under penalty of perjury on this 14th day of January 2008.

_____

Newton Grumbacher

_____

III.   MOTIONS TO DISMISS (*Advanced Legal Writing and Oral Advocacy: Trials, Appeals, and Moot Court*, Chapter 3)

WRITING PROBLEM

1. Based on the following information, prepare a memorandum in support of the motion to dismiss for lack of subject matter jurisdiction or a memorandum in opposition to this motion depending on whichever side you are assigned or choose to represent.

Patricia Piao-Liang Davis is a 20 year old super-model who goes by the professional name "Piao-Liang." She was born in Nanjing, PRC in 1989, but was orphaned at four months of age, and was adopted at six months of age by Clifford and June Davis, U.S. citizens, and raised in Provo, Utah. Piao-Liang is a naturalized citizen of the United States, and is domiciled and resident in Provo, Utah. Piao-Liang has joined a group of other super-models who offer their unfertilized ova for auction on an internet site known as Dezyner-Genes.com. Although she has participated in the web site since January 2007, she has never accepted any bids to purchase her eggs.

While on a photo-shoot for Drop Dead Gorgeous magazine that took her to various locations in China (the Great Wall and Tiananmen Square in Beijing, the Bund in Shanghai, and others), Piao-Liang was approached at West Lake in Hangzhou by a businessman, Mr. Jiang "Jerry" Chuang-ping. Mr. Jiang explained that his wife was infertile, and he was interested in purchasing an ovum from Piao-Liang, and offered her $1 million for it. She was flattered and orally agreed to the transaction. The two drank baijiu and toasted each other several times to celebrate the deal. When she returned to the United States, Piao-Liang's lawyers, Hart, Charles, & LaRouche, reviewed Mr. Jiang's written proposal for the agreement concerning the sale of the ovum, and they accepted the terms, but added a forum selection and choice of law clause in the agreement, specifying that any action arising under the contract would be brought in a state or federal court in California and that the law of California would govern the contract.

The contract was signed by Piao-Liang in New York, NY, on November 2, 2008, and by Mr. Jiang in Taibei, Republic of China (Taiwan), on November 4, 2008. The egg or eggs were to be delivered by June 1, 2009, and the payment of $1 million was to be made immediately upon successful fertilization and implantation.

Jerry Jiang, age 56, is a naturalized American citizen who owns a controlling interest in and supervises four factories producing computer memory chips in Taibei. He was born in Taibei in 1953. He immigrated to the United States in 1979, and was naturalized as a U.S. citizen in 1984. Although he first settled in San Francisco, he now lives and works seven months of the year in Taiwan, and owns a condominium in Taibei. The rest of the year he travels or stays at one of his two homes in San Francisco, California and Aspen, Colorado. His wife, Sun Li, travels with him and stays wherever he is staying throughout the year. (The couple have no children and cannot have any because Sun Li is infertile.) Jiang and Sun have followed this routine every year for the last twelve years, but Jiang has made it known that he intends to retire to Taiwan when he turns 65. He has a California driver's license and a U.S. Passport, but he is still recognized by the government of the Republic of China as having dual-citizenship, and also has a Republic of China passport. He votes, registers his car, and pays taxes in California, but he also pays taxes in Taiwan.

Piao-Liang discovered in late November that Mr. Jiang is the nephew of the late General and President of the ROC, Jiang Ji-shi, better known to the world as Chiang Kai-shek. This horrified her because her Chinese family had been oppressed by the Nationalists prior to the Communist victory in China. She decided to refuse to go through with the sale, and Mr. Jiang sued her in the United States District Court for the Northern District of California.

Piao-Liang has filed a motion to dismiss for lack of subject matter jurisdiction.

UNITED STATES DISTRICT COURT
NORTHERN DISTRICT OF CALIFORNIA

JIANG CHUANG-PING,	)	
	)	
Plaintiff,	)	No. 2:06-CV-2345-K
v.	)	(Judge Kimball)
	)	
PATRICIA PIAO-LIANG DAVIS,	)	JURY TRIAL
A/K/A "PIAO-LIANG",	)	DEMANDED
	)	
	)	
Defendant.	)	

COMPLAINT

NOW COMES Plaintiff Jiang Chuang-ping ("Plaintiff"), and for his complaint against Defendant Patricia Piao-Liang Davis, also known as the supermodel "Piao-Liang" ("Defendant"), states as follows:

PARTIES

1. Plaintiff is a citizen and resident of the City of San Francisco, State of California, and the United States of America. He is domiciled in the State of California in this Northern District of California.

2. Defendant Piao-Liang is a citizen and resident of the State of Utah, United States of America, and is domiciled in Provo, Utah.

JURISDICTION AND VENUE

3. This Court has subject matter jurisdiction over this action under 28 U.S.C. § 1332(a)(1) in that Plaintiff and Defendant have diverse citizenship, and the matter involves over $75,000 in controversy.

4. Personal jurisdiction exists over Defendant because Defendant was served with process in this State and District.

5. Defendant and Plaintiff entered into the Contract attached hereto as Exhibit 1 ("Contract") on November 2 and November 4, 2008, respectively.

6. The contract provides for suit to be brought in a federal court in California and the Contract is to be governed by California law. Contract, section 5.

7. Venue is proper in this district pursuant to the forum selection clause in section 5 of the Contract and pursuant to 28 U.S.C. § 1391 in that Defendant was served with process within this District and Division, and the subject matter of the Contract is present in this District.

COUNT I - BREACH OF CONTRACT

8. On November 2, 2008, Defendant entered into the Contract, promising to deliver to Plaintiff's OB-GYN physician one or more healthy and viable ova from her ovaries at the first available opportunity and no later than June 1, 2009. Upon receipt and successful fertilization and implantation of the egg(s) in Plaintiff's wife's uterus, Plaintiff was to pay Plaintiff by wire transfer the sum of one million United States dollars.

9. On December 18, 2008, Defendant phoned Plaintiff and repudiated the contract by stating that she would not perform her obligations. She then, on that same day, sent by facsimile transmission and U.S. Mail the letter attached hereto as Exhibit 2, again repudiating the Contract and refusing to perform her obligations under the Contract.

10. Plaintiff was and remains ready to perform his obligations under the Contract, and there are no other conditions precedent to the agreement that would prevent its performance.

11. Defendant breached its agreement with Plaintiff by anticipatory repudiation.

12. Plaintiff has no available alternative remedy at law that could replace or compensate Plaintiff for the unique value of the subject matter of the Contract, and seeks specific performance of the Contract, and such further and other relief as the Court deems proper in the circumstances.

COUNT II - SPECIFIC PERFORMANCE

13. Plaintiff realleges the allegations of paragraphs 1-12 of this complaint as though set forth fully in this paragraph.

14. Plaintiff comes to this court seeking equity, with clean hands, and with the equities in his favor. Plaintiff has no available alternative remedy at law. The public policy of this jurisdiction favors the upholding and enforcement of contracts for the provision of a unique subject matter.

15. Defendant has repudiated and breached her obligations under the Contract. The equities and public policy are against Defendant.

16. Plaintiff seeks specific performance of the Contract.

WHEREFORE, Plaintiff requests the Court to order Defendant to deliver to Plaintiff's OB-GYN physician one or more healthy and viable ova from her ovaries at the first available opportunity and no later than June 1, 2009, and to award Plaintiff such further and other relief as the Court deems proper in the circumstances.

JURY TRIAL DEMANDED.

FINLEY & MOORE, LLP

By:_____

        Miriam O. McGuinnis
        Ut Bar No. 02112
        114 Market Street, Suite 2800
        Salt Lake City, Utah 84101
        Phone: 801-555-SU4U

        Attorneys for Plaintiff Jiang Chuang-ping

Purchase and Sale Contract

WHEREFORE, Mr. Jerry Jiang Chuang-Ping (Buyer) and Ms. Patricia Piao-Liang Davis (Seller) wish to enter into an agreement for the transfer of at least one egg from Seller's ovaries to Buyer for the purpose of fertilization of the egg and implantation in Buyer's wife; and

WHEREFORE, the parties, Buyer and Seller, in consideration of the mutual promises stated herein and for other good and valuable consideration; and

WHEREFORE, the parties, Buyer and Seller, wish to complete this transaction at the earliest practicable time, and in no event later than June 1, 2009;

Then the parties covenant and agree to the following:

    1. At the earliest practicable opportunity, and in no event later than June 1, 2009, in New York City, NY or Salt Lake City, UT, or at any other mutually agreeable location, Seller shall deliver to Buyer's OB-GYN physician one or more healthy and viable ova (i.e., eggs) from her ovaries.

2. Upon receipt and successful fertilization of the egg(s), the egg(s) are to be implanted in Buyer's wife's uterus,

3. After successful implantation of the fertilized egg(s) in Buyer's wife's uterus, without miscarriage, for twenty-one days, Buyer shall pay Seller by wire transfer to Osmond National Bank, Account No. 100223456 owned by Seller, the sum of one million United States dollars.

4. In the event that conditions 2 and 3 cannot be successfully completed with the initial supply of the egg(s) from Seller, Seller shall, within six weeks of notification by facsimile or U.S. mail by Buyer of the failure of conditions 2 or 3, supply one or more additional healthy and viable eggs to Buyer's OB-GYN physician in New York City, NY or Salt Lake City, UT, and shall continue to supply eggs in the manner described in this paragraph every six weeks until successful completion of conditions 2 and 3 of this contract.

5. Should any dispute between the parties arise under this agreement, the parties, Buyer and Seller, agree that all disputes shall be resolved in litigation that shall be filed in a state or federal court in the State of California and all conditions and terms and obligations of this contract shall be governed by and interpreted under California law.

Signed by Buyer: Signed by Seller:

_____   _____
Jerry Jiang Chuang-ping   Patricia Piao-Liang Davis
Date: November 4, 2008   Date: November 2, 2008

Piao-Liang® is Beauty
234 Joseph Smith Drive
Provo, UT 84602 USA
(801) 555-piao

December 18, 2008

By Facsimile and Mail:

Mr. Jerry Jiang Chuang-ping
Two Embarcadero Center, Suite 3801
San Francisco, CA 94111-3909
Phone: 415-555-7779
Fax: 888-555-7789

To Mr. Jiang:

I am canceling the deal. I never knew you were connected with the Nationalists. This changes everything. I no longer want to undergo the procedure for you or anyone else.

Sincerely,
Piao-Liang Davis

_____

UNITED STATES DISTRICT COURT
NORTHERN DISTRICT OF CALIFORNIA

JIANG CHUANG-PING,   )
)
     Plaintiff,   )   No. 2:06-CV-2345-K
)
     v.   )
)
PATRICIA PIAO-LIANG DAVIS,   )
)
     Defendant.   )

MOTION TO DISMISS

NOW COMES defendant Patricia Piao-Liang Davis ("Piao-Liang"), and moves this Court pursuant to Fed. R. Civ. P. 12(b)(1), to dismiss this action for lack of subject matter jurisdiction.

Plaintiff seeks this Court to take jurisdiction over the subject matter of this action under 28 U.S.C. § 1332(a)(1), alleging diversity of citizenship of the parties and a proper jurisdictional amount. Diversity cannot be met by Plaintiff because Plaintiff is not a citizen or resident of any State of the United States, and does not possess diverse citizenship within the meaning of 28 U.S.C. § 1332(a)(1). In that Plaintiff is not a citizen and resident of any state of the United States for diversity purposes, this fact defeats the assertion of diversity jurisdiction over the subject matter of this action, and the action must be dismissed.

WHEREFORE, Defendant Piao-Liang prays the Court dismiss this action and award Defendant costs and expenses and such further and other relief as the Court deems appropriate in this matter.

HART, CHARLES, & LAROUCHE P.C.

By:_____

Attorneys admitted *pro*
hac vice by Order of
Court dated 1/6/2009

Sandra LaRouche
Mo. Bar No. 41044
1010 Walnut Street, Suite 200
St. Louis, Missouri 63101
Phone: (314) 555-9900
Fax: (314) 555-9901

Attorneys for Defendant
Patricia Piao-Liang Davis

UNITED STATES DISTRICT COURT
NORTHERN DISTRICT OF CALIFORNIA

JIANG CHUANG-PING,   )
)
                 Plaintiff,   )   No. 2:06-CV-2345-K
        v.   )
)
PATRICIA PIAO-LIANG DAVIS,   )
)
                 Defendant.   )

DECLARATION OF JERRY JIANG CHUANG-PING

I, Jiang "Jerry" Chuang-ping, of lawful age, do swear under penalty of perjury of the laws of the United States and the State of California that I have first hand information concerning the following and the following information is true and correct:

1. I am 56 years old. I am a naturalized United States citizen, and I reside in San Francisco, CA.

2. I am the president and CEO of Jiang Memory Solutions, Ltd., a corporation that has production and distribution facilities in San Jose, CA, Salt Lake City, UT, Redmond, WA, Festus, MO, and Taibei, Republic of China. I supervise four factories producing computer memory chips in Taibei, and the distribution facilities in the United States. Because of these responsibilities, I travel a great deal and am outside the United States on business and for recreation for months at a time. It is common for my business to require me to spend seven or more months outside the United States each year.

3. I have considered California to be my and my wife's home since we immigrated there in 1979. I have no desire to settle in any other state of the United States. My wife and I plan to stay in California for the indefinite future. I have a United States passport and a California driver's license. I have owned a house at 231 Cobb Hill Drive in San Francisco for eleven years, and have leased office space at Two Embarcadero Center, Suite 3801, San Francisco, CA 94111-3909, for seven years. I am registered to vote in California. I have paid taxes to the City and County of San Francisco, the State of California, and the United States from 1979 to the present. I own three vehicles registered in California.

4. I have four bank accounts at BankofAmerica in San Francisco and two bank accounts at BankofAmerica, New York. I also have one account at IBJ Schroeder in Tokyo, Japan, and four accounts at Guomin Bank, Taibei, Republic of China. My checking and commercial line of credit account at BankofAmerica, New York is the largest account I own measured by amount of deposit.

FURTHER DECLARANT SAYETH NAUGHT.

Sworn to under penalty of perjury on this 29th day of December 2008.

_____

Jerry Jiang Chuang-ping

_____

UNITED STATES DISTRICT COURT
NORTHERN DISTRICT OF CALIFORNIA

JIANG CHUANG-PING,	)	
	)	
Plaintiff,	)	No. 2:06-CV-2345-K
v.	)	
	)	
PATRICIA PIAO-LIANG DAVIS,	)	
	)	
Defendant.	)	

DECLARATION OF CHAIM ESCOBAR

I, Chaim Escobar, of lawful age, do swear under penalty of perjury of the laws of the United States and the State of California that I have first hand information concerning the following and the following information is true and correct:

1. I am 36 years old. I am the owner and operator of Chaim's Search and Serve, a private investigatory service in San Francisco, CA.

2. I have personally investigated and obtained the following information about Mr. Jiang Chuang-ping, a/k/a Jerry Jiang, the plaintiff in the above captioned matter.

3. Jerry Jiang was born in Taibei, Taiwan in 1953. He immigrated to the United States in 1979, and was naturalized as a U.S. citizen in 1984.

4. Jiang owns a controlling interest in and supervises four factories producing computer memory chips in Taibei. These factories are his primary source of employment and income.

5. Although he first settled in San Francisco, he now lives and works seven months of the year in Taiwan, and owns a condominium in Taibei. The rest of the year he travels or stays at one of the two homes he owns in San Francisco, California and Aspen, Colorado. His wife, Sun Li, travels with him and stays wherever he is staying throughout the year.

6. Jiang and Sun have followed this routine of living seven or more months in Taiwan every year for the last twelve years.

7. Through interviews with his neighbors, Cliff Zhang and Will Xu, and employees Rajin Sihgn, Carol Patel, and Charlie Wu at his San Jose plant, I have learned that Jiang regularly states that he intends to retire to Taiwan when he turns 65.

8. Jiang has a California driver's license and a U.S. Passport, but he is recognized by the government of the Republic of China as having dual-citizenship, and also has a Republic of China passport. He uses the Republic of China passport on trips throughout Asia, but never when he flies back and forth to the United States.

9. Jiang has four bank accounts in Taibei, Taiwan at the Guomin Bank (National Bank of Taiwan). He has other accounts across the globe in Tokyo, New York, and San Francisco, but his two most active accounts in terms of number of deposits, wire transfers, checks drawn, and other transactions are both at Guomin Bank in Taiwan. He has paid corporate

income taxes and personal income taxes and property taxes to Taiwan every year since 1970 (the earliest year such records are available).

FURTHER DECLARANT SAYETH NAUGHT.

Sworn to under penalty of perjury on this 9th day of January, 2009.

_____

Mr. Chaim Escobar

_____

2. Based on the following information, prepare a memorandum in support of the motion to dismiss for lack of personal jurisdiction or a memorandum in opposition to this motion depending on whichever side you are assigned or choose to represent.

_____

MEMORANDUM

TO: Junior Associate

FROM: Senior Partner

DATE: January 21, 2008

RE: <u>Roger Clemens v. Take Steroids Out of the Ball Game, Inc. and The Sporting News</u> (C87654/34678)

SUBJECT: Motion to Dismiss for Lack of Personal Jurisdiction

Take Steroids Out of the Ball Game, Inc. (TSOOTBG) is a not-for-profit tax exempt organization. It is a private corporation organized and existing under the laws of the State of Illinois with its principal and in fact only place of business being in Champaign, Illinois. TSOOTBG claims that its mission is to eliminate steroids and performance-enhancing drugs from Major League Baseball. TSOOTBG is not affiliated with Major League Baseball, Major League Baseball Players Assoc., Major League Baseball Properties, or the Major League Baseball Players Union, not is it affiliated with government or any government agency. It is solely owned, created, and operated by one person, Marcus McWire, who started the company in December 2007. The company runs a weblog (tsootbg.blogspot.com). It has no other business or other activities except those described below.

Defendant Sporting News is a corporation organized and existing under the laws of the State of Missouri with its headquarters and principal place of business in the County of St. Louis, Missouri within the territory of the United States District Court for the Eastern District of Missouri.

In late 2007, the company used most of its cash on hand to purchase a full page ad in Co-defendant Sporting News's weekly publication. The ad depicted plaintiff Roger Clemens riding a syringe as if it were a rocket and flying over Yankee Stadium, obviously playing off of Clemens' nickname of the "Rocket" and his recent association with steroid use (needle and syringe injections) allegedly undertaken while Clemens was a member of the New York Yankees baseball club.

The ad ran once in Sporting News on December 31, 2007, and at the bottom of the ad in very small but legible lettering was the usual tagline used by TSOOTBG on its weblog along with the address of the blog:

> **Take Steroids Out of the Ball Game is a not-for-profit tax exempt organization that exists solely to put pressure on Major League Baseball to eliminate steroids. We accept donations of any kind --- money, pictures, news stories, whatever. (tsootbg.blogspot.com)**

The ad was reproduced on the TSOOTBG weblog where it has been able to be viewed from January 14 to the present. The ad is in close proximity to a blog entry on Roger Clemens and the Mitchell Report that concerns steroid use in baseball and prominently discusses Clemens' alleged steroid use. The profile listing of the weblog provides instructions on how to donate money or other items to TSOOTBG:

Take Steroids Out of the Ball Game accepts cash donations by PayPal transfer to our account: tsootbg@ gmail.com. Pictures, news stories, and other items may be emailed to us at the same address. Thank you!

TSOOTBG also registered four other web addresses on January 14, 2008: www.RogerClemensComeClean.com, www.RogerClemensHallofFame?.com, www.RogerClemensJuiced.com, and www.RogerClemensSteroidUser.com. All of these web addresses direct users to the **tsootbg.blogspot.com** weblog.

Clemens sued TSOOTBG and Sporting News in the United States District Court for the Eastern District of Missouri for violations of his right of publicity under Missouri law. Subject matter jurisdiction is alleged because Clemens is a citizen and resident of Texas and is diverse from the Missouri and Illinois defendants, and an amount in controversy of over $200,000 is alleged. There is no question that the court has personal jurisdiction over defendant Sporting News because it has its headquarters and its principal place of business within this district. TSOOTBG, on the other hand, has no connections to Missouri or the district of this court except as described above, so TSOOTBG has moved the court pursuant to Fed. R. Civ. P. 12(b)(2) to dismiss the action against it for lack of personal jurisdiction over TSOOTBG.

Our first task is to draft a court brief (Memorandum in Support/ Opposition) regarding the Motion to Dismiss for Lack of Personal Jurisdiction filed by TSOOTBG. See attached court file.

You should assume that the only issue to brief in the motion is whether TSOOTBG had sufficient minimum contacts with the State of Missouri such that it would or would not violate the Due Process Clause of the United States Constitution to sue TSOOTBG in Missouri. Use the complaint and declaration in the court file when you are drafting your memorandum. To the extent that it is relevant, the underlying lawsuit is governed by Missouri law, but federal law (under the Due Process Clause) applies to this motion.

UNITED STATES DISTRICT COURT
EASTERN DISTRICT OF MISSOURI
EASTERN DIVISION

ROGER CLEMENS,	)	
	)	
Plaintiff,	)	No. 04-C-9345 (DJS)
v.	)	
	)	
TAKE STEROIDS OUT	)	
OF THE BALL	)	
GAME, INC., and SPORTING	)	
NEWS,	)	JURY TRIAL
	)	DEMANDED
	)	
Defendants.	)	

COMPLAINT

NOW COMES Plaintiff Roger Clemens ("Clemens"), and for its complaint against Take Steroids Out of the Ball Game, Inc. ("TSOOT-BG") and Sporting News, states as follows:

PARTIES

1. Plaintiff Clemens is an individual domiciled and residing in the State of Texas. Clemens is a citizen of the State of Texas.

2. TSOOTBG is a corporation organized and existing under the laws of the State of Illinois and has its place of incorporation and head-quarters and principal place of business in the State of Illinois. Its sole shareholder and officer, Marcus McWire, is a citizen and domiciliary of the City of Champaign, State of Illinois. All of its operations, facilities, and equipment are located in Champaign, Illinois.

3. Defendant Sporting News is a corporation organized and existing under the laws of the State of Missouri has its place of incorporation and headquarters and principal place of business in the State of Missouri.

VENUE AND JURISDICTION

4. Venue is proper in this district pursuant to 28 U.S.C. § 1391 because the actions alleged herein caused harm to Clemens's publicity rights in the State of Missouri, and the ad was run in a publication based in and emanating from the State of Missouri, and one defendant is a citizen and resident of Missouri and this district, and both defendants are present and amenable to service of process within this United States District Court for the Eastern District of Missouri.

5. Jurisdiction is appropriate in this Court under 28 U.S.C. § 1332 because the citizenship of the plaintiff and the defendants is diverse, and over $75,000 is in controversy in the suit.

COUNT I - RIGHT OF PUBLICITY

6. On December 31, 2007, TSOOTBG purchased a full page advertisement in Sporting News's weekly publication. The ad depicted plaintiff Clemens riding a syringe as if it were a rocket and flying over Yankee Stadium.

7. The ad ran once in Sporting News on December 31, 2007, and at the bottom of the ad in very small but legible lettering was a solicitation used by TSOOTBG in its activities on its weblog along with the address of the blog:

> **Take Steroids Out of the Ball Game is a not-for-profit tax exempt organization that exists solely to put pressure on Major League Baseball to eliminate steroids. We accept donations of any kind --- money, pictures, news stories, whatever. (tsootbg.blogspot.com)**

8. The ad obviously played off of Clemens' nickname of the "Rocket" and used his fame and considerable publicity value of his image and likeness to draw attention to the publication and to attract attention and monetary contributions to TSOOTBG.

9. TSOOTBG used the ad to direct readers of Sporting News' publication to the TSOOTBG's weblog (tsootbg.blogspot.com) where they are solicited to make donations of money to TSOOTBG. The profile listing of the weblog provides instructions on how to donate money or other items to TSOOTBG:

> **Take Steroids Out of the Ball Game accepts cash donations by PayPal transfer to our account: tsootbg@gmail.com. Pictures, news stories, and other items may be emailed to us at the same address. Thank you!**

10. TSOOTBG also registered four other web addresses on January 14, 2008: www.RogerClemensComeClean.com, www.RogerClemensHallofFame?.com, www.RogerClemensJuiced.com, and www.RogerClemensSteroidUser.com. All of these web addresses direct users to the **tsootbg.blogspot.com** weblog.

11. The ad drew attention to the Sporting News publication itself attracting readership and potential subscribers and additional ad revenue by playing off of the enormous publicity value of Clemens' image and persona.

12. Thus, defendants TSOOTBG and Sporting News, acting individually and in concert, did commercially exploit the likeness, image, and

persona to their financial and commercial advantage within the meaning of Missouri right of publicity law.

13. On January 14, 2008, the ad image was posted on the World Wide Web in TSOOTBG's weblog (tsootbg.blogspot.com) where is it visible to anyone and everyone in the State of Missouri who has access to the World Wide Web. As mentioned above, TSOOTBG's weblog contains a solicitation for money from visitors to the site.

14. Thus, defendant TSOOTBG did further commercially exploit the likeness, image, and persona to its financial and commercial advantage within the meaning of Missouri's right of publicity law.

WHEREFORE, Clemens requests the Court to grant it damages in the amount of $200,000, and to award Clemens such further and other relief as the Court deems proper in the circumstances.

BONDS, GIAMBI, PETTITTE, LLC

By:_____
        Barry L. Bonds
        Mo. Bar No. 41042
        211 North Broadway, Suite 3300
        St. Louis, MO 63102
        Phone: 800-NEEDLES
        Fax: 800-SYRINGE

        Attorneys for Plaintiff Roger Clemens

Filed: January 19, 2008

UNITED STATES DISTRICT COURT
EASTERN DISTRICT OF MISSOURI
EASTERN DIVISION

ROGER CLEMENS,   )
)
                 Plaintiff,   )   No. 04-C-9345 (DJS)
         v.   )   Hon. Donald J. Stohr
)
TAKE STEROIDS OUT OF   )
  THE BALL   )
GAME, INC., and   )
SPORTING NEWS,   )
)
                 Defendants.   )

MOTION TO DISMISS

NOW COMES defendant Take Steroids Out of the Ball Game, Inc. ("Defendant TSOOTBG"), and moves this Court pursuant to Fed. R. Civ. P. 12(b)(2) to dismiss this action for lack of personal jurisdiction over Defendant TSOOTBG. In support of this motion, Defendant TSOOTBG states:

Defendant TSOOTBG has never conducted business in Missouri. The only activity engaged in by TSOOTBG having anything to do with Missouri was the ad placed in co-defendant Sporting News' publication and the use of a weblog that is, of course, accessible across the globe and in the State of Missouri. TSOOTBG has not done business or other activity that would create a nexus with the State of Missouri such that the Court may exercise personal jurisdiction over Defendant in this state and judicial district consistent with the minimum contacts requirement of the Due Process Clause of the United States Constitution.

WHEREFORE, Defendant TSOOTBG prays the Court will dismiss this action and award Defendant costs and expenses and such further and other relief as the Court deems appropriate in this matter.

Respectfully Submitted,

DEAN, SLAUGHTER,
SCHOENDIENST & GIBSON

By:_____

Robert Gibson, Mo. Bar No. 32244
201 Market Street, Suite 200
St. Louis, MO 63101
Phone: (888) 555-2006
Fax: (888) 555-1982

Attorneys for Defendant TSOOTBG

UNITED STATES DISTRICT COURT
EASTERN DISTRICT OF MISSOURI
EASTERN DIVISION

ROGER CLEMENS,	)	
	)	
Plaintiff,	)	No. 04-C-9345 (DJS)
v.	)	Hon. Donald J. Stohr
	)	
TAKE STEROIDS OUT	)	
OF THE BALL	)	
GAME, INC., and	)	
SPORTING NEWS,	)	
	)	
Defendants.	)	

DECLARATION OF MARCUS McWIRE

I, Marcus McWire, of lawful age, do swear under penalty of perjury of the laws of the United States and the State of Illinois that I have first hand information concerning the following and the following information is true and correct:

1. I am 42 years old. I am a citizen and resident of Illinois.

2. I am the owner and sole shareholder in and sole officer of the corporation Take Steroids Out of the Ball Game, Inc. ("TSOOTBG"). TSOOTBG was formed on December 12, 2007, by being incorporated on December 12, 2007, and has only existed from that date to the present.

3. TSOOTBG has never conducted business in Missouri.

4. The only activity engaged in by TSOOTBG having anything to do with Missouri was the ad placed in co-defendant Sporting News' publication on December 31, 2007, and the use of a weblog, tsootbg. blogspot.com, created on January 14, 2008. The weblog is, of course, accessible across the globe and in the State of Missouri. The weblog has several alternative addresses: www.RogerClemensComeClean.com, www. RogerClemensHallofFame?.com, www.RogerClemensJuiced.com, and www.RogerClemensSteroidUser.com. All of these web addresses direct users to the tsootbg.blogspot.com weblog.

5. Since creating the weblog, the weblog has received five "visits" from separate individuals who are resident in Missouri. One individual from Missouri visited the site four times and contacted me through PayPal offering to make a $50 donation. This donation has not occurred to date.

6. TSOOTBG has no other activities or contacts with the State of Missouri.

7. TSOOTBG is a not-for-profit tax exempt entity that engages in no commercial activity nor in any activity for profit or gain. In the short time it has existed, it has solely sought to put pressure on Major League Baseball to take action to eliminate steroids from baseball by doing the limited activities described in paragraph 4 above.

FURTHER DECLARANT SAYETH NAUGHT.

Sworn to under penalty of perjury on this 21st day of January, 2008.

Marcus McWire

IV.   MOTIONS FOR SUMMARY JUDGMENT (*Advanced Legal Writing and Oral Advocacy: Trials, Appeals, and Moot Court*, Chapter 4)

WRITING PROBLEM

1. Based on the following information, prepare a memorandum in support of the motion for summary judgment or a memorandum in opposition to this motion depending on whichever side you are assigned or choose to represent.

MEMORANDUM

TO: Junior Associate

FROM: Senior Partner

DATE: January 13, 2009

RE: <u>Abraham Baum v. York Media Holdings, LLC</u>

SUBJECT: Motion for Summary Judgment

Our client is involved in a lawsuit—see attached documents. Defendant York Media Holdings is moving for summary judgment on the complaint. Please prepare a memorandum of law in support of (or in opposition to) the motion.

UNITED STATES DISTRICT COURT
SOUTHERN DISTRICT OF NEW YORK
SOUTHERN DIVISION

ABRAHAM BAUM,   )
)
           Plaintiff,   )
       v.   )   NO. 09-CIV-123 (PKL)
YORK MEDIA HOLDINGS, LLC,)
D/B/A YORK MAGAZINE,   )
)
           Defendant.   )

DEFENDANT YORK MEDIA HOLDINGS' MOTION FOR SUMMARY JUDGMENT

NOW COMES defendant York Media Holdings, LLC ("YMH"), and moves this Court pursuant to Fed. R. Civ. P. 56 for summary judgment on plaintiff's complaint. In support of this motion, YMH states:

As provided in the memoranda of law and attachments submitted herewith, YMH has stipulated to all of the relevant, pertinent, material facts of the complaint, and YMH is entitled to judgment as a matter of law on the sole claim asserted by Plaintiff Baum ("Baum") against YMH. Baum alleges that YMH violated N.Y. Civ. Rights Law §§ 50, 51 (McKinney 2005) when YMH took photographs of Baum on a public street and used them in connection with a news story concerning the effect of the economic climate on the business district and industry in New York City where Baum owns a business and is employed. Furthermore, YMH used the same images incorporated into a newsworthy cover collage as examples of the quality and nature of the contents of its publication in advertising in its magazine, and further used a transformed version of the image of Baum from the newsworthy cover collage in advertising to further reference the quality, contents, and potential readership of YMH's magazine.

Section 51 of the Civil Rights Law is applicable to this private cause of action, and it requires:

> Any person whose name, portrait, picture or voice is used within this state *for advertising purposes or for the purposes of trade* without the written consent first obtained . . . may maintain an equitable action in the supreme court of this state against the person, firm or corporation so using his name, portrait, picture or voice, to prevent and restrain the use thereof . . .

Id. (emphasis added).

YMH did not use the image and likeness of Baum for advertising purposes or for purposes of trade within the meaning of the Civil Rights Law when read in conjunction with the protections of the First Amendment of the United States Constitution whether in the initial use or in the subsequent incidental advertising uses. Therefore, on its face, the complaint fails to state a cause of action upon which relief may be granted and YMH is entitled to judgment as a matter of law on the complaint.

WHEREFORE, Defendant York Media Holdings, LLC, prays the Court will grant summary judgment in its favor and against plaintiff Baum on the sole count and any and all claims asserted in his complaint, and award York Media Holdings, LLC, its costs and expenses and such further and other relief as the Court deems appropriate in this matter.

Respectfully Submitted,

By:_____

Katherine Ivana Weinstein*
Lawrence C. Korn*
Miller, Tolles & Olson LLP
1355 South Grand Avenue
Los Angeles, CA 90071
(213) 678-9100

Attorneys for Defendant York
Media Holdings, LLC

*Appearing Pro Hac Vice by
order of this Court dated
January 12, 2009.

UNITED STATES DISTRICT COURT
SOUTHERN DISTRICT OF NEW YORK
SOUTHERN DIVISION

ABRAHAM BAUM,	)	
	)	
Plaintiff,	)	
	)	
v.	)	NO. 09-CIV-123 (PKL)
YORK MEDIA HOLDINGS, LLC,	)	Jury Trial Demanded
D/B/A YORK MAGAZINE,	)	
	)	
Defendant.	)	

COMPLAINT

NOW COMES plaintiff Abraham Baum ("Baum"), and for his complaint against defendant York Media Holdings, LLC ("York Media"), doing business as "York Magazine," states as follows:

1. Plaintiff Baum is a citizen and resident of the State of New York. Baum is the owner and operator of Abraham Baum Fine Diamonds and Gem Cutting, an S corporation organized and existing under the laws of the State of New York, located at 132 Delancey Street, New York, NY 10002. Baum resides in the Borough of Brooklyn in the area of Williamsburg, at 210 Broadway, Brooklyn, NY 11211.

2. Defendant York Media is a Delaware corporation with its principal place of business in the State of New Jersey. York Media regularly, consistently, and systematically performs business in the State of New York and in this district most obviously through the publication and distribution of its media publications such as York Magazine.

3. Jurisdiction is appropriate in this district under 28 U.S.C. § 1332 because the citizenship of the parties is diverse and plaintiff seeks more than $75,000 in damages. Venue is appropriate in this district

under 28 U.S.C. § 1391 because all of the transactions and events leading to this action and all or most all of the actions causing the injuries to plaintiff were undertaken in this district

COUNT I

4. In November 2008, agents of York Media surreptitiously took a photograph of Baum as he was leaving his place of business.

5. York Media used this photograph on the cover of its publication York Magazine in the December 9, 2008, issue of that magazine.

6. York Media further used this photograph in two commercial advertisements for its York Magazine publication that ran in the December 29, 2008, issue of the magazine and the January 5, 2009, issue of the magazine

7. York Media further distorted and caricatured the image and likeness of Baum by making a cartoon of Baum's face and putting it on a cartoon body and identifying Baum by his first name ("Abe") in the commercial advertisement.

8. York Media did not seek or obtain consent to photograph Baum nor did it seek or obtain consent to use any photograph or image or likeness or the first name of Baum accompanying any image or likeness of Baum in any commercial advertisement or for any use whatsoever.

9. The photographic image and the caricature of Baum as presented and depicted on the cover of York Magazine and in its commercial advertisements is unmistakenly and readily identifiable as that of plaintiff Baum.

10. York Media's publication York Magazine is a general entertainment publication of general and widespread circulation. It is read by tens of thousands of persons in and out of New York, but particularly, it is read by hundreds or thousands of persons in the area of New York City where Baum lives, works, and resides. Furthermore, the commercial advertisements for York Magazine were displayed throughout the boroughs of New York on billboards and on the sides of public transportation buses and in advertising placards in the New York City Subway system.

11. Plaintiff Baum is an Orthodox Hasidic Jew and a member of the Klausenberg Sect, a sect that was almost completely destroyed during the Holocaust. He holds a deep religious conviction that the use of his image for commercial and public purposes violates his religion. In particular he believes that defendants' use of his image violates the Second Commandment prohibition (from the Book of Exodus) against creation and use of graven images.

12. Not only is the use of the image and likeness of Baum in the ways that York Media has used it singularly offensive and inappropriate to Baum and the members of his sect, but the use of the image and caricature of Baum's likeness in combination with the uses of images and caricatures of other, famous New York figures (Robby Day, the famous New York chef who is promoted and self-promoted on cable television's The Food Network and other media; Namon Street, the internationally famous star of Broadway theater, television, and major motion pictures; and Carlita Clausberg, the internationally famous fashion model), all of whose images are used in combination and conjunction with Baum's image, sends the message that Baum intends for his image to be used in the same splashy, promotional (or self-promotional), celebratory ways that the images of the other famous New Yorkers are regularly used in national, international, and local media.

13. York Media's uses of the photographic image and likeness of Baum and its uses of the caricatured image of Baum has caused serious emotional distress, embarrassment, loss of sleep, and other emotional injuries to Baum. Furthermore, most of Baum's cliental in his business are other Orthodox Hasidic Jews who do not approve of the use of a personal image in the ways undertaken by York Media, and therefore York Media has caused business losses to plaintiff Baum. These injuries and losses are on-going, and the injuries and losses to Baum's reputation are irreparable. The equities of the situation described in this complaint favor Baum over York Media.

14. When Baum first discovered that the photograph of his image was being used by York Media in December 2008, he immediately contacted York Media regarding the use. York Media responded that the photographs were not being used for either "advertising" or "trade" and that it believed it was within its legal rights to continue to use the photograph and caricature of plaintiff in the ways that it had been using them. This action ensued.

15. York Media violated N.Y. Civ. Rights Law §§ 50, 51 (McKinney 2005) when it took a photograph of Baum and used it on the cover of York Magazine. It further violated N.Y. Civ. Rights Law §§ 50, 51 when it used the photographic image of Baum in a commercial advertisement for York Magazine, and further violated N.Y. Civ. Rights Law §§ 50, 51 when it used a caricature of the image and likeness of Baum in a commercial advertisement for York Magazine. The image and likeness and first name ("Abe") of Baum were "used within this state for advertising purposes or for the purposes of trade without the written consent first obtained" of plaintiff Baum within the meaning and application of Section 51 of the Civil Rights Law.

WHEREFORE, for the reasons stated above, Baum prays the Court will award him the following relief:

(1) A preliminary and permanent injunction against any use by defendant York Media of the image, likeness, photograph, or caricature of plaintiff Baum;

(2) Monetary compensation and damages in an amount not less than $500,000;

(3) Exemplary and punitive damages in an amount not less than $2,000,000;

(4) Such further and other relief as the Court deems appropriate in this matter.

PLAINTIFF DEMANDS TRIAL BY JURY.

Respectfully submitted,

By:_____

Jerry Goldstein   NY Bar #234566
Law Offices of Jerry Goldstein LLP
24 Delancey Street
New York, NY 10002
Tel: (212) 555-SU4U
Fax: (212) 555-PAYU

Attorney for plaintiff Abraham Baum

UNITED STATES DISTRICT COURT
SOUTHERN DISTRICT OF NEW YORK
SOUTHERN DIVISION

ABRAHAM BAUM,   )
)
            Plaintiff,   )
)
        v.   )   NO. 09-CIV-123 (PKL)
)
YORK MEDIA HOLDINGS, LLC,)
D/B/A YORK MAGAZINE,   )
)
            Defendant.   )

STIPULATION OF FACTS

NOW COME plaintiff Abraham Baum ("Baum"), and defendant York Media Holdings, LLC ("York Media"), doing business as "York Magazine," who stipulate to the following facts:

1. Plaintiff Baum is a citizen and resident of the State of New York. Baum is the owner and operator of Abraham Baum Fine Diamonds and Gem Cutting, an S corporation organized and existing under the laws of the State of New York, located at 132 Delancey Street, New York, NY 10002. Baum resides in the Borough of Brooklyn in the area of Williamsburg, at 210 Broadway, Brooklyn, NY 11211.

2. Defendant York Media is a Delaware corporation with its principal place of business in the State of New Jersey. York Media regularly, consistently, and systematically performs business in the State of New York and in this district most obviously through the publication and distribution of its media publications such as York Magazine.

3. Jurisdiction is appropriate in this district under 28 U.S.C. § 1332 because the citizenship of the parties is diverse and plaintiff seeks

more than $75,000 in damages. Venue is appropriate in this district under 28 U.S.C. § 1391 because all of the transactions and events alleged to be connected to this action were undertaken in this district.

4. In November 2008, a photographer working for York Media took a photograph of Baum as he was leaving his place of business and walking on a public sidewalk on a public street in New York City. Baum was unaware that the photographer had taken his photograph.

5. York Media used this photograph on the cover of its publication York Magazine in the December 9, 2008, issue of that magazine. The December 9, 2008, issue of the magazine contained a story concerning the effect of the 2008 economic climate on the diamond district and diamond sales and gem cutting industry in New York City. Baum owns a diamond and gem cutting business and is employed in the diamond district and in the diamond and gem cutting industry.

6. York Media further used Baum's photograph as depicted on the cover of the December 9, 2008, issue of York Magazine in two subscription page advertisements for its York Magazine publication that ran in the December 29, 2008, issue of the magazine and the January 5, 2009, issue of the magazine.

7. York Media further used and caricatured the image and likeness of Baum by making a cartoon of Baum's face and putting it on a cartoon body and identifying Baum by his first name ("Abe") in the January 2009 subscription page advertisement.

8. York Media did not seek or obtain consent to photograph Baum nor did it seek or obtain consent to use any photograph or image or likeness or the first name of Baum accompanying any image or likeness of Baum in any advertisement or for any use whatsoever.

9. The photographic images and the caricature of Baum as presented and depicted in YMH's commercial advertisements are readily identifiable as reflecting the image and likeness of plaintiff Baum.

10. York Media's publication York Magazine is a biweekly periodical publication of general and widespread circulation. It is read by tens of thousands of persons in and out of New York State, but particularly, it is read by persons in the area of New York City where Baum lives, works, and resides. Furthermore, the advertisements for York Magazine were displayed throughout the boroughs of New York on billboards and on the sides of public transportation buses and in advertising placards in the New York City Subway system.

11. Plaintiff Baum is an Orthodox Hasidic Jew and a member of the Klausenberg Sect. He holds a deep religious conviction that the use of his image for commercial and public purposes violates his religion. In particular he believes that York Media's use of his image violates the Second Commandment prohibition (from the Book of Exodus) against creation and use of graven images.

12. Baum's image and caricature was used in combination with the uses of images and caricatures of other, famous New York figures: Robby Day, the famous New York chef; Namon Street, the famous actor and star of Broadway theater, television, and major motion pictures; and Carlita Clausberg, the internationally famous fashion model. All of these persons' images are used in combination and conjunction with Baum's image.

13. When Baum discovered that the photograph of his image was being used by York Media in December 2008, he immediately contacted York Media regarding the use. York Media responded that the photographs were not being used for either "advertising" or "trade" and that it

believed it was within its legal rights to continue to use the photograph and caricature of plaintiff in the ways that it had been using them. This action ensued.

Respectfully submitted,

By:_____

Jerry Goldstein   NY Bar #234566
Law Offices of Jerry Goldstein LLP
24 Delancey Street
New York, NY 10002
Tel: (212) 555-SU4U
Fax: (212) 555-PAYU

Attorney for plaintiff Abraham Baum

By:_____

Katherine Ivana Weinstein
Lawrence C. Korn
Miller, Tolles & Olson LLP
1355 South Grand Avenue
Los Angeles, CA 90071
(213) 678-9100

Attorneys for Defendant
York Media Holdings, LLC

V.   APPELLATE ADVOCACY: APPEALS, WRITS, AND STANDARDS OF REVIEW (*Advanced Legal Writing and Oral Advocacy: Trials, Appeals, and Moot Court*, Chapter 5)

WRITING PROBLEMS

1. Evaluate the following questions presented from four appellate briefs drafted for submission in the United States Supreme Court. Identify what each does well (if anything) and what you would edit or revise (if anything) in each:

a. Brief of Petitioner in the moot court case: Metropolitan School Dist. of Gotham v. Branch Louisian of the United Church of Christ the Savior

QUESTIONS PRESENTED FOR REVIEW

I.   Whether a public school district violates a religious organization's First Amendment free speech rights by refusing to post information regarding creationism on the school district's web site created to further the educational mission of the school district?

II. Whether a public school district violates the First Amendment's Establishment Clause by sponsoring a religious web page on the district's web site created to increase the educational opportunities for students on topics within the curriculum?

b. Brief of Respondent in the moot court case: Metropolitan School Dist. of Gotham v. Branch Louisian of the United Church of Christ the Savior

QUESTIONS PRESENTED FOR REVIEW

1.   Whether the Fourteenth Circuit Appellate Court erred in holding that Petitioner violated the First Amendment by denying Respondent access to its web site solely on the basis of the religious content of its proposal?

2.   Whether the Fourteenth Circuit Appellate Court erred in holding that Petitioner's conduct in initiating a web site, open for general use to all members of the community, created a limited public forum for the purpose of the right to free speech under the First Amendment?

3.   Whether the Fourteenth Circuit Appellate Court erred in holding that Petitioner's denial of Respondent's proposal, based upon its religious content, is in violation of the First Amendment regardless of the type of forum because the denial constitutes viewpoint discrimination?

4. Whether the Fourteenth Circuit Appellate Court erred in holding that the hosting of Respondent's creationism web pages on Petitioner's web site did not violate the Establishment Clause?

c. Brief of Petitioner in the U.S. Supreme Court case: <u>Capitol Square Review and Advisory Board v. Pinette</u>, 515 U.S. 753 (1995)

QUESTION PRESENTED FOR REVIEW

Whether the unattended display on government property of a purely religious symbol, such as a large, Latin cross, directly in front of a seat of government, such as the Ohio statehouse, violates the establishment clause, even if such display is sponsored by a private group in a public forum?

d. Brief of Respondents in the U.S. Supreme Court case: <u>Capitol Square Review and Advisory Board v. Pinette</u>, 515 U.S. 753 (1995)

QUESTION PRESENTED FOR REVIEW

Whether the temporary, unattended display of a Ku Klux Klan cross on a public forum open to all other political and religious expression violates the Establishment Clause solely because the public forum is in proximity to the seat of government.

2. Evaluate the following statements of the case from four appellate briefs. Identify what each does well (if anything) and what you would edit or revise (if anything) in each:

a. Brief of Petitioner in the moot court case: Metropolitan School Dist. of Gotham v. Branch Louisian of the United Church of Christ the Savior

STATEMENT OF THE CASE

Respondent, Branch Louisian of the United Church of Christ the Savior ("Church"), filed a complaint under 42 U.S.C. § 1983 against

Petitioner, the Metropolitan School District of Gotham, State of New Kent ("School District"), claiming the School District violated Church's rights under the Free Speech and Establishment clauses of the United States Constitution, Amendment I, by refusing to allow the Church's religious web pages on the topic of creationism to be displayed on the School District's Internet web site. (R. at 3.) The District Court of New Kent ruled in favor of the School District and denied Church's Motion for Summary Judgment. (R. at 9.) The Church appealed. The United States Court of Appeals for the Fourteenth Circuit reversed the District Court's decision. (R. at 21.) This Court granted certiorari. (R. at 22.)

Petitioner began operating as an Internet service provider and managing a web server for the purpose of promoting information about the areas of study currently being taught in the School District. (R. at 11.) The School District invites faculty of the School District and other educational institutions in Gotham to propose web pages for inclusion in the site. (R. at 11.) Any entity seeking access to the web site must submit a proposal to the School District. (R. at 11.) The School District then reviews the proposals and determines whether access should be granted based upon whether the web pages are directly related to a topic currently included in the School District's curriculum guide. (R. at 11.)

The School District's home page contains an alphabetical listing of all sponsored web sites and pages that have been accepted and linked to the School District's web page. (R. at 12.) Each listing includes a small icon designed by the creator of the sponsored pages, the title of the web site, a short description of the contents of the pages, and a link to the actual "http" address of the pages. (R. at 12.)

Church applied to the School District for permission to post its web site on March 5, 1999. (R. at 13.) The Church described the proposal as a "thorough examination of the doctrine of Creationism from the Book of Genesis in the Bible… and a comparison and contrasting …with the purportedly scientific doctrines of Evolution and Natural Selection." (R. at 13.) The proposal also included commentary from religious leaders about creationism in text, audio, and video formats and religious depictions of the story of creation in Genesis. (R. at 13.) The School District rejected the proposal because the topic did not directly relate to a subject included in School District's curriculum guide. (R. at 14.)

b. Brief of Respondent in the moot court case: Metropolitan School Dist. of Gotham v. Branch Louisian of the United Church of Christ the Savior

STATEMENT OF THE CASE

Petitioner School District ("Petitioner") is a political subdivision of the State of New Kent. (Record of Transcript [R.] at 10). For the last 150 years, Petitioner has operated all of the public schools in Gotham, New Kent. (R. at 10-11). Petitioner brings this case to the United States Supreme Court on appeal from a decision of the United States Court of Appeals for the Fourteenth Circuit. This Appellant Court found for Respondent, Branch Louisian of the United Church of Christ the Savior ("Respondent"), a religious organization, registered and operating in the State of New Kent. Respondent, a proponent of Judeo-Christian doctrine of Creationism, conducts religious education and worship services each week in a church located in Gotham, New Kent. (R. at 4, 10).

Petitioner is an Internet service provider and hosts web sites from sources outside of the School District system. (R. at 4). Petitioner began operating as an Internet service provider in June 1998. (R. at 11). Petitioner manages the Internet server and operates a web site for the purpose of hosting other web pages on its site. (R. at 11). The home page site reads:

> This site was created by the [School District] for the purpose of promoting information about the areas of study that are currently being taught in the schools of the [School District]. The pages we hope to sponsor will not only highlight topics of interest in the curriculum of the [School District], but also provide resources and information and links to other sources of information that may not be available in the textbooks and other materials provided to our students in the courses taught in the [School District]. In this spirit of expanding the educational potential of this site, we invite faculty of the [School District] and other educational institutions in Gotham, members of the community, and other organizations to propose web pages

for inclusion in the site, as long as the subject matter of each page is tied to topic of education in this [School District]." (R. at 11).

All persons seeking inclusion in the site must submit a written proposal to Petitioner for review describing in detail the title and contents of the proposal. (R. at 11). Petitioner will also review the web site periodically to insure the pages posted on the site meet the requirement being "tied to a topic of education" in the School District's curriculum and are created in such a way "as to uphold the high academic standards of the School District." (R. at 11).

On March 5, 1999, Respondent made a proposal for Petitioner to host its web site on the subject of "Theological Anthropology" the title of which was "Creationism: Past and Present." (R. at 13). The proposal was further described as an examination of the doctrine of Creationism from the Book of Genesis and a comparison and contrasting of the "purportedly scientific" doctrines of Evolution and Natural Selection. (R. at 13). The contents of the proposal were described as a multimedia presentation of commentary from scholars and educators regarding the doctrine of Creationism and five centuries of religious artwork regarding the doctrine of Creationism. (R. at 13). On March 7, 1999, Petitioner denied Respondent's proposal stating that, "its subject matter is not directly related to a topic of education in the district." (R. at 14). On March 11, 1999, Respondent resubmitted its proposal but changed the description of the subject matter to "Social Studies" and "Sociology". (R. at 14) On March 12, 1999, Petitioner once again denied Respondent's proposal on the same grounds as stated before. (R. at 14).

The topics of "Social Studies" and "Sociology" are topics listed under the School District's curriculum guide, however, they do not encompass the topics of Theology, Anthropology, or anything relating to Creationism. (R. at 14). On the other hand, the curriculum guide does include the Darwinian theories of Evolution and Natural Selection, which are currently taught in Biology courses in the School District and have been taught in the District since 1922. (R. at 14-15). Prior to Respondent's proposal, Petitioner had never rejected a proposed web page form a member of the community. (R. at 15). A variety of web pages created by entities having no affiliation with the School District are currently being sponsored on Petitioner's web site. (R. at 12). These entities include, but are not limited to, The Council for Alternative Dispute Resolution with a site on health that features an interview with its founder and director, Reverend Carla Boulevardier, Pastor of St. Peter's AME Church of Gotham, and The Greater Gotham Youth League with a site on health that features an article on suicide written by Fr. John Berrigan, a Roman Catholic Priest of the Gotham Cathedral Church. (R. at 13).

Respondent has made several additional oral requests to have its web pages posted on the Petitioner's web site. Each request was denied. In the hope of exercising its constitutional right to free speech, Respondent filed this lawsuit against the School District on May 15, 1999.

c. Brief of Petitioner in the U.S. Supreme Court case: <u>Capitol Square Review and Advisory Board v. Pinette</u>, 515 U.S. 753 (1995)

STATEMENT OF THE CASE

1. Respondents in this action, the Knights of the Ku Klux Klan (Ohio Realm) and two of their officers, brought this suit originally against the Capitol Square Review and Advisory Board, its executive director, spokesperson, and chairperson. Joint Appendix (J.A. 22-23). The lawsuit sought in effect to compel the State of Ohio to allow Respondents to erect a large, unattended Latin cross directly in front of the Ohio Statehouse during the Christmas season, between December 8, 1993, and December 24, 1993. (J.A. 26). Respondents openly acknowledged that their purpose in seeking to erect the display at this location was to erect "a symbol for our Lord, Jesus Christ" (J.A. 173) in furtherance of their more general purpose to "establish a Christian government in America." (J.A. 144-147).

2. The Capitol Square is owned by the State of Ohio and located in downtown Columbus. It is the site of Ohio's state capitol building, also known as the Ohio Statehouse, which is a large rectangular building that centers the Capitol Square. The Ohio Statehouse, which is a distinctive example of Greek Doric architecture, is topped by a large rotunda. For well over a century, it has housed both chambers of the Ohio General Assembly as well as the offices of the Ohio Governor and other statewide officeholders. (J.A. 96-97). The Ohio Statehouse is the dominant feature of the Capitol Square, and it is plainly and unavoidably visible from every

vantage point on the Capitol Square. See App. A43 (photograph). The District Court held in this case that the Capitol Square is a public forum. See App. A18.

For the past several years, the State of Ohio has allowed certain holiday seasonal displays to be placed on the Capitol Square for limited periods during the month of December. (J.A. 98). The State's traditional policy is to allow a broad range of speakers and other gatherings of people to conduct events on the Capitol Square. (J.A. 98). These displays are generally an exception to that policy because they are unattended structures. The holiday seasonal displays permitted by the State in the past have included a Christmas tree and a menorah. (J.A. 98).

On November 18, 1993, the Capitol Square Review and Advisory Board, which is authorized by law to regulate the uses of the Capitol Square, voted not to permit unattended displays on the Capitol Square during December of 1993. (J.A. 98). That vote was later declared invalid, and on November 23, 1993, the Board voted to approve displays of a Christmas tree and menorah. (J.A. 98-99). The State displayed its own Christmas tree, and a permit application to erect a menorah on the Capitol Square from December 8-16, 1993, which was explicitly stated to be a "seasonal display," was granted. (J.A. 99).

3. On November 29, 1993, Respondents applied for a permit to display a cross on the Capitol Square from December 8-24, 1993. (J.A. 99). The application described the type of event as being to "erect a cross for Christmas." (J.A. 99). Executive Director Keller denied the application on December 3, 1993, "upon the advice of counsel, in a good faith attempt to comply with the Ohio and United States Constitutions, as they have been interpreted in relevant decisions by the Federal and State Courts." (J.A. 99). Respondents later clarified that they sought to erect a cross in the style of a Latin cross,[1] about ten feet high and six feet across and accompanied by a suggested disclaimer open to negotiation. (J.A. 100).

---

1   "Latin cross" is the proper term for any "cross whose base stem is longer than the other three arms." American Civil Liberties Union v. City of St. Charles, 794 F.2d 265, 271, cert. denied, 479 U.S. 961 (1986) (affirming preliminary injunction against display of lighted Latin cross on top of city fire department building during Christmas season because it would violate the Establishment Clause).

On December 9, 1993, Respondents filed an administrative appeal of this action to the full Board; the appeal was perfected on December 13, 1993. (J.A. 100-101). On December 17, 1993, a state administrative appeal was conducted by a hearing examiner who took evidence and heard argument from both sides. On December 21, 1993, the administrative hearing examiner issued a report and recommendation which found that the initial denial of a permit to Respondents was proper. App. A27. The hearing examiner held, among other things, that whereas holiday seasonal symbols have by virtue of that association taken on "cultural significance extending well beyond the religious sphere," the Latin cross "is generally regarded as having a purely sectarian purpose (i.e., to advance or endorse the Christian religion)." App. A34-A35. For that reason, the display of a Latin cross directly in front of the Ohio Statehouse, unlike the display of a Christmas tree or a menorah, was held to violate the Establishment Clause. App. A36. The Board unanimously adopted this report and recommendation as its own final ruling later that day. App. A16.

4. In the meantime, on December 15, 1993, Respondents filed this lawsuit in District court, asserting that the denial of their application for permit to erect a cross violated their constitutional right of free speech. (J.A. 27). The court set the matter for hearing on December 20, 1993, and consolidated the hearing on Respondents' motion for a preliminary injunction with a trial on the merits. At the close of this hearing, the court deferred its ruling pending the outcome of the state administrative appeal process. Once that process was completed on December 21, 1993, the court granted a permanent injunction requiring Petitioners to approve a permit for Respondents to display a cross on the Capitol Square through December 24, 1993. App. A26.

In its ruling, the District Court considered whether Respondents' display of a large, unattended Latin cross directly in front of the Ohio Statehouse would constitute an impermissible "endorsement" of religion under Lemon v. Kurtzman, 403 U.S. 602 (1971), as subsequently interpreted and applied in such "holiday seasonal display" cases as Lynch v. Donnelly, 465 U.S. 668 (1984), and County of Allegheny v. American Civil Liberties Union, 492 U.S. 573 (1989). On the basis of a recent en banc decision by the Sixth Circuit Court of Appeals that addressed essentially the same issue, Americans United for Separation of Church & State

v. Grand Rapids, 980 F.2d 1538 (6th Cir. 1993) (en banc), the District Court held that the unattended religious display in this case would not constitute an impermissible endorsement of religion so as to violate the Establishment Clause. App. A7-A8.

5. Immediately after the District Court issued its ruling, Petitioners moved for a stay pending appeal, which the court denied. Petitioners filed a Notice of Appeal to the Sixth Circuit on the same day -- December 21, 1993 -- and filed a motion for an emergency stay of the injunction pending appeal, which the Sixth Circuit denied on December 22, 1993. App. A40. Petitioners then filed an emergency application for a stay of injunction with Circuit Justice Stevens, which was denied on December 23, 1993. App. A38.

6. Respondents erected a cross on the Capitol Square sometime during the night of December 21, 1993, and it was displayed there the following day until it was apparently vandalized. The cross was displayed by itself in the middle of the lawn directly in front of the Ohio Statehouse, see App. A43 (photograph), located at some distance from the Christmas tree.[2] On December 22, 1993, Petitioners received yet another application from a group of Christian ministers, who sought to erect twenty more Latin crosses in front of the Ohio Statehouse. Petitioners believed themselves obligated, by the force of the District Court's ruling, to grant this further application, and thereafter numerous other crosses were erected and displayed in the same vicinity on December 23-24, 1993. (J.A. 60) (Appendix to Brief In Opposition To Writ Of Certiorari p. RA 31 ("Opp. App.")).

7. On appeal, the Sixth Circuit affirmed the District Court's ruling. App. A1. The Sixth Circuit adhered to its recent en banc decision in Americans United, which "held that a private organization's unattended display of a religious symbol in a public forum does not violate the Establishment Clause." App. A8. The court focused in particular on the nature of the display and the nature of the forum. It essentially held that because this display was privately sponsored, it did not matter what was contained in the display -- for example, a Latin cross in this case as opposed to a menorah in cases like Americans United and County of Allegheny. Because

---

2   The menorah had been removed almost a week earlier, when that permit expired on December 16, 1993.

this display was to be located in a public forum, moreover, it did not matter what kind of location was to exhibit the display -- for example, the Ohio Statehouse in this case as opposed to a public park in cases like Americans United and Lynch. The Sixth Circuit thus determined that a reasonable observer could not conclude that the State of Ohio endorsed Christianity after viewing a large, unattended Latin cross standing directly in front of the Ohio Statehouse because "truly private religious expression in a truly public forum cannot be seen as endorsement by a reasonable observer." App. A9 (quoting Americans United, 980 F.2d at 1553) (emphasis in original). On this ground, the Sixth Circuit held that Respondents' display of a Latin cross directly in front of the Ohio Statehouse did not constitute an impermissible endorsement of religion under the Establishment Clause.

d. Brief of Respondents in the U.S. Supreme Court case: <u>Capitol Square Review and Advisory Board v. Pinette</u>, 515 U.S. 753 (1995)

STATEMENT OF THE CASE

The Knights of the Ku Klux Klan filed this case on December 15, 1993, to challenge, inter alia, the discriminatory refusal of the Capitol Square Review and Advisory Board[3] to grant a permit allowing display of a Ku Klux Klan cross on the public forum on the west side of the Capitol Building in Columbus, Ohio. Hearings to consider the Plaintiffs' requests for injunctive relief were held on December 20-21, 1993, and on January 3, 1994. The order that is the subject of the Petition was entered on December 21, 1993.

a. Background

On October 29, 1993, prior to initiating this case, the Knights of the Ku Klux Klan had applied for a permit to hold a public assembly in the Capitol Square forum. The purpose of the public assembly, which the Klan planned to hold the following January 15, 1994, was to express the organization's political views.

---

3   The Capitol Square Review and Advisory Board is alternatively referred to as the "Board" or the "State" in this brief.

On November 18, 1993, while the application for the January 15th rally was still under consideration, the members of the Capitol Square Review Board met in executive session and discussed the issue of Ku Klux Klan access to the same forum during the holiday season. They feared that the Knights of the Ku Klux Klan might follow the example of another Klan group in Cincinnati by seeking to put up a Ku Klux Klan cross during the Christmas season. RA14, RA18; RA19-RA21. As a result of its discussion in executive session, the Board reconvened in public and voted sua sponte to bar display of both the State Christmas tree and the private display of the Lubavitch sect's menorah from Capitol Square during December 1993. A14. At the time, the Lubavitch Sect had not yet applied for its 1993 permit nor had the Klan yet sought a permit to erect a cross in Capitol Square. Nevertheless, the Petitioners decided to bar the Christmas tree and the anticipated Lubavitch display of its menorah solely to foreclose any claim to equal access that the Klan might present. RA12 (Plaintiffs' Exhibit 33, Broadcast No. 5).

The decision of the State to bar the tree and menorah resulted in a great public uproar. A statement was released by the Office of the Governor objecting to imposition of a ban on all symbols as a means to prevent display of a Klan cross. According to the statement, the "[p]eople of this great State think that we ought to have a Christmas tree and think that we ought to have a menorah at the Statehouse and so do we. We've had a Christmas tree at the Statehouse for tens of years, and you can't let a single group or groups of people dictate to the people of Ohio what they are and aren't going to do." RA14 (Plaintiffs' Exhibit 33, Broadcast No. 6, Statement of Mike Dawson, Press Secretary to the Governor.) Newspaper accounts described the Governor as "disappointed and upset." RA20 (Defendants' Exhibit D, The Columbus Dispatch, November 20, 1993, front page). The Governor was also quoted as saying: "The Board's initial decision was a mistake. I trust this matter will be resolved quickly." Id.

Consistent with these public statements, the Governor and the other State officials who appoint the members of the Board[4] signed and delivered to the Board a letter calling upon the Board to permit the tree and menorah. Id.; RA14; RA19-RA20; JA 167-168, TR I 94. The Board met in special session on November 23, 1993, and resolved into executive session. Immediately following the executive session, the Board

---

4   Ohio Revised Code Section 123.022.

reconvened in public to formally declare its earlier vote invalid. In addition, it approved the State display of its Christmas tree and the private display of a menorah by a nine-to-zero vote. A15; JA 167-168, TR I 94. The vote to approve both the Christmas tree and the menorah was made even though no permit applications for displays on the Capitol Square had been filed. The reason for the change in vote was explained by Board Chairperson Richard Finan (a Petitioner herein): "I've been in politics for twenty-one years. When you get a letter from the Governor, the Speaker, and the President of the Senate, you do respond," he said. RA16 (Plaintiffs' Exhibit 33, Broadcast No. 8).

b. Capitol Square Public Forum

The public forum in question is a large park-like area, a block wide, on one side of the State Capitol building in Columbus.[5] Temporary, unattended[6] displays have been permitted in the public forum for many years. For example, the State of Ohio has erected a Christmas tree annually and has hung a "Seasons Greetings" banner from two of the Statehouse's pillars. 2a. The Lubavitch sect has been granted annual permits to display a large Chanukah menorah in Capitol Square. A14. And, permission has been granted for secular displays, such as United Fund campaign "thermometers" and arts festivals exhibits and booths. JA 159-160. There is no rule or regulation that confines unattended displays to any particular time of year, and they have in fact been present at various times over the years. A16.

In addition to these unattended displays, Capitol Square has been the site of numerous speech activities including gay rights demonstrations, anti-war demonstrations, and religious rallies and marches. A18.

---

5   The forum area at issue in this case is one city block wide and approximately 240 feet deep, JA 96-97 (Stipulations, P12), about 3 1/2 acres. The entire Capitol Square block consists of ten acres, some 435,600 square feet. REDI REALTY ATLAS, City Map Volume I (22nd ed. 1991) p. 397. Views of the public forum are included at Brief of Petitioners, Appendix, at 1a (Plaintiffs' Supplemental Exhibit 104), 3a, (Plaintiffs' Supplemental Exhibit 106), JA 64 (Defendants' Supplemental Exhibit 109), and JA 65 (Defendants' Supplemental Exhibit 110).

6   As used in this brief, "unattended" means that the given display has been permitted to remain at least overnight without accompanying personnel or ongoing ceremonies.

It is undisputed that Capitol Square has "been used from time immemorial for all manner of public gatherings and demonstrations by groups of all kinds, including political parties, charitable and religious groups, labor unions, civil rights groups, and the proponents and opponents of all manner of social and political issues." RA6. As the District Court summarized the record, the Capitol Square "grounds have been made available for speeches and public gatherings by various groups advocating various causes both secular and religious." A14.

c.   Administration of the Capitol Square Forum

The Capitol Square Review and Advisory Board is authorized by law to regulate the uses of Capitol Square. Ohio Revised Code Section 123.022. According to Section 128-4-02 of the Ohio Administrative Code, "Capitol buildings and grounds are available for use by the public . . . for free discussion of public questions" if the applicant adheres to a stated procedure for requesting such use, and if the proposed use:

> (1) Does not interfere with the primary use of the capitol buildings or grounds;
> (2) Is appropriate to the physical context of the capitol buildings or grounds;
> (3) Does not unduly burden the managing authority;
> (4) Is not a hazard to the safety of the public or state employees; and
> (5) Does not expose the state to the likelihood of expenses and/or damages which cannot be recovered.A32 (Report and Recommendation of Hearing Examiner, Conclusions of Law, P2).

Ronald Keller, Executive Director of the Board, is responsible for management of the Capitol Square complex. In this capacity, he grants and denies permits for the use of Capitol Square. TR I 84-85; JA 97, Stipulations, P19. Persons desiring to use Capitol Square submit their requests on the Board's form, "Application For Permit to Use Statehouse Grounds." JA 99, (Stipulations, P27-28); JA 103-111 (Exh. 3,4).

d.   Display of the Menorah and the Tree

On November 29, 1993, Rabbi Chaim Capland submitted an official application for the display -- previously approved by the Board -- of a menorah on Capitol Square from December 8 through December 16, 1993, to coincide with the days of Chanukah. Keller issued Capland's permit on November 29, 1993, the same day the application was submitted. A15, JA 168-169, TR I 97-98. The menorah was erected at the Capitol Square on December 8, 1993.

The State Christmas tree was erected on December 7, 1993. A16.

e.   Denial of a Permit to Display the Ku Klux Klan Cross

The Klan's application for a permit to display its cross on the Capitol Square forum from December 8 through December 24 was also submitted on November 29, 1993. A15. The period covered by the application overlapped the period during which the menorah would be displayed. Executive Director Keller denied the Klan's application by letter of December 3, 1993. Id. Mr. Keller wrote that:

[The denial] . . . was made upon the advice of counsel, in a good faith attempt to comply with the Ohio and United States Constitutions, as they have been interpreted in relevant decisions by the Federal and State Courts. We would direct your attention in particular to controlling decisions recently rendered by the United States Supreme Court under the First Amendment to the United States Constitution.JA 91-93 (Plaintiffs' Exhibit 5); A15 (District Court Findings of Fact, P9).

The Klan filed an administrative appeal of the permit denial. Although the administrative appeal was denied on December 21, 1993, the hearing examiner concluded that:

The evidence adduced at the [administrative] hearing in this matter does not offer a complete explanation of the process or basis for the Board's denial of the Appellant's request. Board Executive Director Keller did, however, advise the Appellant that the Board denied its request on advice of counsel, who had raised constitutional objections to the request.

. . .A33 (Report and Recommendation of Hearing Examiner, Conclusions of Law, P4).

Respondents had filed the instant action prior to the issuance of the hearing examiner's report. On December 21, 1993, following the report, the District Court issued a permanent injunction ordering the State to grant a permit which would allow the Klan to display its cross through December 24. Pursuant to that injunction, the cross was set in place in the early morning hours of December 22, 1993. RA24-RA30 (Plaintiffs' Supplemental Exhibits 102, The Columbus Dispatch, December 23, 1993, front page, and 103, The [Akron] Beacon Journal, December 23, 1993, page B5). It was vandalized a short time later. RA28-RA29, RA31. Meanwhile, on December 22 the Board granted permits to several religious groups that applied to display crosses around the Klan Cross; the purpose of those crosses was to protest the presence of the Klan cross.

f. The Menorah as a Religious Symbol

At the hearing before the District Court, Cantor Jack Chomsky of Tifereth Israel Congregation in Columbus, Ohio, testified that the menorah permitted by the State of Ohio, like other Chanukah menorahs, "is a religious symbol. It is used in conjunction with fulfilling the obligations incumbent upon a Jew for the celebration of the festival of Chanukah." JA 152, TR I 70. Cantor Chomsky explained that Jews have an obligation to "put candles in it as appropriate, as prescribed by our tradition, and they recite blessings which state as part of the blessings that we were commanded to perform this act. Blessings such as this make this into very much a ritual act." JA 155, 75-76. Rabbi Harold Berman also stated that the menorah "is a religious symbol. . . ." JA 53.

g. The Klan Cross

Plaintiff Carr testified that he applied for a permit to display the Klan cross because he had heard that the State was going to permit a tree and a menorah but not a Klan cross. JA 134-137, TR I 42-44. Mr. Carr said that his motivation for filing the request was that "since we were being excluded by the city or the state, the Capitol Square Review and Advisory Board, that we would attempt to obtain a permit to erect a cross for the Christmas season." Id. Mr. Carr also testified that while the cross communicates a religious message, it also conveys a political message: "To us, it is a sacred symbol, but it is also a symbol of going against tyranny, a symbol of freedom." JA 142, TR I 51. He noted that the "Klan's use of the cross originated from the early Scottish clans in Scotland in the 1300's which used the cross as a symbol to rally the clans together to fight against their English oppressors." JA 143. And Mr. Carr observed "the cross was also incorporated in the Confederate battle flag. . . ." JA 150.

In addition, counsel for the Klan informed the State that accompanying the cross would be a disclaimer stating that "this cross was erected by private individuals without government support for the purpose of expressing respect for the holiday season and to assert the right of all religious views to be expressed on an equal basis on public property." A15-16.[7]

h. The Opinion of the District Court

In granting the injunction, the District Court found that the area in question was a traditional public forum, A18, that there was no policy against free-standing displays in Capitol Square, and that for many years a variety of unattended displays have been permitted on Capitol Square for limited periods, including, during December, a free-standing Christmas tree and a free-standing menorah. A16.

The Court observed that one of the Board's reasons for denying the Klan's application -- the purported failure of the Klan to post a bond -- was "not a proper ground for the denial of the permit . . ." and that the State "does not contend that the erection of a cross poses a security risk of any kind." A16. The Court concluded, based on all of the facts, that "the State of Ohio is in no way associating itself with the Klan's display," that there was no appearance of endorsement of religion, and that "the reasonable observer should conclude that the government is expressing its toleration of religious and secular pluralism" in the public forum. The Court then held that "freedom of speech would be meaningless if it did not apply to all groups, popular and unpopular alike." A26.

---

7   Counsel for the Klan also invited State suggestions concerning the content of the disclaimer. Id.

i. The Opinion of the Sixth Circuit

The Sixth Circuit affirmed the District Court on Free Speech, Free Exercise, and Equal Protection grounds. A6-A7, A11-A12. It rejected the Petitioners' claim that there was any endorsement of religion by the State in this case. Instead, it held that a reasonable observer could not conclude that the display of the Ku Klux Klan cross on Capitol Square was a state endorsement of religion. It also concluded that religious groups and groups communicating controversial or offensive messages could not be selectively denied access to a public forum in the name of the Establishment Clause. A11-A12.

---

3. Evaluate the following summaries of the argument from four appellate briefs. Identify what each does well (if anything) and what you would edit or revise (if anything) in each:

   a. **Brief of Petitioner in the moot court case: Metropolitan School Dist. of Gotham v. Branch Louisian of the United Church of Christ the Savior**

SUMMARY OF THE ARGUMENT

The Supreme Court should reverse the appellate court's judgment and grant summary judgment to School District because the School District has not infringed on Church's constitutionally protected free speech rights. The web site at issue is a nonpublic forum due to the control the School District maintained over the forum and because the forum was never opened to the general public. Additionally, the School District properly made a content-based, non-viewpoint centered discrimination of the Church's offered statement on creationism because creationism neither relates to any topic in the school district nor does creationism comport to the policy of the School District in teaching evolution. Finally, regardless of the forum or the type of discrimination, the School District's censorship survives strict scrutiny. Both the School District's interest in providing the best education for children and its duty to abide by the Establishment Clause of the Constitution are compelling state interests.

The censorship at issue was narrowly tailored to fulfill both of these interests as evidenced by the fact that this has been the only restriction of its kind since the inception of the web site.

The Supreme Court should reverse the appellate court's judgment and grant summary judgment to School District because sponsoring of the Church's religious web pages by the School District amounts to a violation of the Establishment Clause of the First Amendment of the Constitution. The Church's web pages are on creationism, a religious doctrine. The Establishment Clause is violated by the School District's sponsorship of the Church's web pages under any test this Court chooses to apply. Sponsoring of the web pages creates a coercive mechanism in which students are coerced to acknowledge the religious doctrine of the Church. The inclusion of the Church's religious web pages on the School District's home page lead a reasonable person to believe that the District is endorsing the religious doctrine of creationism. The purpose of the web server was to provide educational opportunities for the students. This secular purpose is subverted by inclusion of the Church's religious web pages and creating the effect of endorsement of creationism by the School District. The School District monitoring, reviewing, and surveillance of the sponsored web pages leads to an excessive governmental entanglement with the Church and thus a violation of the Establishment Clause if the School District sponsors the Church's web pages.

b. **Brief of Respondent in the moot court case: Metropolitan School Dist. of Gotham v. Branch Louisian of the United Church of Christ the Savior**

SUMMARY OF ARGUMENT

Although the constitutional issues raised pertaining to the right of Free Speech under the First Amendment and the requirement that there be a separation of church and state under the Establishment Clause are not so new, the issue of how these two vital constitutional components are addressed as they pertain to the internet is novel. The judgment of the Fourteenth Circuit Appellate Court should be affirmed because the Metropolitan School District's discriminatory exclusion of the Branch Louisian Church's proposed web pages, solely on the basis of religious content and ideology is in violation of the First Amendment's free speech clause and against public policy. The School District has created a public forum by initiating a web site open to all members of the community and other organizations for the purpose of promoting information regarding current curriculum and providing alternative sources of information that may not be available in the curriculum. Therefore, the School District's conduct in devising the web site for the sole purpose of expressive activities has created a designated public forum. Even if the District's web site is not found to be a pure designated public forum it must qualify as the subset, a limited public forum. Based upon finding the web site a limited public forum, the District's denial of the Respondent's web page solely based upon the religious content therein, constitutes content-based discrimination in violation of the First Amendment's Free Speech Clause. The School District's content-based exclusion of Respondent's web page from its public forum triggers a strict scrutiny analysis. The District offers no compelling state interest to justify content-based discrimination, therefore, the strict scrutiny standard cannot be met. Regardless of the nature of the forum, however, the District's conduct of excluding Respondent's web page based upon Respondent's religious ideology constitutes viewpoint discrimination which is a per se violation of the First Amendment's Free Speech Clause.

The Establishment Clause does not bar the Metropolitan School District from hosting a creationism web page as part of a curriculum focused web site. The inclusion of Respondent's web pages by the Metropolitan School District will be found constitutional because it meets every test articulated by this Court to determine violations of the Establishment Clause. The hosting of Respondent's web pages by the Metropolitan School District respects rather than offends the School District's neutrality towards religion as required by the Establishment Clause. The hosting of Respondent's web pages by the Metropolitan School District comports with the three-pronged <u>Lemon</u> test and, therefore, does not violate the Establishment Clause. The purpose of the District's web site is secular, its primary effect is not the advancement of religion, and the inclusion of the creationism web pages does not create an excessive government entanglement with religion. By including Respondent's web pages on the Metropolitan School District's web site, Petitioners are not intending to endorse nor are they perceived to endorse a particular religious belief. Finally, the District's inclusion in its web site of Respondent's web pages create a policy of religious coercion. Based upon Respondent's arguments, the Appellate Court's ruling should be upheld.

c. Brief of Petitioner in the U.S. Supreme Court case: <u>Capitol Square Review and Advisory Board v. Pinette</u>, 515 U.S. 753 (1995)

SUMMARY OF ARGUMENT

Displays of purely religious symbols at the seat of government, such as the large solitary and unattended Latin cross placed directly in front of the Ohio Statehouse in this case, violate the Establishment Clause of the First Amendment.

A purely religious symbol, such as a Latin cross, the ultimate sectarian symbol of Christianity, conveys a clear message of religion. See <u>American Civil Liberties Union v. City of St. Charles</u>, 794 F. 2d 265 (7th Cir.), cert. denied, 479 U.S. 961 (1986). At the same time, the symbol of the seat of government, in this case the Ohio Statehouse, conveys a clear message of government authority. <u>Kaplan v. City of Burlington</u>, 891 F. 2d 1024 (2nd Cir. 1989), cert. denied, 496 U.S. 926 (1990). The conjunction of the two communicates powerfully to an observer that the message conveyed by each symbol comes from the same source -- the government. Id.

In most circumstances, an observer can easily identify those responsible for speech: the speaker at the microphone, the group chanting a slogan, the person holding a sign or passing out brochures. But when speech is conveyed by an unattended display, the author of the speech is not readily ascertainable and usually is perceived by most reasonable observers to be the owner of the property on which the display stands.

The Establishment Clause protects against religious messages bearing the government's imprimatur. <u>Widmar v. Vincent</u>, 454 U.S. 263 (1981). The juncture of the cross and the government building in an unattended setting creates the danger against which the Establishment Clause guards.

The Court has not addressed whether a union of church and state is legally permissible if it occurs in a public forum. The Sixth Circuit adopted a per se rule that, because a display is privately sponsored in a public forum, there can never be a misperception of the message. But nothing in the Court's precedents removes, for Establishment Clause purposes, the obligation of a court to determine the nature of the message being sent and received. The fact that the message is delivered in a public forum does not give the government the right to advocate religion. Nor may it permit a private party to proffer speech which is likely to be perceived as government speech endorsing religion. Public forum or no public forum, government may not throw its weight behind sectarian evangelism, nor may it permit a private party to create the impression that government supports religion. But just such an impression is created when an unattended, purely religious symbol, such as the Latin cross, is positioned with the state capitol as its backdrop.

The court below incorrectly held that one part of the First Amendment -- the free speech clause -- always trumps another part of the First Amendment -- the Establishment Clause -- when speech is uttered in a public forum. Under such rationale, no inquiry ever need be made whether, under the circumstances of the case, the speaker in the public forum appears to be the government and the speech appears to be endorsement of religion. If the Framers had intended such power of the Free Speech Clause, one would think that they would at least have placed it before the Establishment Clause.

The Court's cases dealing with holiday seasonal displays offer two tests for evaluating the issues in the instant case. See County of Allegheny v. American Civil Liberties Union, 492 U.S. 573 (1989). Each test attempts to strike a proper balance so that government neither advances nor inhibits religion. See Lemon v. Kurtzman, 403 U.S. 602 (1971). This includes not preferring the religious practices of one group at the expense of other groups, or even religious non-adherents. County of Allegheny.

The union of an isolated and unattended religious icon and the seat of government upsets this constitutional balance. Kaplan; Smith v. County of Albemarle, Va., 895 F. 2d 953 (4th Cir.), cert. denied, ___U.S.___, 111 S. Ct. 74 (1990). There is a significant risk that observers of the message conveyed by this union will perceive it as emanating from the government. For that reason, the unattended display in this case violates either test previously established by the Court.

Neither the Court's opinions nor reasoning in its "equal access" line of cases alters this conclusion. The equal access cases dealt with whether the message conveyed by government when allowing or denying access to government property communicates government preference for or intolerance to religion. <u>Widmar; Board of Education of Westside Community Schools v. Mergens</u>, 492 U.S. 226 (1990); <u>Lamb's Chapel v. Center Moriches Union Free School Dist.</u>,___ U.S.___, 113 S. Ct. 2141 (1993). The Court concluded in the context of those cases that equal access was necessary to convey government neutrality toward religion. Although in those cases the Court found no significant risk of misperception of the message conveyed by government, the inquiry was directed toward the perception of the listener or observer under each set of circumstances. See generally id.

In stark contrast, the Sixth Circuit's analysis in this case ceased once the court established that speech was uttered in a public forum by a private non-governmental party. The court below incorrectly limited its analysis to a factual determination of who spoke, rather than, in the circumstances presented, who a "reasonable observer" might rationally conclude spoke.

Government may make distinctions in speech if compelling interests exist for doing so. <u>Lamb's Chapel</u>. Here government has a compelling interest to avoid violating the Establishment Clause. A complete prohibition on purely religious symbols at the seat of government is the only, and, therefore, the most narrowly tailored way to accomplish that goal. Disclaimers are entirely ineffectual and themselves create the risk of government entanglement with religion.

d. Brief of Respondents in the U.S. Supreme Court case: <u>Capitol Square Review and Advisory Board v. Pinette</u>, 515 U.S. 753 (1995)

SUMMARY OF ARGUMENT

The Free Speech and Free Exercise Clauses of the First Amendment and the Equal Protection Clause of the Fourteenth Amendment require a state to permit the temporary unattended display of a Ku Klux Klan cross in a traditional public forum that is open to other political and religious symbols -- even if that forum is near the seat of government -- absent any special indicia of endorsement.

1. The State's discriminatory refusal to permit the display of the Ku Klux Klan cross in a traditional public forum where the State has permitted other secular and religious symbols violates the Free Speech and Free Exercise Clauses of the First Amendment.

In this case, the State has singled out the Ku Klux Klan and has refused to permit the Klan to display its cross in the Capitol Square forum. The cross is symbolic of the Klan's view about politics and religion.

The record establishes that the denial was based upon the controversial communication of a controversial speaker. On that record, the State clearly discriminated among political and religious symbols. Moreover, the discrimination was unlawfully accomplished by means of standardless procedures permitting the exercise of unbridled discretion.

The State's only response to the claim of discrimination is that the Board relied upon the Establishment Clause; however, this explanation rings hollow given the State's tolerance of other religious symbols at the same site.

2. Given the facts of this case, both courts below correctly held that no reasonable observer could conclude that the Ku Klux Klan display of its cross on the Capitol Square public forum constituted an endorsement or appearance of endorsement of religion.

The State erroneously insists that, because of the inherent power of an unattended cross as a symbol, the Establishment Clause automatically bans from the Capitol Square forum the unattended display of the Klan cross at any location at any time under any circumstances. This flat ban is wrong as a matter of law precisely because it forecloses consideration of all relevant facts and circumstances.

The State's contention that the Establishment Clause flatly bans all symbols alleged to be "purely religious" precludes the application of the "reasonable observer" standard set forth by this Court in County of Allegheny v. Greater Pittsburgh ACLU, 492 U.S. 573 (1989) and followed by the courts below. While the State claims that banning the Klan cross is necessary to serve its interest in obeying the Establishment Clause, it ignores its parallel obligation to fulfill the requirements of the Free Speech and Free Exercise Clauses. These interests must be reconciled on a case-by-case basis by use of the "reasonable observer" standard.

The State fails to acknowledge that providing a public forum is not an endorsement of the speech thereon. It also ignores the distinction, recognized in <u>Allegheny</u>, between private religious expression in a public forum and government religious expression.

3. Privately sponsored displays of religious symbols cannot be excluded from a quintessential public forum even at the seat of government, absent some indicia of state endorsement. Indeed, the defining characteristic of a public forum is that the state may not discriminate against speech on the basis of content.

Respondents do not quarrel with the endorsement test under the Establishment Clause as it has been developed by this Court. But, endorsement cannot be presumed from the mere fact of private speech in a public forum. Yet, without this inference, there is no plausible claim of endorsement on the facts of this case, as both lower courts found. The judgment below should therefore be affirmed.

VI. APPELLATE BRIEFS (*Advanced Legal Writing and Oral Advocacy: Trials, Appeals, and Moot Court*, Chapter 6)

WRITING PROBLEMS

1. Evaluate the following sections of argument from four appellate briefs. Identify what each does well (if anything) and what you would edit or revise (if anything) in each. In particular, consider which sections of the arguments contain unsynthesized presentations of case law. Edit and revise these sections to synthesize the presentation of the case law using explanatory synthesis. We have excerpted portions of the arguments for the sake of time and space.

a. **Brief of Petitioner in the moot court case: Metropolitan School Dist. of Gotham v. Branch Louisian of the United Church of Christ the Savior**

ARGUMENT

I. THE UNITED STATES SUPREME COURT SHOULD REVERSE THE APPELLATE COURT'S DECISION GRANTING SUMMARY JUDGMENT TO CHURCH AND GRANT SUMMARY JUDGMENT TO SCHOOL DISTRICT BECAUSE THE SCHOOL DISTRICT'S WEB SITE IS A NONPUBLIC FORUM AND THE SCHOOL DISTRICT IS ALLOWED TO DISCRIMINATE ON THE BASIS OF CONTENT SO LONG AS THE DISCRIMINATION IS REASONABLE AND VIEWPOINT NEUTRAL.

A. <u>Introduction</u>

The First Amendment, applicable to the States via the Fourteenth Amendment, provides protection from unnecessary governmental interference in free speech. <u>Cohen v. California</u>, 403 U.S. 15, 19 (1971). The First Amendment provides, "Congress shall make no law respecting an establishment of religion, or prohibiting the free exercise thereof; or abridging the freedom of speech, or of the press; or the right of the people peaceably to assemble, and to petition the Government for a redress of grievances." U.S. Const. amend. I. In order to invoke First Amendment jurisprudence, the entity claiming a violation of its Constitutional rights ("speaker") must seek access to a "forum." <u>Cornelius v. NAACP Legal Defense & Educ. Fund, Inc.</u>, 473 U.S. 788, 801 (1985). A forum is either public property or private property dedicated to public use. <u>Id.</u>

When a speaker claims a violation of its First Amendment rights after being denied access to a forum, this Court reviews the facts *de novo*. <u>Edwards v. South Carolina</u>, 372 U.S. 229, 235 (1963). Additionally, summary judgment should only be granted when the pleadings, discovery, and all affidavits, if any, "show that there is no genuine issue as to any material fact and that the moving party is entitled to a judgment as a matter of law." Fed.R.Civ.P. 56(c).

Protection of speech rights varies depending upon the nature of the forum. <u>Perry Educ. Ass'n v. Perry Local Educators' Ass'n</u>, 460 U.S. 37, 44-46 (1983). The Court has consistently recognized that a forum is either public, limited public, or nonpublic depending on the historical or present treatment the government has afforded the property. <u>See</u> <u>id.</u> at 44-46. Whether the government can deny a speaker access to a particular forum depends upon whether the forum is public, limited public, or nonpublic.

Furthermore, this Court must give deference to school official's decisions regarding educational matters. <u>Hazelwood Sch. Dist. v. Kuhlmeier</u>, 484 U.S. 260, 273 (1988). This Court has long applied the standard that the education of children is primarily the responsibility of parents, teachers, and state and local school officials, not of federal judges. <u>Id.</u> Additionally, the Court has noted that it is only when the government censors with no valid educational purpose that the First Amendment is "directly and sharply implicated." <u>Id.</u> Moreover, when a party asks the courts to review a genuinely academic decision, the courts should show "great respect for the faculty's professional judgment." <u>Regents of the Univ. of Mich. v. Ewing</u>, 474 U.S. 214, 225 (1985). Educators have the primary freedom to determine who may teach, what may be taught, and how it shall be taught. <u>Sweezy v. New Hampshire</u>, 354 U.S. 234, 263 (1957) (Frankfurter, J., concurring). Finally, the Court has most recently held, "When the government appropriates public funds to promote a particular policy of its own it is entitled to say what it wishes…and it may take legitimate and appropriate steps to ensure that its message is neither garbled nor distorted…" <u>Rosenberger v. Rector and Visitors of the Univ. of Va.</u>, 515 U.S. 819, 833 (1995).

As a final introductory point, web sites, web pages, and web servers are subject to First Amendment forum analysis even though they are somewhat new areas for discourse. <u>See generally</u> <u>Reno v. ACLU</u>, 521 U.S. 844 (1997); <u>Loving v. Boren</u>, 956 F.Supp. 953 (W.D. Okla. 1997); <u>CompuServe, Inc. v. Cyber Promotions, Inc.</u>, 962 F.Supp. 1015 (S.D. Ohio 1997).

The District's decision to exclude the Church's web page discussing creationism was a proper educational decision to which this Court owes great deference. Further, by creating a nonpublic forum, the School District was allowed to engage in content-based discrimination. There is no question that the School District properly made a content-based, non-viewpoint centered censorship in denying access to the Church. Moreover, even if this Court finds that the School District's web page was a limited public forum, the content-based censorship exercised by the School District passes strict scrutiny analysis as it is narrowly tailored to promote a compelling state interest.

* * *

C. The District's web site is a nonpublic forum.

The first issue involves identifying the nature of the forum. The web site at issue is a nonpublic forum. A non-public forum is created when the government does not open the property to the general public. Perry Educ. Ass'n, 460 U.S. at 46. "The First Amendment does not guarantee access to property simply because it is owned or controlled by the government." Id. (quoting U.S. Postal Serv. v. Greenburgh Civic Ass'n, 453 U.S. 114, 129 (1981)). Moreover, "the State, no less than a private owner of property, has power to preserve the property under its control for the use to which it is lawfully dedicated." Id. (quoting Greenburgh Civic Ass'n, 453 U.S. at 129).

In Perry, the Court held that the internal mail system created by the school district to disseminate information to teachers and staff was a non-public forum because neither the district's intent nor its practice opened the mail system to the general public. See generally id. The Court found as dispositive the fact that the district had to grant permission to any person seeking access to the mail system and the fact that permission had not been granted to all who requested it. Id. at 47. The evidence revealed that some groups other than district employees and administrators had been granted access to the mail system. Id. However, the Court concluded that selective access does not create a public forum. Id. See also Cornelius, 473 U.S. at 788 (holding that government run charity drive for nonprofit organizations was nonpublic forum where government retained the power to exclude non-healthcare or non-welfare nonprofit organizations); Arkansas Educ. Television Comm'n v. Forbes, 118 S.Ct. 1633, 1644 (1998) (holding that political debate operated by public television station was nonpublic forum where participation in debate was contingent on the station's permission).

The Court's analysis in <u>Perry</u> strongly supports a finding that the web site at issue here is a nonpublic forum. First, the School District's implementation of standards relating to the type of information the speaker must contribute to the site in order to gain access shows the forum has never been opened to the general public. (R. at 11.) Requiring any speaker's message to relate to a topic of education in the District shows that the forum was not created for the general public because the average person in the community could not be admitted as most people do not possess information pertaining to primary or secondary education. Further, the standards are actively enforced. (R. at 14.) As in <u>Perry</u>, in order to gain access, the speaker must obtain permission from the School District after tendering a written proposal. (R. at 11.) The School District also performs periodic checks of the site for information that is in violation of the policy. (R. at 11.) Finally, the School District maintains the right to remove any non-conforming information. (R. at 11.) Therefore, the District maintained control over the web site by requiring permission, reserving the right to remove information, and setting standards on whom may enter the forum. This control, like in <u>Perry</u>, exhibits the District's purpose that the forum not be opened to the general public. As such, the web site is a nonpublic forum; and the appellate court's decision should be overturned.

D. <u>The District's refusal to allow Church's information regarding Creationism is reasonable, content-based, non-viewpoint discrimination.</u>

Once it has been determined that the web site is a nonpublic forum, the next question is whether the School District properly refused the Church's proposal. It is clear that in this case, the School District properly refused the Church's proposal because its decision was content-based, reasonable, and made irrespective of the Church's viewpoint.

When the forum is characterized as nonpublic, the speaker forbidden access has no First Amendment or other right to the forum. <u>Perry Educ. Ass'n</u>, 460 U.S. at 54. As such, the censorship does not have to be narrowly tailored, the objective does not have to be compelling, and the most efficient means of fulfilling the state's interest do not have to be used. <u>Id.</u> The School District has acted properly as long as its restriction is reasonable and not based on the speaker's viewpoint on the subject. <u>Id.</u> at 46. Distinctions may be drawn between applicants to the site based on subject matter and speaker identity. Id. Furthermore, the reasonableness required need not be the most reasonable or the only reasonable limitation; the state need only show that it was legitimately justified in its actions. Cornelius, 473 U.S. at 808.

1. The District's restriction is reasonable.

Any government restriction on speech in a nonpublic forum must be reasonable. Reasonableness of the restriction on access to a nonpublic forum must be determined in relation to the government's purpose and surrounding circumstances of the forum. Id. at 809. The School District's censorship of the Church's proposal is reasonable in light of Supreme Court precedents.

After determining that the forum in Cornelius was nonpublic, the Court analyzed the government's reasonableness in refusing to allow legal defense and other nonprofit litigation organizations from receiving proceeds from the charity drive designed to support health and welfare nonprofit entities. Id. The Court found the restriction reasonable. Id.

In relation to speech restrictions in nonpublic fora, the reasonableness test requires only a threshold showing that the government has appropriate purposes in limiting access. See generally id. The Court has stated that the government acts reasonably when it discriminates in order to maintain administrative manageability; access to the public can be obtained by the speaker through some other means; where it has denied access in order to avoid the appearance of favoritism to one political group over another; and where it restricts in order to avoid controversy. Id. at 809-810. Furthermore, the government does not have to resort to other agencies' restrictions or findings in different circumstances to determine reasonableness. Id.

Applying Cornelius to the case at bar clearly shows the School District's actions were reasonable. The School District's policy was implemented to supplement the topics listed in the curriculum; and creationism neither is nor ever has been a part of the curriculum for the past 150 years. (R. at 15.) Secondly, the School District reasonably restricted access to the Church to avoid controversy because deeply rooted disagreements may arise over any association between the School District and any particular religious beliefs. The School District also feared jeopardizing the success of the program. Allowing the Church to post information about creationism would inevitably lead to other groups seeking access to post information completely unrelated to any part of the curriculum. This slippery slope would result in the weakening of the evaluative process and would inevitably result in a *de facto* public forum as proper research and analysis of each applicant would become overly consuming of both time and money. For these reasons, the School District reasonably denied access to the Church.

Further, it is clear that the School District had an appropriate purpose in restricting access to the Church in order to maintain neutrality. Like Cornelius, where the Court held limiting the appearance of political favoritism provided reasonable justification, restricting access here to avoid the appearance of religious favoritism shows the reasonableness of the School District's actions. Allowing the Church to post the information would lead non-religious parents in the community to believe that because of their beliefs, their children will be treated differently than those who favor creationism.

Finally, the School District acted properly here because the Church can spread its message to both students and non-students through other means. Traditionally, churches and other religious organizations have spread their message throughout the world by active missionary work. Similarly, the Church can spread its message of creationism throughout the community by distributing pamphlets, door-to-door confrontation, rallies, and persuading non-Christians to visit its services.

The factors set out in Cornelius, as applied to the case at bar, show the reasonableness of the School District's actions. Not only has the School District met the threshold requirement, it has persuasively demonstrated that proper measures were taken in order to maintain the vitality of its program.

2. **The District's restriction is content-based and not viewpoint centered.**

The next issue is whether the School District's restriction is impermissibly viewpoint centered or whether it is appropriate content-based discrimination. The appellate court erred in finding that the School District's restriction was based on the Church's viewpoint. It is clear that the

School District's restriction is appropriate content-based discrimination because creationism does not relate to a topic of education as detailed in the curriculum guide and creationism does not fulfill the School District's purpose in teaching evolution because it is not based on the scientific method. Further, the restriction is content based in the case at bar because creationism does not relate to the areas covered in "Social Studies" or "Sociology" as these courses are taught in the School District. Finally, the deference the Court must give to school districts in educational matters, the recent holding of this Court regarding what constitutes viewpoint discrimination, and the fact that the School District has allowed the communities religious leaders to post information that relates to topics of education in the past lead to the conclusion that the appellate court clearly erred and the School District's actions were appropriately content-based.

"Although a speaker may be excluded from a nonpublic forum if he wishes to address a topic not encompassed within the purpose of the forum, or if he is not a member of the class of speakers for whose especial benefit the forum was created, the government violates the First Amendment when it denies access to a speaker solely to suppress the point of view he espouses on an otherwise includible subject." Cornelius, 473 U.S. at 806. "Viewpoint restrictions pose the inherent risk that the government seeks to suppress unpopular ideals or information." Id. On the other hand, content-based discrimination is acceptable in a nonpublic forum. Perry Educ. Ass'n, 460 U.S. at 54. Although the Court has never explicitly defined viewpoint discrimination, this analysis necessarily involves discussion of public policy, viewpoint discrimination jurisprudence, and the content of the Church's offered material.

Recently, the Court has taken a narrow view on what constitutes viewpoint discrimination. See Arkansas Educ. Television Comm'n, 118 S.Ct. at 1633 (1998); National Endowment for the Arts v. Finley, 524 U.S. 569 (1988). The Court's decisions in these cases allow the government to restrict more liberally without judicial intervention. See Erwin Chemerinsky, *Court Takes a Narrow View of Viewpoint Discrimination*, Trial, Mar. 1999, at 90.

For example, the Finley Court upheld a federal statute requiring artists receiving grants from the NEA to produce art that meets "general standards of decency and respect for the diverse beliefs and values of the American public," as viewpoint neutral. Finley, 524 U.S. at 576. This decision allows an evaluator to use subjective standards when determining whether access should be granted to a nonpublic forum. <u>See</u> Chemerinsky, <u>supra</u>. Therefore, <u>Finley</u> supports the great deference the Court has afforded school faculty and administrators in making access decisions.

In order for the School District's restriction to be viewpoint centered, this Court must find that creationism is related to a topic in the curriculum. If no such relationship exists, creationism information is properly excludable as a content-based restriction. As mentioned previously, the School District's mission in creating the forum was to provide information that has a direct relationship to a specific topic of education included in the curriculum. (R. at 11.) The court of appeals held that evolution was not a topic covered in the curriculum. (R. at 19.) However, it did find that the "origin of humankind" was a topic in the curriculum. (R. at 19.) This is clearly erroneous.

"Topic" is defined as, "a heading in an outlined argument or exposition; the subject of discourse or of a section of discourse." Merriam Webster's Collegiate Dictionary 1244 (10th ed. 1995). Based on this definition, the proper topic for our purposes is what the School District used as a heading in its curriculum. The words "origin of humankind" have never been printed in the curriculum; nor has evolution ever been included in the curriculum. (R. at 15.) On the other hand, biology has been a part of the School District's curriculum of secondary education. (R. at 15.) Instead of interposing its own definition of "topic," the court of appeals should have given deference to the literal meaning of the word. The Court should give deference to the School District and find that for our purposes, biology is the topic covered in the curriculum. As such, creationism is not one view of a topic as listed in the educational curriculum; and the restriction on the Church's proposal to post information regarding the topic was properly declined as a content-based restriction.

Moreover, the School District made a proper content-based restriction in light of its purposes for teaching evolution. Evolution is only part of the biology class offered through the School District. (R. at 15.) The entire course is offered to strengthen and expand students' analytical skills. Biology teaches students to think analytically by introducing them to the scientific method and showing them how scientists in the past used the method to reach a conclusion. <u>See generally</u> <u>Edwards v. Aguillard</u>, 482 U.S. 578 (1987). In other words, through biology, students learn the process of developing a hypothesis based on inferences and observations, testing the hypothesis, making revisions to the hypothesis and re-testing, and eventually drawing a conclusion based on fact. While evolution is discussed, it is not a primary focus of the class and is used overall to teach students how to think for themselves.

In light of the purpose of teaching evolution, it is obvious that creationism is excluded because it was not developed through the scientific method and teaches the students nothing about critical analysis. Id. at 592. Learning creationism requires memorization and regurgitation of material, while biology and evolution forces one to think for one's self both in the laboratory and the outside world. Therefore, the School District denied access to the Church not only because creationism was not listed in the curriculum, but also because, unlike evolution, creationism does not provide an example of the long-standing scientific method. Accordingly, the Court should give deference to the School District as this is an exclusively educational decision and reverse the appellate court's finding that the restriction was based on the Church's views.

The record further states that the Church sought access to the forum by asking that the creationism information be included under the curriculum topics of "Social Studies" and "Sociology." (R. at 14.) However, they were denied access to the site once against because none of the subtopics of Social Studies and Sociology relate to creationism. The list of subtopics include history, geography, government national and international relations, institutions and movements of social change, the human condition of peoples in America and the world, human interactions, social psychology, mass behavior, gangs and cults, deviant behavior, and analysis of social statistical data. (R. at 14.) However, as the District pointed out to the Church, none of these areas encompass the topics of Theology, Anthropology, religion, or anything related to creationism. (R. at 14.) While the exact areas studied under these subtopics are not contained in the record, this Court should give deference to the District as this decision involves the educational mission in creating the web site and find that creationism does not relate to any of those topics. Accordingly, the appellate court's decision should be reversed as the restriction was based on the Church's content.

Like Finley, the Court should allow the District to use some subjectivity in making a decision that not only affects a program that it has created, but ultimately affects the impressionable students. Further, giving the District deference in this situation allows the Court to place more weight on the reasonableness factor that encompasses many of the policies behind allowing restrictions in nonpublic fora. Clearly, had the District tried to indirectly place creationism in one of the sub-fields of Sociology and Social Studies, more and more people would seek access, the reviewing body would become overloaded, and the success of the program would be jeopardized. The web site would also be jeopardized because of the animosity the School District may have caused in parents and students in the community by allowing such a blatantly non-secular topic to be discussed in an educational forum.

Additionally, the Court should take notice that all of the other non-faculty parties who were allowed to post information on the web site had information that directly involved a topic listed in the curriculum. American History, Art, and Health are all covered in the School District's curriculum. (R. at 12-13.) While the web sites relating to Art and American History clearly relate to those purported topics, the extent to which the "health" sites relate to health is not so clear. However, as discussed below, the District properly allowed inclusion of all of the health pages on the web site. Although the reasons stated below are not grounded in the record, the Court should give deference here as it does in other areas when it applies rational basis analysis. In those cases, if the Court can find a reasonable basis for government action, they uphold the statute even if the reasonable basis was not the actual purpose that the government had in mind when enacting a statute. Here, the Court should apply that same standard and adopt the following reasons why the School District allowed the "health" sites even though the reasons are not founded in the record.

The American Red Cross posted a site relating to health and discussing blood properties, collection, and distribution. (R. at 12.) This not only concerns student personal health by providing them with information as to the contents of blood and the dangers and diseases associated with blood, it also advises students of the importance of blood drives for the promotion of the public health. Additionally, the information regarding student mediation and dispute resolution covers topics relating to mental health and brings the issue to a personal level for the students by informing them of their alternatives to fighting. This information ultimately not only relates to their mental health but also their physical health. (R. at 13.) Finally, the site written by a pastor in the community relates to health by covering the issues of teen pregnancy, drug addiction, gangs, and suicide. This clearly follows the health curriculum as all of these topics relate to physical health of the students, as well as, their mental health and safety.

Based upon the reasonableness of the School District's decision, the content-based nature of the censorship, the lack of viewpoint discrimination, and the fact that this Court has consistently given deference to the government when its purpose is educational and it takes steps to maintain its policy, the censorship of the Church's message regarding creationism is constitutional and this Court should reverse the appellate court's judgment.

E. **The appellate court erred in finding that the District's web site was not a nonpublic forum.**

The appellate court erred in finding that the District's web site is not a nonpublic forum. The general public is welcomed to speak in any nonpublic and public fora. In its holding, the appellate court found that the web site was opened to those of the general public who have information pertaining to a topic of education in the District. However, members of the general public who have information regarding a topic of education in the curriculum are not the general public for purposes of forum analysis. Setting standards on who is to be admitted is a key factor in concluding that a forum is not limited public or public. As such, the District appropriately set limitations on those who could be heard on the web site by requiring a nexus between the speaker's information and the curriculum. This precludes the finding that the web site was opened to the general public.

Furthermore, no speaker ever has to obtain permission from the government in order to gain access to a limited public or public forum. As such, the District's requirement that each applicant obtain the District's permission further supports the fact that the web site is a nonpublic forum. Clearly, the School District's web site cannot be characterized as a public forum or limited public forum. Accordingly, the appellate court erred and this Court should reverse the erroneous conclusion.

1. <u>The District's web site is not a public forum.</u>

Public fora are those that "have immemorially been held in trust for the use of the public, and, time out of mind, have been used for purposes of assembly, communicating thoughts between citizens, and discussing public questions." <u>Perry Educ. Ass'n</u>, 460 U.S. at 45 (citing <u>Hague v. Com. for Indus. Org.</u>, 307 U.S. 496, 515 (1939)). Public parks and streets are the quintessential public fora. <u>Id.</u> Any content-based restrictions on communication in public fora must survive strict scrutiny. Therefore, the restriction must be narrowly tailored to necessarily achieve a compelling state interest.

In <u>Hazelwood Sch. Dist.</u>, 484 U.S. at 260, the Court held that even though students do not shed all of their First Amendment rights at the schoolhouse gate, public schools do not possess all of the characteristics of parks, streets and other traditional public fora. <u>Id.</u> at 267. Furthermore, public schools are only public fora if the administrators "by policy or by practice" welcome the general public for indiscriminate reasons. <u>Id.</u> (citing <u>Perry Educ. Ass'n</u>, 460 U.S. at 37). The Court declared in that the school newspaper at issue in <u>Hazelwood</u> was not a public forum. <u>Id.</u> The Court focused on the school's long-standing policy of keeping the content of the newspaper tied to the school's educational curriculum and retaining ultimate control of the newspaper's content by appointing a teacher to make final decisions. <u>Id.</u> Further, the school had not transformed the paper into a public forum by nonchalance or inaction because the district had not deviated from its long-standing policy. <u>Id.</u>

Like the newspaper in <u>Hazelwood</u>, the web site developed and maintained by the School District in the case at bar is by its very nature not a public forum. Not only has the web site never been likened to public streets and parks, the new and developing nature of the World Wide Web excludes it from this category because of the lack of historical precedence. Furthermore, the school specifically declared that its purpose in creating the site was to further the educational goals of the School District in relation to topics covered in the curriculum, not to freely allow the Internet community to post whatever information it desired. (R. at 11.) Additionally, there is no evidence that the School District has turned the site into a public forum by passively allowing the general public to be heard. Therefore, the web site was not a public forum at its inception; nor has it become a public forum through the School District's passivity.

2. <u>The District's website is not a limited public forum.</u>

The limited public forum is a somewhat less-protected category than the public forum. <u>Perry Educ. Ass'n</u>, 460 U.S. at 45. Although these are not the traditional areas like parks and streets that have been classified as public fora, they are protected from overly prohibitive restrictions because the government has opened them to the general public as a "place for expressive activity." <u>Id.</u> at 45-46. Time, place, and content restrictions are allowed once the state opens the limited forum. <u>Id.</u> at 46. In <u>Perry,</u> the Court held that restrictions in limited public fora must also survive strict scrutiny. <u>Id.</u> Since then, however, the Court has first applied the nonpublic forum test before subjecting the restrictions to strict scrutiny. <u>Rosenberger</u>, 515 U.S. at 829.

In <u>Lamb's Chapel v. Center Moriches Union Free Sch. Dist.</u>, 508 U.S. 384 (1993), the Court found a limited public forum where a school district had opened its doors for after-school activities that had "social, civic, and recreational purposes." <u>Id.</u> at 391. Allowing these after-school activities opened the property to the general public because by the terms of the policy almost any activity was allowed after school hours. <u>Id.</u> Therefore, the Court found unconstitutional the school's refusal to allow a group to display a video discussing teenage pregnancy from a religious perspective because a similar video from a non-religious viewpoint would have been admissible. <u>Id.</u>

Comparing the School District's policy in the case at bar with that of the school district's in <u>Lamb's Chapel</u>, it becomes readily apparent that the web site here is not a limited public forum. In <u>Lamb's Chapel</u>, the school's liberal policy of allowing "social, civic or recreational" activity invited the general public onto the school's property. Conversely, the School District here not only restricted the site's participants to those with an educational message, it specifically required that the information be directly related to a topic of education taught in the School District. (R. at 11.) As a result of its policy, the School District maintained control over the web site and forbade the general public from taking part. Therefore, the web site is not a limited public forum.

The District's web site in the case at bar is not a limited public or public forum because the web site is by nature not a long-standing, traditional public forum like parks and streets. Additionally, the School

District has created and maintained a strict policy that does not welcome the general public to enlist in the web site. Furthermore, as mentioned previously, the District requires permission to post information on the web site, which is one of the main characteristics of nonpublic fora. For all of these reasons, this Court should reverse the appellate court's erroneous finding and hold that the District's web site is a nonpublic forum.

F. If the Court finds that the District's web site is a public or limited public forum, restricting access to the Church in order to maintain separation of church and state as mandated by the Establishment Clause satisfies strict scrutiny analysis.

Should the Court find that the School District's restriction is viewpoint centered and/or that the web site is a limited public forum, the Court should still uphold the restriction because it meets strict scrutiny.

As mentioned earlier, the Rosenberger Court used viewpoint, content-based, and reasonableness requirements in striking down a restriction in a limited public forum. Rosenberger, 515 U.S. at 829. However, the Court did not overrule Perry and its progeny that require the Court to use strict scrutiny analysis to any restrictions in a limited public forum. Id. at 842. In fact, the Rosenberger Court, after finding that the restrictions were viewpoint-based, performed a strict scrutiny analysis. Id. Thus, the School District's restrictions may still withstand constitutional challenge, even if found to be viewpoint centered, if the School District can show that the restriction was narrowly tailored to a compelling state interest. Id.

The Court in Rosenberger found that the government would not violate the Establishment Clause if it was forced to give funding to a student-run, religious publication where the university had opened the subsidy program to virtually any group but religious ones. Id. In so finding, the Court held that preventing a violation of the Establishment Clause was not a compelling state interest. Id. The Court's decision in Rosenberger, however, does not preclude the Court from finding here that Establishment Clause issues are a compelling state interest as the finding is largely based on facts unique to each situation. The compelling nature of the Establishment Clause issues can be seen in the section below. Essentially, if the Court finds that posting the Church's information on the web site would be a violation of the Establishment Clause, any restriction under free speech analysis should be upheld as a narrowly tailored means of fulfilling a compelling state interest.

Moreover, the School District also has a compelling state interest in educating its students. As mentioned previously, this Court has stated that educating children is the primary concern of the state. Hazelwood Sch. Dist., 484 U.S. at 273. Also mentioned previously, the Court owes great deference to any decision that the School District may make when the decision is purely educational. Id. Educating children so that they become knowledgeable, self-serving, productive citizens is one of the most important tasks the federal government has left for the states. The Framers of the Constitution recognized the importance of such a responsibility and thought best to leave the decisions to the local administrators who could see the results of their decisions first-hand. States, granted with the power given them by the Framers of the Constitution, have a compelling state interest in seeing that their children are properly educated. Therefore, the School District can survive strict scrutiny by narrowly tailoring its policy to achieve the state interest.

Accordingly, the Court must also consider whether the School District's restriction was narrowly tailored to achieve the compelling state interest. Here, the School District's restriction was narrowly tailored to fulfill a compelling state interest because it only restricted information that was violative of its policy and of the Establishment Clause. The School District did not mandate the exclusion of every religious entity or person from the web site. Moreover, the policy was narrowly drawn to only exclude those speakers who had nothing to contribute to the education in the District. The School District evaluated every piece of information that was proposed for inclusion on the web site. Only after determining that the information was violative of its policy and of the Establishment Clause did the School District restrict the Church's information.

Additionally, one can find further support for the closely tailored nature of the School District's restriction in the fact that this is the only restriction of its kind and that the School District has allowed other religious leaders in the community to contribute to the web site after finding that the information was not religious in nature and that it pertained to primary or secondary education.

The School District's limited actions at issue, taken only when necessary to fulfill its compelling interest of remaining separated from religion and fulfilling its educational policy, is narrowly tailored and survives strict scrutiny analysis. Therefore, even if the Court should find a limited public forum and/or viewpoint discrimination, the Court should still uphold the restriction as a constitutionally necessary censorship.

* * *

CONCLUSION

For the reasons stated above, the decision of the United States Court of Appeals for the Fourteenth Circuit should be reversed, and this Court should grant summary judgment to School District as there are no genuine issues as to any material fact and School District is entitled to judgment as a matter of law.

---

b. Brief of Respondent in the moot court case: Metropolitan School Dist. of Gotham v. Branch Louisian of the United Church of Christ the Savior

ARGUMENT

I. THE JUDGMENT OF THE APPELLATE COURT SHOULD BE AFFIRMED BECAUSE PETITIONER'S DISCRIMINATORY EXCLUSION OF RESPONDENT'S PROPOSED WEB PAGES SOLELY ON THE BASIS OF RELIGIOUS CONTENT AND IDEOLOGY IS IN VIOLATION OF THE FIRST AMENDMENT'S FREE SPEECH CLAUSE AND AGAINST PUBLIC POLICY.

The Appellate Court made a proper decision, in support of public policy, holding that Petitioner's denial of Respondent's web pages violates the Free Speech Clause of the First Amendment. (R. at 19). The Appellate Court accurately found that Petitioner created a public forum by opening its web site to any member of the community wishing to be heard on educational topics that are tied to the School District's curriculum.

Moreover, Petitioner's denial was solely based upon Respondent's religious viewpoint; an act that is presumed unconstitutional. (R. at 19).

The First Amendment provides, in part, that "Congress shall make no law...abridging the freedom of speech." U.S. Const. amend. I. The First Amendment's guarantee of free speech is applicable to restrictions enacted by state and local governments, including public school boards, by way of the Due Process Clause of the 14th Amendment. East High Gay/Straight Alliance v. Board of Edu. of Salt Lake City Sch. Dist., No.CIV.A.2:98-CV-193J, 1999 WL 1103365, at *1 (D. Utah Oct. 6, 1999).

The guarantee of free speech is a vital fundamental right to citizens of the United States upon which our democratic society is built. In Ferlauto v. Hamsher, 88 Cal.Rptr.2d 843 (Cal. Ct. App. 1999). California court held that the "First Amendment's free speech guarantee safeguards a freedom, which is the matrix, and the indispensable condition of nearly every other form of freedom." Id. at 848.

This enumerated freedom, which is the matrix of our great democracy, has begun a recent evolution with the inception of the Internet and cyberspace. This evolution has crept into the realm of authority of the United States Supreme Court, which has set precedent for how this issue must be resolved. In Reno v.ACLU, 521 U.S. 844 (1997), this Court recently addressed the nature of the Internet and held that it most closely resembles books and newspapers and is therefore deserving of the utmost freedom from content-based restrictions. Id. at 885.

In reviewing a constitutional claim, this Court will apply a de novo review of the issue. New York Times Co. v. Sullivan, 376 U.S. 254, 285 (1964). However, when a fundamental right, such as free speech is at issue and the State restriction is content-based, the restriction is subject to strict scrutiny. Widmar v. Vincent, 454 U.S. 263, 263 (1981). Under a strict scrutiny analysis, the restriction is found unconstitutional unless the State can prove that the restriction advances a compelling state interest by the least restrictive means available. Bernal v. Fainter, 467 U.S. 216, 219 (1984). Petitioner is unable to meet this heavy burden.

A private religious expression is entitled to the same protection under the Free Speech Clause as secular private expression. Capitol Square Review and Advisory Board v. Pinette, 515 U.S. 753, 760 (1995). The

State may not discriminate against speakers, by denying them the ability to speak based upon their religious viewpoint. Although the State may not endorse or assist religious activities in a way that violates the Establishment Clause, the State is limited by the First Amendment's Freedom of Speech Clause when it denies benefits to, or imposes burdens on religious speakers. Id. at 760. Petitioner's decision to deny Respondent's proposal based upon its religious content and ideology constitutes an egregious form of discrimination in violation of the First Amendment. The Appellate Court carefully reviewed this vital issue and made a fair and proper ruling in support of Respondent's fundamental right of free speech. Therefore, the decision by the Appellate Court should be affirmed.

A. **Petitioner has created a public forum by initiating a web site open to all members of the community and other organizations for the purpose of promoting information regarding current curriculum and providing alternative sources of information that may not be available in the curriculum.**

In analyzing a regulation of speech under the First Amendment, the nature of the forum involved must be determined because the extent to which the State may restrict access depends upon the type of forum. There are two general categories, public and nonpublic forums. Within the public forum category, however, there are subsets, traditional and designated public forums. The designated public forum category also has a subset, limited public forums. Access to a public forum may only be restricted when necessary to serve a compelling state interest and the exclusion is narrowly drawn to achieve that interest. Access to a nonpublic forum may be limited as to subject matter and speaker identity as long as the distinctions drawn are reasonable in light of the purpose served by the forum. Cornelius v. NAACP, 473 U.S. 788, 807 (1985). This Court first recognized and classified three types of forums in Perry Educ. Ass'n v. Perry Local Educators Ass'n, 460 U.S. 37, 45-46 (1983).

The Court in Perry described a traditional public forum as a place that has a history of being devoted to assembly, debate, and communication between citizens. Id. at 45. Parks, sidewalks, plazas, and streets define a traditional public forum. The rights of the State to limit expressive activity in this type of forum are sharply circumscribed and subject to strict scrutiny. Further, content-based discrimination is only allowed when the

State can prove that the regulation is necessary to serve a compelling state interest and the regulation is narrowly drawn to achieve that interest. Id.

The second type of public forum described in Perry is a designated public forum which is public property not traditionally open to assembly and debate, but which the State has intentionally designated for the purpose of expressive activity. Id. The State is bound by the same standards as a traditional public forum, and strict scrutiny will be applied in reviewing a State regulation. Id. at 46. Therefore, content-based discrimination is prohibited except when it is necessary to serve a compelling state interest and the regulation is narrowly drawn to achieve that end. 460 U.S. at 46. Unlike a traditional forum, however, the State is not required to keep this forum open indefinitely.

A designated public forum may be created for a limited purpose, such as use by certain groups, e.g., Widmar v. Vincent, 454 U.S. 263 (1981) or for the discussion of certain subjects, e.g., Madison Joint Sch. Dist. v. Wisconsin Pub. Employment Relations Comm'n 429 U.S. 167 (1976). This subset of a designated public forum is categorized as a "limited public forum". Within a limited public forum, the State must still show that the restriction is "narrowly drawn to effectuate a compelling state interest". Perry, 460 U.S. at 46. However, the State may also confine the forum's use to the limited purposes for which it is created as long as the regulation is reasonable and not an effort to suppress a speaker's viewpoint. Rosenberger v. Rector of Univ. of Virginia 515 U.S. 819, 829 (1995).

The third type of forum described in Perry is a non-public forum, which is public property that is not by tradition or designation a forum for public communication. 460 U.S. at 46. The State may preserve this forum for its intended purpose, expressive activities, or otherwise, as long as the regulation on speech is reasonable and not an effort to suppress a speaker's viewpoint. 460 U.S. at 46. However, the State has the right to make restrictions to access based upon subject matter and speaker's identity. Id.

1. **Petitioner's conduct in devising the web site for the sole purpose of expressive activities created a designated public forum.**

As stated earlier, the court in <u>Perry</u> addressed the distinctions between the three forums. While the Court did not offer a precise test to determine between a designated public forum and a nonpublic forum, the Court did define the designated public forum as being created by the State for the allocated purpose of expressive activity. 460 U.S. at 45. The nonpublic forum has no such allocation. In <u>Perry</u>, the school district's internal mail system was placed in the third category, nonpublic forum. 460 U.S. at 46. This Court found that the intended function of the mail system was only to facilitate internal communication of school matters and therefore not open to the general public. <u>Id.</u> at 46. This Court further surmised that if the school district's policy was to open the mail system for indiscriminate use by the general public, then it could be considered a designated public forum of the second category. <u>Id.</u>

Petitioner's open access policy clearly meets this "indiscriminate use by the general public" set out in <u>Perry</u>, 460 U.S. at 47. Petitioner created the web site for the sole purpose of sharing ideas related to the curriculum among members in the community. The web site is open to faculty, other educational institutions, members of the community, and other organizations who wish to be heard. This policy is far from the restricted policy of the internal mail system in <u>Perry</u>, which provides a paradigm of a nonpublic forum. Unlike <u>Perry</u>, Petitioner opened its web site to "members of the community, and other organizations" who wished to be heard. (R. at 11). This policy of open access more closely resembles the forum created in <u>Widmar</u>, where a state university made its facilities generally available to all registered student groups. This court held that the university, having opened the forum for use by all registered student groups, created a public forum. 454 U.S. at 263. The forum in the instant case is even more expansive, as it is not open only for use by students or school employees but also for all members of the community, other educational institutions in the community, and other organizations.

Further, this Court held that public school facilities become designated public forums when "school authorities have, by policy or practice, opened those facilities for indiscriminate use by the general public, or by some segment of the public, such as student organizations." <u>Hazelwood</u>

Sch. Dist. v. Kuhlmeier, 484 U.S. 260, 267 (1988). In the instant case, both "policy and practice" compel the conclusion that the web site is a designated public forum. Petitioner states that its policy invites "faculty of the School district, any other educational institution in Gotham, members of the community, and other organizations" to propose web pages for inclusion in the site. (R. at 11). Through its policy, Petitioner has created a forum "generally open to the public" as stated in Hazelwood Sch.Dist. Id. at 267. It is difficult to imagine a more expansive use policy than one explicitly open to "members of the community and other organizations" as expounded in the instant case.

It has been the consistent practice of Petitioner to allow a wide diversity of groups access to the web site. Numerous organizations from the League of Women Voters' to the American Red Cross, to articles written from heads' of churches for the Council for Alternative Dispute Resolution and The Greater Gotham Youth League, have been allowed to post web pages on Petitioner's web site. (R. at 12-13). In fact, no other web pages have been previously denied. (R. at 15). This is a classic example of "indiscriminate use by the general public" as this court called for in Perry and Hazelwood School Dist. 460 U.S. at 47; 484 U.S. at 267.

The very nature of the forum as a web site argues in favor of defining it as a public forum. While the Internet's modernistic nature precludes it from being a traditional public forum it does share many of the same characteristics. Similar to traditional forums, the Internet is devoted to assembly, debate, and expressive communication. Arguably, the Internet is even more dedicated to expressive activities than traditional forums. Traditional forums, such as parks and plazas were not created solely for the purpose of public discourse. One may visit a park for the purpose of relaxing, recreation, or simply to observe and enjoy the serene setting. The Internet, on the other hand, was created for the sole purpose of communication. The "information super-highway" is slowly replacing traditional public forums as an outlet for citizens to express and exchange ideas. As this medium of expression evolves so must our legal definitions.

2. **Even if Petitioner's web site is not found to be a pure designated public forum it must qualify as the subset, a limited public forum.**

The Appellate Court found Petitioner's web site to be a limited public forum as defined in Rosenberger and Perry. (R. at 18). The Court stated that the web site is far from a limited forum where only certain groups or certain subjects may be accommodated to preserve the essential purpose of the forum. Rather, this Court found it to be a limited public forum in that it is open to anyone wishing to be heard as long as the material has some relation to the subjects found in the School Districts curriculum. (R. at 18). It may be argued that the web site is not a "pure" public forum, but rather a "limited" public forum. It is limited in that the material presented on the proposed web pages must be "tied to a topic of education in the School District". (R. at 11). Under a limited public forum, reasonable exclusions made in order to preserve the forum's purpose may be allowed. Perry, 460 U.S. at 46. Petitioner claims that Respondent's web pages were rejected because they were not related to a subject found in the School District's curriculum. (R at 14). Therefore, Respondent is not being discriminated against but being rightfully barred based on the purpose of the forum. However, Petitioner's claim is erroneous. The School District's curriculum includes the creation of humankind as viewed through Darwin's theory of evolution and natural selection. (R. at 15). Respondent's web pages are clearly "tied to a topic of education in the school district" as required by Petitioner's policy. Creationism is merely another theory of the origin of humankind.

Furthermore, Petitioner states the exclusion was necessary to preserve the purpose of the forum it created. Petitioner's purpose explicitly set out on its home web page, states:

> [T]his site was created for the purpose of promoting information about the areas of study currently being taught in the schools. The pages we hope to sponsor will not only highlight topics of interest in the curriculum, but also provide resources and information and links to other sources of information that may not be available in the textbooks and other materials provided to our students in the courses taught. (R. at 11).

Respondent's web pages clearly further the web site's purpose by providing readers with an alternative theory of the creation of humankind, which is not found within the materials taught. Consequently, Petitioner's claim that Respondent's web pages are rightfully barred based on the restrictions of the forum is meritless because the web pages are directly "tied to" theories of the origin of humankind which is included in the District's curriculum and the web pages clearly further the purpose for which the web site was created.

B. **Petitioner's denial of Respondent's web pages solely based upon the religious content therein, constitutes content-based discrimination in violation of the First Amendment's Free Speech Clause.**

By creating a public forum open to all members of the community, Petitioner is barred by the First Amendment from refusing to accommodate Respondent based upon the content of speech. Rosenberger, 515 U.S. at 819. Content-based discrimination is based upon the ideas or information contained in speech. If a restriction occurs because the State objects to the communicative impact of the expression, the State is not being content-neutral. This type of content-based regulation directly suppresses the communicative impact of the speech and therefore must be analyzed under the rigid review of strict scrutiny. Id.

In the instant case, Petitioner's refusal to allow Respondent access to its web site was obvious content discrimination based upon Respondent's religious ideology of creationism. Petitioner has created a public forum by opening up its web site to all members of the community, or organizations who wish to be heard on educational topics that have a connection to the subjects taught in the School District. Concerned with endorsing the separation of church and state, Petitioner objected to the communicative impact of Respondent's web pages because they were based on the religious theory of creationism.

If Respondent wished to address the same topic, the origin of humankind, with the focus on the scientific theory of evolution rather than the religious theory of creationism, then Petitioner would probably have no objection to Respondent's web pages. However, because the web pages include a religious content, Petitioner has denied Respondent's proposal. This is blatant and unconstitutional State content-discrimination of private religious speech.

1. Petitioner's content-based exclusion of Respondent's web pages from its public forum triggers a strict scrutiny test, which Petitioner cannot meet.

When a fundamental right, such as free speech is at issue and the State restriction is content-based, this Court has subjected the regulation to strict scrutiny. <u>Widmar</u>, 454 U.S. at 276. Under a strict scrutiny analysis, the restriction is found unconstitutional unless the State can prove (1) its regulation is necessary to serve a compelling state interest, and (2) that it is narrowly drawn to achieve that interest. <u>Bernal</u>, 467 U.S. at 219. With a fundamental right at issue, such as free speech, few regulations can meet this stringent test.

The strict scrutiny analysis applied to content-based discrimination is based upon policy which was expounded by Justice Holmes in <u>Abrams v. U.S.</u>, 250 U.S. 616 (1919). Justice Holmes stated that there must be "free trade in ideas" and truth will become accepted through the "competition of the market." <u>Id.</u> at 630.

The instant case is analogous to <u>Widmar</u>, where members of a registered religious student organization brought a First Amendment action challenging their exclusion from using university facilities. This Court held that the state university created a public forum by making its facilities available to all registered student organizations, and having done so the university could not discriminate among student groups on the basis of religious content. 454 U.S. at 263. This Court applied the strict scrutiny test and found that the university's discrimination violated the First Amendment. <u>Id.</u> at 268.

Respondent can be analogized to the religious student organization in <u>Widmar</u>. Both Respondent and the student organization are within a class for which the public forum was generally available. Here, the forum is open to all members of the community, and other organizations. In <u>Widmar</u> the forum was open to all registered student organizations. Both Respondent and <u>Widmar</u> were denied access to a public forum based upon religious content of their speech. In accordance with <u>Widmar</u>, this Court should apply strict scrutiny, a constitutional standard that Petitioner cannot satisfy, and find that Petitioner's denial of access to

Respondent based on religious content of the proposed web pages constitutes content discrimination which is unconstitutional under the First Amendment's Free Speech Clause.

2. **Petitioner offers no compelling state interest to justify content-discrimination; hence, Petitioner fails to satisfy strict scrutiny.**

A State may exclude a speaker from a public forum without violating the First Amendment when the exclusion is necessary to serve a compelling state interest and is narrowly drawn to achieve that interest. Arkansas Educ. Television Communication v. Forbes, 523 U.S. 666 (1998). Petitioner has offered no legitimate compelling state interest for excluding Respondent. Petitioner merely argues that the exclusion was necessary to preserve the separation of church and state. While separation of church and state is a compelling state interest on its face, it is ensured under the Establishment Clause and is not violated in the instant case.

The university in Widmar also claimed separation of church and state as a compelling interest allowing content-based discrimination. This Court addressed the claim and held that the State's interest in achieving greater separation of church than is already ensured under the Establishment Clause and is limited by the Free Speech Clause is not sufficiently "compelling" to justify content-based discrimination against religious speech. Widmar, 454 U.S. at 277. Furthermore, this Court found that the forum created by the State was open to a broad spectrum of groups and would provide only an incidental benefit to religion. Id. at 274. In accordance with its prior finding, this Court held that "an open forum in a public university does not confer any imprimatur of state approval on religious sects or practices." Id. Therefore, separation of church cannot be a compelling state interest justifying content-based discrimination.

In Lamb's Chapel v. Center Moriches Union Free School District, 508 U.S. 384 (1993), this Court also rejected the Establishment Clause defense as a compelling state interest. This Court reasoned that the school property, although found to be a nonpublic forum, was open to a wide variety of uses. Moreover, this Court stated that the school district was not directly sponsoring the religious group's activities, and "any benefit to the church would have been no more than incidental." Id. at 395.

Quite obviously, the factors considered by this Court in Lamb's Chapel and Widmar exist here. Petitioner created a public forum open to all members in the community for the purpose of expressing alternative ideas and avenues of materials related to current school curriculum. Petitioner would not be endorsing Respondent's religious ideology on the creation of humankind, it merely would be providing an open public forum allowing alternative viewpoints, whether the viewpoints be religious or secular. Under these circumstances, as in Widmar and Lamb's Chapel, there would be no realistic danger that viewers of the web site would think that Petitioner is endorsing Respondent's religious ideology. Permitting Respondent's web page onto the public web site is not an establishment of religion under any of the Establishment Clause tests articulated by this Court and further illustrated in section two of this argument.

Petitioner offers no compelling state interest to trump the content-based discrimination it imposed on Respondent, therefore, there is no need to look into whether the regulation was narrowly draw to achieve that interest. Unable to prove a compelling state interest, Petitioner has violated Respondent's First Amendment constitutional right to Free Speech.

C. **Regardless of the nature of the forum, Petitioner's conduct of excluding Respondent's web pages based upon Respondent's religious ideology constitutes viewpoint discrimination which is a per se violation of the First Amendment's Free Speech Clause.**

Regardless of the type of forum, restrictions that seek to suppress a speaker's viewpoint are per se unconstitutional in violation of the First Amendment's Free Speech Clause. Arkansas Educ. Television Comm'n, 523 U.S. at 676, Rosenberger, 523 U.S. at 827. Viewpoint discrimination is an egregious subset of content-based discrimination. Id. at 827. While content-based discrimination may be justified by a compelling state interest narrowly drawn to achieve its ends, viewpoint discrimination can never be justified.

As previously stated, Petitioner claims that its web site is a non-public forum and the restriction is based not on the content of the web pages or on Respondent's viewpoint, but rather on the religious subject matter of the web pages and this type of subject-matter discrimination is reasonable in light of a nonpublic forum. (R. at 6). Even if the web site is found to be a nonpublic forum, Petitioner's defense of subject-matter discrimination is not supported by the facts because Petitioner has authorized other web pages that contain religious subject matter. For instance, The Council for Alternative Dispute Resolution has posted a site on "health" which includes an article with founder, Reverend Carla Boulevardier, Pastor of St. Peter's AME Church of Gotham. The Greater Gotham Youth League and North Gotham General Hospital also has a site on "health" including an article written by Fr. John Berrigan, Roman Catholic priest of Gotham Cathedral Church. (R. at 13). Petitioner cannot successfully claim that Respondent is being denied access based on the religious subject matter of the web pages when Petitioner has granted access to web sites that focus on articles written by heads of church.

Moreover, Respondent's perspective on creationism provides a specific premise, a perspective, and a standpoint from which the subject of the origin of humankind may be discussed and considered. The prohibited perspective, creationism, not the general subject matter, origin of humankind, resulted in the refusal to allow Respondent access to Petitioner's public web site, because the subject of the proposed web pages was within the approved category of subjects taught in the School District's curriculum. In arguing subject matter discrimination, Petitioner is merely providing a façade for viewpoint discrimination. Petitioner is not placing the entire topic of the origin of humankind off-limits as it is covered in the School District's curriculum. Instead Petitioner is rejecting Respondent's web pages based upon Respondent's religious ideology of the origin of humankind.

In <u>Lamb's Chapel</u>, this Court found the school district's denial of a church's request to exhibit a film dealing with family and child-rearing issues, to constitute viewpoint discrimination. 508 U.S. at 393. Moreover, this Court found that while opening the school facilities for after school use created a non-public forum, the restriction placed on the church's film was not viewpoint neutral and therefore a violation of the First Amendment. <u>Id.</u> at 393. Furthermore, this Court rationalized its holding by finding that the subject matter of child rearing would ordinarily be permitted; however, it was not permitted in this instance because it was presented from a religious perspective. <u>Id.</u> This rationale was in accordance with this Court's previous finding in <u>Cornelius</u> which held that:

> [A]lthough a speaker may be excluded form a nonpublic forum if he wishes to address topics not encompassed within the purpose of the forum or if he is a member of a class of speakers for whose benefit the forum was created, the government violates the First Amendment when it denies access to speaker solely to suppress point of view he espouses on otherwise includible subject.

473 U.S. at 805.

As established herein, Respondent's proposal encompasses a topic within the purpose of the forum, Respondent is a member of the class of speakers for which the forum was created, and Petitioner has not designated religion as an impermissible subject matter. Therefore, Petitioner's conduct in excluding Respondent's proposal constitutes viewpoint-discrimination, which blatantly violates the First Amendment's Free Speech Clause.

* * *

CONCLUSION

As Chief Justice Burger stated in <u>Lynch v. Donnelly</u>, "in our modern, complex society, whose traditions and constitutional underpinnings rest on and encourage diversity and pluralism in all areas, an absolutist approach in applying the Establishment Clause is simplistic and has been uniformly rejected by the Court." <u>Lynch</u>, 465 U.S. at 678. This case and questions involved cannot be dealt with simplistically. In the case before us, the School District elected to sponsor a web site for the purpose of hosting web pages that would "highlight topics of interest in the curriculum" and provide "information that may not be available in the textbooks" (R-11). Petitioner chose to initiate this web site for the purpose of expressive activities and to promote alternative information tied to the School District's curriculum. By opening this web site to all members of the community, Petitioner created a designated public forum. In doing so, Petitioner must abide by the rules of free speech in accordance with this type of forum. While Petitioner chooses to keep this forum open for general use to all members of the community, it must not discriminate against Respondent's religious viewpoint or the religious content of the proposed web pages. This type of content-based discrimination clearly violates Respondent's First Amendment right to free speech. Ergo, the Appellate Court correctly found that Petitioner's discriminatory behavior in denying Respondent's proposed web pages, violated Respondent's constitutional right to Free Speech.

The School District attempts to justify this First Amendment discriminatory behavior by arguing that it was compelled to do so in order to avoid violating the Establishment Clause. However, the Establishment Clause is not implicated in this case. Every Establishment Clause test articulated by this Court finds the separation of church and state well in place. Allowing the School District to prohibit the Branch Louisian's web pages only does an injustice to the children attending the District's schools. "The classroom is peculiarly the marketplace of ideas. The Nation's future depends upon leaders trained through wide exposure to that robust exchange of ideas which discovers truth out of a multitude of tongues, [rather] than through any kind of authoritative selection." Keyishian v. Board of Regents, 385 U.S. 589, 603 (1967). The School District is failing the children, education, and the Constitution by refusing to host Respondent's web pages and casting a "pall of orthodoxy over the classrooms." Id. The School District's argument loses on both issues. Respondent, therefore, requests that this Court affirm the Appellate Court's decision.

---

c. **Brief of Petitioner in the U.S. Supreme Court case: <u>Capi-</u>**
   <u>tol Square Review and Advisory Board v. Pinette</u>, 515 U.S.
   753 (1995)

ARGUMENT

I. A PURELY RELIGIOUS SYMBOL, SUCH AS A LARGE
   UNATTENDED LATIN CROSS, CLOSELY ASSOCIATED
   WITH THE SEAT OF GOVERNMENT, CONVEYS AN UN-
   MISTAKABLE MESSAGE OF GOVERNMENT IMPRIMA-
   TUR OF RELIGION.

In the Court's line of seasonal holiday display cases, the Court
has confronted the fact-specific nature of each case. That inquiry has
been criticized as dealing with "jurisprudence of minutae". <u>County of</u>
<u>Allegheny v. American Civil Liberties Union</u>, 492 U.S. 573, 674 (1989)
(Kennedy, J., concurring in the judgment in part and dissenting in part).
The Court need not engage in the same analysis in this case. Any isolated,
unattended display of a purely religious symbol at the seat of government violates the Establishment Clause. The combination of symbols
representing church and state conveys too powerful a message that can
easily be misunderstood, especially in a context where an observer has no
readily identifiable source to which to attribute the message, other than
government itself.

Symbols elicit direct and immediate emotions due to their strong
and enduring meaning. A religious, especially sectarian, symbol, no matter what the particular physical setting may be, conveys the unmistakable
message of that symbol's religious doctrine. The Latin Cross is a powerful
example of just such a symbol: ". . . the cross is a symbol par excellence
of Christianity itself as well as of Christ its head. . . . [T]he cross is en-
dowed with transcendent significance." Anderson Affidavit PP 8 and 11
(J.A. 131-132). No ambiguity about the symbolic meaning of the Latin
cross exists.

Similarly, a seat of government such as the Ohio Statehouse stands
inexorably as a symbolic "metaphor for government." <u>American Jewish</u>
<u>Congress v. City of Chicago</u>, 827 F.2d 120, 128 (7th Cir. 1987). When
the universal symbol of Christianity is placed directly in front of the Ohio
Statehouse, it is inseverably linked to the symbolic center of government.

In West Virginia State Board of Education v. Barnette, 319 U.S. 624, 632 (1943), the Court recognized the inescapable association between various symbols:

> Symbolism is a primitive but effective way of communicating ideas. The use of an emblem or flag to symbolize some system, idea, institution, or personality is a short cut from mind to mind. Causes and nations, political parties, lodges and ecclesiastical groups seek to knit the loyalty of their followings to a flag or banner, a color or design. The State announces rank, function, and authority through crowns and maces, uniforms and black robes, the church speaks through the Cross, the Crucifix, the altar and shrine, and clerical raiment. Symbols of State often convey political ideas just as religious symbols come to convey theological ones. (emphasis added).

The meaning of a symbol must be viewed in the overall context of its setting. "The context in which a symbol is used for purposes of expression is important, for the context may give meaning to the symbol." Spence v. Washington, 418 U.S. 405, 410 (1974). Scholars have observed that "people's responses to a symbol will be contingent upon their assessments of the circumstances of its usage." C. Elder & R. Cobb, The Political Uses of Symbols 57 (1983). This is especially true if the symbol is visually linked to other symbols. "When a particular symbol is used in conjunction with several other symbols, they may all become linked in the eyes of the general public." Id. at 77.

Respondents in the instant case were permitted, based upon the lower courts' decisions, to erect a Latin cross at the seat of secular government. Just as the Latin cross conveys a powerful message of religion, the Ohio Statehouse conveys a powerful message of governmental authority. See American Jewish Congress, 827 F.2d at 128 (discussing the symbol of city hall); Kaplan v. City of Burlington, 891 F.2d 1024, 1029-30 (2nd Cir. 1989), cert. denied, 496 U.S. 926 (1990) ("the park involved is not any city park, but rather City Hall park. This Park is bounded on the east by City Hall, the seat and the official symbol of Burlington city government. . . ."). And, just as the Latin cross is the most recognizable symbol of Christianity, the Ohio Statehouse is the single most visible and recognizable symbol of government in the State of Ohio. Any association of the two threatens to blur the distinction between church and state because the observer will view it as government's sponsorship of religion.[8]

The Establishment Clause protects against "any imprimatur of state approval of religious sects or practices." <u>Widmar v. Vincent</u>, 454 U.S. 263, 274 (1981). The combination of the cross and government, in a context where the latter is perceived to support the former, creates this danger.

It has long been recognized that speech may take many forms, including such nonverbal forms as symbolic displays. Not all forms of speech, however, have equivalent impact. Sometimes, such as in this case, speech must be evaluated not only on the basis of its content, but also as to the identity of the speaker. A determination of authorship often is directly determinable from the columnist, the television commentator, the rally speaker, the sign holder. All can be noted directly by the reader or the listener. But in the case of an unattended display, the source of the communication must be inferred. In the absence of clear and direct information to the contrary, an observer reasonably perceives the message conveyed by an unattended display as the message of the landowner.

The grounds of the Ohio Statehouse, in addition to being a public forum, as observed by the Sixth Circuit, are home to statues of historical figures important to Ohio and Columbus. As the record reflects, these grounds have previously housed only two other temporary, unattended displays -- a secular and pluralistic seasonal display and a chart showing the progress of the community's United Way campaign. Observers of these unattended displays correctly will perceive the message conveyed by these symbols as messages supported and approved by the State of Ohio.

The Sixth Circuit declared that since the unattended display of the Latin cross was presented in a public forum, only a "hypothetical dolt" would not realize this message came from private citizens, not the government. Because government can and does convey symbolic unattended

---

8   The Latin cross was not erected as part of a holiday seasonal display but stood majestically by itself in the middle of the front lawn of the Capitol Square. App. A43. Respondents' application specifically requested this location which was apart from and a distance away from where the Christmas tree and menorah were located. (J.A. 43).

messages from the very grounds upon which private speech rallies frequently occur, however, the mere fact that private speech is permitted does not remove the inference that an unattended display on government property is government endorsed.

A battery of cases has held that the display of a cross on government property "dramatically conveys a message of governmental support for Christianity, whatever the intentions of those responsible for the display may be." <u>American Civil Liberties Union v. City of St. Charles</u>, 794 F.2d 265, 271 (7th Cir. 1986), cert. denied, 479 U.S. 961 (1986). See <u>Gonzales v. North Township of Lake County</u>, 4 F.3d 1412, 1423 (7th Cir. 1993) (court held that the cross "does not bear secular trappings sufficient to neutralize its religious message," and indeed "does not convey any secular message, whether remote, indirect, or incidental").

For this reason, courts regularly and persistently have granted injunctions and other proper relief when an Establishment Clause challenge is raised against an attempt by anyone to display a Latin cross on government property. See, e.g., <u>Mendelson v. City of St. Cloud</u>, 719 F. Supp. 1065, 1069 (M.D. Fla. 1989) ("no federal case has ever found the display of a Latin cross on public land by a state or state subdivision to be constitutional"); <u>American Civil Liberties Union v. Mississippi General Services Admin.</u>, 652 F. Supp. 380, 384-85 & n.2 (S.D. Miss. 1987) ("in no other federal case either before or since Lynch v. Donnelly has the public display of a cross by a state or subdivision thereof been found to be constitutional").

This judicial result has been the same whether the Latin cross on government property is large, see, e.g., <u>Jewish War Veterans v. United States</u>, 695 F. Supp. 3, 5 (D.D.C. 1988) (65' illuminated cross serving as war memorial on Marine Corps base; permanent injunction granted); <u>Mendelson</u>, 719 F. Supp. at 1066 (12' cross on city water tower; injunction granted), medium-sized, see, e.g., <u>Libin v. Town of Greenwich</u>, 625 F. Supp. 393, 394 (D. Conn. 1985) (3' X 5' illuminated cross on firehouse; preliminary injunction granted), or quite small, see, e.g., <u>Harris v. City of Zion</u>, 927 F.2d 1401, 1402-04 (7th Cir. 1991), cert. denied, ___U.S.___, 112 S.Ct. 3054 (1992) (Latin cross appeared in one quadrant of municipal corporate seals; permanent injunction granted); <u>Friedman v. Board of County Commissioners</u>, 781 F.2d 777, 779 (10th Cir. 1985) (en banc), cert. denied, 476 U.S. 1169 (1986) (Latin cross appeared on county seal; injunction granted).

In addition, this has been true even when the display of the Latin cross on government property has existed for many years, see, e.g., <u>American Civil Liberties Union v. Rabun County Chamber of Commerce</u>, 698 F.2d 1098, 1101 (11th Cir. 1983) (cross in state park originally dated back almost 30 years; permanent injunction granted); <u>Jewish War Veterans</u>, 695 F. Supp. at 5 (cross on Marine Corps base more than 22 years; permanent injunction granted), and even where it was privately sponsored. See <u>Gonzales</u>, 4 F.3d at 1422-23 (crucifix in public park for more than 40 years; permanent injunction granted). It is this judicial recognition of the inability of an observer to separate the state from the message of the Latin cross that undermines the decision below.

II. THE ESTABLISHMENT CLAUSE MAY REQUIRE A FINDING OF THE UNCONSTITUTIONALITY OF AN UNATTENDED RELIGIOUS DISPLAY, EVEN IF SUCH DISPLAY STANDS IN A PUBLIC FORUM

The decision of the court below is sweeping in scope, creating a per se rule obviating the need to examine how the message is perceived by a reasonable observer. The lower court focused not on the risk that the government's message will be misperceived, but only on the public nature of the forum in which the message is relayed.

The nature of a public forum guarantees broad communication. The Court first recognized the concept of the public forum in <u>Hague v. CIO</u>, 307 U.S. 496 (1939). The Court observed that streets and parks in this country universally have been considered public forums:

> Wherever the title of streets and parks may rest, they have immemorially been held in trust for the use of the public and, time out of mind, have been used for purposes of assembly, communicating thought between citizens, and discussing public questions. Such use of the streets and public places has, from ancient times, been a part of the privileges, immunities, rights, and liberties of citizens.

Id. at 515. See also <u>Lamb's Chapel v. Center Moriches Union Free School District</u>, ___U.S.___, 113 S. Ct 2131, 2146 (1993) ("parks and sidewalks are traditional public fora"); <u>International Soc'y for Krishna Consciousness v. Lee,</u>___ U.S.___, 112 S. Ct. 2711, 2717 (1992) (Kennedy, J., concurring) ("types of property that we have recognized as the quintessential public forums are streets, parks, and sidewalks").

In these traditional public forums, as well as in so-called "designated" or "limited" public forums, the government may not prohibit all communication. <u>Cornelius v. NAACP Legal Defense and Education Fund, Inc.</u>, 473 U.S. 788 (1985); <u>Perry Educ. Assn. v. Perry Local Educators' Assn.</u>, 470 U.S. 37, 45 (1983) ("[I]n places which by long tradition or by government fiat have been devoted to assembly and debate, the rights of the State to limit expressive activity are sharply circumscribed.") (emphasis added).

The public forum doctrine by itself, however, does not require the State of Ohio to permit the erection of any symbol upon government property characterized as a public forum. Just as "[t]he principle that government accommodation of the free exercise of religion does not supersede the fundamental limitations imposed by the Establishment Clause", <u>Lee v. Weisman</u>, ___U.S.___, 112 S.Ct. 2649, 2655 (1992), the public forum doctrine should not be permitted to "swallow up" the Establishment Clause. <u>Kaplan</u>, 891 F.2d at 1029. That a message is delivered in a public forum does not give government the right to advocate religion. Nor may it permit a private party to proffer speech that is likely to be perceived as government speech endorsing religion. Public forum or not, government may not lend its support to a particular religious message or allow private parties to manipulate government for that purpose.

In <u>Burson v. Freeman</u>, ___U.S.___, 112 S.Ct. 1846 (1992), Justice Kennedy squarely recognized the inherent clash between competing constitutional doctrines:

> The same use of the compelling interest test is adopted today, not to justify or condemn a category of suppression but to determine the accuracy of the justification the State gives for its law. There is a narrow area in which the

First Amendment permits freedom of expression to yield to the extent necessary for an accommodation of another constitutional right.

Id., 112 S.Ct. at 1859 (Kennedy, J., concurring). And just as competing doctrines were balanced in that case, they must be balanced here. The Sixth Circuit's holding does not balance competing doctrines. It allows one to trump the other.

* * *

CONCLUSION

For the reasons set forth, this Court should reverse the decision of the court below.

---

d. Brief of Respondents in the U.S. Supreme Court case: <u>Capitol Square Review and Advisory Board v. Pinette</u>, 515 U.S. 753 (1995)

ARGUMENT

I. THE STATE'S DISCRIMINATORY REFUSAL TO PERMIT DISPLAY OF THE KU KLUX KLAN CROSS IN A TRADITIONAL PUBLIC FORUM VIOLATES THE FREE SPEECH AND FREE EXERCISE CLAUSES OF THE FIRST AMENDMENT AND THE EQUAL PROTECTION CLAUSE OF THE FOURTEENTH AMENDMENT

The record in this case clearly establishes that officials of the Capitol Square Review and Advisory Board persistently engaged in a series of discriminatory actions to prevent the Ku Klux Klan from displaying the Klan cross in the public forum at Capitol Square. The maneuvering began after the Ku Klux Klan filed an application to hold a rally at Capitol Square on the birthday of Martin Luther King, Jr. On October 29, 1993, the Board received, but did not act upon, the Klan's permit request. Then, on November 18, 1993, Board Chairman Richard Finan conceded that there was no legal basis to prevent the Klan from holding its rally. RA11.[9] The Board's attention shifted to efforts to forestall the possibility that the Klan might obtain a permit to erect a Klan cross in Capitol Square, because similar applications had been filed in Cincinnati by another Klan group. RA12.

The Capitol Square Review and Advisory Board announced its strategy to forestall possible display of the Klan cross on November 18, 1993. On that date, Board officials stated that the traditional state Christmas tree would not be erected in the Capitol Square during the 1993 Christmas season. They also stated that the Board would not allow the Lubavitch sect to display a menorah that had been permitted in previous years.

The Board's initial strategy crumbled on November 23, 1993, after vigorous public protests and after strong political pressure from the Governor and legislative leaders who appointed the members of the Board. In response to this pressure, the Board suddenly changed course and agreed to permit the menorah and to display the tree. A15; JA 167-168. A few days later, Rabbi Capland applied for a permit to erect the Lubavitch menorah. His permit was granted the same day. A15.

The Board's change of position, which was reported in detail by the press, caused Donnie Carr to file a permit application to display the Klan cross. According to Carr, the permit application was filed to protest the Board's gratuitous policy of denying Klan access to Capitol Square while granting access to the Lubavitch sect. During his testimony at the hearing below he explained that "since we were being excluded by the City or the State, the Capitol Square Review and Advisory Board, that we would attempt to obtain a permit to erect a cross for the Christmas season." JA 136-137.

---

9   The Board did not issue a permit for the Klan rally until ordered to do so by the District Court on January 4, 1994. RA1.

A. The Constitution prohibits discrimination based on political or religious viewpoint.

It was against this record detailing the State's plan to bar the Klan cross that the Court of Appeals for the Sixth Circuit concluded, in a gross understatement, that "there was no indication that Ohio treated the Klan or its display favorably." A10. Indeed, as the Circuit made clear, this case has much less to do with endorsement of the Klan's speech than with discrimination against it. Thus, it commented: "Zealots have First Amendment rights too. Some speech may be distasteful, unpopular and outright offensive, but as Thurgood Marshall so persuasively wrote, the protection found in the First Amendment does not depend on popular opinion[.]" A11. The Sixth Circuit underscored its point by quoting Justice Marshall's statement in Police Department of Chicago v. Mosley, 408 U.S. 92 (1972):

> Necessarily then, under the Equal Protection Clause, not to mention the First Amendment itself, government may not grant the use of a forum to people whose views it finds acceptable, but deny use to those wishing to express less favored or more controversial views. And it may not select which issues are worth discussing or debating in public facilities. There is an "equality of status in the field of ideas," and government must afford all points of view an equal opportunity to be heard. Once a forum is opened up to assembly or speaking by some groups, government may not prohibit others from assembling or speaking on the basis of what they intend to say. Selective exclusions from a public forum may not be based on content alone, and may not be justified by reference to content alone. A11-A12 (30 F.3d at 680), 408 U.S. at 96 (footnote omitted by the Circuit).

This Court has consistently restated this principle in cases decided since Mosley. For example, in Carey v. Brown, 447 U.S. 455, (1980), this Court stated that "[a]ny restriction on expressive activity because of its content would completely undercut the 'profound national commitment to the principle that debate on public issues should be uninhibited, robust, and wide open.'" Id. at 462-63, quoting New York Times v. Sullivan, 376 U.S. 254, 270 (1964). Similarly in R.A.V. v. St. Paul, U.S. , 112

S. Ct. 2538 (1992), this Court stated, "The First Amendment generally prevents government from proscribing speech, see, e.g., Cantwell v. Connecticut, 310 U.S. 296, 309-311 (1940), or even expressive conduct, see e.g. Texas v. Johnson, 491 U.S. 397, 406 (1989), because of disapproval of the ideas expressed. Content based regulations are presumptively invalid." R.A.V., 112 S. Ct. at 2542. According to FCC v. Pacifica Foundation, 438 U.S. 726 (1978)," . . . the fact that society may find speech offensive is not a sufficient reason for suppressing it. Indeed, if it is the speaker's opinion that gives offense, that consequence is a reason for according it constitutional protection." Id. at 745-46.

B. The State's Establishment Clause claim is a pretext for discrimination.

Faced with this overwhelming authority, the State fails to address whether its efforts to prevent display of the Klan cross were motivated by the unpopularity of the Ku Klux Klan and its symbol. Instead, the State prefers to argue that its efforts to prevent display of the Klan cross were motivated solely by a desire to avoid an Establishment Clause violation. According to the State's brief, display of the Klan cross at Capitol Square conveys the "message of government imprimatur of religion" because it is a Latin Cross which, in turn is the symbol of Christianity. Pet. Br. 12-17.

The disingenuousness of the State's Establishment Clause claim is patently apparent. First, contrary to the State's assertion, the Klan itself clearly regards the cross as both a political symbol and a religious symbol. Second, even if it is assumed that the Klan cross is a purely religious symbol, the State may still not discriminate against it nor engage in "maneuvers to bring about a legal ascendancy of one sect over another." Thomas Jefferson, Letter to Elbridge Gerry, January 26, 1799, reprinted in SAUL K. PADOVER, A JEFFERSON PROFILE (1956) 112. Yet, the evidence of discrimination on this record is undeniable. When the menorah was erected in December of 1993, the governor participated in the lighting ceremony. RA23 (The Columbus Dispatch, December 9, 1993). In addition, the menorah has been displayed without state objection for several years. Unlike the permit application for the Klan cross, the application for the menorah was approved in advance of the day it was filed.

Under this Court's well-established precedents, the State may not permit the menorah and bar the cross by selectively invoking the Establishment Clause. For example, in <u>Niemotko v. Maryland</u>, 340 U.S. 268 (1951), the Court unanimously struck down the discriminatory refusal of government officials to allow a Jehovah's Witness group from holding a bible meeting in a public park. Similarly, in <u>Fowler v. Rhode Island</u>, 345 U.S. 67 (1953), this Court found that the First Amendment was violated when a Jehovah's Witness religious service was treated differently than those of Catholics or Protestants. Id. at 69-70.

In <u>Larson v. Valente</u>, 456 U.S. 228 (1982), this Court underscored the constitutional prohibition against discrimination among religions. "The clearest command of the Establishment Clause is that one religious denomination cannot be officially preferred over another." Id. at 244. And, as this Court stated in Allegheny, "[w]hatever else the Establishment Clause may mean . . ., it certainly means that at the very least that government may not demonstrate a preference for one particular sect or creed. . . ." 492 U.S. at 605.

The State's discriminatory motives were highlighted by the Capitol Square Review and Advisory Board's use of ad hoc procedures designed to obstruct Klan access to the Capitol Square. The Board's vacillation over whether to impose a flat ban on all unattended displays at Capitol Square during the Christmas holidays was justified by no published rule or regulation. Nor was any rule or regulation cited as a basis for the anticipatory denial of a permit for the display of the Klan cross.

The ad hoc quality of the Board's permit denial in this case was noted in the findings of the Board's administrative hearing officer. According to these findings:

The evidence adduced at the [administrative] hearing in this matter does not offer a complete explanation of the process or basis for the Board's denial of the Appellant's request. Board Executive Director Keller did, however, advise the Appellant that the Board denied its request on advice of counsel, who had raised constitutional objections to the request. The record does not establish whether other objections were raised by the Board's counsel. A33, P4. The standards applied to the Klan are thus unpublished and unknown. The use of such ad hoc procedures to facilitate discrimination against disfavored speakers is forbidden by the

First Amendment. <u>Forsyth County, Ga. v. Nationalist Movement</u>, U.S., 112 S. Ct. 2395 (1992); <u>Lakewood v. Plain Dealer Publishing Co.</u>, 486 U.S. 750 (1988).

The rule against discrimination is thoroughly consistent with the command of this Court, more than fifty years ago, that no public official "can prescribe what shall be orthodox in politics [or] religion . . .," <u>West Virginia Board of Education v. Barnette</u>, 319 U.S. 624, 642 (1943). The decisions of the District Court and the Court of Appeals were based on this command and therefore should be affirmed.

* * *

CONCLUSION

For the foregoing reasons, the Respondents respectfully urge this Court to affirm the decision of the United States Court of Appeals for the Sixth Circuit.

_____

2. Evaluate the following sections of a petition for a writ of mandamus. Identify what these sections do well (if anything) and what you would edit or revise (if anything) in these sections.

<u>SUMMARY OF THE ARGUMENT AND REASONS WHY MANDAMUS SHOULD ISSUE</u>

This petition for writ of mandamus presents two issues that have been conclusively determined by binding precedent of this circuit: ***first***, that the district court clearly abused its discretion by failing to enforce a valid contractual forum selection clause requiring the dismissal or transfer of the underlying lawsuit. <u>In re Fireman's Fund Insurance Companies</u>, 588 F.2d 93, 95 (5th Cir. 1979) (forum selection clause preempts statutory venue provision); <u>In re Ricoh Corp.</u>, 870 F.2d 570, 572-74 (11th Cir. 1989) (district court clearly abused its discretion in failing to enforce forum selection clause), <u>petition for writ after remand from Stewart Org., Inc. v. Ricoh Corp.</u>, 487 U.S. 22 (1988); and ***second***, that mandamus should issue to correct this manifest error. <u>Ricoh</u>, 870 F.2d at 571-72 (writ of mandamus is to be issued to correct district court's failure to enforce forum selection clause).

This lawsuit arises from a dispute among partners concerning the proper disposition of approximately $23 million in proceeds from the sale of partnership properties in three related partnerships. The partnership agreements contain a forum selection clause calling for any partnership disputes to be brought either in Delaware, the state in which the partnerships are organized, or one of the venues where the partnership properties are located. No properties are located in Florida. Nevertheless, the general partner filed an interpleader action in the U.S. District Court for the Southern District of Florida. The general partner claimed that it was an innocent stakeholder of the disputed proceeds as between the two limited partners, Petitioners and a sister company of the general partner. Plaintiff invoked 28 U.S.C. § 1397, which provides that venue for statutory interpleader actions is appropriate wherever any claimant resides. Both the general partner and its affiliate/limited partner are based in southern Florida.

Petitioners moved pursuant to Fed. R. Civ. P. 12(b)(3) and 28 U.S.C. § 1406 for the case to be dismissed for improper venue because Florida was not one of the contractually agreed-to venues. Alternatively, Petitioners sought transfer to the District of Delaware where a separate action, filed by Petitioners, is pending. The Honorable William J. Zloch, United States District Judge, Southern District of Florida (Respondent), issued two opinions on Petitioners motion. In his initial opinion, he found that:

- The forum selection clause was valid and applicable to this controversy.

- The forum selection clause did **not** permit venue in Florida.

- The forum selection clause was not preempted by 28 U.S.C. § 1397 because even exclusive statutory venue provisions can be waived by contractual agreement of the parties.

After requesting further briefing on the issue of whether 28 U.S.C. § 1404(a) or § 1406 was the proper vehicle to effectuate transfer or dismissal of the case, Judge Zloch issued a second opinion. Without altering any of his initial conclusions, Judge Zloch held that <u>neither</u> § 1404(a) <u>nor</u> § 1406 authorized dismissal or transfer of the case. Judge Zloch held that venue in Florida was not improper as that term is used in 28 U.S.C. § 1406 because venue in Florida was available under the interpleader venue statute, 28 U.S.C. § 1397; therefore, he could neither dismiss nor transfer the action pursuant to §1406. Judge Zloch also refused to transfer the case pursuant to 28 U.S.C. § 1404(a), holding that § 1404(a) was inapplicable because the case could not originally have been brought in the District of Delaware under 28 U.S.C. § 1397. Judge Zloch refused to reconsider his ruling and refused to certify it for interlocutory appeal.

Although mandamus is an extraordinary remedy, it is appropriate where there has been a clear abuse of discretion. Here, Judge Zloch clearly abused his discretion by refusing to enforce the contractual forum selection clause between the parties. The applicable precedent leaves no doubt that the parties contractual selection of venue should be honored even if other venues are specified by statute. <u>Fireman's Fund</u>, 588 F.2d at 95. Indeed, Judge Zloch so found in his initial opinion. His subsequent decision not to give effect to the forum selection clause because of the venue provisions of § 1397 simply cannot be reconciled with his original holding. Nor can it be reconciled with the law.

Petitioners have no other adequate alternative remedy. The option of seeking reversal on venue grounds only after being forced to endure full discovery, litigation, and trial in southern Florida is not only inadequate but is terribly wasteful. This Court has determined that mandamus is appropriate to correct a district court's refusal to enforce a forum selection clause. <u>Ricoh</u>, 870 F.2d at 571-72. This remedy should be granted here.

STATEMENT OF THE ISSUE PRESENTED AND RELIEF SOUGHT

Whether the venue provisions of 28 U.S.C. § 1397 are subject to contractual waiver through a forum selection clause and, if so, whether an action filed in violation of the forum selection clause should be dismissed or transferred to a contractually agreed forum pursuant to either 28 U.S.C. § 1406 or 28 U.S.C. § 1404(a). The district court's opinion denying dismissal or transfer of this case is directly contrary to the following controlling authorities:

In re Fireman's Fund Insurance Companies, 588 F.2d 93 (5th Cir. 1979).

In re Ricoh, 870 F.2d 570 (11th Cir. 1989), petition for writ after remand from Stewart Org. v. Ricoh, 487 U.S. 22 (1988).

The Bremen v. Zapata Off-Shore Co., 407 U.S. 1 (1972).

Carnival Cruise Lines, Inc. v. Shute, 499 U.S. 585 (1991).

Petitioners request this Court to issue a writ of mandamus ordering the district court to dismiss this action for lack of proper venue or, alternatively, to transfer the action to the United States District Court for the District of Delaware pursuant to the forum selection clause applicable to this matter, and to order such further and other relief as the Court deems appropriate in the circumstances.

[We have eliminated the statement of facts and proceedings below sections]

ARGUMENT

I. MANDAMUS IS AN APPROPRIATE REMEDY TO COR-RECT RESPONDENT'S CLEAR ABUSE OF DISCRETION

Mandamus is a proper remedy where the trial court fails to enforce a forum selection clause that requires the dismissal or transfer of an action. In re Ricoh, 870 F.2d 570, 571-72 (11th Cir. 1989), petition for writ after remand from Stewart Org. v. Ricoh, 487 U.S. 22 (1988). It is particularly appropriate for the Court of Appeals to issue the writ when the district court has failed to certify the issue for interlocutory appeal. Id. at 572 n. 4.

The district court clearly abused its discretion when it failed to enforce a valid forum selection clause. In <u>Ricoh</u>, this Court was explicit about the necessity to enforce forum selection clauses by transfer under 28 U.S.C. § 1404(a):

> In considering Ricoh's motion under section 1404(a) to transfer this action to the Southern District of New York, the district court . . . clearly abused its discretion . . .

> . . . [The district court's] deference to the filing forum would only encourage parties to violate their contractual obligations, the integrity of which are vital to our judicial system. See <u>Stewart</u>, [487 U.S. at 33], 108 S.Ct. at 2246 ([E]nforcement of valid forum selection clauses, bargained for by the parties, protects their legitimate expectations and furthers vital interests of the justice system.) (Kennedy, J., concurring); see also <u>Stewart</u>, 810 F.2d 1066, 1075 (11th Cir. 1987) (en banc) (Where, as here, the non-movant has not shown that it would be unjust to honor a forum selection clause that it has freely given, the interest of justice requires that the non-movant be held to its promise.) (Tjoflat, J., concurring). We conclude that when a motion under section 1404(a) seeks to enforce a valid, reasonable choice of forum clause, the opponent bears the burden of persuading the court that the contractual forum is sufficiently inconvenient to justify retention of the dispute.

> In so concluding, we adhere to the reasoning advanced by the Supreme Court in its opinion in this case. See <u>Stewart</u>, [487 U.S. 22] , 108 S.Ct. 2239, 101 L.Ed.2d 22 (1988). . . . [T]he clear import of the Court's opinion is that the venue mandated by a choice of forum clause rarely will be outweighed by other 1404(a) factors.

<u>Ricoh</u>, 870 F.2d at 572-73. The facts of <u>Ricoh</u> parallel the instant case:

> Looking to the specific facts of this case, we note that the instant contract was freely and fairly negotiated by experienced business professionals. . . . Stewart has neither alleged nor shown the presence of fraud,

duress, misrepresentation, or other misconduct that would bar the clause's enforcement. Nor has Stewart demonstrated that because of intervening and unexpected occurrences between the contract's formation and the filing of the suit, the contract's purpose would be frustrated if we were to mandate the transfer of this case to a Manhattan forum. This suit, therefore, does not present the type of exceptional situation in which judicial enforcement of a contractual choice of forum clause would be improper. See <u>Stewart</u>, [487 U.S. at 33], 108 S.Ct. at 2246 (Kennedy, J., concurring). The district court clearly abused its discretion in concluding otherwise.

<u>Ricoh</u>, 870 F.2d at 573-74.

In these circumstances, Petitioners have no other adequate alternative remedy. The only conceivable alternative remedy, "inevitable reversal by this court after the defendants have been forced to endure full discovery, full litigation, and a full trial is scarcely . . . adequate." <u>In re Cooper</u>, 971 F.2d 640, 641 (11th Cir. 1992) (citing <u>In re Watkins</u>, 271 F.2d 771, 775 (5th Cir. 1959)). Therefore, this Court should issue a writ of mandamus to order the Respondent to dismiss or transfer the underlying action.

II. RESPONDENT CLEARLY ABUSED ITS DISCRETION BY DENYING THE MOTION TO DISMISS OR TRANSFER

There is an unbroken line of controlling authorities that require the enforcement of contractual forum selection clauses. <u>The Bremen v. Zapata Off-Shore Co.</u>, 407 U.S. 1 (1972); <u>Carnival Cruise Lines, Inc. v. Shute</u>, 499 U.S. 585 (1991); <u>Stewart Organization v. Ricoh</u>, 487 U.S. 22 (1988); <u>Ricoh</u>, 870 F.2d 570; <u>In re Fireman's Fund Insurance Companies</u>, 588 F.2d 93 (5th Cir. 1979). This point is not disputed by the parties. Judge Zloch concluded, however, that neither § 1406 nor § 1404(a) empowered him to dismiss or transfer the action. This conclusion was clearly in error.

Judge Zloch determined that 28 U.S.C. § 1404(a), rather than § 1406, applied to the motion to dismiss or transfer. Judge Zloch followed what Petitioners believe is a minority opinion among the courts that was triggered by a footnote in the <u>Stewart</u> case, 487 U.S. at 28 n. 8. <u>See</u>, <u>e.g.</u>,

Jumara v. State Farm Ins. Co., 55 F.3d 873, 878-79 (3d Cir. 1995). This position holds that cases are not subject to dismissal under Rule 12(b)(3) or 28 U.S.C. § 1406 on the basis of a forum selection clause because the venue where the case is filed is not made improper by operation of the forum selection clause. Id. Instead, these courts apply 28 U.S.C. § 1404(a) to determine whether the case is to be transferred. Id.

Judge Zloch concluded, however, that § 1404(a) was inapplicable because this case could not have been brought in Delaware under the interpleader venue provision, 28 U.S.C. § 1397. This conclusion is directly contrary to the established law of this circuit, In re Fireman's Fund Ins. Co., 588 F.2d 93, 95 (5th Cir. 1979).

In Fireman's Fund, this Court held that the specific, exclusive venue provision of the Miller Act, 40 U.S.C. § 270b(b), mandating that [e]very suit instituted under this section shall be brought . . . in the United States District Court for any district in which the contract was to be performed and executed and not elsewhere, was nonetheless subject to a forum selection clause between the parties which called for a transfer to a forum where the contract was not to be performed or executed. 588 F.2d at 95. The Court noted that a motion to transfer under 28 U.S.C. § 1404(a) applies to any civil action. Id. Furthermore, the Court noted that even an exclusive venue provision containing the phrase, and not elsewhere, was still subject to alteration by the parties forum selection clause, because venue may be varied by contract. Id.

The Miller Act's exclusive venue provision is worded much stronger than 28 U.S.C. § 1397, yet this circuit recognized that a party's power to contract into another forum is even stronger. This opinion is buttressed by numerous other cases cited by Judge Zloch in the 10/22/96 Order (at pp. 6-7) holding that forum selection clauses preempt the operation of venue statutes, including exclusive venue provisions. B & D Mechanical, 70 F.3d at 1117; FGS Constructors, Inc. v. Carlow, 64 F.3d 1230, 1233 (8th Cir. 1995); Pittsburgh Tank, 62 F.3d at 36; Bense v. Interstate Battery System of America, 683 F.2d 718 (2d Cir. 1982).

Judge Zloch initially followed these authorities in the 10/22/96 Order, specifically holding that "section 1397 . . . is a venue provision and thus subject to contractual waiver." 10/22/96 Order at 7. But he then ignored these authorities in the 12/5/96 Order, concluding that "a contractually designated forum that would not be an appropriate venue for the action under the interpleader venue statue, section1397, is not a court where the action might have been brought under section 1404(a)." 12/5/96 Order at 8.

Judge Zloch cited <u>Hoffman v. Blaski</u>, 363 U.S. 335 (1960), as his sole authority for this proposition. 12/5/96 Order at 8. However, this case is inapposite to the issue because it has nothing whatsoever to do with a forum selection clause or the parties right to make a prior selection of venue by consent or agreement. In <u>Hoffman</u>, the defendants moved under section 1404(a) for transfer to a forum where the defendants had not been amenable to service of process and had no contacts, and where venue was obviously improper at the initiation of the action by plaintiffs. 363 U.S. at 336-37 and n. 2, 338-39 and n. 5. Defendants' motion stated that defendants were willing to submit themselves to the jurisdiction and venue of the alternative forum, if the court would consider the transfer on the basis of convenience to the parties and witnesses. <u>Id.</u> The forum to which defendants sought to be transferred was clearly one in which the case could <u>not</u> have been brought by the plaintiffs when the suit was filed. <u>Id.</u> In these circumstances, the court determined that a transfer to the forum under section 1404(a) was not proper. 363 U.S. at 342-43.

<u>Hoffman</u> is inapposite because in the instant case, plaintiff had every right to bring this action in the forum selected by the Agreements forum selection clause. The controlling authorities hold that forum selection clauses must be enforced unless the opponents of the motion prove that there are exceptional circumstances that render the enforcement of the clause unreasonable and improper. <u>Ricoh</u>, 870 F.2d at 572-74; <u>Stewart</u>, 487 U.S. at 33 (Kennedy, J., concurring). Respondent ignored these authorities, and made a clearly erroneous determination of Petitioner's motion to dismiss or transfer that flies in the face of these authorities and even contradicts Respondent's prior order in the instant case. Therefore, the Court should issue a writ of mandamus to remedy Respondent's clear abuse of discretion and usurpation of judicial power.

CONCLUSION

WHEREFORE, Petitioners respectfully request this Court to issue a writ of mandamus ordering the district court to dismiss this case for lack of proper venue, or to transfer this action to the United States

District Court for the District of Delaware pursuant to the forum selection clause applicable to this matter, and to order such further and other relief as the Court deems appropriate in the circumstances.

_____

Part V

Research and Writing Problems in Upper Division Subjects

I. REMEDIES

WRITING IN THE LAW DISCIPLINE PROBLEMS

1. Based on the following information, prepare a memorandum analyzing whether the contract between Davis and Jiang can be enforced by specific performance:

Patricia Piao-Liang Davis is a 20 year old super-model who goes by the professional name "Piao-Liang." She was born in Nanjing, PRC in 1989, but was orphaned at four months of age, and was adopted at six months of age by Clifford and June Davis, U.S. citizens, and raised in Provo, Utah. Piao-Liang is a naturalized citizen of the United States, and is domiciled and resident in Provo, Utah. Piao-Liang has joined a group of other super-models who offer their unfertilized ova for auction on an internet site known as Dezyner-Genes.com. Although she has participated in the web site since January 2007, she has never accepted any bids to purchase her eggs.

While on a photo-shoot for Drop Dead Gorgeous magazine that took her to various locations in China (the Great Wall and Tiananmen Square in Beijing, the Bund in Shanghai, and others), Piao-Liang was approached at West Lake in Hangzhou by a businessman, Mr. Jerry Jiang (whose Chinese name is Jiang Chuang-ping). Jiang explained that his wife was infertile, and he was interested in purchasing an ovum from Piao-Liang, and offered her $1 million for it. She was flattered and orally agreed to the transaction. The two drank baijiu and toasted each other several times to celebrate the deal. When she returned to the United States,

Piao-Liang's lawyers, Hart, Charles, & LaRouche, reviewed Jiang's written proposal for the agreement concerning the sale of the ovum, and they accepted the terms, but added a forum selection and choice of law clause in the agreement, specifying that any action arising under the contract would be brought in a state or federal court in California and that the law of California would govern the contract. The contract was signed by Piao-Liang in New York, NY, on November 2, 2008, and by Jiang in Taibei, Republic of China (Taiwan), on November 4, 2008. The egg or eggs were to be delivered by June 1, 2009, and the payment of $1 million was to be made immediately upon successful fertilization and implantation.

Piao-Liang discovered in late November that Mr. Jiang is the nephew of the late General and President of the ROC, Jiang Ji-shi, better known to the world as Chiang Kai-shek. This horrified her because her Chinese family had been oppressed by the Nationalists prior to the Communist victory in China. She decided to refuse to go through with the sale, and Mr. Jiang sued her in the United States District Court for the Northern District of California.

Purchase and Sale Contract

WHEREFORE, Mr. Jerry Jiang Chuang-Ping (Buyer) and Ms. Patricia Piao-Liang Davis (Seller) wish to enter into an agreement for the transfer of at least one egg from Seller's ovaries to Buyer for the purpose of fertilization of the egg and implantation in Buyer's wife; and

WHEREFORE, the parties, Buyer and Seller, in consideration of the mutual promises stated herein and for other good and valuable consideration; and

WHEREFORE, the parties, Buyer and Seller, wish to complete this transaction at the earliest practicable time, and in no event later than June 1, 2009;

Then the parties covenant and agree to the following:

1. At the earliest practicable opportunity, and in no event later than June 1, 2009, in New York City, NY or Salt Lake City, UT, or at any other mutually agreeable location, Seller shall deliver to Buyer's OB-GYN physician one or more healthy and viable ova (i.e., eggs) from her ovaries.

2. Upon receipt and successful fertilization of the egg(s), the egg(s) are to be implanted in Buyer's wife's uterus,

3. After successful implantation of the fertilized egg(s) in Buyer's wife's uterus, without miscarriage, for twenty-one days, Buyer shall pay Seller by wire transfer to Osmond National Bank, Account No. 100223456 owned by Seller, the sum of one million United States dollars.

4. In the event that conditions 2 and 3 cannot be successfully completed with the initial supply of the egg(s) from Seller, Seller shall, within six weeks of notification by facsimile or U.S. mail by Buyer of the failure of conditions 2 or 3, supply one or more additional healthy and viable eggs to Buyer's OB-GYN physician in New York City, NY or Salt Lake City, UT, and shall continue to supply eggs in the manner described in this paragraph every six weeks until successful completion of conditions 2 and 3 of this contract.

5. Should any dispute between the parties arise under this agreement, the parties, Buyer and Seller, agree that all disputes shall be resolved in litigation that shall be filed in a state or federal court in the State of California and all conditions and terms and obligations of this contract shall be governed by and interpreted under California law.

Signed by Buyer: Signed by Seller:

_____   _____
Jerry Jiang Chuang-ping   Patricia Piao-Liang Davis
Date: November 4, 2008   Date: November 2, 2008

_____

Piao-Liang® is Beauty
234 Joseph Smith Drive
Provo, UT 84602 USA
(801) 555-piao

December 18, 2008

By Facsimile and Mail:

Mr. Jerry Jiang Chuang-ping
Two Embarcadero Center, Suite 3801
San Francisco, CA 94111-3909
Phone: 415-555-7779
Fax: 888-555-7789

To Mr. Jiang:

I am canceling the deal. I never knew you were connected with the Nationalists. This changes everything. I no longer want to undergo the procedure for you or anyone else.

Sincerely,
Piao-Liang Davis

UNITED STATES DISTRICT COURT
NORTHERN DISTRICT OF CALIFORNIA

JIANG CHUANG-PING,	)	
	)	
Plaintiff,	)	No. 2:06-CV-2345-K
v.	)	(Judge Kimball)
	)	
PATRICIA PIAO-LIANG DAVIS,	)	
A/K/A "PIAO-LIANG",	)	JURY TRIAL
	)	DEMANDED
	)	
Defendant.	)	

COMPLAINT

NOW COMES Plaintiff Jiang Chuang-ping ("Plaintiff"), and for his complaint against Defendant Patricia Piao-Liang Davis, also known as the supermodel "Piao-Liang" ("Defendant"), states as follows:

PARTIES

1. Plaintiff is a citizen and resident of the City of San Francisco, State of California, and the United States of America. He is domiciled in the State of California in this Northern District of California.

2. Defendant Piao-Liang is a citizen and resident of the State of Utah, United States of America, and is domiciled in Provo, Utah.

JURISDICTION AND VENUE

3. This Court has subject matter jurisdiction over this action under 28 U.S.C. § 1332(a)(1) in that Plaintiff and Defendant have diverse citizenship, and the matter involves over $75,000 in controversy.

4. Personal jurisdiction exists over Defendant because Defendant was served with process in this State and District.

5. Defendant and Plaintiff entered into the Contract attached hereto as Exhibit 1 ("Contract") on November 2 and November 4, 2008, respectively.

6. The contract provides for suit to be brought in a federal court in California and the Contract is to be governed by California law. Contract, section 5.

7. Venue is proper in this district pursuant to the forum selection clause in section 5 of the Contract and pursuant to 28 U.S.C. § 1391 in

that Defendant was served with process within this District and Division, and the subject matter of the Contract is present in this District.

COUNT I - BREACH OF CONTRACT

8. On November 2, 2008, Defendant entered into the Contract, promising to deliver to Plaintiff's OB-GYN physician one or more healthy and viable ova from her ovaries at the first available opportunity and no later than June 1, 2009. Upon receipt and successful fertilization and implantation of the egg(s) in Plaintiff's wife's uterus, Plaintiff was to pay Plaintiff by wire transfer the sum of one million United States dollars.

9. On December 18, 2008, Defendant phoned Plaintiff and repudiated the contract by stating that she would not perform her obligations. She then, on that same day, sent by facsimile transmission and U.S. Mail the letter attached hereto as Exhibit 2, again repudiating the Contract and refusing to perform her obligations under the Contract.

10. Plaintiff was and remains ready to perform his obligations under the Contract, and there are no other conditions precedent to the agreement that would prevent its performance.

11. Defendant breached its agreement with Plaintiff by anticipatory repudiation.

12. Plaintiff has no available alternative remedy at law that could replace or compensate Plaintiff for the unique value of the subject matter of the Contract, and seeks specific performance of the Contract, and such further and other relief as the Court deems proper in the circumstances.

COUNT II - SPECIFIC PERFORMANCE

13. Plaintiff realleges the allegations of paragraphs 1-12 of this complaint as though set forth fully in this paragraph.

14. Plaintiff comes to this court seeking equity, with clean hands, and with the equities in his favor. Plaintiff has no available alternative remedy at law. The public policy of this jurisdiction favors the upholding and enforcement of contracts for the provision of a unique subject matter.

15. Defendant has repudiated and breached her obligations under the Contract. The equities and public policy are against Defendant.

16. Plaintiff seeks specific performance of the Contract.

WHEREFORE, Plaintiff requests the Court to order Defendant to deliver to Plaintiff's OB-GYN physician one or more healthy and viable ova from her ovaries at the first available opportunity and no later than June 1, 2009, and to award Plaintiff such further and other relief as the Court deems proper in the circumstances.

JURY TRIAL DEMANDED.

FINLEY & MOORE, LLP

By:_____
          Miriam O. McGuinnis
          Ut Bar No. 02112
          114 Market Street, Suite 2800
          Salt Lake City, Utah 84101
          St. Louis, Missouri 63101
          Phone: 801-555-SU4U
          Fax: (314) 555-9901

          Attorneys for Plaintiff Jiang Chuang-ping

Key Terms: contract, enforceability, subject matter, enforcement against public policy

Launch Point: <u>17A Am. Jur. 2d Contracts § 237</u>

---

2. Based on the following information, research and draft a memorandum analyzing what remedies Lion Forest would be legally entitled to obtain against Newton Grumbacher (including the formula for damages and the possibility of obtaining equitable, injunctive relief) if Forest prevailed against Grumbacher in the lawsuit.

MEMORANDUM

TO: Junior Associate

FROM: Senior Partner

DATE: January 18, 2008

RE: <u>Grumbacher v. Elwood "Lion" Forest</u>

SUBJECT: Motion to Transfer Venue

Defendant Elwood "Lion" Forest is the most famous Native American golfer on the PGA tour. Since his bursting onto the scene in 1999, after winning four consecutive PGA Amateur titles, he has continued to excel, winning ten of the "major" tournaments in the last seven years, and winning the same major (the British Open) in three consecutive years, 2003, 2004, and 2005. He has received an enormous amount of attention from the United States and world press. In the last three years, he has been on the cover of over 180 newspapers and more than 250 sports and news magazines. He has received close to $90 million in product endorsement contracts in 2007, including a deal with TropoOrangie Products for $45 million that put his face on the label of orange juice cartons the world over.

Plaintiff Newton Grumbacher is an artist living in Chicago, Illinois. His medium is oil paint, and he paints outdoors as much as possible. Once, he attended a PGA event at Kemper Lakes Course in Deerfield, Illinois, and saw Lion Forest in action. He sketched the golfer making several shots, and went back to his studio and completed a painting of the golfer in the midst of one of his signature shots. Friends of the artist thought the painting was fantastic, and they encouraged Grumbacher to make some prints of the painting. Grumbacher created a limited series of 200 prints which he began to sell for $600/each. He also created a line of coffee mugs ($8) and golf towels ($10). All the prints, mugs and towels have the same image on them, the painting of Lion Forest with the Artists' name emblazoned across the bottom of the picture.

Lion Forest saw one of the golf towels at an event, and became furious. He immediately had his lawyers draft up a threatening cease and desist letter to Grumbacher. (Complaint, exhibit 1). The letter demanded that Grumbacher cease the distribution or sale of any prints, mugs, towels, or any other article that features the likeness of Lion Forest produced without the consent of Mr. Forest, and retrieve and destroy all existing examples of such items, within 10 days, or Mr. Forest would sue Mr. Grumbacher under Illinois and Federal law for violation of Mr. Forest's right of publicity.

Grumbacher, being no stranger to controversy, got the jump on Mr. Forest and sued him in the Northern District of Illinois for declaratory judgment under Federal False Designation of Origin Act, 15 U.S.C. § 1125 and the Illinois Right of Publicity Act, 765 Ill. Comp. Stat. 1075/30 et seq.

Our first task is draft a court brief (Memorandum in Support/Opposition) regarding the Motion to Transfer Venue filed by Defendant Forest. See attached court file. Use the declarations in the court file when you are drafting your memorandum.

UNITED STATES DISTRICT COURT
NORTHERN DISTRICT OF ILLINOIS
EASTERN DIVISION

NEWTON W. GRUMBACHER,	)	
	)	
Plaintiff,	)	No. 02-C-9345
	)	(Judge Ruben Castillo)
	)	
ELWOOD FOREST, A/K/A "LION"	)	
FOREST,	)	JURY TRIAL
	)	DEMANDED
	)	
Defendant.	)	

COMPLAINT

NOW COMES Plaintiff Newton W. Grumbacher ("Plaintiff"), and for his complaint against Defendant Elwood Forest, also known as the professional golfer "Lion" Forest ("Defendant"), states as follows:

PARTIES

1. Plaintiff is a citizen and resident of the City of Chicago, Cook County, State of Illinois. He is domiciled in the State of Illinois.

2. Defendant Lion Forest is a citizen and resident of the State of Florida, and is domiciled in West Palm Beach, Florida.

JURISDICTION AND VENUE

3. This Court has subject matter jurisdiction over this action under 28 U.S.C. § 1332(a)(1) in that Plaintiff and Defendant have diverse citizenship, and the matter involves over $75,000 in controversy.

4. This Court further has subject matter jurisdiction over this action under 28 U.S.C. § 1331, in that the action arises under federal law, the Federal False Designation of Origin Act, 15 U.S.C. § 1125. This court has supplemental jurisdiction over the portion of the claim that involves the Illinois Right of Publicity Act, 765 Ill. Comp. Stat. 1075/30 et seq.

5. Venue is proper in this district pursuant to 28 U.S.C. § 1391(a)(2) because a substantial part of the events or omissions giving rise to the claims occurred in this district.

COUNT I - DECLARATORY JUDGMENT

6. On June 2, 2007, Plaintiff saw Defendant in person participating in a golf tournament at Kemper Lakes Country Club in Deerfield, Illinois.

7. On that date, Plaintiff made five sketches of Defendant playing golf. Later, he used these sketches to produce an oil on canvas painting which depicts Defendant playing golf.

8. The painting is an artistic creation and a work of art, embodying ideas and images, and reflecting Plaintiff's artistic interpretation and skill. Thus, Plaintiff's painting is protected under state and federal law, including the Federal False Designation of Origin Act, 15 U.S.C. § 1125, and the Illinois Right of Publicity Act, 765 Ill. Comp. Stat. 1075/30 et seq., from claims of infringement or violation of Defendant's rights of publicity.

9. Defendant is a famous public figure. He is one of the most famous golfers currently active on the PGA circuit. His name and image are well know all across the world. Defendant excels at his sport, winning ten of the major tournaments in seven years, and winning the same major

(the British Open) in three consecutive years, 2003, 2004, and 2005. He has received an enormous amount of attention from the United States and world press. In the last three years, he has been on the cover of over 180 newspapers and more than 250 sports and news magazines. He has received close to $90 million in product endorsement contracts in 2007, including a deal with TropoOrangie Products for $45 million that put his face on the label of orange juice cartons the world over. Defendant is a subject worthy of news attention and depiction. Thus, Plaintiff's painting is protected under state and federal law, including the Federal False Designation of Origin Act, 15 U.S.C. § 1125, and the Illinois Right of Publicity Act, 765 Ill. Comp. Stat. 1075/30 et seq., from claims of infringement or violation of Defendant's rights of publicity.

10. Plaintiff has made derivative works of his painting, including a limited edition of 200 high quality, serigraph transfer, individually numbered and signed prints of the painting, worth at least $600 each. Plaintiff has also produced coffee mugs and golf towels bearing the same image of the painting. The image of the painting is modified so as to add the artist's last name on each of the prints, mugs and towels.

11. In that the original painting is protected under state and federal law, including the Federal False Designation of Origin Act, 15 U.S.C. § 1125, and the Illinois Right of Publicity Act, 765 Ill. Comp. Stat. 1075/30 et seq., from claims of infringement or violation of Defendant's rights of publicity, each derivative work produced by the same artist is also protected from claims of infringement or violation of Defendant's rights of publicity.

12. On December 1, 2007, Defendant sent by facsimile transmission and U.S. Mail the letter attached hereto as Exhibit 1, threatening Plaintiff and demanding that Plaintiff cease and desist production, distribution and sale of all prints, mugs, towels, and any other "derivative works" of the painting without the consent of Defendant. The letter also

calls for Plaintiff to destroy the original painting of Defendant and all prints, mugs, towels, and other "derivative works" of the painting now and in the future possession of Plaintiff. The letter threatened a lawsuit within ten days of the letter if its terms were not followed.

13. An actual case and controversy exists between Plaintiff and Defendant based on the letter and the threats of legal action concerning Plaintiff's art contained therein.

WHEREFORE, Plaintiff requests the Court to order a declaratory judgment in favor of Plaintiff and against Defendant, ordering and decreeing that Plaintiff has the right to produce, sell, and distribute the painting of Defendant and prints, mugs, and towels bearing the image depicted in the original painting, and to award Plaintiff such further and other relief as the Court deems proper in the circumstances.

JURY TRIAL DEMANDED.

SMITH, MAPLE, & RUSH, P.C.

By:_____

Andres Smith
Ill. Bar No. 6157980
111 South Michigan Avenue
Chicago, Illinois, 60603-6110
Phone: 800-555-ARTY
Fax: 800-555-SU4U

Attorneys for Plaintiff
Newton W. Grumbacher

Filed: December 8, 2007

Key Terms: right of publicity; unconsented use of name, image, or likeness; First Amendment; freedom of expression; artistic expression; Visual Artists Rights Act

Launch Point: J. Thomas McCarthy, *The Rights of Publicity and Privacy*; 17 U.S.C. § 106A

II. COPYRIGHT

RESEARCH AND WRITING PROBLEMS

1. Are these works original enough for copyright purposes? Explain your answer in 1-2 pages.

    Would you change your answer if you knew they were digital photographs produced by taking light reflected off objects in the natural world and manipulating it with an inventive use of mathematical algorithms to produce the image?

    Key Terms: copyright, originality doctrine, original work of authorship

    Launch Point: 17 U.S.C. § 102

2. Dale Chihuly is one of the most successful modern day artists. Supporters describe him as "the most inventive glass sculptor in the history of the medium." Chihuly is suing former employee Bryan Rubino alleging that Rubino—using techniques he learned while working for Chihuly— reviewed picture books of Chihuly's works and made unauthorized copies. Rubino responded by asserting that Chihuly is attempting to keep other glass artists from

making similar shapes found in nature using basic glass blowing techniques that have been around for centuries. According to Rubino, Chihuly uses ancient techniques to create shapes found in nature. Rubino contends that Chihuly is trying to copyright these techniques, as well as the natural shapes, and in so doing, Chihuly is preventing Rubino from pursuing his livelihood as a glass blower. According to Rubino, the "biomorphic form of asymmetrical glass and/or other features such as colors, arrangements and presentation" are not copyrightable in and of themselves, and Rubino did not infringe Chihuly's copyright by creating biomorphic forms using standard glass blowing techniques. Analyze this dispute under copyright law principles of originality and the idea/expression distinction. Summarize the basic arguments of each side of the dispute.

Key Terms: copyright, originality doctrine, idea vs. expression, procedure, process, system, method of operation, concept

Launch Point: 17 U.S.C. § 102; Maureen O'Hagan, *Glass Artist Chihuly's Lawsuit Tests Limits of Copyrighting Art*, Seattle Times, Dec. 20, 2005, available at http://seattletimes.nwsource.com/cgi-bin/PrintStory.pl?document_id=2002686721&zsection_id=2002111777&slug=chihuly16m&date=20051216

3. Sara paints portraits for Sargent Whistler LLC ("SW"), a commercial studio that takes commissions for painted portraits and assigns them to a stable of artists who have agreed to work 20-30 hours a week for SW. Sara receives 20% of the commission fees for each portrait she paints for SW. SW routinely withholds income taxes, FICA, and state payroll taxes from her payments. SW provides no health insurance, retirement plan, or any other employee benefit to Sara and the other artists working for SW. SW has a large studio where many of the artists work, but Sara prefers the lighting and work space at her own home, and so she routinely performs her work at home with the knowledge and consent of SW. SW supplies paint, thinners and painting media, and canvases to its artists but not their palates, brushes, knives, or other painting tools and cleaning supplies. In any event, Sara prefers to select her own paints and so she rarely uses the paint supplied by SW, again with the knowledge and consent of SW.

Sara, instead, takes a tax write-off for the supplies she expends in her work with SW in the years she earns enough to owe income tax. Sara also accepts her own commissions for portrait work and performs work on those projects in the same place as she does her work for SW; given that the portraits are in oil with its prolonged drying time, Sara often has two or three works in progress for SW sitting in her home studio alongside two or three projects for her own private commissions. Sara has never signed any contract or agreement mentioning ownership of the copyright for works she creates for SW's customers. Analyze and explain in 1-2 pages who owns the copyright over works Sara has created for SW's customers.

Key Terms: copyright, work made for hire

Launch Point: <u>17 U.S.C. § 101</u>; <u>18 Am. Jur. 2d Copyright and Literary Property § 63</u>

---

4. Your firm needs to analyze the claim of a new client, Sarah Clark ("Clark"), the William and Melinda Gates Professor of Legal Writing at Yale Law School. Predict Clark's chances of success in raising a defense of "parody" to allegations of copyright infringement.

    In 2009, Clark started an Attorney Comics Web Page. On these pages, she parodied (or attempted to parody) several well known comic strips: Haggar the Horrible, Peanuts, Dilbert, Calvin and Hobbes, B.C., the Lockhorns, and Grin and Bear It (the "Strips"). Clark claims she attempted to poke fun at the frivolous nature of the Strips by changing the subject matter of the Strips to legal themes and inserting the same or slightly modified versions of the characters of the Strips into legal settings. The strips have new names in Clark's versions—Harry the Litigator, Penal-Nuts, Gilbert, Cardozo and Holmes, J.D., the Lockjaws, and Grin and Pay It, respectively—and all of the characters in her strips make humorous and ironic statements about the law, the criminal justice system, and the litigious atmosphere in this country. The characters in Clark's attempted parodies bear an uncanny resemblance to the characters in the original Strips except for the changes in the names of the strips and the characters' names and the changes in the roles and dialogue of the characters who now play legal roles and discuss legal themes. Clark does not identify or make any specific reference to the original authors or owners of the Strips. The owner of the copyrights of the Strips, United Feature Syndicate ("UFS"), recently stumbled upon Clark's parodies of the strips and did not find them amusing. UFS sued Clark in the United States District Court for the District of Connecticut for copyright infringement.

You first need to evaluate whether Clark can claim that these works are a bona fide parody as that term is interpreted and defined under 17 U.S.C. § 107 on "fair use" of copyrighted works. Pay particular attention to the definition of parody – taking a large or small portion of the original work sufficient to conger up the original, and using it in a "transformative" manner for the purpose of parody. You should assume that Clark's comics do infringe on the copyrights of UFS unless she can prove that she made a "fair use" of them.

You should answer in 1-3 pages the legal question: Is Clark's work a fair use within the meaning of 17 U.S.C. § 107? Several factors of the section 107 fair use test appear to be established here and will not need to be examined in detail. The nature of the copyrighted work appears to be a non-issue here because the Strips are publicly known, expressive works and are copyrightable. Clark's motives had nothing to do with commercial gain; she created the web site purely for her own amusement and the amusement of the viewers who stumble on to it. Nor is it possible to predict the effect of her website on the market for the original works as this will require more fact finding, and it may be moot if Clark is found to have failed the parody definition.

Key Terms: copyright, infringement, fair use, purpose and character of the use, comment, criticism, parody

Launch Point: 17 U.S.C. § 107, *Campbell v. Acuff-Rose Music,* 510 U.S. 569 (1994); *Leibovitz v. Paramount Pictures Corp.,* 137 F.3d 109 (2nd Cir. 1998); *Dr. Seuss Enter. v. Penguin Books USA,* 109 F.3d 1394 (9th Cir. 1997)

DRAFTING PROBLEM

1. In 2009, Clark started an Attorney Comics Web Page. On this page, she wants to parody or satirize several well known comic strips owned by United Feature Syndicate ("UFS"): Haggar the Horrible, Peanuts, Dilbert, Calvin and Hobbes, B.C., the Lockhorns, and Grin and Bear It (the "Strips"). Clark wants to poke fun at the frivolous nature of the Strips by changing the subject matter of the Strips to legal themes and inserting the same or slightly modified versions of the characters of the Strips into legal settings. The strips have new names in Clark's versions—Harry the Litigator, Penal-Nuts, Gilbert, Cardozo and Holmes, J.D., the Lockjaws, and Grin and Pay It, respectively—and all of the characters in her strips make humorous and ironic statements about the law, the criminal justice system, and the litigious atmosphere in this country. The characters in Clark's works will bear an uncanny resemblance to the characters in the original Strips except for the changes in the names of the strips and the characters' names and the changes in the roles and dialogue of the characters who now play legal roles and discuss legal themes. Clark has not yet contacted the owner of the Strips. Draft a license agreement whereby UFS will grant Clark the rights to modify and create deriviative works based on the Strips in the manner described above.

   Key Terms: license, copyrighted works, derivative works, parody, satire

   Launch Point: http://comics.com/terms/; Lindey on Entertainment, Publishing and the Arts 3d, Chapter 13A. Commercial Exploitation: Merchandising, § 13A:5. Checklist for drafting merchandising license agreements, § 13A:6. Nonexclusive license of specified rights; Eckstrom's Licensing in Foreign and Domestic Operations: The Forms and Substance of Licensing, Copyright and Media Licenses, Forms, § 8:2

2. Based on the following information, draft a negotiation statement (a short summary of your client's legal position intended for submission to a neutral and to your opponent in a negotiation) on behalf of Newton Grumbacher making the argument that Lion Forest would not be legally entitled to injunctive relief against

Newton Grumbacher that involved destroying Grumbacher's original painting under the Visual Artist's Rights Act, 17 U.S.C. § 106A, even if Forest prevailed against Grumbacher in the lawsuit.

MEMORANDUM

TO: Junior Associate

FROM: Senior Partner

DATE: January 18, 2008

RE: <u>Grumbacher v. Elwood "Lion" Forest</u>

SUBJECT: Motion to Transfer Venue

Defendant Elwood "Lion" Forest is the most famous Native American golfer on the PGA tour. Since his bursting onto the scene in 1999, after winning four consecutive PGA Amateur titles, he has continued to excel, winning ten of the "major" tournaments in the last seven years, and winning the same major (the British Open) in three consecutive years, 2003, 2004, and 2005. He has received an enormous amount of attention from the United States and world press. In the last three years, he has been on the cover of over 180 newspapers and more than 250 sports and news magazines. He has received close to $90 million in product endorsement contracts in 2007, including a deal with TropoOrangie Products for $45 million that put his face on the label of orange juice cartons the world over.

Plaintiff Newton Grumbacher is an artist living in Chicago, Illinois. His medium is oil paint, and he paints outdoors as much as possible. Once, he attended a PGA event at Kemper Lakes Course in Deerfield, Illinois, and saw Lion Forest in action. He sketched the golfer making several shots, and went back to his studio and completed a painting of the golfer in the midst of one of his signature shots. Friends of the artist thought the painting was fantastic, and they encouraged Grumbacher to make some prints of the painting. Grumbacher created a limited series of 200 prints which he began to sell for $600/each. He also created a line of coffee mugs ($8) and golf towels ($10). All the prints, mugs and towels have the same image on them, the painting of Lion Forest with the Artists' name emblazoned across the bottom of the picture.

Lion Forest saw one of the golf towels at an event, and became furious. He immediately had his lawyers draft up a threatening cease and desist letter to Grumbacher. (Complaint, exhibit 1). The letter demanded that Grumbacher cease the distribution or sale of any prints, mugs, towels, or any other article that features the likeness of Lion Forest produced without the consent of Mr. Forest, and retrieve and destroy all existing examples of such items, within 10 days, or Mr. Forest would sue Mr. Grumbacher under Illinois and Federal law for violation of Mr. Forest's right of publicity.

Grumbacher, being no stranger to controversy, got the jump on Mr. Forest and sued him in the Northern District of Illinois for declaratory judgment under Federal False Designation of Origin Act, 15 U.S.C. § 1125 and the Illinois Right of Publicity Act, 765 Ill. Comp. Stat. 1075/30 et seq.

Our first task is draft a court brief (Memorandum in Support/Opposition) regarding the Motion to Transfer Venue filed by Defendant Forest. See attached court file. Use the declarations in the court file when you are drafting your memorandum.

UNITED STATES DISTRICT COURT
NORTHERN DISTRICT OF ILLINOIS
EASTERN DIVISION

NEWTON W. GRUMBACHER,	)	
	)	
Plaintiff,	)	No. 02-C-9345
	)	(Judge Ruben Castillo)
	)	
ELWOOD FOREST, A/K/A "LION"	)	
FOREST,	)	JURY TRIAL
	)	DEMANDED
	)	
Defendant.	)	

COMPLAINT

NOW COMES Plaintiff Newton W. Grumbacher ("Plaintiff"), and for his complaint against Defendant Elwood Forest, also known as the professional golfer "Lion" Forest ("Defendant"), states as follows:

PARTIES

1. Plaintiff is a citizen and resident of the City of Chicago, Cook County, State of Illinois. He is domiciled in the State of Illinois.

2. Defendant Lion Forest is a citizen and resident of the State of Florida, and is domiciled in West Palm Beach, Florida.

JURISDICTION AND VENUE

3. This Court has subject matter jurisdiction over this action under 28 U.S.C. § 1332(a)(1) in that Plaintiff and Defendant have diverse citizenship, and the matter involves over $75,000 in controversy.

4. This Court further has subject matter jurisdiction over this action under 28 U.S.C. § 1331, in that the action arises under federal law, the Federal False Designation of Origin Act, 15 U.S.C. § 1125. This court has supplemental jurisdiction over the portion of the claim that involves the Illinois Right of Publicity Act, 765 Ill. Comp. Stat. 1075/30 et seq.

5. Venue is proper in this district pursuant to 28 U.S.C. § 1391(a)(2) because a substantial part of the events or omissions giving rise to the claims occurred in this district.

COUNT I - DECLARATORY JUDGMENT

6. On June 2, 2007, Plaintiff saw Defendant in person participating in a golf tournament at Kemper Lakes Country Club in Deerfield, Illinois.

7. On that date, Plaintiff made five sketches of Defendant playing golf. Later, he used these sketches to produce an oil on canvas painting which depicts Defendant playing golf.

8. The painting is an artistic creation and a work of art, embodying ideas and images, and reflecting Plaintiff's artistic interpretation and skill. Thus, Plaintiff's painting is protected under state and federal law, including the Federal False Designation of Origin Act, 15 U.S.C. § 1125, and the Illinois Right of Publicity Act, 765 Ill. Comp. Stat. 1075/30 et seq., from claims of infringement or violation of Defendant's rights of publicity.

9. Defendant is a famous public figure. He is one of the most famous golfers currently active on the PGA circuit. His name and image are well know all across the world. Defendant excels at his sport, winning ten of the major tournaments in seven years, and winning the same major (the British Open) in three consecutive years, 2003, 2004, and 2005. He has received an enormous amount of attention from the United States and world press. In the last three years, he has been on the cover of over 180 newspapers and more than 250 sports and news magazines. He has received close to $90 million in product endorsement contracts in 2007, including a deal with TropoOrangie Products for $45 million that put his face on the label of orange juice cartons the world over. Defendant is a subject worthy of news attention and depiction. Thus, Plaintiff's painting is protected under state and federal law, including the Federal False Designation of Origin Act, 15 U.S.C. § 1125, and the Illinois Right of

Publicity Act, 765 Ill. Comp. Stat. 1075/30 et seq., from claims of infringement or violation of Defendant's rights of publicity.

10. Plaintiff has made derivative works of his painting, including a limited edition of 200 high quality, serigraph transfer, individually numbered and signed prints of the painting, worth at least $600 each. Plaintiff has also produced coffee mugs and golf towels bearing the same image of the painting. The image of the painting is modified so as to add the artist's last name on each of the prints, mugs and towels.

11. In that the original painting is protected under state and federal law, including the Federal False Designation of Origin Act, 15 U.S.C. § 1125, and the Illinois Right of Publicity Act, 765 Ill. Comp. Stat. 1075/30 et seq., from claims of infringement or violation of Defendant's rights of publicity, each derivative work produced by the same artist is also protected from claims of infringement or violation of Defendant's rights of publicity.

12. On December 1, 2007, Defendant sent by facsimile transmission and U.S. Mail the letter attached hereto as Exhibit 1, threatening Plaintiff and demanding that Plaintiff cease and desist production, distribution and sale of all prints, mugs, towels, and any other "derivative works" of the painting without the consent of Defendant. The letter also calls for Plaintiff to destroy the original painting of Defendant and all prints, mugs, towels, and other "derivative works" of the painting now and in the future possession of Plaintiff. The letter threatened a lawsuit within ten days of the letter if its terms were not followed.

13. An actual case and controversy exists between Plaintiff and Defendant based on the letter and the threats of legal action concerning Plaintiff's art contained therein.

WHEREFORE, Plaintiff requests the Court to order a declaratory judgment in favor of Plaintiff and against Defendant, ordering and decreeing that Plaintiff has the right to produce, sell, and distribute the painting of Defendant and prints, mugs, and towels bearing the image depicted in the original painting, and to award Plaintiff such further and other relief as the Court deems proper in the circumstances.

JURY TRIAL DEMANDED.

SMITH, MAPLE, & RUSH, P.C.

By:_____

Andres Smith
Ill. Bar No. 6157980
111 South Michigan Avenue
Chicago, Illinois, 60603-6110
Phone: 800-555-ARTY
Fax: 800-555-SU4U

Attorneys for Plaintiff
Newton W. Grumbacher

Filed: December 8, 2007

Key Terms: Visual Artists Rights Act; right of integrity; right of publicity; unconsented use of name, image, or likeness

Launch Point: 17 U.S.C. § 106A; J. Thomas McCarthy, *The Rights of Publicity and Privacy*

WRITING IN THE LAW DISCIPLINE PROBLEM

1. Mark Murphy, a St. Louis artist, wishes to license his paintings of flowers and floral scenes that he painted from photographs he took at the Missouri Botanical Gardens. First, determine whether Murphy must obtain a license or other permission from the

Missouri Botanical Gardens before embarking on this venture and write up your conclusions in 1-3 pages. Second, draft a license form for Murphy's works that would be suitable for the works to be republished in various media—notecards, illustrations for books and magazines, calendar companies, and other media outlets.

Key Terms: license, copyrighted works, derivative works, republication rights

Launch Point: Lindey on Entertainment, Publishing and the Arts 3d, Chapter 13A. Commercial Exploitation: Merchandising, I. Grant of License, § 13A:5. Checklist for drafting merchandising license agreements, § 13A:6. Nonexclusive license of specified rights; Eckstrom's Licensing in Foreign and Domestic Operations: The Forms and Substance of Licensing, Copyright and Media Licenses, Forms, § 8:2

III.   RIGHT OF PUBLICITY

RESEARCH AND WRITING PROBLEMS

1. David Beckham is an internationally known football (soccer) star. Shortly after Beckham obtained a release from his multi-million dollar contract with the Los Angeles Galaxy soccer club in 2009, Toro Sports International Ltd. starting giving out small hand-squeezable stress relievers shaped like soccer balls at international trade shows and to buyers and sales persons at major sports retailers worldwide. The stress relievers had the image of Beckham on them along with the distinctive "T" (for Toro) logo and Toro Sports Int'l Ltd. mark. Each stress reliever also bore the following message:

> "I'll retire in ~~England Spain Los Angeles~~ Italy? Wherever they pay me the mo$t!"

There were versions of the ball created with the text in English, Chinese, French, German, Italian, Japanese, Portugese, and Spanish. Beckham did not authorize this use of his image and he seeks advice on how to combat this blatant theft of his image and persona in the United States. Draft a 2-3 page memorandum analyzing Beckham's claims against Toro and Toro's potential defenses to these claims.

Key Terms: right of publicity; unconsented use of name, image, or likeness; First Amendment; freedom of expression; comment or criticism of public figure; sports as a matter of public interest

Launch Point: J. Thomas McCarthy, *The Rights of Publicity and Privacy*

2. You represent Abraham Baum, the plaintiff in a suit brought pursuant to New York Civil Rights Law §§ 50-51 against York Media Holdings, LLC, for violation of Mr. Baum's right of privacy. Draft a client letter to Mr. Baum explaining the following order of the court in the litigation:

UNITED STATES DISTRICT COURT
SOUTHERN DISTRICT OF NEW YORK
SOUTHERN DIVISION

ABRAHAM BAUM,	)	
	)	
Plaintiff,	)	
	)	
v.	)	NO. 09-CIV-123 (PKL)
	)	
YORK MEDIA HOLDINGS, LLC,	)	
D/B/A YORK MAGAZINE,	)	
	)	
Defendant.	)	

ORDER AND JUDGMENT

PETER K. LEISURE, J.

    The underlying action, brought under N.Y. Civil Rights Law § 51, concerns defendant's use of a photograph of plaintiff, concededly without his consent. The motion before the court brought by defendant York Media Holdings, LLC ("YMH"), is for summary judgment seeking dismissal of the complaint.

DISCUSSION

YMH claims that the challenged photograph was initially used in the context of and as an illustration of a newsworthy article in YMH's York Magazine publication ("the Magazine") and therefore is exempt from the application of New York State privacy laws because it is protected free speech by a member of the press under the United States and New York State Constitutions. All subsequent uses of this image, it is asserted, were undertaken to advertise the initial use in incidental or ancillary second-ary uses, or were independently justified as First Amendment protected artistic expression.

In this motion, certain facts are not in dispute or are stipulated to:

Plaintiff Baum ("Baum") is an Orthodox Hasidic Jew and a mem-ber of the Klausenberg Sect, a sect that was almost completely destroyed during the Holocaust. He holds a deep religious conviction that the use of his image for commercial and public purposes violates his religion. In particular he believes that each of YMH's uses of his image violates the Second Commandment prohibition (from the Book of Exodus) against creation and worship of graven images.

In December 2008, a photographer working for YMH took a photograph of Baum as he was leaving his place of business and walking on a public sidewalk on a public street in New York City. Baum was un-aware that the photographer had taken his photograph.

YMH used this photograph on the cover of its publication, the Magazine, in the December 9, 2008, issue of the Magazine. This use is shown in Exhibit 1 to the Complaint in this matter. The December 9, 2008, issue of the Magazine contained a story concerning the effect of the 2008 economic climate on the diamond district and diamond sales and gem cutting industry in New York City. Baum owns a diamond and gem cutting business and is employed in the diamond district and in the diamond and gem cutting industry.

YMH further used Baum's photograph as depicted on the cover of the December 9, 2008, issue of the Magazine in two subscription page advertisements for its York Magazine publication that ran in the December 29, 2008, issue of the magazine and the January 5, 2009, issue of the magazine. These uses are shown in Exhibits 2 and 3 attached to the Complaint.

YMH further used the image and likeness of Baum by making a cartoon of Baum's face and putting it on a cartoon body and identifying Baum by his first name ("Abe") in the subscription page advertisement shown in Exhibit 3 attached to the Complaint.

YMH did not seek or obtain consent to photograph Baum nor did it seek or obtain consent to use any photograph or image or likeness or the first name of Baum accompanying any image or likeness of Baum in any advertisement or for any use whatsoever.

The photographic image and the caricature of Baum as presented and depicted in Exhibits 1, 2, and 3 to the Complaint are readily identifiable as reflecting the image and likeness of plaintiff Baum.

YMH's publication York Magazine is a biweekly periodical publication of general and widespread circulation. It is read by tens of thousands of persons in and out of New York State, but particularly, it is read by persons in the area of New York City where Baum lives, works, and resides. Furthermore, the advertisements shown in Complaint, Exhibits 2 and 3 were displayed throughout the boroughs of New York on billboards and on the sides of public transportation buses and in advertising placards in the New York City Subway system.

When plaintiff first discovered the photograph of his image in early December 2008, he immediately contacted defendants regarding the use. YMH responded that the photographs were not being used for either "advertising" or "trade" and that it believed it was within its legal rights to continue use the photograph of plaintiff in the manner it had been using them. This action ensued.

N.Y. Civil Rights Law §§ 50 and 51 prohibit the unconsented use of identity within the State of New York "for advertising purposes or for the purposes of trade." The rights contained in these statutory sections are the exclusive remedies allowed in New York State for an unauthorized use of one's likeness. Howell v. Post, 81 N.Y.2d 115 (1993). Right of privacy laws are intended to defend the average person from unwanted public exposure and the potential emotional damage thereby inflected. Weisfogel, Fine Arts v. Uncertain Protection: The New York Right of Privacy Statute and the First Amendment, 20 Columbia-VLA J.L. & Arts 91 (1995). New York's Privacy laws were enacted to strike a balance between the right to privacy, on the one hand, and the right to First Amendment free speech and free press on the other. Arrington v. New York Times, 55 N.Y.2d 433 (1982).

The elements of a privacy claim under Civil Rights Law §§ 50 and 51 are: (1) use of plaintiff's name, portrait, picture or voice, (2) for advertising purposes or for trade, (3) without consent, and (4) within the State of New York. Hoepker v. Kruger, 200 F.Supp.2d 340 (SDNY 2002). YMH concedes facts that establish elements 1, 3 and 4 of a privacy cause of action. It claims, however, that as a matter of law, the photograph of Baum was not used for "advertising" or "trade" purposes. YMH claims that the photograph of Baum was used in a "newsworthy" way in the context of the reporting of a news story and that this type of use is expressly not included within the privacy protections under New York's statute. It further contends that the publication of newsworthy photos and illustrations of newsworthy stories cannot constitutionally be within the protection of New York's privacy laws because it is constitutionally protected speech. U.S. Const. amend. I; N.Y. Const. art. I, § 8.

Baum denies that the photograph was used in a proper manner to illustrate a news story. He argues that YMH's intended purpose was to pick a random but interesting-looking image of a person found on the street in the general vacinity of a diamond and gem business and to exploit that image to attact attention to the cover of its magazine and sell more magazines through the initial use and the two subsequent uses of the image in commercial subscription advertisements in the Magazine. Baum claims that each use of his photograph constitutes a commercial use in trade or advertising that is actionable under the privacy laws.

Baum urges that privacy cases require a balancing of competing constitutional interests. Baum argues that freedom of expression is not an absolute guaranty, but requires a trier of fact to weigh Baum's constitutional rights to privacy and his right to practice his religion against YMH's competing interests.

The N.Y. Court of Appeals has repeatedly held that the New York statutory right of privacy restricts the use of one's likeliness against use for advertising and trade only and nothing more. It is a strictly construed statute enacted with sensitivity to the potentially competing values of privacy protection versus free speech. <u>Messenger v. Gruner</u>, 94 N.Y.2d 436 (2000); <u>Finger v. Omni Publs. Int.</u>, 77 N.Y.2d 138 (1990); <u>Arrington v. New York Times</u>, 55 N.Y.2d 433 (1982).

There are recognized categories of protected uses that are not actionable under Civil Rights Law §§ 50 and 51. The most widely recognized protected category is for matters that are "newsworthy." <u>Messenger v. Gruner</u>, supra. The courts also recognize that as long as the primary purpose of the use is newsworthy, incidental or ancillary commercial use of the image does not otherwise turn a protected use into an unprotected use. <u>Arrington v. New York Times</u>, supra; <u>Altbach v. Kulon</u>, 302 A.D.2d 655 (3rd Dept. 2003). Thus, for example, use of a likeness in connection with advertising or selling newspaper subscriptions does not convert an excepted use into an actionable use under the New York State privacy laws. <u>Messenger v. Gruner</u>, supra; <u>Velez v. VV Pub. Cap</u>, 135 A.D.2d 47 (1st Dept. 1988), leave to app. den'd, 72 N.Y.2d 808 (1988). Moreover, a profit generating motive will not convert an otherwise newsworthy use of someone's likeness into one that is used for advertising or trade purposes. <u>Dworkin v. Hustler Magazine, Inc.</u>, 867 F.2d 1188 (9th Cir.), cert. denied, 110 S.Ct. 59 (1989).

The Court is satisfied that the initial use of Baum's image by YMH on the cover of the Magazine was an appropriate and protected newsworthy use of the image in conjunction with a news story that ran in the same issue of the Magazine. Baum works in and owns a business in the diamond and gem industry in New York City and was photographed on a public street leaving his diamond and gem business. The fact that Baum is no celebrity and is not the singular "face of the New York City diamond and gem industry," as repeatedly asserted by Baum, does not change the fact that he has a connection and association with the diamond and gem industry that is sufficient to allow the use of his image to illustrate a news story on that industry, and the use was not simply "an advertisement in disguise." See <u>Rogers v. Grimaldi</u>, 875 F.2d 994 (2d Cir. 1989); <u>Parks v. LaFace Records</u>, 329 F.3d 437 (6th Cir. 2003).

Nor is the second use of the image of Baum a violation of Baum's privacy rights. As long as the primary purpose of the use was newsworthy, incidental or ancillary commercial use of the image does not otherwise turn a protected use into an unprotected use. Arrington v. New York Times, supra; Altbach v. Kulon, 302 A.D.2d 655 (3rd Dept. 2003). Thus, for example, use of a likeness in connection with advertising or selling news media subscriptions does not convert an excepted use into an actionable use under the New York State privacy laws. Messenger v. Gruner, supra; Velez v. VV Pub. Cap, 135 A.D.2d 47 (1st Dept. 1988), leave to app. den'd, 72 N.Y.2d 808 (1988). Uses such as the reproduction of a magazine cover in a subsequent advertisement to sell subscriptions of the same magazine are not actionable even if the person depicted on the cover complains and refuses to consent to the second use. See Namath v. Sports Illustrated, 371 N.Y.S.2d 10 (App. Div. 1st Dept. 1975), aff'd, 352 N.E.2d 584 (N.Y. 1976).

The third use of Baum's image in cartoon form gives the Court the most pause. YMH asserts that this is just one more incidental or ancillary use of Baum's image. I do not agree. The consensus of the case law in this area requires the use of the image to advertise the quality and nature of the <u>contents</u> of the publication. The modified cartoon image of Baum did not appear in the Magazine prior to its use in advertising for subscription sales in the January 5, 2009, issue of the Magazine. Thus, the advertisement was not showing any "contents" of the Magazine at all, it was just showing a newly doctored version of an image that did appear earlier on the cover of the Magazine.

Perhaps in recognition of this fact, YMH has raised the alternative defense to its use of the cartoon image that the use is "artistic" in nature and is sufficiently related to the earlier protected uses but transformed in an artistic way that it still is exempted from action under the N.Y. Civil Rights Law §§ 50 and 51. I turn to this argument now.

In recent years, some New York courts have addressed the issue whether an artistic use of an image is a use exempted from action under New York States Privacy Laws. Altbach v. Kulon, 302 A.D.2d 655 (3rd Dept. 2003); Simeonov v. Tiegs, 159 Misc.2d 54 (N.Y. Civ. Ct. 1993); Hoepker v. Kruger, 200 F.Supp.2d 340 (SDNY 2002). They have consistently found "art" to be constitutionally protected free speech, that is so exempt. The Court agrees.

Even while recognizing "art" as potentially exempted use removed from the reach of New York's privacy laws, the problem of sorting out what allegedly artistic expressions may or may not legally receive the benefits of this protection remains a difficult one. Some states for example, limit art to transformative and not duplicative likenesses. See, e.g., Comedy III Productions, Inc. v. Gary Saderup, Inc., 25 Cal.4th 387 (2001), cert. denied, 534 U.S. 1078 (2002) [only transformative art was entitled to First Amendment protection in California]. Other states have limited exempted use to original works of fine art, but not to distribution of reproductions. Martin Luther King, Jr. Center for Social Change, Inc. v. American Heritage Products, Inc., 250 Ga.135, 296 S.E.2d 697 (1982).

New York has been fairly liberal in its protection of what constitutes art. Altbach v. Kulon, supra; Simeonov v. Tiegs, supra; Hoepker v. Kruger, supra. In Hoepker v. Kruger, the court recognized that art can be sold, at least in limited editions, and still retain its artistic character. This analysis recognizes that First Amendment protection of art is not limited to only starving artists. The analysis in Hoepker is consistent with the primary purpose and incidental purpose doctrines, that have developed in connection with the newsworthy exemptions to privacy protections. A profit motive in itself does not necessarily compel a conclusion that art has been used for trade purposes. DiGregorio v. CBS, Inc., 123 Misc.2d 491 (Sup Ct N.Y. Co 1984).

In its moving papers, YMH has made a prima facie showing that the cartoon image of Baum is "art." This is not a subjective determination, and cannot be based upon the personal preferences of either party or the court. YMH has demonstrated that the image is virtually the same as the image used in the earlier, protected uses on the cover and in the initial subscription advertisement; this is obvious just by looking at the cartoon. To the extent it is different, it is only because the image has been transformed in an artistic way, which further supports protection from suit under section 51 because artistic transformation is a form of speech that is encouraged and protected by the First Amendment freedom of expression public policy.

Baum complains that YMH's use of his image is different because of his religious beliefs and the need to protect them as supported by the public policy underlying the free exercise clause of the First Amendment and the general constitutional protections of privacy derived from the prenumbra of the Bill of Rights of the U.S. Constitution. The facts of this case, in and of themselves, however, do not otherwise convert news or art or other protected expression into something used in trade. They do not raise a sufficient factual basis to challenge YMH's prima facie showing that the photograph was used for newsworthy purposes and to advertise these newsworthy uses, and that the cartoon use further is protected as art.

The free exercise clause, however important to our country and the values upon which it was founded, restricts state action. <u>Zelman v. Simmon-Harris</u>, 122 S.Ct. 2460 (2002). There is no state action complained of in this case, only the private actions of defendants. Thus, this situation is distinguishable from circumstances where the government required a photograph that was claimed to be a violation of a fundamental religions belief. See <u>Quarnes v. Peterson</u>, 728 F.2d 1121 (9th Cir. 1984). The issues raised by Baum do not rise to constitutional consideration.

Clearly, Baum finds the use of the photograph bearing his likeness deeply and spiritually offensive. The sincerity of his beliefs is not questioned by YMH or this Court. While sensitive to Baum's distress, it is not redressable in the courts of civil law. In this regard, the courts have uniformly upheld Constitutional First Amendment protections, even in the face of a deeply offensive use of someone's likeness. Thus, in Arrington, supra, the Court of Appeals recognized that an African American man's image was being used in a manner that conveyed viewpoints that were offensive to him. It nonetheless found the use of the image protected. In <u>Costlow v. Cusimano</u>, 34 A.D.2d 196 (4th Dept.) the court held that the parents of children who died by suffocation when they trapped themselves in a refrigerator could not assert a privacy claim to prevent defendant from publishing an article with photographs of the premises and the deceased children, because the article was "newsworthy." These examples illustrate the extent to which the constitutional exceptions to privacy will be upheld, notwithstanding that the speech or art may have unintended devastating consequences on the subject, or may even be repugnant. They are, as the Court of Appeals recognized in Arrington, the price every person must be prepared to pay for in a society in which information and opinion flow freely. 55 N.Y.2d at 442.

The Court, therefore, finds that Baum has failed to state a cause of action under New York Civil Rights Law § 51. Summary judgment is granted on such basis.

CONCLUSION

In accordance with the aforementioned, it is hereby:

ORDERED that defendant, YMH's motion for summary judgment dismissing the complaint is granted in its entirety; and it is further

ORDERED that the clerk is directed to enter a judgment in favor of YMH dismissing the complaint, with prejudice.

Any relief request not expressly granted herein is denied.

This shall constitute the decision and order of the Court.
Date: February 6, 2009

Key Terms: right of privacy and publicity, New York Civil Rights Law, freedom of the press, publication of matters of public interest, incidental advertising

Launch Point: New York Civil Rights Law §§ 50-51

WRITING IN THE LAW DISCIPLINE PROBLEMS

1. Based on the following information, research and draft a memorandum analyzing what remedies Lion Forest would be legally entitled to obtain against Newton Grumbacher (including the formula for damages and the possibility of obtaining equitable, injunctive relief) if Forest prevailed against Grumbacher in the lawsuit.

MEMORANDUM

TO: Junior Associate

FROM: Senior Partner

DATE: January 18, 2008

RE: <u>Grumbacher v. Elwood "Lion" Forest</u>

SUBJECT: Motion to Transfer Venue

Defendant Elwood "Lion" Forest is the most famous Native American golfer on the PGA tour. Since his bursting onto the scene in 1999, after winning four consecutive PGA Amateur titles, he has continued to excel, winning ten of the "major" tournaments in the last seven years, and winning the same major (the British Open) in three consecutive years, 2003, 2004, and 2005. He has received an enormous amount of attention from the United States and world press. In the last three years, he has been on the cover of over 180 newspapers and more than 250 sports and news magazines. He has received close to $90 million in product endorsement contracts in 2007, including a deal with TropoOrangie Products for $45 million that put his face on the label of orange juice cartons the world over.

Plaintiff Newton Grumbacher is an artist living in Chicago, Illinois. His medium is oil paint, and he paints outdoors as much as possible. Once, he attended a PGA event at Kemper Lakes Course in Deerfield, Illinois, and saw Lion Forest in action. He sketched the golfer making several shots, and went back to his studio and completed a painting of the golfer in the midst of one of his signature shots. Friends of the artist thought the painting was fantastic, and they encouraged Grumbacher to make some prints of the painting. Grumbacher created a limited series of 200 prints which he began to sell for $600/each. He also created a line of coffee mugs ($8) and golf towels ($10). All the prints, mugs and towels have the same image on them, the painting of Lion Forest with the Artists' name emblazoned across the bottom of the picture.

Lion Forest saw one of the golf towels at an event, and became furious. He immediately had his lawyers draft up a threatening cease and desist letter to Grumbacher. (Complaint, exhibit 1). The letter demanded that Grumbacher cease the distribution or sale of any prints, mugs, towels, or any other article that features the likeness of Lion Forest produced without the consent of Mr. Forest, and retrieve and destroy all existing examples of such items, within 10 days, or Mr. Forest would sue Mr. Grumbacher under Illinois and Federal law for violation of Mr. Forest's right of publicity.

Grumbacher, being no stranger to controversy, got the jump on Mr. Forest and sued him in the Northern District of Illinois for declaratory judgment under Federal False Designation of Origin Act, 15 U.S.C. § 1125 and the Illinois Right of Publicity Act, 765 Ill. Comp. Stat. 1075/30 et seq.

Our first task is draft a court brief (Memorandum in Support/Opposition) regarding the Motion to Transfer Venue filed by Defendant Forest. See attached court file. Use the declarations in the court file when you are drafting your memorandum.

UNITED STATES DISTRICT COURT
NORTHERN DISTRICT OF ILLINOIS
EASTERN DIVISION

NEWTON W. GRUMBACHER,	)	
	)	
Plaintiff,	)	No. 02-C-9345
	)	(Judge Ruben Castillo)
	)	
ELWOOD FOREST, A/K/A "LION"	)	
FOREST,	)	JURY TRIAL
	)	DEMANDED
	)	
Defendant.	)	

COMPLAINT

NOW COMES Plaintiff Newton W. Grumbacher ("Plaintiff"), and for his complaint against Defendant Elwood Forest, also known as the professional golfer "Lion" Forest ("Defendant"), states as follows:

PARTIES

1. Plaintiff is a citizen and resident of the City of Chicago, Cook County, State of Illinois. He is domiciled in the State of Illinois.

2. Defendant Lion Forest is a citizen and resident of the State of Florida, and is domiciled in West Palm Beach, Florida.

JURISDICTION AND VENUE

3. This Court has subject matter jurisdiction over this action under 28 U.S.C. § 1332(a)(1) in that Plaintiff and Defendant have diverse citizenship, and the matter involves over $75,000 in controversy.

4. This Court further has subject matter jurisdiction over this action under 28 U.S.C. § 1331, in that the action arises under federal law, the Federal False Designation of Origin Act, 15 U.S.C. § 1125. This court has supplemental jurisdiction over the portion of the claim that involves the Illinois Right of Publicity Act, 765 Ill. Comp. Stat. 1075/30 et seq.

5. Venue is proper in this district pursuant to 28 U.S.C. § 1391(a)(2) because a substantial part of the events or omissions giving rise to the claims occurred in this district.

COUNT I - DECLARATORY JUDGMENT

6. On June 2, 2007, Plaintiff saw Defendant in person participating in a golf tournament at Kemper Lakes Country Club in Deerfield, Illinois.

7. On that date, Plaintiff made five sketches of Defendant playing golf. Later, he used these sketches to produce an oil on canvas painting which depicts Defendant playing golf.

8. The painting is an artistic creation and a work of art, embodying ideas and images, and reflecting Plaintiff's artistic interpretation and skill. Thus, Plaintiff's painting is protected under state and federal law, including the Federal False Designation of Origin Act, 15 U.S.C. § 1125, and the Illinois Right of Publicity Act, 765 Ill. Comp. Stat. 1075/30 et seq., from claims of infringement or violation of Defendant's rights of publicity.

9. Defendant is a famous public figure. He is one of the most famous golfers currently active on the PGA circuit. His name and image are well know all across the world. Defendant excels at his sport, winning ten of the major tournaments in seven years, and winning the same major (the British Open) in three consecutive years, 2003, 2004, and 2005. He has received an enormous amount of attention from the United States and world press. In the last three years, he has been on the cover of over 180 newspapers and more than 250 sports and news magazines. He has received close to $90 million in product endorsement contracts in 2007, including a deal with TropoOrangie Products for $45 million that put his face on the label of orange juice cartons the world over. Defendant is a subject worthy of news attention and depiction. Thus, Plaintiff's painting is protected under state and federal law, including the Federal False Designation of Origin Act, 15 U.S.C. § 1125, and the Illinois Right of Publicity Act, 765 Ill. Comp. Stat. 1075/30 et seq., from claims of infringement or violation of Defendant's rights of publicity.

10. Plaintiff has made derivative works of his painting, including a limited edition of 200 high quality, serigraph transfer, individually numbered and signed prints of the painting, worth at least $600 each. Plaintiff has also produced coffee mugs and golf towels bearing the same image of the painting. The image of the painting is modified so as to add the artist's last name on each of the prints, mugs and towels.

11. In that the original painting is protected under state and federal law, including the Federal False Designation of Origin Act, 15 U.S.C. § 1125, and the Illinois Right of Publicity Act, 765 Ill. Comp. Stat. 1075/30 et seq., from claims of infringement or violation of Defendant's rights of publicity, each derivative work produced by the same artist is also protected from claims of infringement or violation of Defendant's rights of publicity.

12. On December 1, 2007, Defendant sent by facsimile transmission and U.S. Mail the letter attached hereto as Exhibit 1, threatening Plaintiff and demanding that Plaintiff cease and desist production, distribution and sale of all prints, mugs, towels, and any other "derivative works" of the painting without the consent of Defendant. The letter also calls for Plaintiff to destroy the original painting of Defendant and all prints, mugs, towels, and other "derivative works" of the painting now and in the future possession of Plaintiff. The letter threatened a lawsuit within ten days of the letter if its terms were not followed.

13. An actual case and controversy exists between Plaintiff and Defendant based on the letter and the threats of legal action concerning Plaintiff's art contained therein.

WHEREFORE, Plaintiff requests the Court to order a declaratory judgment in favor of Plaintiff and against Defendant, ordering and decreeing that Plaintiff has the right to produce, sell, and distribute the painting of Defendant and prints, mugs, and towels bearing the image depicted in the original painting, and to award Plaintiff such further and other relief as the Court deems proper in the circumstances.

JURY TRIAL DEMANDED.

SMITH, MAPLE, & RUSH, P.C.

By:_____

> Andres Smith
> Ill. Bar No. 6157980
> 111 South Michigan Avenue
> Chicago, Illinois, 60603-6110
> Phone: 800-555-ARTY
> Fax: 800-555-SU4U
>
> Attorneys for Plaintiff
> Newton W. Grumbacher

Filed: December 8, 2007

Key Terms: right of publicity; unconsented use of name, image, or likeness; First Amendment; freedom of expression; artistic expression; Visual Artists Rights Act

Launch Point: J. Thomas McCarthy, *The Rights of Publicity and Privacy*

---

2. Based on the following information, prepare a memorandum analyzing the viability of plaintiff's claims and defendant's defenses in the law suit <u>Clemens v. Take Steroids Out of the Ball Game</u>. (Do not analyze the claims or defenses of The Sporting News).

MEMORANDUM

TO: Junior Associate

FROM: Senior Partner

DATE: January 21, 2008

RE: <u>Roger Clemens v. Take Steroids Out of the Ball Game, Inc. and The Sporting News</u> (C87654/34678)

SUBJECT: Motion to Dismiss for Lack of Personal Jurisdiction

Take Steroids Out of the Ball Game, Inc. (TSOOTBG) is a not-for-profit tax exempt organization. It is a private corporation organized and existing under the laws of the State of Illinois with its principal and in fact only place of business being in Champaign, Illinois. TSOOTBG claims that its mission is to eliminate steroids and performance-enhancing drugs from Major League Baseball. TSOOTBG is not affiliated with Major League Baseball, Major League Baseball Players Assoc., Major League Baseball Properties, or the Major League Baseball Players Union, not is it affiliated with government or any government agency. It is solely owned, created, and operated by one person, Marcus McWire, who started the company in December 2007. The company runs a weblog (tsootbg.blog-spot.com). It has no other business or other activities except those described below.

Defendant Sporting News is a corporation organized and existing under the laws of the State of Missouri with its headquarters and principal place of business in the County of St. Louis, Missouri within the territory of the United States District Court for the Eastern District of Missouri.

In late 2007, the company used most of its cash on hand to purchase a full page ad in Co-defendant Sporting News's weekly publication. The ad depicted plaintiff Roger Clemens riding a syringe as if it were a rocket and flying over Yankee Stadium, obviously playing off of Clemens' nickname of the "Rocket" and his recent association with steroid use (needle and syringe injections) allegedly undertaken while Clemens was a member of the New York Yankees baseball club.

The ad ran once in Sporting News on December 31, 2007, and at the bottom of the ad in very small but legible lettering was the usual tagline used by TSOOTBG on its weblog along with the address of the blog:

Take Steroids Out of the Ball Game is a not-for-profit tax exempt organization that exists solely to put pressure on Major League Baseball to eliminate steroids. We accept donations of any kind --- money, pictures, news stories, whatever. (tsootbg.blogspot.com)

The ad was reproduced on the TSOOTBG weblog where it has been able to be viewed from January 14 to the present. The ad is in close proximity to a blog entry on Roger Clemens and the Mitchell Report that concerns steroid use in baseball and prominently discusses Clemens' alleged steroid use. The profile listing of the weblog provides instructions on how to donate money or other items to TSOOTBG:

Take Steroids Out of the Ball Game accepts cash donations by PayPal transfer to our account: tsootbg@ gmail.com. Pictures, news stories, and other items may be emailed to us at the same address. Thank you!

TSOOTBG also registered four other web addresses on January 14, 2008: www.RogerClemensComeClean.com, www.RogerClemensHallofFame?.com, www.RogerClemensJuiced.com, and www.RogerClemensSteroidUser.com. All of these web addresses direct users to the **tsootbg.blogspot.com** weblog.

Clemens sued TSOOTBG and Sporting News in the United States District Court for the Eastern District of Missouri for violations of his right of publicity under Missouri law. Subject matter jurisdiction is alleged because Clemens is a citizen and resident of Texas and is diverse from the Missouri and Illinois defendants, and an amount in controversy of over $200,000 is alleged. There is no question that the court has personal jurisdiction over defendant Sporting News because it has its headquarters and its principal place of business within this district. TSOOTBG, on the other hand, has no connections to Missouri or the district of this court except as described above, so TSOOTBG has moved the court pursuant to Fed. R. Civ. P. 12(b)(2) to dismiss the action against it for lack of personal jurisdiction over TSOOTBG.

Our first task is to draft a court brief (Memorandum in Support/ Opposition) regarding the Motion to Dismiss for Lack of Personal Jurisdiction filed by TSOOTBG. See attached court file.

You should assume that the only issue to brief in the motion is whether TSOOTBG had sufficient minimum contacts with the State of Missouri such that it would or would not violate the Due Process Clause of the United States Constitution to sue TSOOTBG in Missouri. Use the complaint and declaration in the court file when you are drafting your memorandum. To the extent that it is relevant, the underlying lawsuit is governed by Missouri law, but federal law (under the Due Process Clause) applies to this motion.

UNITED STATES DISTRICT COURT
EASTERN DISTRICT OF MISSOURI
EASTERN DIVISION

ROGER CLEMENS,	)	
	)	
Plaintiff,	)	No. 04-C-9345 (DJS)
v.	)	
	)	
TAKE STEROIDS OUT	)	
OF THE BALL	)	
GAME, INC., and	)	
SPORTING NEWS,	)	JURY TRIAL
	)	DEMANDED
	)	
Defendants.	)	

COMPLAINT

NOW COMES Plaintiff Roger Clemens ("Clemens"), and for its complaint against Take Steroids Out of the Ball Game, Inc. ("TSOOT-BG") and Sporting News, states as follows:

PARTIES

1. Plaintiff Clemens is an individual domiciled and residing in the State of Texas. Clemens is a citizen of the State of Texas.

2. TSOOTBG is a corporation organized and existing under the laws of the State of Illinois and has its place of incorporation and headquarters and principal place of business in the State of Illinois. Its sole shareholder and officer, Marcus McWire, is a citizen and domiciliary of the City of Champaign, State of Illinois. All of its operations, facilities, and equipment are located in Champaign, Illinois.

3. Defendant Sporting News is a corporation organized and existing under the laws of the State of Missouri has its place of incorporation and headquarters and principal place of business in the State of Missouri.

VENUE AND JURISDICTION

4. Venue is proper in this district pursuant to 28 U.S.C. § 1391 because the actions alleged herein caused harm to Clemens's publicity rights in the State of Missouri, and the ad was run in a publication based in and emanating from the State of Missouri, and one defendant is a citizen and resident of Missouri and this district, and both defendants are present and amenable to service of process within this United States District Court for the Eastern District of Missouri.

5. Jurisdiction is appropriate in this Court under 28 U.S.C. § 1332 because the citizenship of the plaintiff and the defendants is diverse, and over $75,000 is in controversy in the suit.

COUNT I - RIGHT OF PUBLICITY

6. On December 31, 2007, TSOOTBG purchased a full page advertisement in Sporting News's weekly publication. The ad depicted plaintiff Clemens riding a syringe as if it were a rocket and flying over Yankee Stadium.

7. The ad ran once in Sporting News on December 31, 2007, and at the bottom of the ad in very small but legible lettering was a solicitation used by TSOOTBG in its activities on its weblog along with the address of the blog:

> **Take Steroids Out of the Ball Game is a not-for-profit tax exempt organization that exists solely to put pressure on Major League Baseball to eliminate steroids. We accept donations of any kind --- money, pictures, news stories, whatever. (tsootbg.blogspot.com)**

8. The ad obviously played off of Clemens' nickname of the "Rocket" and used his fame and considerable publicity value of his image and likeness to draw attention to the publication and to attract attention and monetary contributions to TSOOTBG.

9. TSOOTBG used the ad to direct readers of Sporting News' publication to the TSOOTBG's weblog (tsootbg.blogspot.com) where they are solicited to make donations of money to TSOOTBG. The profile listing of the weblog provides instructions on how to donate money or other items to TSOOTBG:

> **Take Steroids Out of the Ball Game accepts cash donations by PayPal transfer to our account: tsootbg@gmail.com. Pictures, news stories, and other items may be emailed to us at the same address. Thank you!**

10. TSOOTBG also registered four other web addresses on January 14, 2008: www.RogerClemensComeClean.com, www.RogerClemensHallofFame?.com, www.RogerClemensJuiced.com, and www.RogerClemensSteroidUser.com. All of these web addresses direct users to the **tsootbg.blogspot.com** weblog.

11. The ad drew attention to the Sporting News publication itself attracting readership and potential subscribers and additional ad revenue by playing off of the enormous publicity value of Clemens' image and persona.

12. Thus, defendants TSOOTBG and Sporting News, acting individually and in concert, did commercially exploit the likeness, image, and persona to their financial and commercial advantage within the meaning of Missouri right of publicity law.

13. On January 14, 2008, the ad image was posted on the World Wide Web in TSOOTBG's weblog (tsootbg.blogspot.com) where is it visible to anyone and everyone in the State of Missouri who has access to the World Wide Web. As mentioned above, TSOOTBG's weblog contains a solicitation for money from visitors to the site.

14. Thus, defendant TSOOTBG did further commercially exploit the likeness, image, and persona to its financial and commercial advantage within the meaning of Missouri's right of publicity law.

WHEREFORE, Clemens requests the Court to grant it damages in the amount of $200,000, and to award Clemens such further and other relief as the Court deems proper in the circumstances.

JURY TRIAL DEMANDED.

BONDS, GIAMBI, PETTITTE, LLC

By:_____

Barry L. Bonds Mo. Bar No. 41042
211 North Broadway, Suite 3300
St. Louis, MO 63102
Phone: 800-NEEDLES
Fax: 800-SYRINGE

Attorneys for Plaintiff Roger Clemens

Filed: January 19, 2008

Key Terms: right of publicity; unconsented use of name, image, or likeness; First Amendment; freedom of expression; artistic expression; Visual Artists Rights Act

Launch Point: J. Thomas McCarthy, *The Rights of Publicity and Privacy*

IV. ADVANCED CONSTITUTIONAL LAW, FIRST AMENDMENT, AND FREEDOM OF EXPRESSION

RESEARCH AND WRITING PROBLEMS

1. The Dudes, a relatively new and little-known religion, wants to erect a ten foot monument in a public park in Sweet City, Texas. The monument will contain the Great Eight Dudisms, which they believe were handed down to them by their supreme being, The Man. The members believe these rules are sacred and must be followed. Currently, a five foot monument of the Ten Commandments exists in the park. It was donated by a private group and is the only religious monument in the park. The Dudes applied to have their monument erected, but Sweet City has rejected their petition. As a result, The Dudes have come to your law

firm wondering if they have a First Amendment right to erect the monument. Draft a 3-5 page memo to your senior partner detailing the success of such a lawsuit.

Key Terms: freedom of expression, government speech, Ten Commandments, religious speech, free exercise of religion

Launch Point: Pleasant Grove City, Utah v. Summum, --- S.Ct. ---, 2009 WL 454299 (Feb. 25, 2009)

2. Zeli is distributing videos with graphic sexual content from an internet website. Each video is completely computer generated— no humans were involved as actors or models. In fact, the only person involved in any way in the production of the videos is Zeli himself, the programmer. Zeli uses an advanced animation technique that makes the videos appear to be slightly grainy super-8 video footage of actual persons and events. Several of Zeli's video offerings show what appears to be teenage girls or boys involved in sexual activities with adults. Discuss the potential censorship of Zeli's internet videos as child pornography under United States law.

Key Terms: first amendment, obscenity, internet, censorship, animated or computer-generated child pornography

Launch Point: *United States v. Williams*, 128 S. Ct. 1830 (2008); *Ashcroft v. Free Speech Coalition*, 535 U.S. 234 (2002))

DRAFTING PROBLEMS

1. Draft a city ordinance that would allow Sweet City, Texas, to make determinations regarding the erection of fixed monuments or other structures bearing expression on public property of Sweet City. Follow the guidelines of the United States Supreme Court's decision, particularly *Pleasant Grove City, Utah v. Summum, --- S.Ct. ---, 2009 WL 454299 (Feb. 25, 2009*. Make sure the ordinance would cover the situation described in Research and Writing Problem 1 above in this section.

Key Terms: freedom of expression, government speech, Ten Commandments, religious speech, ordinance or law regulating speech

Launch Point: <u>Pleasant Grove City, Utah v. Summum, --- S.Ct. ---, 2009 WL 454299 (Feb. 25, 2009)</u>

2. The City of Pleasanton, Wyoming, wants to control the proliferation of "adult" businesses in the city. Draft an ordinance for the town that will control the placement of adult businesses (adult book stores, nude or partially nude exotic dancing, and the like) through strict zoning requirements that will concentrate all adult businesses in a small area of the city. Review United States Supreme Court case law to determine the requirements for such an ordinance.

Key Terms: freedom of expression, obscenity, adult business, zoning, due process

Launch Point: <u>*City of Littleton, Colo. v. Z.J. Gifts D-4, L.L.C.,* 541 U.S. 774 (2004)</u>; <u>*City of Los Angeles v. Alameda Books, Inc.,* 535 U.S. 425 (2002)</u>; <u>*City of Renton v. Playtime Theatres, Inc.,* 475 U.S. 41 (1986)</u>

3. The town of Sunnyton, Minnesota, has decided that it wants to control the proliferation of "adult" businesses in the town not by concentrating them in one place but by dispersing them away from each other and by keeping them away from schools and churches in the town. Draft an ordinance for the town that will control the placement of adult businesses (adult book stores, nude or partially nude exotic dancing, and the like) through "reverse zoning" requirements that will disperse all adult businesses in the town away from each other and away from schools and churches. The town calculates that even if every adult business is kept 2000 feet away from any school or church or other adult business, this still will leave 15,000 acres or roughly 23% of the the developable area of the town left open for adult businesses. Review United States Supreme Court case law to determine the requirements for such an ordinance.

Key Terms: freedom of expression, obscenity, adult business, reverse zoning, due process

Launch Point: *City of Littleton, Colo. v. Z.J. Gifts D-4, L.L.C.,* *541 U.S. 774 (2004)*; *City of Los Angeles v. Alameda Books, Inc.,* *535 U.S. 425 (2002)*; *City of Renton v. Playtime Theatres, Inc., 475* *U.S. 41 (1986)*

WRITING IN THE LAW DISCIPLINE PROBLEMS

1. A series of cartoons depicting the Prophet Muhammad were published in a newspaper in the United States. The cartoonist who created them did so in reaction to an article which detailed an author's struggle to find an artist willing to help him illustrate a book entitled "The Qur'an and the life of the Prophet Muhammad. The cartoons are particularly offensive to Muslims because there is a strict prohibition on the creation or display of any depiction of the Prophet Muhammad under Islamic law and tradition, and protests against the newspaper publishing the cartoons and against American journalists and against many other media-related institutions that picked up and republished the story have grown violent causing the death of three persons and the injuring of dozens more. Draft a comprehensive report relating to the possibility of government censorship of the cartoons in the United States. In addition, analyze whether a prior restraint on their publication could have been ordered.

    Key Terms: first amendment, censorship, public health or safety, national security, prior restraint doctrine

    Launch Point: *Doe v. Gonzales, 127 S. Ct. 1 (2005)*; *CBS, Inc.* *v. Davis, 510 U.S. 1315 (1994)*; *U.S. v. Progressive, Inc., 467 F.* *Supp. 990 (W.D. Wis. 1979)*

2. Ding Li has created an internet application on his MySpace.com page that allows you to alter an avatar of a world leader wearing a military uniform. You can change the face of the subject from George W. Bush to Vladimir Putin to Jalal Talabani to Moktada al-Sadr to Mahmoud Ahmadinejad or to many other world leaders. The uniforms also can be changed. Eventually, the user can chose

a "method of destruction" such as improvised explosive device, car bomb, machine gun fire, or rocket propelled grenade, which triggers a brief animation in which the avatar suffers the method of destruction chosen by the user. This image is replaced by a grim reaper figure that laughs caustically while the screen displays the message "Death to all warmongers" in the native language of the person chosen for the display — English, Russian, Arabic, Farsi, or other. After creating the vignette, the user can email it to any number of recipients. Draft a comprehensive report relating to the possibility of government censorship of this web application in the United States. In addition, analyze whether a prior restraint on its publication could have been ordered.

Key Terms: first amendment, censorship, internet, public health or safety, national security, prior restraint doctrine

Launch Point: *Doe v. Gonzales*, 127 S. Ct. 1 (2005); *CBS, Inc. v. Davis*, 510 U.S. 1315 (1994); *U.S. v. Progressive, Inc.*, 467 F. Supp. 990 (W.D. Wis. 1979)

†